DISCORD
AND HARMONY

Readings in International Politics

DISCORD
AND HARMONY
Readings in International Politics

Edited by
IVO D. DUCHACEK
The City College of the City University of New York

THE DRYDEN PRESS INC.
HINSDALE, ILLINOIS

To Dr. Karel Steinbach

Preface

This collection of readings in international politics brings together selections reflecting both a high standard of analysis and careful juxtaposition of conflicting views. Studies written by prominent scholars in the field are contrasted with several case studies. Thus theory is tested against practice, foresight against error, fact against fiction, rational plan against accident, strategic insight against improvisation, and despair against wishful thinking. Identical problems are constantly viewed from different, usually opposing, angles. The purpose is to stimulate a meaningful discussion—in class and outside—on the basis of varying theoretical approaches and knowledge of relevant facts.

The book is divided into fourteen chapters, grouped into three parts: I. States and Nations; II. Decisions in Foreign Policy; and III. War, Deterrence, and Diplomacy. From the features of international politics with which a student may already have some familiarity—states, nationalism, and national self-determination—the book successively leads the student toward the more complex problems of international relations such as international law, the controversial concept of national interest and power, the role of perception and misperception, the influence of ideologies and morality on the conduct of foreign policy, nuclear and conventional deterrence, tacit bargaining, and the assumptions, practice, and limits of peaceful accommodation by diplomacy.

Each of the fourteen groups of readings is preceded by a brief introduction, and each of the forty-six reading selections is introduced by a headnote that guides the reader toward the main thesis and possible controversy. In addition, the readings mutually challenge each other within each chapter on both the theoretical and practical levels: scholars are contrasted with statesmen and scholars with other scholars. Thus, for instance, the chapter on national interest records the controversy between Morgenthau and Hoffmann; it is followed by a case study on the Bay of Pigs invasion as described by a participant-observer of the then process of determining United States national interest, Arthur M. Schlesinger, Jr. The chapters on nationalism and national self-determination group Karl W. Deutsch with Mao Tse-tung, Rupert Emerson with Chiang Kai-shek, and Ernest Renan with Frantz Fanon and Sekou Touré. The problem of adequate information, reliable data, and appropriate guessing—as well as *ex post facto* rationalization—is analyzed by such scholars as Ole R. Holsti and Thomas C. Schelling but is also documented by the case study of the Cuban missile crisis by Theodore C. Sorensen. In a chapter on ends and means in international politics we find side by side the Quakers, Trotsky, Max Weber, Kautilya, and Machiavelli; a connected case study focuses on the decision to use the first atomic bomb on Hiroshima. The chapter on the role of ideology in international politics juxtaposes the controversy between Lenin and Kautsky and between Moscow and Peking to Richard J. Barnet's critique of American interventions in the Third World. The chapters on war and deterrence contain not only Clausewitz and Herman Kahn and his critics Amitai Etzioni and Philip Green but also the secret documents from the German diplomatic archives to illustrate how World War II came about. International law is approached from both the cautiously optimistic angle (Falk and Fried) and the more skeptical viewpoint (de Visscher, Lissitzyn, and Morgenthau). The analyses of the consequences of the nuclear stalemate by Kenneth N. Waltz and John H. Herz are followed by a critical appraisal of the United States options in the case of future post-Vietnam crises.

The combination of case studies with scholarly controversies aims at providing the student with the knowledge of those past international developments that still mark our era. The emphasis is on an appropriate conceptual and analytical framework rather than on chronological history or on contemporary events; the latter will invade the class from all directions in any event, supplying additional challenges to, or confirmations of theory. Thus, it is hoped, the student will be equipped with tools and concepts essential for a relevant analysis of present and future conflicts and cooperation among nations.

In preparing an anthology of a modest length that deals with such a vast subject as politics among nations, some aspects of international affairs had to be passed by; some painful decisions to abridge or eliminate important essays at the last moment have proved unavoidable.

The book is organized so that the fourteen chapters are independent and their sequence can easily be altered to fit the organization of any currently popular text. It can be used without change with *Nations and Men,* Second Edition, 1971, by Ivo D. Duchacek, also published by Holt, Rinehart and Winston.

No author can properly thank everyone who has contributed to the preparation and completion of a book of this kind. I can only mention those whose assistance in this project was outstanding.

My first thanks are addressed to my friend Dr. Harry Gold whose help and understanding have now resulted in the completion of a third volume under his hospitable roof.

The publishers and authors who have given me their permission to use—and usually abridge—their work deserve my thanks. In most cases the abridgment necessitated the omission of all or nearly all footnotes.

I should like to express my thanks and appreciation for the cooperation and help extended to me by several student research assistants: Miss Sarah Edell, Joel Wachs, Martin Rosenblum, and Paul Stillman.

New York, New York   I.D.D.
August 1971

Contents

X Chapter 9 / The Role of Ideology 181

Chapter 10 / On Noble Ends and Ignoble Means   216

Part III / War, Deterrence, and Diplomacy

Chapter 11 / Politics and Guns   257

Chapter 12 / Nuclear Deterrence   301

DISCORD AND HARMONY

Readings in International Politics

Part I

States and Nations

1

The Territorial Dimension of International Politics

There are over 135 national governments on this Earth, each representing and acting on behalf of its respective community. All over the globe, national boundaries indicate that there are territorial limits to a national government's authority to give and enforce law. The physical expanse of a national community and its political system is known as the territorial state (sometimes called nation-state). The way in which nations and states interact determines the nature of international politics, which is the subject of our study.

Economic groups, political movements, ideologies, governments, and states derive considerable strength from being based on and identified with a clearly delineated territorial community. The platforms, goals, and manipulations of political parties reflect the interests of territorial subdivisions such as electoral districts, regions, or units in a federation, as well as those of the national community. Functional interest groups, which promote and defend nonterritorial interests such as labor, business, agriculture, and religion, cannot escape the territorial pull; they are, for the most part, organized on a geographically determined basis—cells or chapters, local or regional chambers of commerce, provincial cooperatives, parishes or dioceses, and so on. It seems that man as a political being is foremost a territorial being.[1]

No one can say for certain when territorial dividing and subdividing first occurred. It is probably as old as humanity. It may well have begun with the first delineation of boundaries between several clusters of inhabited caves and their respective hunting grounds. Here, man may have organized his immediate "friends" for the cooperative purposes of division of labor and protection against outsiders. The most dynamic feature of "modern" nationalism—the desire to acquire and maintain one's own independent state—may be seen as directly related to the territorial organization of cave settlers, afraid of, and yet in an inevitable contact with, alien outsiders. Peace and order among peoples have often issued from mutual understanding and respect of the geographic limits of each other's control of a given area and use of its natural resources. Yet, all too frequently contention over the extent of respective territorial domains has been a cause of disputes and wars among us.

The selections in this chapter examine the reasons for modern man's stubborn insistence on being fenced into a territorial state. Often, such structures prove unviable and fail to provide welfare and security to their inhabitants. However, territorial parochialism continues despite those unifying compulsions of modern technology which permit both destruction and cooperation on a universal scale, and despite the mass exchange of ideas, persons, goods, and so on. Certainly the growing awareness of the worldwide interdependence of nations and men should result in a new attitude toward the territorial state. "The rationale for change has been established," noted Nobel Peace Prize winner, Canadian statesman Lester B. Pearson. "The will to make it has not."[2]

It may be that long habit and deliberate indoctrination has made men since tender childhood think of the world in terms of separate and contrasting territorial compartments, as Boulding considers. Or it may be that man is driven by an innate territorial instinct, as Ardrey suggests. Or perhaps it is an inevitable individualistic reaction to the menacingly big size of modern global problems. In a world threatened, as Herz discusses, by the "ongoing rush of mankind into technological conformity of a synthetic planetary environment" the territorial state may have a new and important role to play: custodian of life and culture, guarantor of group identity, protection, and welfare. Some students of international politics argue that the emergence of ministates and the reassertion of territorial nationalisms are directly related to the superpowers' mutual nuclear paralysis, which prevents them from not only using but even credibly menacing with nuclear punishment. Under the giant "nuclear umbrella" all territorial

[1] See Ivo D. Duchacek, *Comparative Federalism: The Territorial Dimension of Politics* (New York: Holt, Rinehart and Winston, Inc., 1970), p. 3.

[2] Lester B. Pearson, "Beyond the Nation-State," *Saturday Review* (February 15, 1969), 54.

states actually have become less vulnerable and more self-confident than they otherwise would have been in a nonnuclear age.

The division of mankind into territorial compartments has failed so far to show symptoms of decline. The territorial state remains the favored political vehicle of modern times because it seems to meet three basic requirements: the sense of *identity*, which unites men in cooperative action; the creation and acceptance of central *authority*, which is a prerequisite for order and organization of larger groups; and *equality* of inhabitants, which encourages participation in the common affairs of the community.[3]

Certainly other forms of large-group cooperation and action are conceivable. Several scholars, notably J. David Singer, anticipate an emergence of transnational nongovernmental organizations (NGO's)—international pressure groups (of a sort) that could be formed by labor, business, churches, scientists, technicians, ecologists, or students. The functional goals and voices of the NGO's, internationally coordinated, may significantly influence the policies and actions of national governments and perhaps even erode the walls of the territorial state.

Analyzing the present situation, however, the division of humanity into territorial states continues to appear to most nations and their leaders as more acceptable and more efficient than any other known alternative. Some men may regret the fact of territorial preference, but, in the study of international politics, they cannot overlook it.

1 / The Map-Shape of Nations

Kenneth E. Boulding

Every single square mile of the inhabited surface of the globe has been placed under direct or indirect control of one of the territorial states. The very few remaining dependent territories and peoples in Africa, Asia, and the Caribbean represent administrative extensions of nation-states, mostly West European. In due time, these dependent territories are expected to obtain and

From pp. 123–124 of Kenneth E. Boulding, "National Images and International Systems," *The Journal of Conflict Resolution*, 3 (June 1959). Reprinted by permission of the author and the publisher.

[3] Dankwart A. Rustow, *A World of Nations: Problems of Political Modernization* (Washington, D.C.: The Brookings Institution, 1967).

administer their own territorial states. Singly, territorial states own and administer their portions of the world; collectively, they influence the whole of it.

A nation is, to many, the colored shape or the land mass that is depicted on a map. This selection explains why the concept of nation as an inhabited physical expanse of a specified size and shape is important for the study of conflict and cooperation among nations; the *exclusiveness* of territorial occupation means that generally one nation can increase its territorial possession only at the expense of a decrease in the territory of another. This situation makes for a potential, though certainly not inevitable, conflict.

... It is perhaps the most striking single characteristic of the national state as an organization, by contrast with organizations such as firms or churches, that it thinks of itself as occupying, in a "dense" and exclusive fashion, a certain area of the globe. The schoolroom maps which divide the world into colored shapes which are identified as nations have a profound effect on the national image. Apart from the very occasional condominium, it is impossible for a given plot of land on the globe to be associated with two nations at the same time. The territories of nations are divided sharply by frontiers carefully surveyed and frequently delineated by a chain of customs houses, immigration stations, and military installations. We are so accustomed to this arrangement that we think of it as "natural" and take it completely for granted. It is by no means the only conceivable arrangement, however. In primitive societies the geographical image is not sharp enough to define clear frontiers; there may be a notion of the rough territory of a tribe, but, especially among nomadic peoples, there is no clear concept of a frontier and no notion of a nation as something that has a shape on a map. In our own society the shape on the map that symbolizes the nation is constantly drilled into the minds of both young and old, both through formal teaching in schools and through constant repetition in newspapers, advertisements, cartoons, and so on. A society is not inconceivable, however, and might even be desirable, in which nations governed people but not territories and claimed jurisdiction over a defined set of citizens, no matter where on the earth's surface they happened to live.

The territorial aspect of the national state is important in the dynamics of international relations because of the *exclusiveness* of territorial occupation. This means that one nation can generally expand only at the expense of another; an increase in the territory of one is achieved only at the expense of a decrease in the territory of another. This makes for a potential conflict situation. This characteristic of the nation does not make conflict inevitable, but it does make it likely and is at least one of the reasons why the history of international relations is a history of perpetual conflict.

The territorial aspect of international relations is complicated by the fact that in many cases the territories of nations are not homogeneous but are

... "empires," in which the populations do not identify themselves with the national image of the dominant group. Thus when one nation conquers another and absorbs the conquered territory into an empire, it does not thereby automatically change the culture and allegiances of the conquered nation.[4]

2 / The Territorial Imperative

Robert Ardrey

Ethology, the study of patterns of animal behavior with possible insights into human behavior, was pioneered by Austria's Konrad Lorenz and Holland's Niko Tinbergen in the 1930s.[5] A comparative study of animal and human behavior was popularized later by Robert Ardrey in his two books, *The Territorial Imperative* and *African Genesis;* the latter is quoted in this selection. Ardrey's central thesis is that possession of a territory is an absolutely necessary condition for the fulfillment of man's basic needs such as security (as opposed to anxiety), stimulation (as opposed to boredom), and, above all, identity (as opposed to anonymity). For man, as for the animal, territory works toward satisfying genetically predetermined needs; territory must be protected at any cost. As proof of the depth of the impulse to protect one's own territorial possession, Ardrey cites the small nations' resistance to great powers (Finnish war against the Russians and the Greek war against the Italian and German armies). He also stresses the electrifying effect that the Japanese attack on Pearl Harbor had on American public opinion, ridden until that day with doubts and indecision about the war, even though Hitler had been victorious in Europe for two years.

Several social scientists have challenged the theory of a primarily instinctive territorial urge among men. They note that, motivated by glory or ideology

From pp. 12–20 *(passim)* of *African Genesis* by Robert Ardrey. Copyright © 1961 by Literat S.A. Reprinted by permission of Atheneum Publishers and William Collins Sons & Co. Ltd. Author's Footnotes have been omitted.

[4] Chapter 3, Selection 8, will deal with the effects of the principle of national self-determination on international relations in more detail.——Ed.

[5] Lorenz's book, *On Aggression,* was published in the United States in 1963.

(making the world safe for democracy, communism, socialism, and so on), men often covet more territory than they instinctively or materially need. Also, unlike animals, men are rationally able to accept a loss of their territory to their enemies or a territorial merger with their friends. Ardrey adds to his territorial thesis an important qualification: Territorial nationalism of men differs from the social territoriality of the primate by "man's capacity to form coalitions." Thus, human groups may select either to establish, or not to establish, interterritorial cooperation in forms of alliances, common markets, or federal unions. In matters of territorial behavior, man's instincts compete with both reason and complex emotions, whereas animals are guided primarily by instinct. (Selection 3, the essay by John H. Herz, contains a critique of the instinctive territorial imperative.)

Territoriality—the drive to gain, maintain, and defend the exclusive right to a piece of property—is an animal instinct approximately as ancient and powerful as sex. . . . There are birds like the swallow and jackdaw, and fish like the herring and cod, who form societies based on other than the territorial urge. But in the family of primates to which our human stream has been confined for seventy million years, to be deprived of territory is to be deprived of society; and to be deprived of society is very nearly to be deprived of all. . . .

Three fundamental drives for territory, for status and for organized society become evident in the primates, those creatures closest to ourselves. And behind all three looms the vague outline of a fourth force, deep-set, unaccountable, and perhaps unprovable: a mysterious need for order. What more may be out there, we cannot yet know. . . .

Birdsong takes place when and if the male gets his territory. So long as buntings are joined in flocks on the neutral feeding ground, the male never sings. Only when he finds that perch which will be the advertisement of his territorial existence—his alder, his gate, his willow bough—does the will to sing enchant him. . . .

Birdsong from the female is unquestionably an announcement of sexual readiness. But it occurs in response to the male's announcement of territorial readiness. . . .

The male bird sings of his possession. His call is distinctive throughout all his species since it is directed to the ears of his species alone. He sings to all other males that he is a bird of property and is prepared to defend what is his own. When he sings to the female, it is not to advise her that he is sexually ready—since he is a male his readiness may be assumed—but that being a bird of property he is worthy of her notice. It is a piece of information essential to the female ear. . . .

The rhesus monkeys transported from India . . . were about three hundred and fifty in number; went to pieces morally on the voyage; and,

resettled on the little Puerto Rican island, within about a year divided their thirty-six acres into territories, established their societies and regained their self-respect. In the light of what happened later one must keep in mind that these territories were new and perhaps lacked to a degree the authority over behaviour that older territories might exert. If this was so, however, it was not reflected in rhesus behaviour. Each group quickly established its proper hostility for neighbouring groups, and in customary isolation quickly welded its social life into an amiable, xenophobic whole.
. . .

If man is a part of the natural world, then he possesses as do all other species a genetic inheritance from ancestry as long as life itself. The territorial urge, as part of that inheritance, may in the human species be wrong or right, bad or good, destructive or constructive, wasting or conservative. But if man is a part of the natural world then his competitive drive cannot be erased by the elimination of private property, an institution itself derived from his animal ancestry; the drive can only be shifted—as happens in those social animals holding territory in common—from an expression of individuality through control of material objects to an expression of individuality through dominance over his fellow human beings. . . .

The territorial drive, as one ancient, animal foundation for that form of human misconduct known as war, is so obvious as to demand small attention. When Sir Arthur Keith found himself too old for any active contribution to the Second World War, his broodings produced the marvellous volume, *Essays on Human Evolution,* and the conclusion: "We have to recognize that the conditions that gave rise to war—the separation of animals into social groups, the 'right' of each group to its own area, and the evolution of an enmity complex to defend such areas—were on earth long before man made his appearance." Such an observation of a human instinct probably more compulsive than sex throws into pale context the more wistful conclusions of the romantic fallacy: that wars are a product of munitions makers, or of struggles for markets, or of the class struggle; or that human hostility arises in unhappy family relationships, or in the metaphysical reaches of some organic death force.

Permanence of territory acts as a factor reducing conflict. But also there prevails throughout all territorial animals a varying respect for the rights of the neighbour. The respect exists despite the universal law that territorial neighbours live in eternal and unremitting hostility. The bird attacks an intruder not with the objective of destroying him or seizing his territory in reprisal. Victory is accomplished by driving him away. . . .

It is a law of nature that territorial animals—whether individual or social—live in eternal hostility with their territorial neighbours. If civilized man on occasion demonstrates for his territorial neighbours a tolerance somewhat greater than that of the rhesus monkey, then one need only reflect on what a miraculous transformation is brought to the nature of the civilized man when aggression threatens his territory. It seem probable that the demands of civilization, not the yearnings of an inherently genial nature, account for any temporary lapses in human belligerence. . . .

Nationalism as such is no more than a human expression of the animal drive to maintain and defend a territory. It differs from the social territoriality of the primate only to the degree of man's capacity to form coalitions. . . .

3 / The Territorial State Revisited

John H. Herz

In the 1950s John H. Herz published an essay on the rise and demise of the territorial state.[6] He anticipated the demise of the territorial state in favor of supranational universalism under a combined impact of the growing economic and technological interdependence of nations, mass communications, air warfare, and the specter of nuclear warfare. Herz' article, elaborated upon in his later book,[7] had a greater influence on scholars than on statesmen and men in general. In their study of geography and international politics, for instance, Harold and Margaret Sprout[8] refer to Herz's study and similarly conclude that the combination of nuclear explosives and missiles had made "the territorial nation-state as unviable as the medieval castle became after the development of artillery."

"Political scientists are no more likely than other human beings to admit

Abridged from pp. 12–18 of John H. Herz, "The Territorial State Revisited," *Polity*, 1:1 (September 1968). Reprinted by permission of the author and the publisher. Author's footnotes have been omitted; footnotes added by the editor are so marked.

Another portion of Herz's study is reproduced in Selection 39. It focuses on the link between the unavailability of nuclear force for the purpose of protection, on the one hand, and the rise of nonaligned nationalism and the increased use of interventionist practices, on the other.

[6] "Rise and Demise of the Territorial States," *World Politics*, 9:4 (1957), 473.

[7] *International Politics in the Atomic Age* (New York: Columbia University Press, 1959).

[8] "Geography and International Politics," *The Journal of Conflict Resolution*, 4:1 (March 1960). 160.

mistakes—particularly when the mistakes have appeared in print," notes the journal *Polity,* which, in 1968, published Herz's new essay on the same subject in which he "handsomely retracts some of his previously stated ideas." Some readers may believe that Herz was actually right in his first optimistic article that expressed the hope for an early advent of supranational universalism. Others may agree with his later, more pessimistic estimate of the situation and his expressed fear lest chaos instead of universalism be our future. Still others may argue that Herz's present thesis is not pessimistic enough since it contains an expression of hope for amicable cooperation among territorial states that may preserve both peace and cultural diversity. This selection is from Herz's partial reversal of his original thesis on the demise of the territorial state.

Despite the conspicuous rise of international organization and supranational agencies in the postwar world and despite the continuing impact on international affairs of subnational agents such as business organizations (in the West) and "international" parties (in the East), the states remain the primary actors in international relations. Indeed, as the rush into "independent" statehood shows, being a sovereign nation seems to be the chief international status symbol as well as to furnish the actual entrance ticket into world society.

In 1957 I published an article entitled—perhaps rashly—"Rise and Demise of the Territorial State." Its chief thesis was to the effect that for centuries the characteristics of the basic political unit, the nation-state, had been its "territoriality," that is, its being identified with an area which, surrounded by a "wall of defensibility," was relatively impermeable to outside penetration and thus capable of satisfying one fundamental urge of humans —protection. However, so my argument proceeded, territoriality was bound to vanish, chiefly under the impact of the developments in the means of destruction which render defense nugatory by making even the most powerful "permeable." What was going to take the place of the now obsolete nation-state? I said that, rationally speaking, only global "universalism," affording protection to a mankind conceiving of itself as one unit, was the solution. . . .

Developments have rendered me doubtful of the correctness of my previous anticipations. The theory of "classical" territoriality and of the factors threatening its survival stands. But I am no longer sure that something very different is about to take its place. There are indicators pointing in another direction: not to "universalism" but to retrenchment; not to interdependence but to a new self-sufficiency; toward area not losing its impact but regaining it; in short, trends toward a "new territoriality." . . .

Why do we speak of "new territoriality"? If territory and statehood are to continue or resume their accustomed role, in what respect are they new? I suggest the term because now they will exist in an environment of nuclear penetrability, and they will have to assert themselves in an environment of vastly and rapidly increasing technological, economic, and general inter-relationships of a shrinking world. . . .

. . . Decline of empires, reduction in the role of penetrating force—developments such as these create preconditions for continuation of a national role as a basic constituent of international relations. They are necessary but not sufficient factors. In a positive way, nations, in order to be effective actors in international relations, must prove to be "legitimate" units, that is, entities which, generically and individually, can be and are being considered as basic and "natural" for the fulfillment of essential purposes, such as the protection and welfare of people. We must, therefore, search for factors that enable them to play this role, and also deal with the obstacles they encounter. . . .

To one watching the seemingly unending appearance of (by now over 130) "nation-states" upon the international scene—a veritable population explosion of nations—raising doubts about the ongoing power of the nation-state idea may sound strange. But all of us are aware of the turmoil and travail, the difficulties and doubts that accompany the process. Can one put into one and the same category The Gambia and France, Barbados and China, the Congo and Argentina? It is a commonplace to point out the synthetic nature of units formed on the accidental basis of boundaries drawn at the European conference table in the age of colonialism; the artificiality of "nations" built on the tearing apart or throwing together of several coherent entities, such as tribes; the doubtful identity of nations themselves proclaiming to be parts of an overarching nation (such as Arab states in relation to an overall "Arab nation"); the linguistic and similar centrifugal forces that threaten even apparently solid nations such as India; the nonviability of tiny or excessively weak nations, devoid of sufficient population and/or resources; the lack of territorial integration of widely separate island groups.

What, then, renders a nation-state legitimate? Legitimacy originates from the feelings and attitudes of the people within as well as neighbors and others abroad in regard to the unit, its identity and coherence, its political and general "way of life." Where there is positive valuation, that is, an impression or even a conviction that the unit in question "should be" the one on the basis of which a particular group organizes its separate and distinct existence as a "nation," there is legitimacy. The legitimacy of the territorial state that emerged from the Middle Ages in Europe was chiefly founded on defensibility against foreign attack (its protective function) and on the two successive principles of "legitimate" dynastic rule and, later, common nationality. One might distinguish between the legitimacy of the unit as such and that of its internal system (regime, socio-political structure). In regard to the former, in an age of nationalism units may range all the way from

illegitimacy to complete legitimacy. Mere possession of the outward paraphernalia of statehood (independent government in *de facto* control of an
area) does not suffice. For instance, with the growth of national unification
movements in the areas later constituting the German Empire and the
Italian Kingdom, existing sovereign states in these areas became increasingly
illegitimate. Today, the partition of Germany leaves the legitimacy of both
German units in doubt. Independence movements rendered empires increasingly illegitimate as indigenous nationalism rose against colonialism. But in
many of the new states that emerged from decolonization, absence of
minimally strong feelings of identity and solidity still prevents their being
considered as fully legitimate. There is, of course, a good deal of variation.
Where, as in Algeria, or now in Vietnam, a population previously little
integrated even in its own image has to fight long and doggedly for independence, it is likely to emerge more strongly consolidated as a national
entity than where a "nation," carved out with accidental boundary lines, had
independence thrown upon it without much popular exertion. Being compelled to fight for or defend one's territory generates true nationhood.

Internal legitimacy (without which the legitimacy of the unit as such can
provide little real solidity) in our day is closely related to democracy in the
broad sense of people having the conviction that they control their destinies
and that government operates for their welfare. . . .

Outlook and Conclusions

A good deal of attention has recently been paid to discoveries in the
relatively young science of animal behavior (ethology); they relate to the
so-called territorial nature of certain animal species. Biologists such as
Konrad Lorenz and, following their lead, popularizers such as Robert
Ardrey,[9] have given us vivid descriptions of how animals in every major
category (fish, birds, mammals) stake out an area as "their own," fix
boundaries, defend their territory (singly, with a mate, or in small groups)
against intruders, are motivated by their "territorial instinct" more powerfully when close to the center of their territory than when at a distance
from it, and so forth. To perceive analogies to these striking phenomena in
human affairs, and particularly in relations of nations to each other, is
tempting, and the authors mentioned have not hesitated to jump to such
conclusions. "The territorial nature of man is genetic and ineradicable."
The "territorial imperative" not only motivates individuals, such as peasants
threatened with collectivization of their holdings, but accounts for the behavior patterns of nations and other human collectivities. For those of us in
the social sciences who have previously emphasized the role of "territori-

[9] See Selection 2.——Ed.

ality," especially in international relations, it is tempting to find in these phenomena a biological and thus vastly more fundamental confirmation of their theories. If the "territorial imperative" that motivates the basic units of international relations is rooted in the nature of humans as animal species we do not have to worry about the future of the nation-state. Contrariwise, approaches that look forward to eventual replacement of territorial units with something nonterritorial, such as world government, would truly be proved utopian.

I suggest that we suspend judgment, however—at least for the time being. It seems that the ethological findings themselves are contested exactly in the area of our ancestors, or closest relatives, the primates. And an unwarranted jumping to conclusions becomes patent when no evidence is offered that a genetically inherited instinct prevails in humans as it does in certain, but *only* certain animal species, or that what motivates individual animals (or possibly humans) or very small groups (like families or clans) the same way, that is, instinctively, motivates large societies, such as nations. Ardrey, for instance, is inconsistent when he claims that the territorial imperative that motivated Russian peasants tenaciously clinging to their plot of land was destroyed by collectivization (thus "proving" the eternal, because instinct-based, nature of private property) while at the same time asserting that the much larger collectivity, the nation, as such reacts instinctively to intrusion on "its" territory. Why, then, do not *kolkhozes* develop their territorial instinct? True, in cases of threats to their very existence (such as we have discussed in connection with Israel, Algeria, etc.) nations' defensive behavior seems to be motivated by very elementary and powerful "imperatives." But even here there is no proof of instinctive behavior. And outside such marginal and truly "existential" situations the analogy is even less convincing. The more "normal" condition of nations competing for power (including territory) and thus getting involved in expansionism, armament races, and wars seems to go back rather to what I have called the "security dilemma," that is, the fear that competing units may deprive them of their land, resources, independence, and political existence. Animals do not "know"—as does man—that conspecific groups may become competitors for "hunting grounds" or other means of living; they do not "realize" that, if "their" territory proves insufficient to support a given number of them, they can solve this problem by invading others' territory, or, by the same token, that conspecific groups may attack them for these purposes.

It is thus a realization specific and unique to man that explains (in part, at least) competition for territory and scarce resources and accounts for intergroup conflicts, territorial defense and aggrandizement, and so forth. The social constellation deriving from this realization is different from one that would derive from genetically inherent instincts. For, if it is conscious competition for scarce resources rather than a territorial and/or aggressive instinct that in the past has been the prime motive of humans and human societies, the outlook for the future of international relations must differ vastly from one based on the assumption of biological drives. Under the latter, territorial units must forever go on fighting for land and resources. But the security dilemma can at least be attenuated through scientific-technological progress that "modernizes" mankind and thus frees it from scarcity. Modernization thus raises the hope that nationhood could become stabilized, not on the basis of a territorial instinct, but on that of providing plenty for those it comprises. . . .

For the presently underdeveloped nation modernization means liberation from economic dependencies (such as those of the present one-crop and one-resource countries). Modernization and economic development would also serve to confer on many units that legitimacy which, as pointed out before, they lack because of the absence or weakness of a "national" elite that would integrate them, despite ethnic and similar disparities, into a modern nation. . . .

But whether such consolidation of the nation-state and corresponding stability of the state system will be attained depends on whether at least a large proportion of the underdeveloped will be able to modernize themselves. Modernized countries have proved relatively stable, also, generally, they do not desire territory from others: not the Soviet Union from the United States, or vice versa, nor even, by now, Germany from France. But the underdeveloped are beset by every type of turmoil, radicalism, and foreign interventionism. It is therefore a problem of development and development policies; a question of whether the affluent nations will be able and willing to make the sacrifices that are required of them even though they themselves have their own problems of development and equity; above all, it is the problem of preventing overpopulation. The rapidly growing pressure of population outrunning resources not only prevents the underdeveloped from modernizing but may actually lead to conditions deteriorating so badly that territory may assume overwhelming importance again. Unless there is rapid and drastic population planning, excess populations will press against boundaries separating them from—for the most part equally overpopulated—neighbors, and wars may ensue with the violence of the primitive, elementary struggle for "hunting grounds" and "water holes," only now on a global plane. Territory would become an object of expansionism and conquest again, and nationalism assume, or reassume, the nature of antagonism and despair. The big and wealthy would withdraw into their poverty-surrounded nuclear fortresses, or else engage in renewed "international civil war." For the time being, so it appears, it is not internationalism, "universalism," or any other supranational model that constitutes the alternative to the territorial, or nation-state, system, but genuine, raw chaos.

Such chaos would lead to a system or, rather, a nonsystem of international relations in which the terms territoriality and statehood would hold scant meaning. If we consider how little has been done in these decisive decades to forestall such a development—hardly anything, for instance, in the vital areas of population control and of the widening gap between the under-developed and the affluent nations—the pessimistic conclusion that it is almost too late for the development of a system of "new territoriality" seems, realistically, to impose itself. Assuming, however, that the "almost" still leaves room for more hopeful potentialities, let us recall the hypotheses made above by summing up the most basic requirements for a development under which the new-old nation-state, the polity of the last decades of this century, might emerge.

First among these, I would list the spread of political, economic, and attitudinal modernity to the areas where legitimate nation-states have still to be established through such processes of modernization. What this pre-supposes demographically, technologically, economically has already been mentioned.

Second, to make sure that new states, as well as some of the old, do not fall prey to continual quarrels over territorial issues, such issues among them must be settled in such a way that boundaries encompass populations which consider themselves and are recognized by others as nationally satisfied and self-sufficient entities. This is a large order, and all devices of diplomacy, all procedures of international organization, all rules of law and institutions of adjudication must be utilized, developed, and possibly im-proved for their solution.

Third, we must count upon the continuing deradicalization of systems originally based on world-revolutionary doctrines, and a corresponding in-clination of the other states to leave the choice of internal structure to the respective nations without trying to influence, interfere, or control. Among other things, this would imply that programs of foreign assistance be sepa-rated from political policies and/or transferred increasingly to international agencies, and that even in case of civil war outside powers abstain from assisting either side, including the one they consider the "legitimate govern-ment" of the unit in question; new international law might be developed to spell out the corresponding legal rules and commitments.

Last, but not least, under such hypotheses recourse to international violence would be reduced to two major categories: action in self-defense when, and only when, one's own territory is directly attacked or invaded; in the event the invader succeeds in occupying the area, continued resistance of its population through a combination of guerilla warfare and nonviolent resistance to render the aggressor the "fly on the flypaper." . . .

The function, then, of the future polity would still or again be that of providing group identity, protection, and welfare; in short, the legitimate function of the nation. And this neo-territorial world of nations, in addition, might salvage one feature of humanity which seems ever more threatened by the ongoing rush of mankind into the technological conformity of a synthetic planetary environment: diversity of life and culture, of traditions and civilizations. If the nation can preserve these values, it would at long last have emerged as that which the philosophers of early nationalism had expected it to be: the custodian of cultural diversity among groups mutually granting each other their peculiar worth. In the past that other, opposite type of nationalism, the exclusivist, xenophobic, expansionist, oppressive one, has rendered their expectation nugatory, causing instability and infinite suffering of nations and people. This small world of ours can no longer live with it. Chaotic instability is too high a price to pay for its fleeting triumphs in an inflammable world. Neo-territoriality will function only if and when the danger of nuclear destruction and the interdependence of humans and their societies on the globe will have made nations and their leaders aware that the destiny awaiting us is now common to all.

4 / Trends away from the Nation-State

J. David Singer

In contrast to Herz's reluctant recognition of the probable durability of the territorial state as a basic component of the international system, Singer considers that it may have begun to lose the loyalty of its citizens. Singer accuses the territorial state of being less capable of protecting its citizens materially, less viable as a basis for economic organization, and more demanding of popular support. In its place, a multitude of extranational associations of intranational groups will emerge, and, being more "natural" than the territorial state, according to Singer, these associations will tend to replace it as the dominant component of the global system.[10]

From pp. 2–3, 10 of J. David Singer, "The Global System and Its Sub-systems: A Developmental View," a paper presented at the American Political Science Association, New York, 1966. Reprinted by permission of the author. Author's footnotes have been omitted.

[10] A similar expectation of an emergence of transnational values and groups is expressed by Richard A. Falk in his essay on the future of international law (Selection 15).

Even though the national state was already emerging as a potent form of social organization in Europe by 1648 and the close of the Thirty Years' War, its really preponderant role in Continental politics was probably not established until both Germany and Italy had been unified, just a century ago. And today, even as Asian and African nationalists struggle to establish viable states out of economic and social chaos and against powerful countervailing tendencies, the national states of Europe and North America begin to show the early indications of ultimate demise. A variety of signs suggest that, as objects of loyalty, the Western industrialized states are becoming less salient and less attractive to increasing sectors of their citizenry, and that as allocators and redistributors of valued objects, the upward trend at the expense of other social organizations has begun to flatten out and may well be heading back down in the decades immediately ahead.

If these assertions are correct—and they would seem to be susceptible of empirical disconfirmation via opinion surveys, content analysis and studies of budget trends—how do we account for it? One set of factors would seem to be that of the increasing permeability of national boundaries, reducing their capacity to resist unwanted inputs of both information and energy. On the energy side, due to weapons technology, national states have lost what Boulding . . . refers to as "unconditional viability"; aircraft, missiles, and their payloads now make each nation's physical survival largely conditional on the policies and capabilities of other nations. Not only can national boundaries no longer interdict all enemy weapons, but they can no longer interdict unwanted information. Even at this early point in communications technology, it is relatively simple to penetrate a nation's boundaries via radio, television, and paper; and with communication satellites and miniature receivers, the problem will be even simpler. Combined with this is another consequence of industrialization: more people can travel more rapidly and economically to more remote places than ever before, although in this case, governments can easily prohibit it. Even though there is still far more domestic than international communication and tourism, and some evidence that the gross increase in intra-national communication continues to outstrip that in extra-national communication, the opportunities and incentives for an increase in the latter are clearly present. Moreover, the critical factor may well be the communication experiences of the opinion makers and reference figures rather than that of the masses, and there is little doubt that these sectors are already enjoying an increase in foreign vis-à-vis domestic information exchange.

The interaction of these two sets of phenomena is by no means fully understood yet, but one interpretation might be that it could, and may already, produce some serious dissonance. As the nations decline in their capacity to protect their citizens militarily, the regimes may be expected to counteract that weakness by greater efforts at political and psychological mobilization. But such "mobilization" depends on the credibility of those very tribal superstitions which are the most likely victims of the increased access to cosmopolitian information.

On the economic side, however, it might be argued that as the industrial nations have embraced Keynsian economics and welfare state practices, the citizen becomes more closely dependent upon and bound to the national state. While it is true that these policies have led to increasing real income, and somewhat more equal distribution thereof . . . , as well as less severe fluctuations in the business cycle, the modern economics have also created some serious new problems for national regimes. Because expectations regarding economic well-being have risen, governments are less free to solve some of the perpetual problems by traditional means; in earlier days, for example, any serious discrepancy in a nation's balance of payments could be handled by devaluation of the currency, import quotas, tariff increases, tax increases, interest rate increases, and other measures of that sort. The resulting economic dislocation used to be accepted as a normal concomitant of a free economy, but such measures today would produce widespread dissatisfaction in the industrial nations. These and related developments suggest that even as a basis for economic organization, the national state is inadequate. As this paper is written, we see a dramatic illustration of all these tendencies in Britain, which has not only been able to do precious little to assure its citizens of military protection, but seems increasingly incapable of functioning as a viable economic system.

Whether these speculations turn out to be premature, or even erroneous, and the national state does not soon begin to experience an absolute decline in the loyalty it receives, there is little doubt that other secondary organizations (of an intra- and extra-national nature) will experience a relative increase in attractiveness and legitimacy at the state's expense. This tendency is perhaps best illustrated in the United States where the provincial ("state") governments are being bypassed by direct social welfare linkages between the federal government and the municipalities. More important of course, and almost unnoticed by students of American politics, is the increasing role of *ad hoc,* non-governmental, citizens groups. As in the agricultural control programs begun in the New Deal period, groups of citizens linked by profession or common organizational memberships rather than by territorial unit, are serving as decisional and executive surrogates (if not substitutes) for traditional units of government. Such non-governmental groupings have always played some sort of role in national states, if only as pressure groups, but if the impression of their rising importance is correct, it may be yet another indication that the trend away from nation-state dominance is stronger than that toward it. . . .

The basic direction of that tendency and which of the many classes of sub-system is likely to emerge as the successor to today's national state—if at all—is far from clear, and a more solid research base could suggest which trends are the strongest. On the basis of the very limited evidence now available, however, some rash, but tentative, speculations might be ventured; all of this assumes, of course, that major nuclear war is somehow avoided. First, the national state will decline in potency as it increases in permeability and diminishes in efficacy on the socio-economic as well as the military side. In its place, most likely to emerge as more potent sub-systems of the global system will be associations which are more adaptive than the nation has been or can, by its basic nature, be. They will be considerably less territorial in their base, less vulnerable to serious internal cleavage because they will embrace somewhat more homogeneous interests and ideologies, and will have fewer external threats to overcome. Moreover, their leaders will not find themselves in the nearly insoluble predicament which faces the early and mid-twentieth century elites, caught as they are between the demands of the international system and the temptations of the domestic sub-system.

Whereas the functionalist outlook anticipates a global polity of *national* sub-systems which have somehow "learned" to cooperate, the point of view expressed here predicts the displacement of national entities by extra-national associations of intra-national groups which are based more on such attributes as social class, ideology, profession (including managers, technocrats, etc.) and somewhat less on the accident of birth, ethnicity and language. As these more natural associations become more integrated and influential via the gradual assumption of many functions now handled by the national state (or not handled at all), they will develop into coalitions of NGO's and begin to compete successfully for influence in the pluralistic setting at the headquarters of the various emerging global institutions. Inevitably they will demand more than observer status and will begin to share with national governments the representative function in the various legislative bodies.

As I suggested above, these speculations flow from an extremely fragile base. Though a few students of world politics have begun to produce some imaginative and plausible scenarios of the future, the empirical base is such that plausibility is all that we dare claim.

2
Nationalism

The renowned historian, Arnold J. Toynbee, defined nationalism as a "state of mind in which we give our paramount loyalty to one fraction of the human race—to a particular tribe of which we happen to be tribesmen."[1] A territorial state is the ideal form of political organization for a group that feels as a nation. Of course, such supreme loyalty may be felt toward a state that already exists or toward a state that may be established at some future date in the wake of a successful secession, anticolonial revolution, or national liberation war. Nationalism in the process of acquiring a state is usually referred to as national self-determination.[2]

Long and controversial is the list of reasons for the existence and strength of modern nationalism. Historians and social scientists usually identify a territorial base in combination with common institutions and culture (such as language, religion, history including myths and legends, and hopes or plans for a common future) as the most plausible sources of nationalistic feelings. Yet none of these factors, taken singly, can explain the origin and continuing force of nationalism. Other scholars attribute nationalism to deliberate socialization of men into national beings: Man's awareness of common territorial fate, language, traditions, history, institutions, and anticipation of a common future is primarily a

[1] Arnold J. Toynbee, "Again Nationalism Threatens," *The New York Times Magazine* (November 3, 1963), 23.

[2] This aspect of nationalism will be the subject of further analysis in Chapter 3.

result of indoctrination and education by the family, the school, and the mass media. Displays of national symbols (flags, military uniforms), political oratory (especially on days commemorating national glories or tragedies), and daily mass media outputs combine to produce a mighty stream of ethnocentric messages. Although not all citizens accept or absorb the avalanche of self-centered admiration or pity uncritically, the majority does. A citizen who normally displays no nationalistic emotion may find himself surprisingly elated when he sees his national flag raised and hears the national anthem played at the Olympics, for example. Nationalistic feeling showers on the winning athlete who, in principle, should have competed as an individual instead of a nation's representative. All national governments see to it that their achievements are appropriately brought to the attention of their people. In 1969 the Americans were supposed to be particularly gratified as a nation at the sight of the Stars and Stripes on the surface of the moon. The same year, the Chinese government recommended that the first explosion of a Chinese hydrogen bomb (September 29, 1969) be celebrated, as the Chinese press agency Hsinhua put it, as "another fruitful result of the Great Proletarian Revolution . . . at a time when hundreds of millions of army-men and civilians throughout China were warmly celebrating the glorious festive occasion of the twentieth anniversary of the foundation of the great People's Republic of China."[3] It is fascinating as well as depressing to observe the strange ways in which national leaders all over the world hope to make a citizen proud of and loyal to his nation.

In his study of the growth of nations, Karl W. Deutsch identified eight patterns that seem to recur and, to a limited extent, seem to be comparable among different regions, periods, and cultures. The eight uniformities of growth are:

1. Subsistence agriculture shifts to *exchange economy*.
2. Rural populations in *core areas* of denser settlement and more intensive exchange are subject to social mobilization.
3. Growth of *towns* is accompanied by the growth of social mobility within them and between town and country.
4. *Basic communication grids,* linking important rivers, towns and trade routes in a flow of transport, travel and migration, begin to grow.
5. Accumulation and *concentration of capital* and skills, and sometimes of social institutions, have the effect of *"lift-pump"* on other areas and populations, with the successive entry of different social strata into the nationalistic phase.
6. Rise of the concept of individual and group *"interest"* and the growth of *individual self-awareness* and awareness of one's predispositions to join a particular group united by language and communication habits.

[3] *The New York Times* (October 5, 1969).

7. *Ethnic awareness* is awakened and *national symbols* accepted.
8. Ethnic awareness merges with attempts at *political compulsion,* sometimes transforming one's own people into a privileged group in a polyethnic system.[4]

One of the most disturbing aspects of nationalistic emotion is the frequent combination of inner-directed love, trust, amity, and self-admiration with outer-directed hatred, distrust, enmity, and contempt of all outsiders. Symptomatically, soldiers in defense of their nation are to love and protect their people and country by hating and destroying their enemy.

The following Selections 5 and 6 examine the reciprocal influence of seemingly mutually exclusive concepts of self-centered nationalism and proletarian international solidarity. Selection 7 analyzes a possibly beneficial influence of a more just distribution of world wealth upon envy and hatred among nations.

5 / Nationalism Socialized: Socialism Nationalized

Edward Hallett Carr

The famous charter of proletarian internationalism, the Marx-Engels manifesto of 1848, concludes with a hope and call for supranational unity of the laboring classes: "Working Men of All Countries, Unite!" The text of the manifesto, however, recognizes the inescapable territorial dimension of the proletarian action and advises the revolutionaries to wrench the control of their national communities from the hands of their territorial rulers and exploiters: "The working men have no country. We cannot take from them what they have not got. Since the proletariat must first of all acquire political supremacy, must

From pp. 18–24, 26–33 *(passim)* of Edward Hallett Carr, *Nationalism and After,* 1945. Reprinted by permission of St. Martin's Press, Inc., New York, The Macmillan Company of Canada, and Macmillan & Co., Ltd. Some author's footnotes have been omitted or placed in the text; footnotes added by the editor are so marked.

[4] Karl W. Deutsch, "The Growth of Nations: Some Recurrent Patterns of Political and Social Integration," *World Politics,* 5:2 (January 1953), 168–195.

rise to be the leading class of the nation, must constitute itself *the* nation, it is to this extent itself national, though not in the bourgeois sense of the word."

Since 1848 the rhetoric of proletarian internationalism has had to be grafted onto nationalist egoism and emotionalism; the early Marxist hope for international class brotherhood has adapted itself to the fact that, as an African socialist put it: "Nation is the first reality in the twentieth century."[5] The English historian E. H. Carr argues below that a state which, in accordance with the socialist concept, becomes a promoter and protector of the nation's standard of living nationalizes not only the means of production but the socialist creed itself.

The rise of new social strata to full membership of the nation marked the last three decades of the 19th century throughout western and central Europe. Its landmarks were the development of industry and industrial skills; the rapid expansion in numbers and importance of urban populations; the growth of workers' organizations and of the political consciousness of the workers; the introduction of universal compulsory education; and the extension of the franchise. . . . The "democratization" of the nation in the earlier part of the century had resulted in the establishing of popular control over the functions of maintaining law and order. . . . The "socialization" of the nation which set in towards the end of the century brought about a far more radical change. . . . Henceforth the political power of the masses was directed to improving their own social and economic lot. The primary aim of national policy was no longer merely to maintain order and conduct what was narrowly defined as public business, but to minister to the welfare of members of the nation and to enable them to earn their living. The democratization of the nation in the second period had meant the assertion of the political claims of the dominant middle class. The socialization of the nation for the first time brings the economic claims of the masses into the forefront of the picture. The defence of wages and employment becomes a concern of national policy and must be asserted, if necessary, against the national policies of other countries; and this in turn gives the worker an intimate practical interest in the policy and power of his nation. The socialization of the nation has as its natural corollary the nationalization of socialism.

The 20th-century alliance between nationalism and socialism . . . in its modern form . . . dates from Bismarck, who, schooled by Lassalle, showed the German workers how much they had to gain from a vigorous and ruthless nationalism. . . . In the same period the word "jingoism"[6] was coined

[5] Léopold Sédar Senghor, President of Senegal, in his book *African Socialism* (New York: Frederick A. Praeger, Inc., 1964), p. 47.

[6] Jingoism has been probably derived from "by jingo," which was part of a bellicose and patriotic song current at the time of English-Russian tension over the eastern Mediterranean in 1878. The verse was: "We don't want to fight, but by jingo if we do, We've got the ships, we've got the men, We've got the money too."——Ed.

in Great Britain to describe something that had not hitherto existed—the nationalism of the masses. . . . National policy was henceforth founded on the support of the masses; and the counterpart was the loyalty of the masses to a nation which had become the instrument of their collective interests and ambitions.

In a work originally published in 1907 the Austrian Social Democrat, Otto Bauer, argued that socialism meant "an increasing differentiation of nations, a sharper emphasis on their peculiarities, a sharper division between their characters," and attacked those who believed that socialism would "diminish or even remove the differences between nations." . . . Writers on international relations in English-speaking countries had less insight; for the most part they were content to congratulate themselves on the increasing "popular" interest in international affairs and believed that this would promote international concord.

. . . In the 19th century, when the nation belonged to the middle class and the worker had no fatherland, socialism had been international. The crisis of 1914 showed in a flash that, except in backward Russia, this attitude was everywhere obsolete. The mass of workers knew instinctively on which side their bread was buttered; and Lenin was a lone voice proclaiming the defeat of his own country as a socialist aim and crying treason against the "social-chauvinists."[7] International socialism ignominiously collapsed. Lenin's desperate rear-guard action to revive it made sense only in Russia, and there only so long as revolutionary conditions persisted. Once the "workers' state" was effectively established, "socialism in one country" was the logical corollary. The subsequent history of Russia and the tragi-comedy of the Communist International are an eloquent tribute to the solidarity of the alliance between nationalism and socialism.

. . . The democratic nationalism of the 19th century had proved manageable and compatible with some kind of international order precisely because its aspirations were predominantly political and could be satisfied within the framework of the 19th-century *laissez-faire* . . . state. The social nationalism (or national socialism) of the 20th century, by shifting the ground from political to economic aspirations, brought about the abdication of the *laissez-faire* state in favor of the "social service" state. . . . Henceforth the functions of the nation-state were as much economic as political. . . . Nationalism had invaded and conquered the economic domain from which the 19th century had so cunningly excluded it. The single world economy was replaced by a multiplicity of national economies, each concerned with the well-being of its own members. . . .

---

[7] Derived from the name of Nicholas Chauvin of Rochefort. His demonstrative patriotism and attachment to Napoleon at the time of the Empire came to be ridiculed by his comrades. *Chauvinism* is now applied to a vainglorious, bellicose, or intolerant form of patriotism.——Ed.

Eco + Political

As custodians of the living standards, employment and amenities of their
whole populations, modern nations are, in virtue of their nature and function, probably less capable than any other groups in modern times of reaching agreement with one another.

The contrast between the comparatively law-abiding habits of members
of a national community and the law-breaking proclivities of nation members of the international community has long been a truism; and recent rapid
decline in the observance of international law is common ground among all
observers. . . . Paradoxically enough, it was Bismarck who first diagnosed
the symptoms of decline and ascribed it to the unreliability of democracies.
The diagnosis was too narrow. The decline was due not to any particular
form of government or constitution, but to the socialized nation of which
Bismarck was one of the first promoters. . . .

. . . The first obligation of the modern national government, which no
other obligation will be allowed to override, is to its own people. It would be
absurd to lament this state of affairs as proof of increased human wicked-
ness; it might equally well be regarded as proof of a sharpened social conscience. But whatever view we take of it, it would be folly to neglect the
overwhelming evidence that modern national governments cannot and will
not observe international treaties or rules of international law when these
become burdensome or dangerous to the welfare or security of their own
nation. Any so-called international order built on contingent obligations
assumed by national governments is an affair of lath and plaster and will
crumble into dust as soon as pressure is placed upon it.

6 / Can a Communist Be a Patriot?

Mao Tse-tung

Chairman Mao believes that a Communist who is also an internationalist
must be a patriot if he is a citizen of a nation that has become victim of an
imperialist aggression. This thesis was contained in a report submitted by Mao
to the plenary session of the Central Committee of the Chinese Communist

From pp. 196–197 of Mao Tse-tung, *Selected Works*, Vol. 2 (1937–1941) (Peking:
Foreign Languages Press, 1961–1965).

Party in 1938, the second year of Japan's aggressive war against China. The polemical tone of the excerpt reflects the then discussion among the Chinese Communists on the subject of Mao's recommendation to join forces with Chiang Kai-shek's Nationalist armies and defend China against Japan. Mao's point was that defeatism was an appropriate attitude for the Communists of the aggressor nations such as imperial Japan or Nazi Germany while patriotism was an appropriate attitude for the Chinese Communists. The first portion of Mao's statement on patriotism was again reproduced in 1966 in the little red book of the Chinese cultural revolution, *Quotations from Chairman Mao Tse-tung.*[8]

Can a Communist, who is an internationalist, at the same time be a patriot? We hold that he not only can be but must be. The specific content of patriotism is determined by historical conditions. There is the "patriotism" of the Japanese aggressors and of Hitler, and there is our patriotism. Communists must resolutely oppose the "patriotism" of the Japanese aggressors and of Hitler. The Communists of Japan and Germany are defeatists with regard to the wars being waged by their countries. To bring about the defeat of the Japanese aggressors and of Hitler by every possible means is in the interests of the Japanese and the German people, and the more complete the defeat the better. This is what the Japanese and German Communists should be doing and what they are doing. For the wars launched by the Japanese aggressors and Hitler are harming their own people as well as the people of the world. China's case is different, because she is the victim of aggression. Chinese Communists must therefore combine patriotism with internationalism. We are at once internationalists and patriots, and our slogan is, "Fight to defend the motherland against the aggressors." For us defeatism is a crime and to strive for victory in the War of Resistance is an inescapable duty. For only by fighting in defence of the motherland can we defeat the aggressors and achieve national liberation. And only by achieving national liberation will it be possible for the proletariat and other working people to achieve their own emancipation. The victory of China and the defeat of the invading imperialists will help the people of other countries. Thus in wars of national liberation patriotism is applied internationalism. For this reason Communists must use their initiative to the full, march bravely and resolutely to the battle front of the war of national liberation and train their guns on the Japanese aggressors. For this reason, immediately after the Incident of September 18, 1931, our Party issued its call to resist the Japanese aggressors by a war of national defence, and later proposed a national united front against Japan, ordered the Red Army to reorganize as part of the anti-Japanese National Revolutionary Army and to march to the front, and instructed Party members to take their place in the forefront of the war and defend the motherland to

[8] (Peking: Foreign Languages Press, 1966), pp. 175–176.

the last drop of their blood. These are good patriotic actions and, far from running counter to internationalism, are its application in China. Only those who are politically muddle-headed or have ulterior motives talk nonsense about our having made a mistake and abandoned internationalism.

7 / Nationalism and World Unity

Karl W. Deutsch

In this selection Deutsch combines his estimate of the continuing importance of nationalism with a cautious expectation that the same process of mass mobilization and modernization that created nationalism may in the future turn against it. This reversal is likely when the economic inequality among nations is replaced by a more just distribution of world wealth. Deutsch's hope is also expressed by Sekou Touré and many other leaders of the Third World.

It should not be assumed, of course, that material advancement will, by itself, remove aggressive tendencies and intolerance among nations and men. "The recent history of the world," according to Inis L. Claude, "fails to confirm the existence of a direct correlation between national economic backwardness and aggressiveness; it was advanced Germans, not primitive Africans, who shattered world peace in 1939."[9] Underdeveloped Africa and Asia played indeed only a minor part in the history of intolerant and expansive nationalism and in the war designs of the developed major powers both before and during World War II. As one representative of the Third World, Charles Malik of Lebanon, stated: "The poor, the sick, the dispossessed must certainly be done justice to. But to suppose that there will be peace when everybody is materially happy and comfortable, is absolute nonsense."[10]

Deutsch also warns against premature hopes for an early merger of nations into supranational communities, either on a regional or world basis. An emerging bloc of nations rarely views itself as a stepping stone to a world government and world peace; regional blocs are often being established in opposition to and

Reprinted from pp. 190–193 of *Nationalism and Social Communication: An Inquiry into the Foundations of Nationality* (1953) by Karl W. Deutsch by permission of The MIT Press, Cambridge, Mass.

[9] Inis L. Claude, Jr., *Swords into Plowshares: The Problems and Progress of International Organization* (New York: Random House, 1959), p. 384.
[10] *United Nations Bulletin* (May 1, 1951), 459.

in defense against similarly motivated international groupings. The British historian E. H. Carr (see also Selection 5) points out that "a division of the world in a small number of large multinational units . . . would be simply the old nationalism writ large."[11]

. . . [T]here seems to be considerable propects for the increasing importance of nationalism in the years ahead. . . .

Yet the same processes which made nationalism probable may soon come to turn against it.

Nationalism was associated with the mass mobilization of precommercial, preindustrial peasant peoples. Their mobilization and their transition to an industrial economy should be substantially completed within the next two generations. Barring a general atomic war, capital equipment by then should become far more widely distributed over the world's more backward regions.

Tying the mobilized populations into national communities and social classes has tended to separate peoples from each other for a time; but it made them fundamentally more alike, and taught many of them to adjust to new and changing patterns of communication.

The unfinished part of the task should not be underestimated. The economic inequality between different groups or classes within each country has been matched, and in some instances in part replaced, by the inequality between different countries and peoples. Since the Industrial Revolution, nationalism has drawn much of its strength from the successively lower levels of material civilization—the *Kulturgefaelle,* as the Germans called it —met in each country by many travelers journeying eastward from America to China, or going southward from the temperate zone to the equator. Everywhere on this ladder of economic inequality, nationalists found richer neighbors to resent and envy; poorer neighbors to despise and fear; but few, if any, equals to respect.

The fact of inequality was perhaps not decisive, but its vast extent, and its tendency to shrink so slowly, or sometimes even to increase was decisive. Economic growth has been so much faster in some countries than in others that today the living standards of Australian and Hindu farmers may well be even farther apart than they were a hundred years ago. That the difference in poverty is so great, and that the world's poorest peoples are so numerous—comprising, as they do, more than one-half of mankind—these are perhaps the fundamental facts behind much of today's nationalistic insistence on national separateness and economic and political barriers. Not before the bottom of the barrel of the world's large peoples has been reached, not before inequality and insecurity will have become less extreme,

[11] Edward Hallett Carr, *Nationalism and After* (New York: Saint Martin's Press, Inc., 1945), p. 35.

not before the vast poverty of Asia and Africa will have been reduced substantially by industrialization, and by gains in living standards and in education—not before then will the age of nationalism and national diversity see the beginning of its end.

Thus far, the age of nationalism has grouped people apart from each other, and may for a time continue to do so. But at the same time it is preparing them, and perhaps in part has already prepared them, for a more thoroughgoing world-wide unity than has ever been seen in human history.

Even the growth of national consciousness may under certain circumstances contribute to this end. It can become a blinding curse to those who have accepted it uncritically. Like all consciousness, however, it draws much of its strength from being an awareness of something which exists. To reveal what is, to show the true state of affairs for part of the political problems of a part of mankind may serve as a preparation for teaching men to be aware of the whole pattern of their affairs, and of the single problem of mankind on its painful way to unity. As men attain this insight into the essential unity of their fate on this planet, the age of nationalism and of the growth of nations may recede into its proper historical perspective.

Nationalistic parties and leaders have characteristically led their peoples along part of this way. They seem unlikely to lead them to its end. They have tended to be more successful in the stages of national protest than in the tasks of national construction. In underdeveloped countries, nationalists often have been more successful in building parties rather than armies; armies rather than schools; schools rather than factories; and factories rather than fundamental changes in village life. Often they have been political beneficiaries of a process of social mobilization which they had not created and over which they had little influence. They were riding a wave, not channeling a river, and they would drift as far as they were carried by the current. In general they did not come to grips with the fundamental productive forces of their countries, and they left their peoples often not much less poor and not much better organized than the large and largely anonymous processes of economic growth would make them.

. . . It may take national leaders and movements of deeper realism and greater stature than the nationalists of the years between 1900 and 1950, if the majority of the peoples and nations of mankind are to outgrow the present age of national separation and conflict.

The same considerations apply to the growth of regional blocks, or of blocks cemented by ties of economics, ideology, or power. Such blocks exist already, and for the near future their growth seems more probable than that of any major institutions of world government. All such blocks will be characterized by uneven internal structures based on underlying cluster patterns of settlement, capital, natural resources, and facilities for social communication. The expansion of all such blocks will be subject, therefore, to very real geographic and social limitations, although there might be a lesser limitation on their ability to inflict military damage on each other.

In the long run, the decisive question for any such block will be the same as that for any state or nation of today: Will it prove an instrumentality of inner development and growth or an engine of stagnation and destruction? What may matter most in the end will be not so much the size of the bite as the quality of the chewing. How much of a living unity, how much actual and mutual communication, how much cultural and economic growth will there be among the masses of the populations throughout the territories of each block? From the viewpoint of democracy, genuine freedom and development within a limited block of countries should be preferable to stagnation within a larger area or under an inadequate or premature world government.

3

Multinational States and Stateless Nations

This chapter focuses on the widely recognized and acclaimed principle of national self-determination, which, in essence, states that a community that feels itself to be a nation has the right to acquire and maintain its own territorial state. The primary problem in accepting this principle is one of distinguishing *any* dissatisfied group from a group that is a potential nation (that is, a territorial community internationally entitled to statehood). Rupert Emerson examines this basic problem in Selection 8.

If nations and states are to be made to coincide territorially, administratively, politically, and emotionally, two different processes may achieve such an aim: assimilation (amalgamation or integration which may be either voluntary or forcible) or territorial secession.

Many a polytribal, multiracial, or multinational (polyethnic) territorial community has been transformed into a relatively homogeneous nation by a process of more or less forcible assimilation. Some nations have issued, as it were, from a central authority's (medieval king or dictator) power to impose obedience and integration, render services, assure protection, and manipulate the contents and means of national socialization. The history of royal France and imperial Germany are good examples. In brief, a nation may *postdate* a territorial state.

The second process is actually territorial disintegration by means of secession. Nations often claim and obtain separation from a multinational state or empire. Thus, the emotional and political cohesion of a community may *predate* its own territorial state, which is the source and justification of national self-determination. A nation in quest of a state may be called stateless nation; in a multinational state such a stateless nation is usually called a national minority and in a colonial empire it is called a dependent people. A stateless nation, then, is a group that feels itself to be a nation; it is a *potential* state and therefore an actor on the international stage. For this reason potential nation-states and their composites (multinational states or colonial empires) are of major interest to any student of international politics.

Internal tensions within a territorial state or its colonial extension tend to transform a basically domestic political scene into one resembling the international arena. For instance, in a revolution or a civil war where one side expresses its ultimate goal in terms of territorial secession, a nation-state actually splits into two or more units, each controlling a portion of the national (or imperial) territory and engaging in an independent search for external support; that is, a seceding segment may conduct its own foreign policy, the very attribute of a full-fledged sovereign state. Thus, not only established states but also potential nation-states assume an active role in international politics. The Palestinian guerilla movement in the 1970s is a good example of the power of a potential nation-state. In the present era of global interdependence, no internal strife, whether ideological or ethnic, is immune to internationalization. Subnational groups in revolt against their territorial government assume, expect, ask for, are promised, and generally receive support from an established state. The extent of this support is usually not related to the justice of the revolting group's demands but is determined by the foreign nation's interest in weakening the hold of the tottering government over its people.

This chapter contains Renan's classic statement on the nation in spiritual rather than territorial or economic terms—"a nation is a soul"—and modern nationalist leaders' expressions of fear that in our interdependent world of unequal nations their nation may lose its soul by slavish imitation or cultural conquest.

8 / National Self-Determination

Rupert Emerson

When a community develops its consciousness of a separate political entity, should its claim for an independent territorial statehood be an *absolute* right irrespective of circumstances? Or is a demand for national self-determination in terms of independent statehood to be treated as only one of several competing interests and conflicting principles, and therefore only a *relative* right? A relative right is a right that may or may not be implemented according to circumstances such as the community's strategic location, population size, political maturity, economic viability, or effect of its agitation and action on domestic as well as international peace and order. The following excerpt from one of the best studies of nationalism in the second half of the twentieth century examines possible answers to the questions posed above.

Since the state is in modern times the most significant form of organization of men and embodies the greatest concentration of power, it is inevitable that there should have been, and should still be, a great and revolutionary struggle to secure a coincidence between state and nation. The nation seeks to take over the state as the political instrument through which it can protect and assert itself. Less than a century ago Lord Acton could lay down the dictum that "A state may in course of time produce a nationality; but that a nationality should constitute a state is contrary to the nature of modern civilization"; but the nation has in fact become the body which legitimizes the state. As in earlier times the state achieved legitimacy through, say, its monarch or its religion, it is now legitimate if it is the embodiment and expression of a nation. Where the state is based on any principle other than the national one, as is by definition the case in any imperial system, its foundations are immediately suspect in a nationalist age. Once the people of such a state have come to a consciousness of national identity, the presumption is that the state will shortly be swept away, to be replaced by another cleaving as closely as possible to the national foundations. Where the peoples of several nations are seriously intermingled, as they are at so many points on the face of the globe, discord and trouble are the almost inevitable result. . . .

Excerpted by permission of the publishers from pp. 9, 43–45, 96, 297–299, 380, 397–399, 405–407 (*passim*), of Rupert Emerson, *From Empire to Nation,* Cambridge, Mass.: Harvard University Press, Copyright, 1960, by the President and Fellows of Harvard College. Footnotes omitted.

The principle of self-determination derives from a familiar set of doctrines, whose apparent simplicity conceals a multitude of complications. The prime starting point is presumably the eighteenth-century proposition that governments must rest upon the consent of the governed, to which the nineteenth and twentieth centuries added the assumption that, since man is a national animal, the government to which he will give his consent is one representing his own nation. For full-blown self-determination to emerge it was only necesary to secure recognition of a new principle of natural law which entitles nations to possess their own states and, as the other side of the coin, renders illegitimate states with a non-national base. As Woodrow Wilson put it, the Central Empires had been forced into political bankruptcy because they dominated "alien peoples over whom they had no natural right to rule." With the aid of a little sleight of hand the original claim that individuals must consent to or contractually establish the governments ruling them is thus transmuted itno the natural right of nations to determine their own statehood. . . .

. . . In the current temper of world opinion no one can in principle oppose what has come to be the almost self-evident right of peoples to dispose of their own destinies, but it is unfortunately equally impossible to formulate this right in such terms as to make it meaningfully applicable to reality. Who can say the nations nay, and yet who can say what nations are and when and how they may assert themselves? . . .

If the issue is put in its most drastic terms, to accept the right of self-determination in blanket fashion is to endow social entities which cannot be identified in advance with a right of revolution against the constituted authority of the state, and even to obligate the state to yield to the demands of the revolutionaries. . . .

This is one key facet of the question—that peoples and even nations are uncertain quantities which from time to time assert themselves with irresistible force but which cannot be known in advance with any assurance. Even if nations are taken for granted as given—a not unreasonable assumption since nations will at all events make themselves heard in their own good time—when they come to self-determination they are inevitably exercising a revolutionary right. In its most extreme version the right of self-determination could mean the right of any group of disaffected people to break away at their pleasure from the state to which they presently belong and establish a new state closer to their heart's desire. As far back as 1793 in the setting of the French Revolution Carnot reported to the National Assembly that:

> If . . . any community whatever had the right to proclaim its will and separate from the main body under the influence of rebels, etc., every country, every town, every village, every farmstead might declare itself independent. . . .

Traditionally it has been by making trouble—at the extreme by turning to revolution in the fashion inaugurated by the Americans—that dependent peoples have called attention to their demands. If they made enough of a nuisance of themselves, holding on to them ceased to be worth while. Only since World War II has the ending of colonialism found anything approaching general acceptance as the present goal of colonial policy. . . .

Self-determination when self-exercised involves revolution. With revolution confronting them, the colonial or imperial powers resorting to repression have habitually pleaded that they were doing no more than enforcing the law or treaties legally made whereas the nationalists were carrying on illegal activities which deserved the full authorized penalties. Within the limits of the existing order this is a position whose formal correctness cannot be challenged any more than can the proposition that, in normal circumstances, a government must and will defend itself against attack. This invocation of legality is, however, irrelevant and unimpressive to the nationalists against whom it is invoked since they deny the validity of both the source and the content of the law or treaty to which the governing power turns for justification. They may be branded as rebels by the imperial authorities, although they see themselves as patriots. Formally they are lawbreakers or treaty violators; in a larger and more realistic view what is actually involved is the clash of two fundamentally opposed systems of law: the positive law of empire and the "higher law" of the nationalists. For the members of the Indian National Congress it was a point of pride to have been imprisoned by the British, and Nkrumah and his followers in the Gold Coast took to themselves the title of Prison Graduates. . . .

In illustration of this age-old conflict between established order and revolutionary aspiration one might turn to a debate in 1956 on the Algerian question. The French representative in the Security Council, denying the competence of the United Nations, stated:

> France is doing no more in Algeria than exercising one of the most normal attributes of domestic sovereignty. It is endeavoring to maintain public order which has been disturbed by rebellious citizens; it is trying to prevent, or, if that has proved impossible, to punish the killings, the brutalities, fires and robberies which certain French Algerians are committing against other French Algerians, whether Christians or Mohammedans.

Speaking for the thirteen states which had brought the matter up, the Iranian representative contended on the contrary that, since the Algerian question was purely colonial, it was squarely within the UN domain. As he saw it, the right of the Algerians to self-determination was inalienable, and he suggested that the legitimacy of many of the states present, including the United States, rested upon a revolutionary base. To the Algerian nationalists who were carrying on the struggle in the field the position was clear: they were prepared to negotiate with France the terms on which Algerian independence would be secured, but not to recognize French sovereignty or the law flowing from it.

A stand is made on the high line: "We cannot yield to force"; yet when force is absent or abandoned, why yield at all? . . . A more rational principle should no doubt have been established than that a state or people attracts attention to its grievances by making trouble; regrettably there is little evidence that it has. In general it remains true, as I. L. Claude put it, that "states are likely to get what they want if they raise a sufficient fuss and unlikely to get it if they fail to do so." . . . At least until the unlikely event of the creation of an international organ empowered to decide when and how each colony should attain self-government, the dependent peoples who receive an international hearing will usually be those who have resorted to self-help. . . .

Self-determination constitutes formal recognition of the principle that nation and state should coincide, but the plain fact is that the state structure derived from the past only occasionally and accidentally coincided with the national make-up of the world. That is, indeed, what all the furor was about. . . .

The simple truth is that, once a certain stage of development is passed, colonial peoples will not accept good government as a substitute for self-government. Their own version of what they want coincides with the answer given to Lord John Russell in 1854 when he suggested that if the Italians would only keep quiet Austria would be more humane and grant them more privileges than they could secure by insurrection. To this proposition Daniel Manin, defender of Venice, replied:

> We do not ask that Austria be humane and liberal in Italy—which, after all, would be impossible for her even if she desired; we ask her to get out. We have no concern with her humanity and her liberalism; we wish to be masters in our own house.

In point of fact, good government, far from being a substitute for self-government, appears to be one of the prime keys to the emergence of clamorous political demands. It is not the most down-trodden who rise in their wrath, but those who have made a good start on the path of advance: "A population that rebels is a population that is looking up, that has begun to hope and to feel its strength." . . .

Paradoxical as it may seem, colonial nationalism is far less a response to oppression or neglect than to the widened horizons opened up by progressive colonial governments. . . . There is ample ground for condemnation of the governments of the imperial countries for their past failure to devote themselves to the social welfare and advancement of the alien communities overseas which they had come to dominate in a generally haphazard process of expansion. Such condemnation is idly divorced from historical reality, however, if it overlooks the fact that, until quite recently, these and other governments assumed no such responsibility for their own people at home. In addition, a substantial time lag usually separates the adoption of benevolent policies at home from their translation to overseas dependencies. . . .

To peoples emerging from imperial overlordship the major immediate contributions of nationalism are a sense of independent worth and self-respect and a new social solidarity to replace the traditional bonds. It is the sword and shield of those who are achieving independence. From being "natives" they rise to the honorable title of nationals. Through national self-assertion they achieve the spiritual satisfaction of demonstrating that they can make their own the forms on which the superior imperial powers pride themselves. They achieve also the more tangible satisfaction of overcoming that lack of social-political cohesion which earlier played so large a role in rendering them unable to resist the imperial pressure of consolidated nations. . . . The new states which have come into existence, such as Ghana or Indonesia, or the old ones which have reasserted themselves, such as Thailand or Afghanistan, can certainly not be ordered around on the old imperial terms, but neither can they cope singly with the overwhelming tasks which confront them. The most intransigent of nationalisms must live in a world of which interdependence has become a central feature; no state acting alone can guarantee its own security or assure its own well-being.

9 / Nation: A Soul

Ernest Renan

A nation can be better defined by its history experienced in common and by its determination to share a common future than by territorial boundaries, religion, language, race, or economic interests. This thesis was the subject of a now-classic lecture that the French historian Ernest Renan (1823–1892) delivered at the University of Paris on March 11, 1882. Renan's conclusion,

Translation from pp. 202–205 of *Modern Political Doctrines,* edited by Alfred Zimmern, published by Oxford University Press, 1939. Reprinted by permission.

reproduced below, recognizes the threat of dissolution of established nations by emotional secessionism and expresses a cautious hope for a confederation of the European nations in the distant future. His spiritual concept of a nation as a soul may seem elusive yet it would be wrong to underestimate its force. It is certainly comparable and often more decisive than economic, territorial, or institutional causes of modern nationalism.

A nation is a soul, a spiritual principle. Two things, which are really only one, go to make up this soul or spiritual principle. One of these things lies in the past, the other in the present. The one is the possession in common of a rich heritage of memories; and the other is actual agreement, the desire to live together, and the will to continue to make the most of the joint inheritance. . . . To share the glories of the past, and a common will in the present; to have done great deeds together, and to desire to do more— these are the essential conditions of a people's being. . . . The Spartan song "We are what ye were, and we shall be what ye are," is, in its simplicity, the abridged version of every national anthem.

In the past, a heritage of glory and of grief to be shared; in the future, one common plan to be realized; to have suffered, rejoiced and hoped together; these are things of greater value than identity of custom-houses and frontiers in accordance with strategic notions. These are things which are understood, in spite of differences in race and language. I said just now "to have suffered together," for indeed common suffering unites more strongly than common rejoicing. Among national memories, sorrows have greater value than victories; for they impose duties and demand common effort. Thus we see that a nation is a great solid unit, formed by the realization of sacrifices in the past, as well as of those one is prepared to make in the future. A nation implies a past; while, as regards the present, it is all contained in one tangible fact, viz., the agreement and clearly expressed desire to continue a life in common. The existence of a nation is (if you will forgive me the metaphor) a daily plebiscite, just as that of the individual is a continual affirmation of life. . . .

We have excluded from politics the abstract principles of metaphysics and theology; and what remains? There remains man, with his desires and his needs. But you will tell me that the consequences of a system that puts these ancient fabrics at the mercy of the wishes of usually unenlightened minds, will be the secession and ultimate distintegration of nations. . . . Human wishes change indeed: but what in this world does not? Nations are not eternal. They have had beginnings and will have ends; and will probably be replaced by a confederation of Europe. But such is not the law of the age in which we live. Nowadays it is a good, and even a necessary, thing that nations should exist. Their existence is the guarantee of liberty, which would be lost, if the world had but one law and one master.

10 / Fear of Losing National Soul

Chiang Kai-shek
Mao Tse-tung
Frantz Fanon
Sekou Touré

The preceding statement by Ernest Renan is Europe-centered. When Renan affirms that nations, as guarantors of liberty, should exist, he has in mind France, Spain, England, and Germany, and not their colonial extensions or imperial denials of nationhood in Africa and Asia. It is therefore useful to juxtapose Renan's concept of a nation as a soul with the African and Asian fear of losing national identity and culture under foreign domination and subsequent excessive imitation of the "invader." The danger of losing national soul is particularly acute in the period of postcolonial modernization when developing countries try to catch up with the more advanced countries by imitating their seemingly successful models.

It is hard to imagine a greater contrast in personality and conditions under which Chiang Kai-shek and Frantz Fanon, or Mao Tse-tung and Sekou Touré, expressed their warnings; yet their words possess an identical flavor of urgency and anxiety.

Slaves of Western Culture

Chiang Kai-shek

This statement by the leader of Nationalist China, President Chiang Kai-shek, is an excerpt from his book *China's Destiny* written in the early 1940s. In a bitter analysis Chiang Kai-shek denounced the imposition of unequal treaties by Western powers upon China in 1842, following the Opium War. These unequal treaties (annulled by the United States and Britain one hundred years later, in 1942) opened the so-called treaty ports to foreign trade and industrialization; the Chinese government was not allowed to fix its own tariffs on foreign goods, subject foreigners to Chinese laws, or prohibit the importation of opium. Treaty ports became foreign enclaves on the Chinese soil and thus effective channels for importation of foreign concepts and ideologies. The Chinese slavishly imitated foreign culture, a behavior that Chiang Kai-shek particularly deplored.

From pp. 72–73, 80–83, of Chiang Kai-shek, *China's Destiny* (New York: The Macmillan Company, 1947).

Originally the Chinese people took to learning Western[1] culture because they would not be slaves. But the result was contrary to what had been expected: by learning Western culture they unknowingly became its slaves.

After the Student Movement of May the Fourth,[2] 1919, two currents of thought, ultra-individualistic liberalism and class-struggle communism, found their way into Chinese academic circles, and later became widespread in the country. On the whole, Chinese academic circles desired to effect a change in our culture, forgetting that it had certain elements which are immutable. . . . The dispute between so-called liberalism and communism was nothing more than a dispute concerning Anglo-American and Soviet ideologies in their imitated and distorted form. All these imitated and distorted theories and political doctrines not only could not meet the needs of China's national life, but they were also inconsistent with the inherent spirit of China's culture: for any one of us to advocate these theories and doctrines indiscriminately is to forget completely that he is a Chinese and to miss completely the object of learning which is to make use of what is learned for the benefit of China. The result was only to make Chinese culture sink into a state of decay and disintegration. . . . Foreign personages and things were praised to the skies while the history of the fatherland was cast aside like a pair of worn-out slippers. Self-confidence was undermined and defeatism set in. The people became like a heap of loose sand and the country tottered on the verge of dissolution and dismemberment. The people failed to realize that if the nation should fall to pieces, the individuals in it would also perish.

China's Culture: National in Form. People's Democratic in Content

Mao Tse-tung

The second excerpt contains Mao's warning against "uncritical gulping of foreign material," and advocates China's own way to a new system, one op-

From pp. 61–63 of Mao Tse-tung, *On New Democracy* (Peking: Foreign Languages Press, 1966).

[1] It should be noted that from the Chinese point of view Marxism-Leninism as well as liberal democracy represent imports from the West. In many areas of the world the American and Western European usages of terms "East" for the Communist world, and "West" for the advanced democracies, make no sense either geographically or conceptually.——Ed.

[2] The May 4th movement of 1919 was a great movement of students and intellectuals that marked the beginnings of China's modern revolutionary history. It was both anti-imperialist and antifeudal, and represented the reaction of Chinese intellectuals to the turbulent new forces unleashed by World War I. In specific protest

posed to that of Chiang Kai-shek yet also consciously Chinese. The statement is an excerpt from Mao's pamphlet *On New Democracy* written in January 1940. In the 1970s his pamphlet is still being circulated in China and throughout the Western world in several translations; and millions of copies have been sold.

... To nourish her own culture China needs to assimilate a good deal of foreign progressive culture, not enough of which was done in the past. We should assimilate whatever is useful to us today not only from the present-day socialist and new-democratic cultures but also from the earlier cultures of other nations, for example, from the culture of the various capitalist countries in the Age of Enlightenment. However, we should not gulp any of this foreign material down uncritically, but must treat it as we do our food— first chewing it, then submitting it to the working of the stomach and intestines with their juices and secretions, and separating it into nutriment to be absorbed and waste matter to be discarded—before it can nourish us. To advocate "wholesale westernization" is wrong. China has suffered a great deal from the mechanical absorption of foreign material. Similarly, in applying Marxism to China, Chinese communists must fully and properly integrate the universal truth of Marxism with the concrete practice of the Chinese revolution, or in other words, the universal truth of Marxism must be combined with specific national characteristics and acquire a definite national form if it is to be useful, and in no circumstances can it be applied subjectively as a mere formula. ... Chinese culture should have its own form, its own national form. National in form and new-democratic in content—such is our new culture today.

... A splendid old culture was created during the long period of Chinese feudal society. To study the development of this old culture, to reject its feudal dross and assimilate its democratic essence is a necessary condition for developing our new national culture and increasing our national self-confidence, but we should never swallow anything and everything uncritically. It is imperative to separate the fine old culture of the people which had a more or less democratic and revolutionary character from all the decadence of the old feudal ruling class. China's present new politics and new economy have developed out of her old politics and old economy, and her present new culture, too, has developed out of her old culture; therefore, we must respect our own history and must not lop it off. However, respect for history means giving it its proper place as a science, respecting its

---

against the terms of the Treaty of Versailles as they affected China, and against the terms of Japan's infamous Twenty-One Demands, huge student demonstrations were held in Peking on May 4, 1919, to denounce the pro-Japanese Peking government.——Ed.

dialectical development, and not eulogizing the past at the expense of the present or praising every drop of feudal poison. . . . As far as the masses and the young students are concerned, the essential thing is to guide them to look forward and not backward. . . .

Behold, New China is within sight. Let us all hail her!

Her masts have already risen above the horizon. Let us all cheer in welcome!

Raise both your hands. New China is ours!

"Let Us Decide Not to Imitate Europe"

Frantz Fanon

The third excerpt is from Frantz Fanon's famous book *The Wretched of the Earth*. His passionate appeal is addressed to the Third World peoples whom he urges to "leave this Europe where they are never done talking of Man, yet murder men everywhere they find them, at the corner of every one of their streets, in all the corners of the globe." Fanon includes the United States in his indictment of European inhumanism. Fanon (1925–1961), a distinguished black psychiatrist and one of the leading spokesmen of the Algerian revolution, was born in Martinique. His anti-European appeal was originally written in French.

Let us decide not to imitate Europe, let us combine our muscles and our brains in a new direction. Let us try to create the whole man, whom Europe has been incapable of bringing to triumphant birth.

Two centuries ago, a former European colony decided to catch up with Europe. It succeeded so well that the United States of America became a monster, in which the taints, the sickness, and the inhumanity of Europe have grown to appalling dimensions.

Comrades have we not other work to do than to create a third Europe? . . .

We today can do everything, so long as we do not imitate Europe, so long as we are not obsessed by the desire to catch up with Europe.

So, comrades, let us not pay tribute to Europe by creating states, institutions, and societies which draw their inspiration from her.

Humanity is waiting for something from us other than such an imitation, which would be almost an obscene caricature. . . .

It is a question of the Third World starting a new history of Man, a history which will have regard to the sometimes prodigious theses which Europe has put forward, but which will also not forget Europe's crimes, of which the most horrible was committed in the heart of man, and consisted

From pp. 312–315 of Frantz Fanon, *The Wretched of the Earth* (New York: Grove Press, Inc., 1968).

of the pathological tearing apart of his functions and the crumbling away of his unity.

Colonialism's Greatest Misdeed

Sekou Touré

The last statement is the voice of the President of Guinea, Sekou Touré. It is an excerpt from his article written for the American quarterly *Foreign Affairs,* in 1962.

[I]t is a question of affirming our "Africanity," that is to say our personality, without attempting to dress it up in Western or Eastern costume. What must be constructed harmoniously and rapidly is an Africa that is authentically African. Africa has her own needs, concepts and customs. She does not seek to deck herself out in borrowed clothing that does not fit. . . .

We of course know that the world today is interdependent, and Africa, which cannot live in isolation, does not intend to remain at the margin of this modern world. She thinks she is entitled to benefit from the experience of other nations as well as from the fruits of her own efforts. In turn, she must contribute actively to the creation of a world society in which each nation, while retaining its own personality, will be considered on an equal footing with the others and will, like them, take on its proper share of international responsibilities. . . .

Colonialism's greatest misdeed was to have tried to strip us of our responsibility in conducting our own affairs and convince us that our civilization was nothing less than savagery, thus giving us complexes which led to our being branded as irresponsible and lacking in self-confidence. Our greatest victory, then, will not be the one we are winning over colonialism by securing independence but the victory over ourselves by freeing ourselves from the complexes of colonialism, proudly expressing Africa's authentic values and thoroughly identifying ourselves with them. Thus the African peoples will become fully conscious of their equality with other peoples.

From pp. 141–150 (*passim*) of Sekou Touré, "Africa's Future and the World," *Foreign Affairs,* 41:1 (October 1962).

4

Contacts
and Cooperation
among Nations

Contacts among nations may be cooperative or hostile, unintentional or deliberate, haphazard or systematic, interpenetrating or marginal, desired or dreaded. Whatever their form, intensity, or purpose, such contacts are *inevitable*. No doubt the first territorial community to emerge in history (or prehistory) soon realized that a similar process of territorial organization must be occurring in other areas. Men, tribes, and nations were quickly to learn that they were not to be alone in the world. The most isolationist nation could not avoid contact with at least its immediate neighbors. Today especially, in the age of over-population, rapid transportation, and mass media nations are in constant contact with one another.

This chapter expands our focus from single nations and states to the inter-acting composite, the international system. By repeated interaction and mutual influence, nations and states create a pattern of behavior that reflects their experience with international contacts as well as the anticipation of more or less foreseeable reactions on the part of others.

Several scholars have recommended shifting from the traditional concentration on individual states and their leaders to the analysis of the system as a whole: a shift from the components to the composite. These advocates of *systemic analysis*, as it is called, hope to discover a repeatable and characteristic behavior of states, a behavior that reflects and results from the existing structure and nature of the system of states. In other words, this theory holds that the international system of states mirrors its components, and that the system, likewise, indelibly reflects upon every component unit's perspective and action. Given the presence of certain circumstances, general patterns of political behavior may be hypothesized or predicted. Morton A. Kaplan explains this thesis in his pioneering study on international system and process.[1] His hypotheses are similar to those used by physical scientists who, for instance, can hypothesize characteristic behavior of a mass of gas molecules in a container providing certain stated conditions of temperature and pressure in the tank hold; the prediction obviously cannot hold if the temperature or pressure of the tank is changed or the container removed from the experimental room. In Selection 11, J. David Singer examines the advantages and disadvantages of studying the system rather than its individual components, the nations and their leaders.

The characteristics of the international system change with the changing ideologies and technology and with the increase or decrease in number of states, neutrals, and small, medium, great, and supergreat powers; the system is also influenced by the nature of those international organizations which it has produced. International *organizations* such as alliances, customs unions, common markets, international functional agencies (for instance, Universal Postal Union, International Labor Organization, and International Monetary Fund), or the United Nations result from deliberate planning and purposeful action of the founding member-states. Every nation decides for itself whether to adhere to any of the existing international organizations. In contrast, the structure and nature of the international *system* are not the result of a deliberately planned and purposefully creative effort on the part of its components. Every new nation automatically becomes a member of the system and is subject to its patterns whether it wants to or not. Even such revolutionary superpowers as the Soviet Union and China finally had to adapt themselves to the forms and patterns of the international system, despite their rhetorics to the contrary.

When nations freely decide to establish international organizations and agencies, they expect that the benefits to be derived from their collective pooling of resources, skills, and wills will be greater than the disadvantages that may result from some sacrifices, such as payment of membership dues and a pledge to circumscribe their future freedom of action. Since nations remain uncertain of their future benefits, they proceed very cautiously before accepting any important limitation upon their sovereignty; they either limit their membership to a specific period of *time* (many alliances are limited to twenty years even though

[1] *System and Process in International Politics* (New York: John Wiley & Sons, Inc., 1957).

they also provide for renewal) or reserve for themselves the right of *withdrawal* at any time; another limitation is a provision that no decision of an international body is binding upon its members unless all, singly and collectively, consent to it. So far, nations have proved quite reluctant to delegate to an international agency the authority to make binding decisions in vital matters. The delegation of decision-making power to the United Nations Security Council represents only a seeming departure from this general principle of self-sufficiency. The Security Council, on behalf of all the UN members, has the right to determine the existence of any threat to peace and decide what economic or military measures should be applied against the aggressor. Approval of a measure requires a majority of nine out of fifteen members, and must include the concurring votes of the five great powers (United States, Britain, France, Soviet Russia, and China). If the five superpowers ganged up effectively and nuclearly against the rest of the United Nations members, they could, in theory and according to the Charter, establish a great power dictatorship through the United Nations. But, since unanimity of great powers seems a remote possibility, the member nations have actually surrendered very little of their sovereignty to the universal international organization.

Like men who both need and dread the power of their national government (and therefore institute elaborate systems of checks and balances) nations, too, both need international organization and dread its potentially dictatorial power. Unlike men, nations still firmly believe in their capacity to go it alone most of the time; this is why they create only very loosely structured and, on the whole, ineffective organizations. Nations do not wish to create a supranational world government, but, at best, a forum for "harmonizing the actions of nations in the attainment of common ends."[2] The "common ends" seem very few indeed.

Clearly, even the United Nations organization, as defined by its Charter, realistically recognizes that the time for a universal amalgamation of nations and men into a supranational global system has not come yet. In the existing system of states, nations are expected to pursue their own separate national interests with the hope that, here and there, these interests will be brought into harmony through the United Nations, or other means. As succinctly stated by Inis L. Claude:

> In creating the United Nations [statesmen] meant that it should be an instrument for promoting national interests and purposes, including that of making it possible for the multistate system to operate tolerably well. Tell a United States Senator that the United Nations assists our sovereign nation in conducting

[2] From the wording of Article 1 of the Charter. No excerpts from the United Nations Charter are reproduced in this reader. The United Nations headquarters in New York has published a vest pocket edition of the Charter (10 cents) which also contains the Statute of the International Court of Justice. It should be assigned or consulted in conjunction with Chapters 4 and 5. Chapter 12 on the meaning and process of deterrence will deal with the United Nations provisions for collective security in more detail.

its affairs in the modern world and he may support it; tell him that it is the first step toward the eliminaion of national sovereignties, and he is likely to show hostility.[3]

11 / Territorial States and Their System

J. David Singer

In international politics as in any other area of study there are several ways to approach the subject. A student or scholar may choose to focus upon either the components or the whole. In other words, he may choose between the flowers *or* the garden, the president *or* the whole executive branch of a national government. A study that concentrates on the parts is called microlevel analysis; a study focused on the system is called macrolevel analysis. The selection of one or the other focus is, as Singer suggests, a matter of conceptual convenience, but it is never an easy choice. In international relations, the responsible scholar must be prepared to evaluate the relative utility and implications of either the microlevel analysis, which focuses on nations, or the macrolevel analysis, which concentrates on their system. Singer's main essay deals comparatively with the advantages and disadvantages of both approaches. It is preceded by his brief analysis of the international system as environment.

It is a truism that every living organism, from the nerve cell to the nation, exists in an environment and interacts with other organisms which exist within the confines of that environment. But the truism fails to answer two more specific questions. First, exactly what constitutes that environment? What are its limits and boundaries, and where is the conceptual line of demarcation between the actors and their environment? Second, what is the nature of the environment's impact on the actors? Or, more specifically, in what directions and to what extent does the environment affect and influence the behavior of these actors? . . .

From pp. 35–37 of J. David Singer, *Human Behavior and International Politics: Contributions from the Social-Psychological Sciences,* 1965. Reprinted by permission of Rand McNally & Company. This selection, entitled "The International System as Environment," is part of Singer's introduction to the first part of the symposium. Footnotes omitted.

[3] Inis L. Claude, Jr., *Swords into Plowshares: The Problems and Prospects of International Organization* (third ed.; New York: Random House, 1964), 9.

[I]n world politics, any one of the following might be selected as the actor: the head of state, the foreign minister, the foreign ministry, the delegation at the United Nations, the entire government, all or part of the population of a nation, the economic or social elites, or the opinion-makers, to mention a few of the tangible—but by no means easily identifiable—possibilities. Or one may select as his actors the abstraction known as the "state." Or he may decide that one or several international organizations is the most important, and, hence, most theoretically useful, actor.

Traditionally, however, the "nation" has come to be regarded as the key actor in this field, and that choice is reflected in the name normally given to the field: international (or inter-nation) relations. Although a persuasive case can be made for others, I still consider the nation the most important and most useful choice, . . .

Having made that choice, however, there still remains the problem of defining and delimiting the nation, so that it may be differentiated from its environment. This brings up the concept of the international system as a large and complex social system. . . . [consisting of] not only the nations, but all the other discernible and relevant groups which affect relations among nations but which are outside of any particular nation. Individuals and groups *within* any single nation are conceived of as *components of the nation,* but those groupings that exist across, or *outside of,* several nations are seen as *components of the system.* Regional and global organizations are the most important, and they may be either intergovernmental, such as the League of Nations or the U.N., their specialized agencies, O.A.S., alliances, lighthouse commissions, and customs unions, or *non*governmental, such as trade union organizations, industrial cartels, Red Cross, Rotary International, World Association of World Federalists, International Political Science Association, and so on.

The international—or any other social—system, however, is more than the sum or aggregate of its subnational, national, cross-national, or supranational components. It has certain distinguishing characteristics of its own, varying over time, and these systemic characteristics are most usefully thought of as falling into three classes. First there is its *technological* character, which refers to the degree to which human ingenuity and resourcefulness permit men and their social organizations to control, adapt to, or overcome the physical characteristics of the earth and its relevant environment. Second, there is the *cultural* (some might call it the attitudinal) dimension. This is the general body of norms, values, and expectations which most of the world's politically relevant people in any given period believe in—and believe that others believe in. In other words, there is a folklore of widely, but by no means globally, shared preferences and predictions regarding what nations *ought* to do and are *likely* to do in their relations with one another, with their own citizens, and with the cross-national and international organizations.

Finally, the environment has a *structural* or institutional dimension, and among the variables which might be used to describe this systemic characteristic are:

a. the number of nations and dependencies in the system;
b. the number of discrete coalitions and alliances;
c. the number of nonaligned nations;
d. the ease with which nations may move into or out of alliances;
e. the number and ratio of super, major, minor, and small powers;
f. the ease with which nations may move up or down in the power hierarchy; and
g. the degree of formal and informal organization in the total system, ranging from near-anarchy to world empire, with balance of power, collective security, and federation as three major intermediate degrees of organization.

Admittedly none of these three classes of systemic characteristics is found to be equally distributed among the nations. In the technological realm, for example, not all nations will have the same degree of access to knowledge, an equal number of people to apply it, or similar industrial or natural resources in order to exploit it. But even though the distribution and application of technological knowledge may be radically uneven, and its impact widely different from nation to nation, it cannot be thought of primarily as an *actor* characteristic; it exists in the larger international system and can be expected—no matter how tight the secrecy—to spread in its effects over most of the system. Likewise, the structural or the cultural characteristics of the system, though found and experienced differentially around the globe, are still most usefully conceived of as systemic—rather than actor—characteristics.

Professor Singer's main essay—dealing with the advantages and disadvantages of both the macrolevel and microlevel analyses—follows.

The International System as Level of Analysis

Beginning with the systemic level of analysis, we find in the total international system a partially familiar and highly promising point of focus. First of all, it is the most comprehensive of the levels available, encom-

J. David Singer, "The Level-of-Analysis Problem in International Relations." From *The International System: Theoretical Essays*, 1961, eds. Klaus Knorr and Sidney Verba. Published for the Center of International Studies, Princeton University, pp. 77–90. Reprinted by permission. Some author's footnotes have been omitted.

passing the totality of interactions which take place within the system and its environment. By focusing on the system, we are enabled to study the patterns of interaction which the system reveals, and to generalize about such phenomena as the creation and dissolution of coalitions, the frequency and duration of specific power configurations, modifications in its stability, its responsiveness to changes in formal political institutions, and the norms and folklore which it manifests as a societal system. In other words, the systemic level of analysis, and only this level, permits us to examine international relations in the whole, with a comprehensiveness that is of necessity lost when our focus is shifted to a lower, and more partial, level. For descriptive purposes, then, it offers both advantages and disadvantages; the former flow from its comprehensiveness, and the latter from the necessary dearth of detail.

As to explanatory capability, the system-oriented model poses some genuine difficulties. In the first place, it tends to lead the observer into a position which exaggerates the impact of the system upon the national actors and, conversely, discounts the impact of the actors on the system. This is, of course, by no means inevitable; one could conceivably look upon the system as a rather passive environment in which dynamic states act out their relationships rather than as a socio-political entity with a dynamic of its own. But there is a natural tendency to endow that upon which we focus our attention with somewhat greater potential than it might normally be expected to have. Thus, we tend to move, in a system-oriented model, away from notions implying much national autonomy and independence of choice and toward a more deterministic orientation.

Secondly, this particular level of analysis almost inevitably requires that we postulate a high degree of uniformity in the foreign policy operational codes of our national actors. By definition, we allow little room for divergence in the behavior of our parts when we focus upon the whole. It is no coincidence that our most prominent theoretician—and one of the very few text writers focusing upon the international system—should "assume that [all] statesmen think and act in terms of interest defined as power."[4] If this single-minded behavior be interpreted literally and narrowly, we have a simplistic image comparable to economic man or sexual man, and if it be defined broadly, we are no better off than the psychologist whose human model pursues "self-realization" or "maximization of gain"; all such gross models suffer from the same fatal weakness as the utilitarian's "pleasure-pain" principle. Just as individuals differ widely in what they deem to be pleasure and pain, or gain and loss, nations may differ widely in what they consider to be the national interest, and we end up having to break down

[4] Hans J. Morgenthau, *Politics Among Nations,* 3rd ed., New York, 1960, pp. 5-7. Obviously, his model does not preclude the use of power as a dimension for the differentiation of nations. [See also Selection 16.——Ed.]

and refine the larger category. Moreover, Professor Morgenthau finds himself compelled to go still further and disavow the relevance of both motives and ideological preferences in national behavior, and these represent two of the more useful dimensions in differentiating among the several nations in our international system. By eschewing any empirical concern with the domestic and internal variations within the separate nations, the system-oriented approach tends to produce a sort of "black box" or "billiard ball" concept of the national actors.[5] By discounting—or denying—the differences among nations, or by positing the near-impossibility of observing many of these differences at work within them, one concludes with a highly homogenized image of our nations in the international system. And though this may be an inadequate foundation upon which to base any *causal* statements, it offers a reasonably adequate basis for *correlative* statements. More specifically, it permits us to observe and measure correlations between certain forces or stimuli which seem to impinge upon the nation and the behavior patterns which are the apparent consequence of these stimuli. But one must stress the limitations implied in the word "apparent"; what is thought to be the consequence of a given stimulus may only be a coincidence or artifact, and until one investigates the major elements in the causal link—no matter how persuasive the deductive logic—one may speak only of correlation, not of consequence.

Moreover, by avoiding the multitudinous pitfalls of intra-nation observation, one emerges with a singularly manageable model, requiring as it does little of the methodological spohistication or onerous empiricism called for when one probes beneath the behavioral externalities of the actor. Finally, as has already been suggested in the introduction, the systemic orientation should prove to be reasonably satisfactory as a basis for prediction, even if such prediction is to extend beyond the characteristics of the system and attempt anticipatory statements regarding the actors themselves; this assumes, of course, that the actors are characterized and their behavior predicted in relatively gross and general terms.

These, then, are some of the more significant implications of a model which focuses upon the international system as a whole. Let us turn now to the more familiar of our two orientations, the national state itself.

---

[5] The "black box" figure comes from some of the simpler versions of S-R psychology, in which the observer more or less ignores what goes on within the individual and concentrates upon the correlation between stimulus and response; these are viewed as empirically verifiable, whereas cognition, perception, and other mental processes have to be imputed to the individual with a heavy reliance on these assumed "intervening variables." The "billiard ball" figure seems to carry the same sort of connotation, and is best employed by Arnold Wolfers in "The Actors in International Politics" in William T. R. Fox, ed., *Theoretical Aspects of International Relations,* Notre Dame, Ind., 1959, pp. 83-106. . . .

The National State as Level of Analysis

The other level of analysis to be considered in this paper is the national state—our primary actor in international relations. This is clearly the traditional focus among Western students, and is the one which dominates almost all of the texts employed in English-speaking colleges and universities.

Its most obvious advantage is that it permits significant differentiation among our actors in the international system. Because it does not require the attribution of great similarity to the national actors, it encourages the observer to examine them in greater detail. The favorable results of such intensive analysis cannot be overlooked, as it is only when the actors are studied in some depth that we are able to make really valid generalizations of a comparative nature. And though the systemic model does not necessarily preclude comparison and contrast among the national sub-systems, it usually eventuates in rather gross comparisons based on relatively crude dimensions and characteristics. . . .

But just as the nation-as-actor focus permits us to avoid the inaccurate homogenization which often flows from the systemic focus, it also may lead us into the opposite type of distortion—a marked exaggeration of the differences among our sub-systemic actors. While it is evident that neither of these extremes is conducive to the development of a sophisticated comparison of foreign policies, and such comparison requires a balanced preoccupation with both similarity and difference, the danger seems to be greatest when we succumb to the tendency to overdifferentiate; comparison and contrast can proceed only from observed uniformities.

One of the additional liabilities which flow in turn from the pressure to overdifferentiate is that of Ptolemaic parochialism. Thus, in overemphasizing the differences among the many national states, the observer is prone to attribute many of what he conceives to be virtues to his own nation and the vices to others, especially the adversaries of the moment. That this ethnocentrism is by no means an idle fear is borne out by perusal of the major international relations texts published in the United States since 1945. Not only is the world often perceived through the prism of the American national interest, but an inordinate degree of attention (if not spleen) is directed toward the Soviet Union; it would hardly be amiss to observe that most of these might qualify equally well as studies in American foreign policy. The scientific inadequacies of this sort of "we-they" orientation hardly require elaboration, yet they remain a potent danger in any utilization of the national actor model. . . .

Another and perhaps more subtle implication of selecting the nation as our focus or level of analysis is that it raises the entire question of goals, motivation, and purpose in national policy. Though it may well be a peculiarity of the Western philosophical tradition, we seem to exhibit, when confronted with the need to explain individual or collective behavior, a strong proclivity for a goal-seeking approach. The question of whether national behavior is purposive or not seems to require discussion in two distinct (but not always exclusive) dimensions.

Firstly, there is the more obvious issue of whether those who act on behalf of the nation in formulating and executing foreign policy consciously pursue rather concrete goals. And it would be difficult to deny, for example, that these role-fulfilling individuals envisage certain specific outcomes which they hope to realize by pursuing a particular strategy. In this sense, then, nations may be said to be goal-seeking organisms which exhibit purposive behavior.

However, purposiveness may be viewed in a somewhat different light, by asking whether it is not merely an intellectual construct that man imputes to himself by reason of his vain addiction to the free-will doctrine as he searches for characteristics which distinguish him from physical matter and the lower animals. And having attributed this conscious goal-pursuing behavior to himself as an individual, it may be argued that man then proceeds to project this attribute to the social organizations of which he is a member. The question would seem to distill down to whether man and his societies pursue goals of their own choosing or are moved toward those imposed upon them by forces which are primarily beyond their control. Another way of stating the dilemma would be to ask whether we are concerned with the ends which men and nations strive for or the ends toward which they are impelled by the past and present characteristics of their social and physical milieu. Obviously, we are using the terms "ends," "goals," and "purpose" in two rather distinct ways; one refers to those which are consciously envisaged and more or less rationally pursued, and the other to those of which the actor has little knowledge but toward which he is nevertheless propelled.

Taking a middle ground in what is essentially a specific case of the free will vs. determinism debate, one can agree that nations move toward outcomes of which they have little knowledge and over which they have less control, but that they nevertheless do prefer, and therefore select, particular outcomes and *attempt* to realize them by conscious formulation of strategies.

Also involved in the goal-seeking problem when we employ the nation-oriented model is the question of how and why certain nations pursue specific sorts of goals. While the question may be ignored in the system-oriented model or resolved by attributing identical goals to all national actors, the nation-as-actor approach demands that we investigate the processes by which national goals are selected, the internal and external factors that impinge on those processes, and the institutional framework from which they emerge. . . .

There is still another dilemma involved in our selection of the nation-as-actor model, and that concerns the phenomenological issue: do we examine our actor's behavior in terms of the objective factors which allegedly influence that behavior, or do we do so in terms of the actor's *perception* of these "objective factors"? Though these two approaches are not completely exclusive of one another, they proceed from greatly different and often incompatible assumptions, and produce markedly divergent models of national behavior.

The first of these assumptions concerns the broad question of social causation. One view holds that individuals and groups respond in a quasi-deterministic fashion to the realities of physical environment, the acts or power of other individuals or groups, and similar "objective" and "real" forces or stimuli. An opposite view holds that individuals and groups are not influenced in their behavior by such objective forces, but by the fashion in which these forces are perceived and evaluated, however distorted or incomplete such perceptions may be. For adherents of this position, the only reality is the phenomenal—that which is discerned by the human senses; forces that are not discerned do not exist for that actor, and those that do exist do so only in the fashion in which they are perceived.[6] Though it is difficult to accept the position that an individual, a group, or a nation is affected by such forces as climate, distance, or a neighbor's physical power only insofar as they are recognized and appraised, one must concede that perceptions will certainly affect the manner in which such forces are responded to. As has often been pointed out, an individual will fall to the ground when he steps out of a tenth-story window regardless of his perception of gravitational forces, but on the other hand such perception is a major factor in whether or not he steps out of the window in the first place. The point here is that if we embrace a phenomenological view of causation, we will tend to utilize a phenomenological model for explanatory purposes.

The second assumption which bears on one's predilection for the phenomenological approach is more restricted, and is primarily a methodological one. Thus, it may be argued that any description of national behavior in a given international situation would be highly incomplete were it to ignore the link between the external forces at work upon the nation and its general foreign policy behavior. Furthermore, if our concern extends beyond the mere description of "what happens" to the realm of explanation, it could be contended that such omission of the cognitive and the perceptual linkage would be ontologically disastrous. How, it might be asked, can one speak of "causes" of a nation's policies when one has ignored the media by which external conditions and factors are translated into a policy decision? We may observe correlations between all sorts of forces in the international system

[6] The problem of perception and misperception is analyzed in Chapter 8 (Introduction) and in Chapter 9 (Selection 21 by Holsti).——Ed.

and the behavior of nations, but their causal relationship must remain strictly deductive and hypothetical in the absence of empirical investigation into the causal chain which allegedly links the two. Therefore, even if we are satisfied with the less-than-complete descriptive capabilities of a non-phenomenological model, we are still drawn to it if we are to make any progress in explanation.

The contrary view would hold that the above argument proceeds from an erroneous comprehension of the nature of explanation in social science. One is by no means required to trace every perception, transmission, and receipt between stimulus and response or input and output in order to explain the behavior of the nation or any other human group. Furthermore, who is to say that empirical observation—subject as it is to a host of errors —is any better a basis of explanation than informed deduction, inference, or analogy? Isn't an explanation which flows logically from a coherent theoretical model just as reliable as one based upon a misleading and elusive body of data, most of which is susceptible to analysis only by techniques and concepts foreign to political science and history?

This leads, in turn, to the third of the premises relevant to one's stand on the phenomenological issue: are the dimensions and characteristics of the policy-makers' phenomenal field empirically discernible? Or, more accurately, even if we are convinced that their perceptions and beliefs constitute a crucial variable in the explanation of a nation's foreign policy, can they be observed in an accurate and systematic fashion? Furthermore, are we not required by the phenomenological model to go beyond a classification and description of such variables, and be drawn into the tangled web of relationships out of which they emerge? If we believe that these phenomenal variables are sytematically observable, are explainable, and can be fitted into our explanation of a nation's behavior in the international system, then there is a further tendency to embrace the phenomenological approach. If not, or if we are convinced that the gathering of such data is inefficient or uneconomical, we will tend to shy clear of it.

The fourth issue in the phenomenological dispute concerns the very nature of the nation as an actor in international relations. Who or what is it that we study? Is it a distinct social entity with well-defined bondaries—a unity unto itself? Or is it an agglomeration of individuals, institutions, customs, and procedures? It should be quite evident that those who view the nation or the state as an integral social unit could not attach much utility to the phenomenological approach, particularly if they are prone to concretize or reify the abstraction. Such abstractions are incapable of perception, cognition, or anticipation (unless, of course, the reification goes so far as to anthropomorphize and assign to the abstraction such attributes as will, mind, or personality). On the other hand, if the nation or state is seen as a group of individuals operating within an institutional framework, then it makes perfect sense to focus on the phenomenal field of those individuals who participate in the policy-making process. In other words, *people* are capable of experiences, images, and expectations, while institutional abstractions are not, except in the metaphorical sense. Thus, if our actor cannot even have a phenomenal field, there is little point in employing a phenomenological approach.

These, then, are some of the questions around which the phenomenological issue would seem to revolve. Those of us who think of social forces as operative regardless of the actor's awareness, who believe that explanation need not include all of the steps in a causal chain, who are dubious of the practicality of gathering phenomenal data, or who visualize the nation as a distinct entity apart from its individual members, will tend to reject the phenomenological approach. Logically, only those who disagree with each of the above four assumptions would be *compelled* to adopt the approach. Disagreement with any one would be *sufficient* grounds for so doing.

The above represent some of the more significant implications and fascinating problems raised by the adoption of our second model. They seem to indicate that this sub-systemic orientation is likely to produce richer description and more satisfactory (from the empiricist's point of view) explanation of international relations, though its predictive power would appear no greater than the systemic orientation. But the descriptive and explanatory advantages are achieved only at the price of considerable methodological complexity.

Conclusion

Having discussed some of the descriptive, explanatory, and predictive capabilities of these two possible levels of analysis, it might now be useful to assess the relative utility of the two and attempt some general statement as to their prospective contributions to greater theoretical growth in the study of international relations.

In terms of description, we find that the systemic level produces a more comprehensive and total picture of international relations than does the national or sub-systemic level. On the other hand, the atomized and less coherent image produced by the lower level of analysis is somewhat balanced by its richer detail, greater depth, and more intensive portrayal. As to explanation, there seems little doubt that the sub-systemic or actor orientation is considerably more fruitful, permitting as it does a more thorough investigation of the processes by which foreign policies are made. Here we are enabled to go beyond the limitations imposed by the systemic level and to replace mere correlation with the more significant causation. And in terms of prediction, both orientations seem to offer a similar degree of promise. Here the issue is a function of what we seek to predict. Thus the policy-maker will tend to prefer predictions about the way in which nation *x* or *y* will react to a contemplated move on his own nation's part, while the scholar will probably prefer either generalized predictions regarding the behavior of a given class of nations or those regarding the system itself.

Does this summary add up to an overriding case for one or another of the two models? It would seem not. For a staggering variety of reasons the scholar may be more interested in one level than another at any given time and will undoubtedly shift his orientation according to his research needs. So the problem is really not one of deciding which level is most valuable to the discipline as a whole and then demanding that it be adhered to from now unto eternity.[7] Rather, it is one of realizing that there is this preliminary conceptual issue and that it must be temporarily resolved prior to any given research undertaking. And it must also be stressed that we have dealt here only with two of the more common orientations, and that many others are available and perhaps even more fruitful potentially than either of those selected here. Moreover, the international system gives many indications of prospective change, and it may well be that existing institutional forms will take on new characteristics or that new ones will appear to take their place. As a matter of fact, if incapacity to perform its functions leads to the transformation or decay of an institution, we may expect a steady deterioration and even ultimate disappearance of the national state as a significant actor in the world political system.

12 / The Superpowers and the United Nations

John G. Stoessinger

The author of the following essay analyzes the theory and practice of Article 27 of the United Nations Charter. This core provision guarantees that no

From pp. 3–17 of *The United Nations and the Superpowers,* 2d ed., by John G. Stoessinger. Copyright © 1965, 1970, by Random House, Inc. Reprinted by permission. Footnotes omitted.

[7] It should also be kept in mind that one could conceivably develop a theoretical model which successfully embraces both of these levels of analysis without sacrificing conceptual clarity and internal consistency. In this writer's view, such has not been done to date, though Kaplan's *System and Process in International Politics* seems to come fairly close.

major political or military decision may be adopted without the concurrence of the five great powers. Veto by one of them annuls a decision even if fourteen out of the fifteen members of the Security Council support it. According to Stoessinger, the veto provision is not a source of major weakness of the United Nations but, on the contrary, a realistic principle of international politics in an era in which an effort to imitate the democratic method of decision by numerical majority would only embitter international relations.

One of the more persistent myths surrounding the United Nations concerns the use of the veto power by the Soviet Union and the United States. It is an established fact that by 1969 the Soviet Union had vetoed 105 Security Council resolutions, whereas the United States had yet to cast its first veto. Hence, it is said that the Soviet Union's frequent use of the veto has hampered and weakened the United Nations by preventing it from acting, while the United States has exercised remarkable self-discipline by never using the veto at all.

This chapter will show that neither part of this myth is accurate. On the one hand, the ultimate effect of the Soviet veto on UN action has been considerably exaggerated. On the other, while it is technically correct to say that the United States has never cast a veto, we shall see that the United States has, in fact, developed a "hidden veto," which it has used frequently and effectively. In short, it is one thesis of this chapter that the difference in the behavior of the superpowers on the use of the veto is more apparent than real; both have tried to protect their national interests, although by different parliamentary tactics. Moreover, we shall attempt to show that the interaction between the superpowers on the veto has not necessarily had a negative effect on the development of the United Nations. On the contrary, the United Nations has responded to the challenge with imagination and flexibility, and this response has led to important constitutional and political changes within the Organization. One reason why the United Nations today is a different—and stronger—organization from the one established in 1945 has been its ability to rise to the challenge of the superpower veto.

The framers of the Charter gave the Security Council extensive powers to keep the peace. The Council was to consist of eleven members, five of which—the United States, the Soviet Union, Great Britain, France, and China—were to be permanent. In addition, six nonpermanent members were to be elected by the General Assembly for two-year terms. The Charter empowered the Security Council to recommend means of peaceful settlement of disputes; and, if a nation committed an act of aggression, the Council was to have the power to apply sanctions against the aggressor. Such sanctions might range from the severance of diplomatic relations all the way to collective military action.

The Big Five were clearly intended to dominate the Council. It was hoped that no aggressor would then be able to challenge such an overwhelming agglomeration of power. The Big Five, in return for their primary responsibility to keep the peace, received commensurate privileges: a permanent seat on the Council and the veto power, by which each of the Big Five could prevent the Security Council from taking action on a substantive issue. Three of the Great powers at San Francisco—the United States, the Soviet Union, and Great Britain—insisted on the right of veto and none of them would have acceded to the United Nations without it. China and France at first took a more flexible position, but the rigid stand of the Big Three soon resulted in their equally firm insistence on the veto rule.

The exact wording of Article 27 of the Charter, which established the veto power, is as follows:

1. Each member of the Security Council shall have one vote.
2. Decisions of the Security Council on procedural matters shall be made by an affirmative vote of seven members.
3. Decisions of the Security Council on all other matters shall be made by an affirmative vote of seven members including the concurring votes of the permanent members; provided that in decisions under Chapter VI, and under paragraph 3 of Article 52, a party to a dispute shall abstain from voting.

While a major power was required to abstain from voting on resolutions related to the peaceful settlement of disputes to which it was a party, it was technically free to veto all other nonprocedural matters. In addition, the powers agreed that the decision whether a matter was substantive or procedural was itself a substantive question and hence subject to veto. Thus, by a double veto system—one veto to decide whether the issue was substantive or procedural and the second on the issue itself—a Great Power could veto anything it chose, with the single exception of questions regarding the peaceful settlement of disputes to which it was a party. Or, to put it the other way around, all the Great Powers had to be in agreement before the Security Council could act. Clearly, it seemed that close cooperation among the Big Five would be a necessary prerequisite for an effective Security Council. Yet, the deepening split between the superpowers and the 9 vetoes cast by the Soviet Union during 1946 adumbrated to many observers a succession of paralyzing vetoes that could jeopardize the effectiveness of the entire United Nations.

In January 1966, the Security Council was enlarged from eleven to fifteen members. The four new nonpermanent members were all to be selected from the new nations of the world. An affirmative vote by the Council now required 9 votes rather than 7. The veto power of the Big Five remained unaffected by the Charter amendment.

The Soviet Union and the Veto

The Soviet Union has been responsible for 105 of the 113 vetoes cast by 1969, or over 90 percent of the total. But the figures themselves do not adequately explain the picture. One must see what effect the vetoes had on the United Nations *after* they were cast.

A Soviet veto could meet one of three different fates. First, it could "stick" completely, meaning that no significant further action on the vetoed issue was taken by other organs of the United Nations or by states outside the United Nations. For example, the Soviet veto of an investigation of the Indian invasion of Goa "stuck." Second, a veto could be "circumvented" if another organ of the United Nations provided alternative machinery. In some cases, this alternative machinery could continue the effective direction of the action in place of the paralyzed Security Council. For example, the General Assembly effectively circumvented the Soviet vetoes cast during the Korean War by directing the "police action" itself. In other cases, the United Nations could try another approach, but still fail to resolve the issue. . . . Thus, our criterion of a circumvented veto is not necessarily the successful settlement of an issue but the capacity of the United Nations to provide alternative machinery to fill the breach left by a paralyzed Security Council. As a third fate, a veto may be superseded either because the disputants negotiated the issue directly, as happened in the Berlin Blockade, or because changing circumstances may resolve the dispute. . . . In sum, therefore, a Soviet veto can "stick," be circumvented, or be superseded.

In general, one can distinguish four major areas in which the USSR has used the veto to protect and promote its national interest: vetoes cast in direct U.S.-Soviet confrontations; vetoes cast on behalf of a Communist ally; vetoes cast on behalf of a state outside the Communist bloc; and vetoes cast against candidates for UN membership. Let us now examine in greater detail the consequences of Soviet vetoes in each of these.

The Soviet Union has used the veto eighteen times to protect its national interest in a direct clash with the United States. It vetoed 5 resolutions calling for UN action in such cold-war confrontations as the Berlin Blockade, the Hungarian Revolution, the destruction of a U.S. RB-47 airplane (2 vetoes), and the Czechoslovak crisis of 1968. The USSR twice vetoed the election of a Secretary-General whom the United States favored strongly. It also vetoed five measures related to disarmament and cast 6 vetoes at various points during the UN Operation in the Congo.

Not all of these vetoes have prevented further UN action. When the General Assembly voted to extend the term of Secretary-General Trygve Lie during the Korean War, it circumvented one Soviet veto. When the Soviet Union vetoed an American draft resolution on the Hungarian crisis, an emergency session of the General Assembly passed a more strongly worded resolution recommending that the Secretary-General investigate the situation and suggest methods of ending the foreign intervention. Neither the Secretary-General nor a Special Committee appointed by him could secure the cooperation of the new Soviet-sponsored government in Hungary and thus the matter was eventually dropped. From the UN point of view, however, the immediate cause of failure was not the Soviet veto. The Organization did develop compensatory if somewhat token machinery, but the attitude of the Hungarian government prevented further action. The 6 vetoes cast during the Congo Operation were all circumvented. The vetoed proposals were enacted by the Assembly in similar if not always identical language and the basic objective of the USSR—the obstruction of the Congo Operation—was not achieved. Two further issues which elicited Soviet vetoes—the Berlin Blockade and the RB-47 incident—were resolved through negotiation between the superpowers without direct UN involvement. The remaining 7 vetoes, however, did stick and no further action was taken inside or outside the world organization.

A second group of 16 vetoes was cast by the Soviet Union not to protect itself directly, but to assist a Communist ally. By vetoing two resolutions the USSR prevented a UN inquiry into the new Communist government in Czechoslovakia in 1948. One veto on behalf of Albania over the Corfu Channel dispute with Great Britain was resolved outside the United Nations by an agreement of the parties to submit the issue to the International Court of Justice. Another veto—on behalf of North Vietnam against Thailand's charge of Communist infiltration—was superseded by changed circumstances. The Soviet Union vetoed five resolutions during the Korean War, but these vetoes, like those cast during the Congo Operation, did not prevent the United Nations from achieving its basic objectives. Six vetoes cast to protect Greece's Communist northern neighbors during the Greek Civil War were effectively circumvented by General Assembly action. Finally, a Soviet veto on a resolution concerning the overthrow of the Communist government in Guatemala in 1954 was superseded. In sum, only the 2 vetoes cast over Czechoslovakia were final; 11 others were circumvented by UN action; and 3 were bypassed by events outside the United Nations.

Sixteen vetoes cast by the Soviet Union may be described as proxy vetoes or vetoes cast on behalf of neutralist states with which the USSR wished to gain favor. Eleven of these were used on behalf of Arab states against former colonial powers or against Israel. Four of them—1 on the diversion of the river Jordan and 3 cast at various points in the continuing Syrian-Israeli dispute—were final.

The very first veto in the Security Council was cast in 1946 against a resolution expressing confidence that the British and French would withdraw their forces from Syria and Lebanon. This veto was superseded outside the United Nations as the two powers expressed their intention to withdraw and did so promptly. Another pro-Arab veto was also superseded outside the United Nations when the USSR refused to support Iraq's claim to Kuwait. The remaining 4 pro-Arab vetoes were all circumvented by UN action. Two of the 4 were cast on behalf of Egypt. One vetoed resolution concerned the passage of Israeli cargoes through the Suez Canal. As noted above, Secretary-General Hammarskjöld reached an agreement with the Egyptian government, but at the last moment the scheme failed. The second pro-Egyptian veto was cast in 1956 against a resolution calling on Egypt, the United Kingdom, and France to continue their negotiations and for Egypt to submit guarantees that the Canal would be managed effectively. Despite the veto, the talks continued under the guidance of the Secretary-General. When the Canal was reopened in April 1957, Egypt deposited an instrument with the United Nations acknowledging its treaty obligations under international law and later accepted the jurisdiction of the International Court of Justice on matters of interpretation.

Two Soviet vetoes were cast during the Lebanon crisis of 1958, and both were circumvented by General Assembly action.

Three of the vetoes by proxy were used on behalf of India. The first, on the Kashmir problem, stuck. A second veto on Kashmir, cast against fuller negotiations, was bypassed when the United States succeeded in bringing India and Pakistan together for talks in exchange for U.S. aid to India during the Chinese invasion of that country. The third, on Goa, struck. Finally, 2 vetoes cast over Indonesian independence were circumvented by Assembly action, but a veto cast in the 1964 Indonesian-Malaysian dispute has stuck. In sum, therefore, 7 proxy vetoes for neutralist states have stuck; 6 were circumvented by UN action; and 3 were superseded by outside circumstances.

The largest number of vetoes, 51, was used to block the admission of new members to the United Nations. This total, however, is not as staggering as it appears, since 34 of these 51 vetoes were "repeats." Italy, for example, was vetoed 6 times, and Portugal, Jordan, Ireland, Ceylon, South Korea, South Vietnam, and Japan were vetoed 4 times each. One Soviet objective in vetoing the admission of these states was to force the United States to admit such Communist states as Albania, Bulgaria, Hungary, and Rumania to the world organization. In an effort to break this membership deadlock, the two superpowers negotiated directly and in 1955 reached agreement on a "package deal" that made possible the admission of sixteen new members, including most of the protégés of both superpowers. In one sense, therefore, the Soviet vetoes attained their end: the admission of the Communist applicants. But in another sense, they were superseded, since all the U.S. candidates against which vetoes had been cast—save South Korea and South Vietnam—were also admitted to membership. A decision of the superpowers taken outside the United Nations effectively resolved the membership stalemate. In all, forty-three of the membership vetoes were superseded by the "package deal" and only eight—four against South Vietnam and four against South Korea—have stuck.

Four early Soviet vetoes—in 1946 against Spain—do not fit into any of the above categories, but their fate is clear. They were cast in order to obtain more severe action against the Franco regime for its association with the Axis during World War II. While the Assembly passed resolutions similar to some of the vetoed proposals, the rapid development of the cold war and Spain's increasing value to the West prevented further action. In effect, these vetoes were superseded by changing circumstances.

The following table presents the above material in summary form.

SOVIET VETOES 1946–1969

	Stuck	Circumvented	Superseded	Total
Direct				
confrontations	7 (39%)	8 (44%)	3 (17%)	18
For Communist				
allies	2 (12%)	11 (69%)	3 (19%)	16
Proxy vetoes	7 (44%)	6 (38%)	3 (18%)	16
Membership				
vetoes	8 (16%)	—	43 (84%)	51
Spanish				
question	—	—	4	4
	24 (23%)	25 (24%)	56 (53%)	105

An analysis of the table suggests several conclusions. First, it is a startling fact that nearly 80 percent of the Soviet Union vetoes have been rendered less effective in one way or another and 24 percent have been circumvented by action of the United Nations itself. The "circumventability" of a veto depends on several factors. The identity of the veto's beneficiary is of great importance and often determines the degree of political incentive to override a veto or the degree of political caution against such action. The legal-constitutional situation may also play an important part. Here one must ask how rigid the Charter is on a given point. On the membership question, for example, the Charter seems to exclude circumvention. Some states toyed with the idea, but the World Court refused to go along with their scheme. Then, there is a point at which the legal and political issues meet: given some latitude in the constitution and the political desire to circumvent a veto, is it *politically* possible to exploit the *constitutional* possibility? The Indian "liberation" of Goa is a case in point. The Soviet veto stuck in this case not because there was no alternative machinery that might have been used against it—the General Assembly could have served—but because it was clear that, in voting terms, the Assembly would have endorsed the Soviet position. The United States believed, probably correctly, that the Assembly would have supported the Soviet view of "liberation," not the Western view of "aggression." Hence, the veto served in this case as an instrument of the majority view of the United Nations rather than a device for blocking the majority position.

A second general conclusion emerging from our table concerns the Soviet vetoes that have stuck. The Soviet Union has been more successful in direct confrontations with the United States (39 percent) and in proxy vetoes cast on behalf of neutralist states (44 percent) than in vetoes on behalf of Communist allies (12 percent). In short, along with its own direct national interest, the USSR has been better able to protect the interests of neutrals than those of allies.

It is clear from the above that, in direct superpower confrontations, the United States and other UN members acknowledge the power realities of the situation. Pushing the United Nations too far in situations like the Hungarian Revolution or the Czechoslovak crisis, for example, runs the risk of shattering it altogether. The durable character of the proxy vetoes has also been an expression of cold-war realities: first, the United States has been reluctant to seek to upset a veto cast on behalf of a neutralist state, since, like the Soviet Union, it is anxious to win neutralist support. Moreover, the political realities noted above would make it difficult to mobilize a majority for such circumvention in the General Assembly. On the other hand, the United States has taken a strong interest in circumventing vetoes cast on behalf of Communist allies when the American national interest has been at stake. The five circumvented vetoes during the Korean War were cases in point. In all instances, the attitude of the two superpowers has been crucial to the durability of the veto.

A third general conclusion from the record suggests that the 105 vetoes have not constituted as formidable an obstacle to the solution of international problems as one might expect. In the first place, this total is somewhat misleading, since 34 of the membership vetoes were "repeats." More important, however, is the fact that in nearly 80 percent of the cases in which a veto had been cast, some further action was forthcoming. In 53 percent of the vetoed cases, the issues were settled outside the United Nations by direct negotiations or changing circumstances. Even in these cases however, the United Nations sometimes played a "good-offices" role. For example, the preliminary discussions about lifting the Berlin Blockade were held between Soviet and American officials at the United Nations.

The significant fact is that 24 percent of the vetoed issues, including important peace and security operations, were circumvented directly by compensatory UN action. In these instances, the USSR paralyzed the Security Council, but not the United Nations *in toto*. General Assembly action, as in the extension of Secretary-General Lie's term in 1950, and joint action by the Assembly and the Secretary-General, as in the Congo Operation, have been the major forms of UN compensatory machinery.

On balance, the evidence suggests that the United Nations, far from being helpless in the face of the Soviet veto, has responded to the challenge with imagination and flexibility. It has moved cautiously when the direct interest of a superpower has been at stake. In four-fifths of the cases, however, either the United Nations has been able to devise means to circumvent the veto, although not necessarily to solve the problem, or the issue has been effectively settled by outside events. In short, the veto has not been an insurmountable obstacle to the resolution of international issues.

Before considering the United States and the veto, it is interesting to note the fate of vetoes cast by members other than the Soviet Union: 4 by France, 3 by Great Britain, and 1 by China. All of these were either circumvented by UN action or superseded by events. The creation of the United Nations Emergency Force by the General Assembly in 1956 after British and French vetoes paralyzed the Security Council is a well-known case in point.

The United States and the Veto

The companion myth to the paralyzing Soviet veto is that of American self-denial. Western observers never tire of pointing out that the United States has never used the veto.[8] Some observers go so far as to question whether the United States ever favored the inclusion of the veto power in the UN Charter. Even so well-informed a statesman as Senator John Sherman Cooper, former Ambassador to India, asked in 1954 whether it was not true that the United States, at the time of the approval of the Charter, "was opposed to the veto."

To assert that the United States objected to the inclusion of the veto power in incorrect. To say that the United States has never used the veto power is literally correct, but highly misleading in a broader sense. The implication would be that one superpower had selfishly put national interest above international considerations while the other had unselfishly sub-

[8] On March 17, 1970, the United States cast what may be considered its first veto. The United States did so as it joined with Britain in rejecting an Afro-Asian resolution that would have condemned England for not using force to eliminate the white-minority government of Rhodesia. Britain's veto would have been, of course, sufficient to defeat the resolution if all the other fourteen members of the Security Council had voted for it. The vote was Britain's fourth use of the veto. It is the United Nations practice to record the negative votes of all permanent members as vetoes when their result is a defeat of a majority decision. Consequently in the United Nations record the United States vote of March 17, 1970, is, technically, a veto.—— Ed.

ordinated national interests in order to further international cooperation. The fact of the matter is that the United States has not used the veto because it has been able to protect and promote its national interest in other ways. By obtaining majority votes against resolutions it opposes, the United States has never been forced to cast a veto. The key to this American "hidden veto" has, of course, been the composition of the Security Council. It is a fact that until the enlargement of the Council from eleven to fifteen in 1966, a majority of its members usually were military allies of the United States. In 1958, Premier Khrushchev lashed out against what, in his view, was clear American domination of the Council:

> It is common knowledge that the majority in the Security Council is composed of the votes of countries dependent, in one way or another, primarily economically, on the USA. Thus, the Security Council in its present composition cannot be regarded as an impartial arbiter, and that is why it has of late ceased to play the important role in the maintenance of international peace and security which devolved upon it by virtue of the United Nations Charter.

When Khrushchev made this statement, eight votes on the Council were controlled by military allies of the United States in NATO and SEATO. Two members—Iraq and Sweden—were neutral in the East-West struggle. In the following year, Sweden was replaced by Italy, a member of NATO, and Iraq by Tunisia, another neutral.

Thus, in 1959, the United States had good reason to expect nine of the eleven Security Council members to support its position on any major East-West issue....

There are numerous cases on record which suggest that the United States has used its considerable influence to persuade members of the Council to form a negative majority for its position and thus avoid having to cast a veto. For example, during the protracted controversy over the admission of new members, the United States repeatedly blocked the admission of Soviet-sponsored candidates, not by a veto, but by prevailing upon its allies to back its position. The USSR, on the other hand, had to cast fifty-one vetoes to block American-sponsored candidates. The U-2 episode in 1960 was another typical case of the American "hidden veto" in action. In May of that year, the Soviet Union brought the case before the Security Council and introduced a resolution branding the flights by American planes over Soviet territory as "acts of aggression." Two states—the USSR and Poland —voted in favor of the Soviet motion; seven states voted against: Argentina, China, Ecuador, France, Italy, the United Kingdom, and the United States —all members of the Western alliance system. Two neutralist states— Ceylon and Tunisia—abstained.

This pattern began to change somewhat in 1966, when four nonpermanent members were added to the Security Council. The passage of a resolution now required 9 affirmative votes instead of 7. Since the enlargement of the Council was undertaken primarily for the benefit of the new nations, most of which were "neutralist" on East-West issues, it now became more difficult for the United States to control the Council. For example, in 1966, the United States attempted to have the Vietnam question inscribed on the Council's agenda, and found itself dependent upon the vote of Jordan. The move succeeded, but just barely. The days of an automatic American majority or of a "hidden veto," exercised by mobilizing this majority against a Soviet-sponsored resolution, were over. U.S. influence was still very great, but now had to depend on bargaining and persuasion rather than reliance on an absolute majority.

In considering the American position on the veto, one must also take notice of the considerable power the United States can exercise within UN organs before a vote is ever taken. At the present time, the United States pays approximately 40 percent of the total operating cost of the United Nations. It is largely this contribution that allows the Organization to maintain its present precarious hold on financial solvency. If the United States were to be sufficiently displeased with a project to consider withholding even just its voluntary contributions, UN planners would debate seriously before going ahead. On occasion, the United States has actually exercised this "financial veto" in order to attain objectives, such as the termination of the International Refugee Organization and the prevention of SUNFED, the Special United Nations Fund for Economic Development. In addition, the threat of a veto has at times been as effective as the actual casting of one. When, in 1950, the United States let it be known that it was determined to veto any candidate but Trygve Lie for the office of Secretary-General, the threat itself was sufficient. His term was extended by the General Assembly after the USSR had cast a veto in the Security Council.

In sum, the evidence demonstrates that the United States, like the Soviet Union, seeks to protect its national interest against any hostile action by the Security Council. However, because of its powerful position on the Security Council and in the United Nations generally, it has never been forced to resort to the casting of a veto. On the whole, therefore, the two superpowers have employed different parliamentary strategies to attain similar ends: the protection of the national interest.

The Veto and the United Nations

It now remains to be seen what effect the interaction of the two superpowers on the veto problem has had on the political evolution of the United Nations itself.

It is clear from the above discussion that the actual exercise of the veto power has not proved to be as great a threat to the effective functioning of the United Nations as it might have been in theory. In the first place, the Security Council has tended to narrow rather than expand the scope of the veto power. It established the principle that the abstention of a Great Power was not tantamount to a veto, thus giving states the opportunity to avoid commitment on a difficult choice without preventing UN action. In the Korean police-action decision of 1950, the Security Council went even further, by declaring that the absence of a Great Power should merely be regarded as an abstention, not a veto *in absentia*. Finally, the threat of the "double veto," the parliamentary device that would allow a Great Power to veto practically anything it chose, has not materialized in practice. While it still exists as a potential weapon, the "double veto" was used only three times, the last occasion arising in 1948.

Second, to blame the veto power for the strains and difficulties in re-solving international problems is to confuse the symptoms with the causes. The Security Council veto might be viewed simply as the formal parlia-mentary expression of the real "veto" which any superpower actually has as a fact of life in a system of sovereign nation-states. The temptation of a voting assembly is to mistake its majority decisions as accurate and en-forceable expressions of power realities. They are not, especially not in the nuclear age. The veto power has forced the Security Council to de-emphasize majority rule as far as the superpowers are concerned in favor of the more realistic unanimity principle: slow and frequently laborious negotiations to accommodate divergent points of view until both superpowers prefer to acquiesce rather than upset the system. The veto is thus a lesson in *Realpolitik*.

In fact, one may argue that the abolition of the veto might increase, not diminish, international tensions and the danger of war, since the majority might then be tempted to vote an action against a recalcitrant superpower. The technique of arriving at political decisions by counting votes without regard for power is a democratic luxury that the world may not be able to afford, particularly in the nuclear age. The principle of voting and living by majority decisions does make sense in a homogeneous political context, but in a world of profound schisms, negotiating with the opponent rather than outvoting him may be the wiser method of settling differences.

5

International Law and World Community

There has been a long and inconclusive controversy concerning the existence, nature, validity, and enforceability of international law (law of nations). Many scholars emphatically affirm the existence of international law and point to numerous legal rights and obligations among nations by which most governments scrupulously abide, especially in matters of international commerce, communications, or diplomatic immunities (Selection 14). According to others international law is, at best, weak because it is primitive and underdeveloped. Hans J. Morgenthau (Selection 14) compared the law of nations with "the kind of law that prevails in certain preliterate societies, such as the Australian aborigines or the Yurok of northern California. It is a primitive type of law primarily because it is almost completely decentralized law."[1] And still other scholars argue that the term international law is merely a premature and wishful label applied by its advocates—mostly professors of international law—to their moral, ideological, or class preferences in an attempt to endow them with

[1] Hans J. Morgenthau, *Politics among Nations* (Fourth ed.; New York: Alfred A. Knopf, 1967), p. 265.

legal sanctity. All who study it, however, seem to agree that international law such as it exists today fundamentally differs from national law.

Four obvious differences between international and national legal systems seem relatively noncontroversial:

(1) In a national legal system most laws are created centrally either by the national legislature, representing the common interests and values of the national community, or by a dictator who can assure enforcement of laws, regardless of the interests and values of his community. In an international legal system there is no central law-making agency with a recognized authority to enact legal norms binding upon all members of the international community.

Legal rights and obligations among nations are created in a highly decentralized fashion. The Statute of the International Court of Justice (Article 38) identifies three primary sources of international law:

(a) International conventions: treaties or contracts that establish rights and obligations for those nations which have consented to them;

(b) International custom: "custom" means more than habitual behavior or conduct. "It is usage felt by those who follow it to be an obligatory one," explains one authority on international law.[2]

(c) The general principles of law recognized by civilized nations: this rather obscure category seems to refer to concepts that cannot be proved either by international treaty or international custom but that may be detected in the decisions of national courts or even deep in the hearts and legal consciences of men.

If international law is primarily created by treaties and general practice accepted as law, can it be placed above nations? Or can it represent only an aggregate of written contracts and mutually accepted patterns of behavior binding upon some but not all nations? L. F. L. Oppenheim, an authority on international law whose opinion is included in Selection 13, asserted that "the Law of Nations is usually regarded as law between, not above the several states . . . as, apart from International Law, there is as yet no superior authority above sovereign states."[3] However, a dissenting argument by J. L. Brierly, another authority, is equally assertive: "if states are the subjects of international law, as Oppenheim admits they are, the law must surely be above them, and they must be subordinate to it."[4]

(2) Internationally, no real counterpart to a national judicial system (criminal and civil courts) exists. The International Court of Justice, sometimes called World Court, cannot deal with international crimes such as armed assault, atomic blackmail, rape of a country, or genocide. The Nuremberg and Tokyo

---

[2] J. L. Brierly, *The Law of Nations: An Introduction to the Law of Peace* (Sixth ed.; London: Oxford University Press, 1963), p. 60.

[3] L. F. L. Oppenheim, *International Law: Peace*, Vol. I (London: Longmans, Green and Co., Ltd., 1955), p. 4.

[4] Brierly, p. 47.

War Crimes tribunals, established by the victors after World War II, were very special temporary courts to deal with specific actions connected with that war; their purpose was to publicize and punish crimes committed by the defeated enemies; the question of whether the Numerberg and Tokyo verdicts established also a valid precedent is debatable.

Furthermore, even in noncriminal cases the World Court cannot assume jurisdiction unless both the plaintiff and the defendant agree that the World Court is the proper agency to deal with their dispute, which they both deem legal rather than political.[5] The line between a legal and a political dispute is not clear. A legal dispute is usually an issue that calls for interpretation of, or reallocation of rights and duties under, an international treaty or custom, which the contending parties recognize as mutually and legally binding. If, however, the main issue is the *change* of a given law or legal system, nations must either negotiate and agree on a new treaty or use violence to replace the old order by a new one. Similarly, a citizen in a national community goes to the judge when he wants a law or a contract interpreted; but if he wants the law to be changed, he either writes to his congressman or becomes a revolutionary.

Among nations, the obvious problem is who should determine which dispute is dominantly legal and therefore suitable to judicial settlement and which is political and therefore solved by diplomacy or violence; the inseparable problem, however, is what measure will be used to make the initial determination. The Covenant of the League of Nations (Article 13/1) distinguished between disputes that are suitable to judicial settlement and disputes that can be satisfactorily settled by diplomacy, but it failed to provide a clear indication of which is which. Similarly, the United Nations Charter (Article 36/3) recommends that, as a general rule, parties should refer their legal disputes to the International Court of Justice. "Whatever the formula," as Louis B. Sohn noted,

> ... the states of the world are going to evade the Court's jurisdiction whenever they deem it unsuited for the decision of their disputes with other states. No definition of legal disputes can be made so narrow as to prevent the adjudication of disputes involving to some extent non-legal issues, and the state will always reserve the right to claim that a particular dispute cannot be satisfactorily adjudicated by a court, even the ideal court.[6]

It seems that the problem of deciding whether a dispute is legal, mixed (legal and political), or purely political is in itself political. Realistically, albeit with regret, many international lawyers concur in this conclusion. For instance, one British lawyer suggests that all conflicts in international politics could be "reduced

---

[5] Nations usually submit their legal disputes to the World Court on the basis of a special agreement that refers to the specific issue; or, they may choose to accept the obligation to submit all their future legal disputes to the Court (the so-called Optional Clause, provided for in Article 36 of the Statute of the International Court of Justice).

[6] Louis B. Sohn, "Exclusion of Political Disputes from Judicial Settlement," *American Journal of International Law*, 38:4 (October 1944), p. 698.

to contests of legal nature" and then he adds: "The only decisive test of the justiciability of the dispute is the *willingness* of the disputants to submit the conflict to the arbitration of law" (italics added).[7]

(3) The third difference between domestic and international law is the existence of centralized national law enforcement and the absence of any central supranational agency with the right and power to enforce law on the international scene. Self-help is an exception under a national law but it is a rule under international law (Morgenthau, Selection 14). The possibility of observing the law without enforcement in both national and international law is discussed by John H. E. Fried in Selection 14.

(4) A fourth difference between national and international legal systems should be mentioned. It is more fundamental than the previously mentioned contrast between nationally centralized and internationally decentralized law-making, law-adjudicating, and law-enforcing. This crucial difference is between the existence of clearly common interests and values that bind individuals and groups together in a national community, on the one hand, and the absence of common interests and values among nations, on the other. For this reason sovereign and self-centered nations can hardly form a real community or society.

The following selections represent but a small fragment of the controversy as reflected in voluminous international legal literature and numerous scholarly articles and essays.

[7] Sir Hersch Lauterpacht, *The Function of Law in the International Community* (London: Oxford University Press, 1933), pp. 158, 164. Compare with Hans Kelsen, *Peace through Law* (Chapel Hill, N. C.: University of North Carolina Press, 1944), pp. 26, 29: "Any conflict between States as well as between private persons is economic or political in character; but that does not exclude treating the dispute as a legal dispute. . . . A positive legal order can always be applied to any conflict whatever."

13 / The Myth and Reality of World Community: A Controversy

L. F. L. Oppenheim
J. L. Brierly
Oliver J. Lissitzyn
Stanley Hoffmann
Charles de Visscher

The five authors represented in this selection share a positive attitude toward the constructive role international law may or should play. They differ, however, in their estimates of the capability and willingness of the existing nation-states—long established or newly emerging, poor or rich, communist, fascist, or democratic—to form a true global community from which a common legal superstructure might issue.

"The Existence of a Community Is . . . A Reality"

L. F. L. Oppenheim

The essential conditions of the existence of Law are . . . threefold. There must, first, be a community. There must, secondly, be a body of rules for human conduct within that community. And there must, thirdly, be a common consent of that community that these rules shall be enforced. . . . If we find this definition of Law correct, and accept these three essential conditions of Law, the existence of Law is not limited to the State community only, but is to be found everywhere where there is a community. . . .

. . . [T]he question arises, whether an international community exists whose Law could be the Law of Nations. . . . This question had already, before the First World War, been decided in the affirmative, as far as the states of the civilized world were concerned. . . . Though the individual States are sovereign and independent, though there is no international government above them, there exists a powerful unifying factor, namely their common interests. The influence of that unifying factor is liable to

From pp. 6–18 (*passim*) of L. F. L. Oppenheim, *International Law: Peace,* Vol. I (London: Longmans, Green, and Co., Ltd., 1955). The author is a former Professor of International Law at the University of Cambridge. His two volumes on international law (the first volume on the law of peace and the second on the law of war) are considered among the most authoritative books on the subject.

suffer a set-back whenever economic nationalism, political intolerance, and the pursuit of self-sufficiency on the part of sovereign states tend to create artifical barriers among the people composing them. Whenever that happens the authority and reality of International Law are likely to weaken. But such retrogression, being contrary to the natural tendencies of development and to the realities of international intercourse between States, must be regarded as temporary and as leaving essentially intact the existence of an international community. . . .

Thus the first essential condition for the existence of law. . . . the existence of a community. . . . is, at least, in the long run, a reality.

"Material Bonds Are Not Enough"

J. S. Brierly

Material bonds [such as international commerce] . . . are not enough without a common social consciousness; without that they are as likely to lead to friction as to friendship. Some sentiment of shared responsibility for the conduct of a common life is a necessary element in any society, and the necessary force behind any system of law; and the strength of any legal system is proportionate to the strength of such a sentiment. . . . Law can only exist in a society, and there can be no society without a system of law to regulate the relations of its members with one another. If then we speak of the "law of nations," we are assuming that a "society" of nations exists, and the assumption that the whole of civilized world constitutes a single society or community is one which we are not justified in making without examination.

Three Divisions of the World

Oliver J. Lissitzyn

The concept of an international law originated among a few kindred nations of Western Europe, conscious of their common background in the Greek,

From p. 43 of J. L. Brierly, *The Law of Nations: An Introduction to the Law of Peace* (Sixth ed.; London: Oxford University Press, 1963), p. 43.

From pp. 3, 14–17, 37–39 (*passim*) of Oliver J. Lissitzyn, "International Law in a Divided World," *International Conciliation*, No. 542 (March 1963). Reprinted by permission of Carnegie Endowment for International Peace. Some author's footnotes have been omitted; footnotes added by the editor are so marked.

Roman, and Christian civilizations. Is the nature of the Western origin of international law an invitation or an impediment to its universal adoption by the modern world, which is so deeply divided by contrasting traditions, ideologies, levels of development, and legal doctrines? The challenge to the Western European concepts of international law comes from two sources: the communist bloc and the Third World.

According to communist doctrine, any law is a reflection of a class interest; thus, Western law is a tool of the exploiting classes, while the communist law allegedly expresses the interest of the working class. "Laws and norms of law are subordinated to the laws of the class struggle and the laws of social development," reasserted the so-called Brezhnev Doctrine in 1968. If the class conflict is truly irreconcilable, how can there be a community among states ruled by irreconcilably hostile classes? Could a communist nation ever accept a doctrine of universal law that subjects all violence to its binding rules, including revolutionary class violence?

The universality of international law has also been questioned by the new states in Africa and Asia. As seen by them international law was originally created and then nurtured in the culture of their former colonial masters; when international law was extended to Asia, Africa, and Latin America, it was frequently invoked to protect the national or private industrial interests of the advanced and powerful Western states.

The author of the following analysis examines the opposition to, and the practice of partial adherence to, international law in a world that is not only divided into over 135 national states but also into three major blocs: the communist states, the West, and the Third World.

Fifty years ago, echoing the optimism of the nineteenth century, the author of a standard British treatise on international law confidently asserted that "immeasurable progress is guaranteed to International Law, since there are eternal moral and economic factors working in its favour."[8] Today many Western jurists are asking, with varying degrees of pessimism, whether or not there is still something that can be properly called universal international law, and, if so, whether or not the universality of international law can long be maintained in the face of the cold war and the rise to statehood of an ever growing number of nations of non-Western antecedents.

As early as the inter-war period, some Western jurists saw a threat to international law in the rejection by the rulers of the Soviet Union of the fundamental values and premises of Western public order. At that time the Soviet Union was hardly strong enough to defy the West, and the Soviet challenge to the foundations of international law was soon overshadowed by that of the aggressive nihilism of the Axis powers, particularly Nazi Germany. The emergence of the Soviet Union after World War II as one of the superpowers, however, could not but increase the anxiety of Western

[8] Oppenheim, p. 83.——Ed.

observers, some of whom saw in the resulting "disunity" of mankind a threat to the very existence of international law. . . .

Nothing in the background of the Communist leaders who seized power in Russia in 1917 predisposed them favorably toward international law. Like all law, it was to be regarded by Marxists as an instrument of the policy of the ruling class—namely, the "capitalist" class, under whose rule it had been developed. But the young Soviet republic, surrounded by "capitalist" states it was too weak to defy openly, needed peace and trade. Unhesitatingly, the Soviet leaders turned to international law as a means of protection and of necessary cooperation with the outside world. They were prompt to invoke international law against the hostile activities of Western powers. As early as 1921, "international law" was expressly laid down in a German-Soviet bilateral agreement as a standard to be applied in certain matters by these countries in their relations with each other.

The basic Soviet attitude toward international law was developed fairly rapidly under the combined pressure of practical need and Marxist doctrine. The problem of reconciling the apparent acceptance of an international law binding on Communist and non-Communist governments alike with the Marxist conception of law has been a perennial source of difficulty for Marxist legal theoreticians; but it has not been allowed to stand in the way of the pragmatic use of international law in the interests of Soviet policy. This pragmatic approach has remained substantially the same to this day, despite frequent variations in formulation and sometimes acrimonious discussion of the finer points by Soviet jurists. All doctrines, formulations, and applications of international law are appraised in terms of their usefulness to the Communist cause. . . .

. . . In the late Stalin era, F. I. Kozhevnikov baldly stated the Soviet attitude in these words:

> Those institutions in international law which can facilitate the execution of the stated tasks of the USSR are recognized and applied by the USSR, and those institutions which conflict in any manner with these purposes are rejected by the USSR. . . .

. . . International law, however, is also useful to the Soviet Union, as it is to other states, in preventing excessive friction with the outside world and in facilitating such relations of a cooperative nature with the "capitalist" states as the policies of the governments concerned permit. There has been a large measure of routine compliance by the Soviet Union with the generally accepted norms in such areas as diplomatic immunities and jurisdiction on the high seas. The Soviet Union, moreover, has entered into a great number of bilateral and multilateral treaties and agreements with non-Communist states. A recent comprehensive study shows that in the first forty years of its existence (1917–1957) the Soviet state entered into

2,516 treaties and agreements, and the tendency appears to be toward an increase in Soviet treaty obligations and relationships. Only a small proportion of these treaties and agreements have been primarily political in character. Most have been in the functional areas of world affairs—trade, communications, transport, consular relations, health, conservation of natural resources (such as certain stocks of fish, seals, and whales). In these areas, Communist and non-Communist states have often deemed it mutually advantageous, if only temporarily, to cooperate with each other, and international law has provided the framework for the desired cooperation.

The attitudes of the newly independent and other less developed nations and their leaders toward international law cannot be identified and described as easily as those of the Soviet ruling elite. Unlike the latter, the leaders of these nations do not for the most part think and act within the framework of a single comprehensive philosophical and political system such as Marxism-Leninism. . . . The less developed nations, furthermore, differ in cultural background, levels of education, political orientation, and specific interests. Within each nation, moreover, there may be significant differences in attitudes toward international law among the various groups participating in the policy-making process. . . . Yet many of these nations show certain common tendencies in their attitude toward international law. These tendencies are a product of resentment of past foreign domination and attitudes of superiority, and of a low level of economic development with resulting economic and technological dependence on the more advanced countries. None of the less developed nations officially denies the existence or the binding force of international law. All have at various times invoked its norms in disputes with other states and in debates in international organizations. With varying degrees of interest, they have participated in diplomatic conferences for the codification and development of international law, and in the work of the Assembly's Sixth Committee. All have entered into numerous treaties, including many general multilateral conventions, thus extending the scope of the application of international law. Several have submitted disputes to the International Court of Justice.

Yet, among the less developed nations, there is a perceptible current of discontent with traditional international law. This discontent generally does not lead to a denial or depreciation of the role of international law in world affairs. Indeed, spokesmen for the less developed countries often stress the need for the further development of international law in order to increase its importance in relations among nations. But development means change, and the desire for the development of international law in part reflects a feeling that the traditional norms are a creation of a limited number of Western states and do not necessarily serve the needs and aspirations of the less developed and, particularly, the newly independent nations. Consequently, it is felt, the traditional norms are not, or should not be, binding on them.

The "expansion" of international law to Asian and African nations is said to be proceeding at the price of a "continuous dilution of its content, as it is reinterpreted for the benefit of the newcomers."[9]

The discontent of the less developed nations with existing international law reflects more than the feeling that some of its norms may be outmoded or opposed to the interests of the weaker states and the newly independent states. There is also a desire to incorporate in it certain principles that have been usually regarded in the West as political rather than legal and that, by their very generality and flexibility of application, lend themselves to manipulation.[10]

A Judgeless World Where No One Is Innocent

Stanley Hoffmann

A community's legal system mirrors the nature of the community itself. It can hardly be much better or much worse than the community's leaders, values, and interests. Using this principle, Hoffmann suggests that the state of conflict among nations largely determines the flaws of the international legal system. This selection contains a number of challenging, though hardly encouraging, points.

The permanent plight of international law is that, now as before, it shows on its body of rules all the scars inflicted by the international state of war. The tragedy of contemporary international law is that of a double divorce: first, between the old liberal dream of a world rule of law, and the realities of an international system of multiple minidramas that always threaten to become major catastrophes; second, between the old dream and the new requirements of moderation, which in the circumstances of the present system suggest a *downplaying* of formal law in the realm of peace-and-war issues, and an *upgrading* of more flexible techniques, until the system has become less fierce. The interest of international law for the political

From pp. xii–xix of Stanley Hoffmann, "Introduction," in Lawrence Scheinman and David Wilkinson (Eds.), *International Law and Political Crisis: An Analytic Casebook* (Boston: Little, Brown & Company, 1968).

[9] J. Stone, *Quest for Survival: The Role of Law and Foreign Policy* (Cambridge, Mass., Harvard Univ. Press, 1961), p. 88.

[10] These include such political-legal issues as self-determination, decolonization, the right to dispose of one's own national resources, including the problem of past and future foreign investments or protecting fishing rights beyond territorial waters against unfair competition by fishing fleets of the well-equipped advanced industrial nations. ——Ed.

scientist is that there is no better way of grasping the continuing differences between order within a national society and the fragile order of international affairs than to study how and when states use legal language symbols and documents, and with what results. . . .

. . . *[T]he nature of the international system condemns international law to all the weaknesses and perversions that it is so easy to deride.* International law is merely a magnifying mirror that reflects faithfully and cruelly the essence and the logic of international politics. In a fragmented world, there is no "global perspective" from which anyone can authoritatively assess, endorse, or reject the separate national efforts at making international law serve national interests above all. Like the somber universe of Albert Camus' Caligula, this is a judgeless world where no one is innocent.

World Community as a Civilizing Idea

Charles de Visscher

The author of the following analysis is a Belgian jurist of world reputation, former judge of the International Court of Justice, and former president of the Institute of International Law. In contrast to Oppenheim, he expresses considerable doubts as to the reality of the world community today. The intermittent contacts and material bonds among nations, though necessary and welcome, cannot be regarded as manifestations of true common social consciousness, nor of true community.

Yet de Visscher, who denies the existence of a true world community, is not a pessimist. For him the international community, capable of producing an enforceable legal system, is a *potential* order in the minds of men, a positive force that may generate political and social change.[11]

Merely to invoke the idea of an international community, as the habit is, is immediately to move into a vicious circle, for it is to postulate in men, shut in their national compartments, something that they still largely lack, namely the community spirit, the deliberate adherence to supranational values. . . . If the international community, or more accurately the sense of such a community, finds so little echo in individual consciences, this is less because power obstructs it than because the immense majority of men are still infinitely less accessible to the doubtless real but certainly remote solidarities that it evokes than to the immediate and tangible solid-

From pp. 88–92, 98–100 (*passim*) of Charles de Visscher, *Theory and Reality in Public International Law* (Princeton, N.J.: Princeton University Press, 1968).

[11] In Selection 15, Richard A. Falk will deal with international law as a generative force in greater detail.

arities that impose themselves upon them in the framework of national life. ... It is in contact with the world outside that any social group differentiates and becomes conscious of itself; only against the stranger does its solidarity fully assert itself. The modern State owes its historical cohesion and strong individualization to external pressures and the sentiments of loyalty to the national collectivity that they have generated and stimulated. National solidarities have triumphed over internal tensions, even the most deep-rooted, such as those between class and class. The international community has no such decisive factor of social cohesion. It has no substitute for it save the infinitely less powerful appeal to sacrifice, to a common supranational good. And this, a perception which is the source of all progress, is hardly accessible to the immense majority of men. ... The international community is a potential order in the minds of men; it does not correspond to an effectively established order. ... The idea of an international community belongs to those great intuitions, to those "civilizing ideas" which, though slow in their action and subject to eclipses, are nevertheless positive forces that generate political and social change.

14 / Observance and Enforcement of International Law

John H. E. Fried
Hans J. Morgenthau

International law is often described as being more violated than observed. By contrast, national communities generally adhere to their own legal system and only exceptionally or marginally violate it. Is this contrast a correct description of facts of national and international life?

According to John H. E. Fried, the answer is negative. First, most international rules and obligations have been constantly observed by nation-states because their mutual interests depended on such observance; enforcement was not necessary because violation was neither contemplated nor perpetrated. To the question, "How efficient is international law?" Fried replies: "It is at least as efficient as is domestic law."[12]

[12] John H. E. Fried, "How Efficient Is International Law," in Karl W. Deutsch and Stanley Hoffmann (Eds.), *The Relevance of International Law* (Cambridge, Mass.: Schenkman Publishing Co., Inc., 1968), p. 132.

Enforcement of national laws appears effective whenever the consensus and force of an organized community are pitted against individual violators who are more often than not comparatively weak and unorganized. The picture changes, however, when the will and power of a community to coerce and punish deviant behavior has been challenged by a multitude of violators who are armed and organized, as is often the case of criminal gangs or revolutionary organizations. When a national consensus collapses and the nation is split asunder by a controversy between two or more powerful entities, the domestic scene becomes a close parallel to the international: lawlessness, brutality, inhumanity, and wanton destruction characterize both the defenders and challengers of a given national order.

On the international scene we have noted the absence of a global consensus and the ensuing absence of an international authority with the right and power to give and enforce international law. In such a situation nations rely on the mutuality of their interests (which may be very strong, as Fried demonstrates, especially in their commercial contacts in which national survival is not at stake) or self-help as a remedy against potential or actual violation of a rule. But self-help is a remedy that evidently favors the mighty and leaves the small nations at the mercy of a bully. This circumstance leads Hans J. Morgenthau to conclude that in the absence of a world community of shared values only a balance of power can prevent a powerful nation from violating the rights of smaller nations: "Where there is neither community of interests nor balance of power, there is no international law." Paradoxically, in the nuclear era, balance of power can perhaps protect a nonaligned nation but it cannot protect a small allied nation against its own superpower ally. Precisely because there was a balance (or nuclear stalemate) between the Soviet Union and the United States, Czechoslovakia, a small ally of the Soviet Union, could rely neither on the balance of power nor on self-help to protect itself against conquest and occupation by the allied armies of the Soviet Union in 1968.

Respecting Law without Enforcement

John H. E. Fried

There is widespread belief that international law is more often broken than observed. . . .

One paradoxical reason for this widespread misunderstanding is the very fact that in many ways international law functions relatively so well that the problems involved and the efforts that were needed to solve them remain unnoticed. Whenever a radio station adapts its wave-lengths in a manner as not to interfere with those of a station abroad; whenever a customs officer

From pp. 106–108 of John H. E. Fried, "For a New Image of International Law," *Main Currents in Modern Thought,* 21:5 (May–June 1965). Reprinted by permission.

calculates the duty due according to a tariff agreement; whenever a freighter anchors in a foreign port and then our breakfast coffee is loaded onto it; whenever any organ of the U.N. or of any of the numerous other international and regional intergovernmental organizations sits down for deliberations; wherever an embassy or consulate functions; whenever investments are made abroad, or anybody crosses a frontier; whenever water is diverted for irrigation from a river flowing through two or more countries; whenever the spread of epidemic diseases or illegal traffic in dangerous drugs is being combatted; whenever foreign patents are used; whenever a plane traverses the ocean—and many more matters could be added to this list—it is international law in action, and appreciation is due to the honest effort and cooperation that had to go into the making of the rules and functioning of the institutions, arrangements and facilities which make these things possible.

Furthermore, whenever a new treaty comes into force (hundreds do every year!) or a decision is rendered by the World Court or by a mixed commission or by any other organ endowed by international law with the jurisdiction to render it, and whenever a new multinational or bilateral agency is created or a new function is entrusted to it, something has been added to the world legal order.

No doubt, international law, just as any other law, can be, and sometimes is being, twisted. But this does not make it a bag of tricks. The question is whether such sophistries or outright disregard for obligations can be blamed on international law. The answer is evidently in the negative. Otherwise, by the same token, the surgical knife, designed to save lives, could be blamed if it is being used for improper purposes.

What then, should be done in case of disregard for international obligations? This brings us to the most frequently made criticism of international law:

"International law is not enforceable; this is its fatal weakness."

At first sight, comparison with domestic law seems to show international law at a decisive disadvantage: "If I drive my car through a red light, or steal, the cop will arrest me—but where is the cop when a State commits a wrong?" This argument can soberly be dealt with only by a series of considerations, ranging from statistics to basic aspects of the philosophy of law. In briefest outline, the answer would have to raise the following points:

First of all, the argument implies that States constantly commit wrongs and, indeed, *criminal* wrongs (for, be it noted also, domestic law provides neither cop nor jail for the far vaster field of *civil* obligations). The argument is already much weakened by the empirical fact, mentioned above, that by and large international obligations are being honored.

The argument also oversimplifies a penological doctrine which even in domestic law, where the psychology of individuals is of the essence, is by no means uncontested—namely, that obedience to law will be proportionate to the fear of punishment. . . .

The argument implies that domestic law *guarantees,* as it were, either fulfilment or punishment, and that the risk of punishment increases the probability of fulfilment. But everyday experience shows that in spite of the most highly developed enforcement systems, many debts remain unpaid, many other obligations unfulfilled, and countless crimes unpunished. In fact, it is highly questionable whether statistical data would not reveal a proportionately higher percentage of violations of domestic than of international law.

All of these considerations greatly reduce the persuasiveness of the "non-enforceability" argument. However, to them must be added the really decisive counter-argument:

At every level of law, the most difficult question is enforcement (and even ascertainment of who is "right" and who is "wrong") in controversies of *major* importance between *powerful* entities. For these cases, the analogy with the traffic cop is altogether inappropriate. States are large, powerful entities. The law regarding important disputes between them can therefore be compared, if at all, only with such branches of domestic law, particularly *constitutional* law, which regulate the relations between powerful entities of the same country—for example, between a federal government and state governments. What do we see then? We see, for example, that in most countries neither written nor customary constitutional law permits "judicial review"; and that even where judicial review and enforcement of such judgments are legally permitted, the enforcement machinery will hardly ever be put in motion because, as, for example, Professor Quincy Wright pointed out, the consequence would be civil war. Similarly, it is instructive to notice that the vast majority of industrialized countries do *not* provide for judicial or other enforceable determination of major collective industrial disputes. Hence, the question of enforcement cannot even come up.

Does all this mean that the legal order has to abdicate in the face of major conflicts? Not at all. It means that the law, being concerned with rationality and order, will avoid potentially self-defeating rules. But it will, for example, for major collective wage disputes, lay down and enforce measures designed to minimize the probability of disorders, prescribe "cooling-off" periods, etc. It will, above all, bend every effort to provide settlement machinery long before a major industrial dispute explodes.

The situation is not dissimilar, only vastly more serious, in the case of major international crises. A single violation of the obligation not to commit military aggression may have consequences immeasurably more serious than those of all traffic violations and all failures to pay debts put together. It is also true, as U Thant pointed out, that the sanctions would have to be so extreme (namely, the very conflagration which the entire fabric of international law is designed to *prevent*) as not to be rationally or realistically feasible.

This, however, does not prove the futility of the international legal order. On the contrary. It proves the rationality and usefulness of those rules, devices and institutions which are designed to make certain that the danger point will not be reached; which provide for *peaceful* settlement; which at least can de-fuse problems that, if they were left unchecked, might escalate into catastrophe.

Balance of Power and the Rule of Law

Hans J. Morgenthau

International law does not ... provide for agencies and instrumentalities for the purpose of enforcement apart from the agencies and instrumentalities of the national governments. ... Only under very exceptional and narrow conditions, in the form of self-help and self-defense [intentional killing in self-defense is authorized by most national legal systems], does domestic law give the victim of a violation of the law the right to take the law into his own hands and enforce it against the violator. What is a narrowly circumscribed exception in domestic law is the principle of law enforcement in international law. According to this principle, the victim, and nobody but the victim, of a violation of the law has the right to enforce the law against the violator. Nobody at all has the *obligation* to enforce it.

There can be no more primitive and no weaker system of law enforcement than this; for it delivers the enforcement of the law to the vicissitudes of the distribution of power between the violator of the law and the victim of the violation. It makes it easy for the strong both to violate the law and to enforce it, and consequently puts the rights of the weak in jeopardy. A great power can violate the rights of a small nation without having to fear effective sanctions on the latter's part. It can afford to proceed against the small nation with measures of enforcement under the pretext of a violation of its rights, regardless of whether the alleged infraction of international law has actually occurred or whether its seriousness justifies the severity of the measures taken.

The small nation must look for the protection of its rights to the assistance of powerful friends; only thus can it hope to oppose with a chance of success an attempt to violate its rights. Whether such assistance will be forthcoming is a matter not of international law but of the national interest as conceived by the individual nations, which must decide whether or not to come to the support of the weak member of the international community. In other words, whether or not an attempt will be made to enforce international law and whether or not the attempt will be successful do not depend primarily upon legal considerations and the disinterested operation of law-enforcing mechanisms. Both attempt and success depend upon political considerations and the actual distribution of power in a particular case. The protection of the rights of a weak nation that is threatened by a strong one is then determined by the balance of power as it operates in that particular situation. Thus the rights of Belgium were safeguarded in 1914 against their violation by Germany, for it so happened that the protection of those rights seemed to be required by the national interests of powerful neighbors. Similarly, when in 1950 South Korea was attacked by North Korea, their concern with the maintenance of the balance of power in the Far East and of territorial stability throughout Asia prompted the United States and some of its allies, such as France and Great Britain, to come to the aid of South Korea. On the other hand, the rights of Colombia, when the United States supported the revolution in 1903 which led to the establishment of the Republic of Panama, and the rights of Finland, when attacked by the Soviet Union in 1939, were violated either with impunity or, as in the case of Finland, without the intervention of effective sanctions. There was no balance of power which could have protected these nations.

15 / International Law: A New Approach

Richard A. Falk

In the following essay Falk focuses on two major themes. First: he admonishes international lawyers to place themselves above the narrow horizons of their own national affiliation—not an easy assignment in our nationalist era. Relying on the ambiguities of international law, these experts are currently willing and able to justify almost any national policy and action—the United States war in Vietnam or the Soviet occupation of Czechoslovakia—in "legal" terms. Instead of this service to the national government, so-called international lawyers should, according to Falk, provide their nations and the world with impartial standards to measure and appraise controversial national actions.

The question is, of course, whether in international politics a "denationaliza-tion" of truth and law is possible. Even if successfully detached from their national bias, legal experts may still distort their understanding of international law by their personal, ideological, or religious preferences. Like anybody else, they may find it extremely difficult to be "objective" in world affairs.

The second theme is Falk's thought-provoking analysis of the new horizontal links among people (compare with Singer in Selection 4) which cut across the boundaries of national sovereignty. In theory and practice there have been several departures from the concept of international law as law between sovereign nation-states only. For example, the racist policies of the Nazi government with regard to its own inhabitants and the racist apartheid policies of the South African government now tend to be viewed as matters of international legal concern rather than as matters of sovereign domestic jurisdiction. Falk points to the role of subnational, nongovernmental, and regional bodies in international law, the legal influence of the majority decisions of the United Nations General Assembly, the importance of domestic institutions (especially courts), and individual claimants for expansion of the application of international legal consensus.

The study of international law has been decisively influenced by a number of conditioning factors in international life:

1. The increasing expectation that legal rules, procedures, and institutions are relevant to the prohibition, regulation, and settlement of violent international conflict. The avoidance of World War III is here the most dramatic objective.

2. The aftermath of decolonization as reflected in the active participation in international society of a large number of states at various stages of economic and political development. These states are pressing demands for a restructuring of international relationships that points toward the creation of an international welfare system.

3. The emergence of actors other than nation-states that contribute to the creation, maintenance, and destruction of order and justice in world affairs. These include individuals, political groupings (e.g. "blocs"), regional organizations, functional agencies, and international institutions.

4. The steady erosion of the idea of exclusively domestic jurisdiction in contemporary world affairs in such crucial areas as civil strife and human rights. Such erosion indicates the need for new conceptions of international law adequate to deal with the international implications of domestic

phenomena as well as to examine the traditional range of legal concerns—
the regulation of the relations between the units constituting the international system.

5. The emerging need to discover ways to control the social and
political impacts of technology and thereby to respond to such challenges
as overpopulation, radioactive contamination, subliminal manipulation,
weather and climate modification.

6. The role of subnational actors (especially individuals) and
transnational groups (for instance, political parties, business associations,
religious groups) in invoking the authority of international law to challenge
and restrain the exercise of power by nation-states.

7. The role of regional and community consensus in mobilizing the
international system, or portions of it, to legitimate sanctioning procedures
and even to authorize uses of force for the common welfare (for instance,
to eliminate *apartheid* in South Africa).

These are among the issues and developments impinging upon traditional
conceptions of international law and leading to new directions and methods
of inquiry. The process of change in international society in recent decades
has been so drastic that the presence of a doctrinal and methodological lag
in the discipline of international law is not surprising. A sovereignty-
oriented, state-centered image of international society has dominated international legal thought for several centuries. The present period is an
exciting one for international law, calling for adaptation to a much more
complicated structure of international society, a structure within which the
basic organizing distinction between matters of domestic jurisdiction and
matters of international jurisdiction has grown far less helpful and within
which the limits of state discretion can no longer be satisfactorily described
by the obligations undertaken voluntarily and formally through a national
government's manifestation of an intention to be bound.

New Trends in Observation
and Assessment in
International Legal Studies

International law is both a contemplative academic subject and an
active ingredient of diplomatic process in world affairs. The failure to maintain the clarity of this distinction accounts for considerable confusion about
the nature and function of international law in the world today. An international lawyer is also a citizen of a nation-state who often holds strong views
as to preferred courses of foreign policy. One way for him to vindicate these

views is to demonstrate their compatibility or incompatibility with governing rules of international law. . . .

If an international lawyer determines that his scholarly analysis confirms the foreign policy of his country, then he has a choice of making such an argument or maintaining silence. It would seem preferable that the legal argument be made, provided that it strengthens the movement to make international law serve as the arbiter of foreign policy rather than its servant. To enable such a contribution it is essential that the scholar avoid polemical rhetoric, offer legal authority for the conclusions reached, acknowledge areas in which international law is indefinite, and consider facts and arguments that oppose the legal conclusions reached. In effect, an important contribution of international lawyers is to provide an independent criterion by which to appraise controversial action of national governments. This contribution can be maintained only if there is a convincing distinction evident between scholarly analysis and national affiliation. If national affiliation is a total indicator of legal analysis, then there is no reason to seek guidance as to the nature of permissible behavior in international society from the writings of international lawyers. One might expect, however, at this stage of international history to acquire superior insight into the character of legal expectations by consulting legal analyses of controversial conduct which have been made by international lawyers located in countries not directly involved as participants in the controversy. A tradition of such impartial commentary, if it could be encouraged, might serve to enhance the stature and influence of international law.

The international lawyers of the period after World War I, dominated by approaches associated with legal positivism or natural law, achieved a different sort of policy irrelevance from the policy justifications of recent years. These earlier international lawyers detached law from the political context of world affairs and made very rigid analyses of the regulation of state conduct by invoking supposedly fixed and unambiguous rules of restraint. They relied for a new system of world order upon agreed legal rules, but they failed to develop an adequate appreciation of the social and political difficulties of making these rules into effective behavioral norms. The Covenant of the League, the Kellogg-Briand Pact, and the general seriousness with which prohibitions upon the use of aggressive force were taken by international lawyers are indicative of this general failure to understand the limited effect of rules of restraint upon the central activities of the nation-state in a social system as decentralized in its distribution of power and as horizontal in its institutional structure as is international society.

In the 1940's and 1950's, new critiques of international law as legalistic and moralistic were salutory efforts to persuade well-intentioned governments away from any general reliance upon such rules in the pursuit of their interests and the defense of their values. A modicum of realism suggests that rules governing recourse to violence can be manipulated; the complementarity of a system of legal rules assures that a legal pretext, at least, will always be available to a government.

And given the absence of impartial procedures to review contradictory legal claims put forward by nation-states in a dispute, there is no very persuasive means to appraise the relative merits of the legal argument. The understanding of a legal order, then, must be expanded to include an awareness of the prospects for upholding a fairly stable set of expectations about what is permissible and what is impermissible conduct, an awareness that shifts inquiry from the rules to the social and institutional means available for their effective implementation. The leading international lawyers in the period following World War II have been increasingly sensitive to this need to examine the role of law in light of the overall setting of international politics. . . . [that is, to] give great attention to the definition of realistic goals for international law in light of the decentralized character of international society. There is almost a consensus present among contemporary international lawyers that such an intellectual orientation is essential to the fruitful study of international law. The result of this orientation is to bring the study of international law into ever closer association with the outlook, method, and concerns of the social scientist.

In his analyses, the international lawyer cannot afford to hold constant the context within which law is created and applied or within which legal controversy takes place. For the student of domestic law the institutional social context is fairly clearly established and can more easily be taken for granted, although the bearing of changing pressures and values upon the development of all phases of law is not widely accepted. For international lawyers the first task, in a sense, is to find functional equivalents for the legislature, court, and executive and then to measure the degree to which these equivalents produce law-conditioned behavior in international affairs. So long as international lawyers conceived of the search for functional equivalence in terms of mechanical identity, the results of their labors produced either artificial enthusiasm or premature despair. Such a mechanical approach tends to give exaggerated prominence to the central institutions that do exist in international society—especially to the International Court of Justice—and produces either an attitude that such institutions as do exist constitute the international legal system or the conclusion that despite the formal existence of equivalent institutions their impact on international behavior is so marginal and sporadic as to deprive of legal quality the ordering of relations among states.

The development of a more sophisticated approach to the notion of functional equivalence makes it possible to achieve a richer sense of the character of international law. In particular, increasing stress is now being put upon the distinctive ordering characteristics of an international society conceived of in predominantly horizontal and decentralized terms. The most pronounced consequence of this stress is to shift the focus of inquiry from the activities of primitive international institutions to the activities of national legal institutions in generating, enforcing, and repudiating the rules and expectations associated with international law. It is a commonplace hypothesis that it is necessary to correlate patterns of authority with patterns of power in an effective social order. One can thus infer, in a manner relevant to the study of international law, that the effective locus of authority will be on the national level. Systematic attention is now being given for the first time to the role of national institutions and decision-makers in upholding and developing international law. . . .

. . . There are certain international situations of conflict and crisis in which the overriding goals of national policy are chosen almost independently of what the law, impartially assessed, might be supposed to require. Consequently there exists a rather misleading and destructive tendency to conclude that international law has nothing whatever to do with the behavior of states or with the maintenance of international stability in this sort of political setting. Government lawyers are called in, if at all, to provide legal arguments for a decision taken on other grounds, so that official action will seem legally defensible, especially in the eyes of domestic public opinion. Certainly this rationalizing function of international law seems dominant with respect to U.S. military participation in Vietnam or to the armed intervention of 1965 in the Dominican Republic. And in Soviet international practice there is almost no indication that international lawyers in their role as experts on international law advise on policy or are permitted to comment objectively on the relationship between Soviet practice and relevant rules of international law. The role of international law has in these situations been restricted to one of rationalization, and there is little indication that the existence of international law has had much bearing on the execution of the various phases of foreign policy. Such an exclusion of law from the procedures of political decision-making does suggest a willingness to conceive of national interest as exclusively defined by national will and by the relative capabilities of interested parties to assert control over the event in question.

But political decision-making need not require the exclusion of international law. By the formulation of the political position in terms of a distinct legal claim, the nature of an international controversy may be clarified and the rival actor made somewhat less likely to overreact. International law can operate as an assured medium of diplomatic communication, allowing for processes of claim and counterclaim to delimit the area of dispute and clarify the stakes of a particular conflict. The degree to which international law facilitates international communication is a new subject for scholarly investigation. An informed awareness of legal expectations in a situation of crisis may also strengthen inclinations to exercise maximum self-restraint in achieving the political end in view. One way to command support for or to minimize opposition to political claims, especially those involving the use of force, is to show a high regard for relevant rules of international law. The interdiction by the United States of Soviet "offensive" missiles bound for Cuba in 1962 is a prominent example of structuring a political claim to reinforce rather than to detract from the relevance of international law to the conduct of foreign policy. . . .

. . . The Soviet Union's endorsement of support for wars of national liberation—a departure from the Charter conception of permissible use of force—provides a complex example of unintended consequences flowing from an original departure in doctrine and practice from legal expectations. Among the consequences of such a departure is that it weakens the impact of Soviet objections to the more militant posture of the Chinese and to the interventionary anti-Communist policies and practices of the United States. Likewise the unilateral nature and the scale of the United States role in support of the Saigon government in Vietnam are generating precedents (with regard to outside participation in civil wars) that seem to impair existing precedents of neutrality and limited intervention that might have been strengthened had the United States chosen an alternative course of action.

Part of the inquiry directed at the role of international law on the domestic level is to take note of the increasing use of international law by private citizens, at least in democratic societies, as a way to restrain, or dramatize opposition to, the undertakings of their own national government. This development is attributable, in part, to a withering of nationalist sentiment in the developed countries, both reflecting a universal humanistic ethic popular among intellectuals of all countries and expressing a widespread fear that even the most powerful nations must act with caution in the nuclear age. The existence of this trend is some indication that international lawyers are adopting an outlook based on an extranationalistic view of international law, which can serve as a transnational source of judgment on issues of disputed legality. Dramatic evidence of this outlook is the effort to present cases in domestic courts to test the willingness of these courts to question the legality under international law of government conduct. Notions of sovereign immunity are giving way as barriers to such challenges on behalf of international law. The idea that international law is of concern only in state-to-state relations is also giving way, undermined, in part, by the imposition after World War II of criminal responsibility on the leaders of Germany and Japan because of their alleged violation of international law. The precedent of the Nuremberg Judgment is now being invoked against those who helped to create it, the argument being that if individuals have a duty to avoid violating rules of international law, then this duty of the individual must be protected by the domestic system, and thus that a domestic court must not decline to determine whether or not its own government is violating international law (just as it determines whether or not its own government is violating domestic law).

By and large these attempts to make use of domestic courts in this fashion have failed, the court refusing to regard the plaintiff as competent to raise the issue or itself as competent to decide it. . . . However, the mere presence of these cases on court dockets is significant to the extent that it can dramatize a shift in the locus of loyalty from the national scene to the common law of mankind. To the extent that domestic courts dismiss such claims because the conduct of foreign policy is a nonreviewable exercise of executive discretion, these cases serve to highlight prerogatives claimed by a state in its foreign affairs that it would not dare claim for domestic affairs. Further, these cases call attention to the discrepancy between the appeals of statesmen for the rule of law in world affairs and their insistence upon the nonreviewability of their own conduct within their own domestic courts. Surely if the conduct of foreign policy is not subject to review in a forum as sympathetic with national perspectives as a domestic court is normally inclined to be, then the outlook for entrusting vital legal disputes to international tribunals is indeed dim.

The relevant point here is that the study of international law can benefit greatly by more systematic and comparative attention to the extent and manner of domestic institutions' application of international law. . . .

A Japanese domestic court in the *Shimoda* case provides the only example of an attempt by a legal tribunal to assess the legality of the atomic attacks upon Hiroshima and Nagasaki. The court's decision is particularly significant, first, because it involves a review under international law of belligerent action carried out in the course of a major war by the victorious powers and, second, because the review was undertaken at the instance of individuals, five survivors of the attacks. The conclusion reached by the Tokyo court that the atomic raids violated international law has an impact, the ultimate strength of which is as yet unmeasurable, upon the status of nuclear weapons as legitimate military weapons. To the extent that such an impact exists it illustrates how the growth of international legal standards may be the result of determinations of law reached at the domestic level. The case illustrates as well that individuals may be beginning to make a legislative input to the international system, thereby complicating further the notion that rules of international law can be formed only by the consent of sovereign states.

Contemporary approaches to international law are searching for ways to encompass the role of actors other than nation-states, ways that are descriptive of the relevance of law to international behavior. Wolfgang Friedmann has called attention to the relevance of regional actors to the growth of effective international law in a world divided on such fundamental matters as human rights and the ownership of private property. As yet no adequate work has been done on the degree to which regional actors are bound either by the rules governing nation-states in their relations with other regional actors or by some nascent interregional law of a distinctive sort. . . . There are important issues involving the danger of regional aggression against a state that opposes the regional consensus in some fundamental way, as Israel opposes the Arab League, Cuba the Organization of American States, and South Africa the Organization of African Unity. International lawyers are growing sensitive to the need to adapt their framework of inquiry to take account of the contemporary structure of international society, especially the relevance of regional actors and international institutions to the regulation of all sorts of behavior with transnational implications.

A different source of regulatory authority arises from the efforts of bloc actors to moderate the limits of conflict by establishing rules of the game in their relations *inter se*. The significance of these rules depends upon the degree to which certain relations are perceived in bipolar terms and upon the acceptance of and reliance upon processes of communication to establish commonly perceived limits of conflict. The Soviet Union and the United States are both competing for political influence in the new states of Asia and Africa. One consequence of this competition is the manipulation of civil strife so as to produce desired outcomes; another, in special cases, is intervention with overt military power. At the same time, these two preeminent world powers seek to avoid an escalation of small wars above certain thresholds. Therefore, rules of the game that limit the extent and nature of participation in civil wars would seem to serve the common interest of both powers without unduly interfering with their freedom of political action. Among the most significant of these rules is a prohibition upon the use of nuclear weapons to support one's proxy faction. Another calls for the confinement of the geographical scope of violence to the territorial limits of the state that is the scene of the violence. The decision in February of 1965 to extend the war in Vietnam by bombing north of the seventeenth parallel is a very significant challenge to this rule unless the civil war is viewed as a struggle between North Vietnam and the Saigon elite in South Vietnam. Given the inability of the United Nations to interpose itself effectively in situations of cold war violence, these informal rules of the game are an important ingredient of contemporary world order, and their importance is to some extent dependent upon their character as norms being perceived and understood by relevant decision-makers. If law is identified with community expectations and a violation of law consists of the disappointment of these expectations, then there is no real problem presented by assimilating this kind of "rule" into the analysis used to deal with rules created by the more traditional procedures associated with treaty-making and customary international law.

In fact, one of the major issues challenging time-honored approaches to international law is the development of a more adequate theory of the basis of legal obligation in international society. C. Wilfred Jenks has been particularly articulate in suggesting the need to supplant a sovereignty-oriented notion of consent with a community-oriented notion of consensus. Considerable recent attention has been given to the law-creating potential of various sorts of resolutions passed by the General Assembly. Considerable work needs to be done to formulate the conditions under which and the extent to which various categories of resolutions do have a law-creating impact. It is also necessary to investigate the interaction between resolutions and attitudes toward permissible and impermissible behavior and thereby to achieve some understanding of when and how the General Assembly can exert an effective influence, as well as to identify some of the occasions upon which its actions are likely to be futile.

Some authoritative insight into the juridical status of these issues has been given in several of the Dissenting Opinions in *The South West Africa Cases* decided by the International Court of Justice in June of 1966. In the course of this complex litigation the argument was made that the practice of *apartheid* is "illegal" because of the law-creating effect of formal acts of the General Assembly supported by an over-whelming majority of the membership. . . . The main point is that the traditional dichotomy between what is obligatory and what is permissive is crumbling and that therefore international lawyers need a more adequate and comprehensive theory of legal obligation than that developed to serve an international society consisting only of states in which the existence of law subserves the ideology of national sovereignty.

Part II

Decisions in Foreign Policy

6

National Interest and Power

In the study of international politics no other phrase stimulates a more passionate and inconclusive controversy than "national interest." Its exact meaning has eluded scholars and politicians. The concept of national interest in terms of the pursuit of power is central to the theory of political realism, developed by Hans J. Morgenthau (Selection 16). It assumes that the will and capacity of a nation-state to survive in a hostile international environment represents the core meaning of national interest. In order to justify his practical and realistic approach to international politics, Morgenthau pointed to the morality of national interest:

> In a world where a number of sovereign nations compete with and oppose each other for power, the foreign policies of all nations must necessarily refer to their survival as their minimum requirement. Thus all nations do what they cannot help but do: protect their physical, political and cultural identity against encroachments by other nations.... If an American statesman must choose between the promotion of universal liberty, which is a moral good, at the risk of American security and, hence, of liberty in the United States, and the promotion of American security and of liberty in the United States, which is another moral good, to the detriment of the promotion of universal liberty, which choice ought he to make? The utopian will not face the issue squarely and will deceive him-

self into believing that he can achieve both goods at the same time. The realist will choose the national interest on both moral and pragmatic grounds; for if he does not take care of the national interest nobody else will.[1]

Furthermore, national interest is not only moral but also practical since, according to Morgenthau, it rests on obvious and solid realities that can be objectively ascertained, and not on changing opinions and passions. This thesis is supported by many examples from history; they indicate that some nations' major needs and goals have remained unchanged over long periods of time. Even the replacement of the ruling elites by their revolutionary rivals does not seem to affect the concept of national interest; in democracies, following national elections a new leader seems to follow basically the same foreign policy as his predecessor. One specific example is the United States' continuous involvement in and sensitivity to Latin American affairs; there does not seem to be a major difference between the basic approaches of Presidents Monroe, both Roosevelts, Kennedy, or Nixon. Another example is Russia's continuous search for warm-water ports and control of the western and southern approaches to Russia in eastern Europe and the eastern Mediterranean. This desire to secure areas of access to Russia has played a significant role in the foreign policies of the czars as well as the present leaders of Soviet Russia; the differences in the concepts of Russia's national interest under such opposing forms of government appear minimal.

Continuity of national interest seems to be primarily a matter of geography and logistics; the national leaders must take into account these two immutable factors—in fact, they are their "captives." But there are also other elements in the situation: despite their new rhetorics, new elites remain to some extent also captives of the national past, including the international commitments, decisions, and plans that have been subscribed to by their predecessors or former rivals. One scholar has noted several reasons why specific foreign policy goals and methods are carried over from the past to the present and reinforced in the process:

> In the first place, enunciated objectives tend to become imbedded in the information states of the decision makers who choose them and also in the information states of those decision makers who come to office later. In the second place, once an objective or means of implementation is pursued, the investment in that objective is lost if a change is made. Other actors [the allies, for instance] have already pledged their cooperation. Claims have publicly been made. Reversals would cloud the entire issue and make policies appear arbitrary. Besides, time, money, and personnel have already been expended.

[1] Hans J. Morgenthau, *Dilemmas of Politics* (Chicago: University of Chicago Press, 1958), pp. 66, 73–74. According to Morgenthau the determination of the residual meaning of national interest is relatively simple, "for it encompasses the integrity of the nation's territory, of its political institutions, and of its culture." The last two of Morgenthau's "irreducible minima" seem so broad as to open rather than conclude a discussion on the core meaning of national interest.

Moreover, the organization is structured to scan for information which seems consonant with the given objective and to ignore information which appears to conflict. This is particularly true at non-political levels in the administration. Furthermore, these levels in the administration brief political appointees and play a large role in directing their attention toward given courses of action and away from other equally plausible courses of action.[2]

The American fiasco at the Bay of Pigs (see Selection 18) certainly confirms the impact of past commitments and the strong influence of "experts": however great his misgivings were, President Kennedy finally did approve the execution of the Eisenhower-Nixon-CIA plan to topple Castro by an American-led and American-organized invasion of armed Cuban exiles. Eisenhower's and Kennedy's concepts of American national interest in the matter seemed to coincide.

Critics of the concept of national interest challenge its relevance and usefulness as a guide to national policy mostly on two accounts: they deny, first, that it is permanent and stable, and, second, that it can be so clearly and objectively defined that controversies over its meaning and ways of promoting it may be eliminated. In particular, several students of international politics oppose the tendency to endow the concept of national interest with

> ... the sanctity of a fixed historical law for each state, immutable over long periods and always properly understood by intelligent and imaginative statesmen, misunderstood and bungled by those who did not really appreciate the position and interests of their country in world affairs.[3]

The problem of establishing an exact meaning of "national interest" in any given situation (often unforeseen or unforeseeable by the leaders) is indeed central. If national interest is defined in such noncontroversial terms as national security or international peace it means all things to all men; so, too, do such other popular generalities as common welfare, justice, and order. Nearly everybody favors peace, security, welfare, justice, and order. But can such broad and vague terms guide actual policy? Moreover, the very vagueness of the concept, as its critics point out, permits the power-holders to claim that national interest is what they say it is and to invoke their personal concept for the purpose of silencing dissent.

Furthermore, even when, instead of generalities, specific, concrete goals are identified (that is, *what* is to be preserved or promoted), the controversy inevitably shifts to the means (that is, *how* to promote national interest). Both the definition and the implementation of national interest are subject of bitter controversies and recriminations among parties, interest groups, mass media, diplomats, generals, and political leaders in free societies, and between per-

---

[2] Morton A. Kaplan, *System and Process in International Politics* (New York: John Wiley & Sons, Inc., 1957), pp. 153–154. A paperback edition of this book was published in 1964.

[3] Ernst B. Haas, "The Balance of Power as a Guide to Policy-Making," *The Journal of Politics*, 15:3 (August 1953), 379.

sonalities and/or factions in totalitarian systems. We have evidence—in the form of purges and subsequent accusations and explanations—that the definition and implementation of national goals have often been subject to most violent disputes in Nazi Germany, Stalinist Russia, Mao's China, or Castro's Cuba. Focusing on pluralistic Western societies, Ernest B. Haas succinctly concludes:

> There is no unified, immutable, and stable conception of national interest. Different groups entertain different policy motivations at any one time and tend to change their motivations over a period of time. . . . The conception of national interest which prevails at any one time is no more than an amalgam of varying policy motivations which tend to pass for a "national" interest as long as the groups holding these opinions continue to rule. These motivations may be homogeneous or conflicting, depending on the nature of the ruling group. Homogeneity in outlook, and motivations can by no means be taken for granted even in a given parliamentary majority or coalition of elites. Nor does a single ruling elite necessarily imply agreement among its members on the nature of the national interest.[4]

The controversy over the meaning of national interest and its usefulness as a guideline for foreign policy does not mean, of course, that the critics of the concept deny that "interest" and its companion, "power"—that is, the capacity to produce intended effects by persuasion and/or coercion of men—have ever ceased or should be expected to cease to be part of the national and international scene. Men will continue to use the power of an eloquent argument, the power of intimidatory bluff, the power of coercion, and the power of organization to convince, deter, or coerce for the protection and promotion of what they believe to be their important interests. Pressure groups, political parties, ideological movements, and territorial states all are dedicated to the furtherance of a collective interest by organized power. (A territorial state represents today the most extensive and most effectively organized pressure group; it is, in fact, a *national interest group*.) The furtherance of collective interest becomes a questionable pursuit in concrete cases where Morgenthau's three "irreducible minima"—territorial integrity, political institutions, and culture—do not seem to be immediately and directly threatened. This situation frequently confronted the United States, which in the twentieth century, with the exception of Pearl Harbor, has never been subject to a clear-cut direct attack; the dangers to its security seemed to be rather distant and projected into the future than immediate and direct (for example, Nazi Germany in World War II, and the crises in Korea, Vietnam, the Middle East, Cambodia, Cuba, and Berlin). The United States' broad and geographically undetermined concept of national interest was warmly praised by Joseph Stalin who, at a banquet during the Yalta Conference (in February 1945, three months before V-E Day), raised and proposed a toast to President Roosevelt. In his toast Stalin contrasted Mr. Churchill's and

[4] *Ibid.*, 382.

his own simple decisions concerning the defense of their nations' vital interests with the more complex decisions of the President of the United States. Russia and Britain, after all, Stalin said,

> ...had been fighting for their very existence against Hitlerite Germany but there was a third man whose country had not been seriously threatened with invasion, but who had had perhaps a broader conception of national interest and even though his country was not directly imperilled had been the chief forger of the instruments which had led to the mobilization of the world against Hitler. He mentioned in this connection Lend-Lease as one of the President's most remarkable and vital achievements in the formation of the Anti-Hitler combination and in keeping the allies in the field against Hitler.[5]

A second aspect of the controversy over national interest concerns the availability of means and concrete methods of action. What seems politically desirable may not be feasible in terms of available power. Nations and men are neither omniscient nor omnipotent. National power to persuade, deter, or coerce other nations is limited. Some goals and values must be therefore sacrificed so that other goals and values may be maximized. Choice—the very essence of all politics—is always difficult and almost always controversial.

It is important to note that national power is not only a means, and therefore potentially limiting, but it is also a generator of new goals and interests. What is materially feasible may become politically desirable. Furthermore, national leaders ask not only what they *have* in order to promote national interest but also what capabilities they *need* and therefore must have. While national capabilities place some obvious limits on national goals, it is also true that in the light of national needs existing capabilities may be substantially increased and new resources added or improvised.

No inventory of national capabilities can avoid the mutual influence of the ends and means—of interest and power, respectively. One study on this subject suggests an interesting analogy in which a national power inventory is triangulated by two searchlight beams: beam number 1 is "resources" and beam number 2 is "national strategy." Groping through the darkness of international relations, the beams finally intersect on the target and so indicate the measurable distance, that is the attainability of national goals.[6] The first beam represents the usual checklist of national power ingredients—area, human resources, industrial establishment, and weaponry—and must be related to the strategic second beam. Harmony between the two is not necessarily determined by available resources but, to some extent at least, by the intensity and scope of national need and interest which, in fact, may mobilize and/or augment resources.

[5] Quoted by Robert E. Sherwood, *Roosevelt and Hopkins: An Intimate History* (New York: Harper & Row, Publishers, Inc., 1948), p. 869.

[6] Stephen D. Jones, "The Power Inventory and National Strategy," *World Politics*, 6:4 (July 1954), 421–452.

16 / The Key Concept of Political Realism: Interest in Terms of Power

Hans J. Morgenthau

Morgenthau's theory of international relations is known as political realism. Its key assumption is that national leaders think and act in terms of interest defined as power. According to its adherents and advocates, a realist theory of international politics prevents a student or practitioner of international politics from losing his way when he observes or moves through the landscape of world affairs; political realism allegedly provides a reliable "map" of international politics; the map describes the essence of politics among nations to all those who can read it. In particular, political realism guards students and practitioners of international politics against two popular fallacies: the concern with the personal motives and ideological preferences of statesmen. Personal motives may be interesting but are the most illusive of all psychological data; and ideologies have proved unreliable indicators of actual foreign policy decisions, as Chapters 9 and 10 will illustrate. According to Morgenthau, the survival of a nation (preservation of its identity) is the irreducible minimum, the necessary element of its interest vis-à-vis other nations.

Speculation concerning both the assumptions and usefulness of political realism and Morgenthau's concept of national interest has occupied the center of the political and academic scene for several decades. One systematic critique of the theory follows in Selection 17.,

---

Political realism believes that politics, like society in general, is governed by objective laws that have their roots in human nature. In order to improve society it is first necessary to understand the laws by which society lives. . . .

Human nature, in which the laws of politics have their roots, has not changed since the classical philosophies of China, India, and Greece endeavored to discover these laws. Hence, novelty is not necessarily a virtue in political theory, nor is old age a defect.

Interest as Power

The main signpost that helps political realism to find its way through the landscape of international politics is the concept of interest defined in

From pp. 5–10, 25–29 (*passim*) of *Politics among Nations,* by Hans J. Morgenthau. Copyright 1948, 1954, © 1960, 1967 by Alfred A. Knopf, Inc. Reprinted by permission of the publisher. Author's footnotes have been omitted. Three headings are added by the editor.

terms of power. This concept provides the link between reason trying to understand international politics and the facts to be understood. It sets politics as an autonomous sphere of action and understanding apart from other spheres, such as economics (understood in terms of interest defined as wealth), ethics, aesthetics, or religion. Without such a concept a theory of politics, international or domestic, would be altogether impossible, for without it we could not distinguish between political and nonpolitical facts,, nor could we bring at least a measure of systematic order to the political sphere.

We assume that statesmen think and act in terms of interest defined as power, and the evidence of history bears that assumption out. That assumption allows us to retrace and anticipate, as it were, the steps a statesman— past, present, or future—has taken or will take on the political scene. We look over his shoulder when he writes his dispatches; we listen in on his conversation with other statesmen; we read and anticipate his very thoughts. Thinking in terms of interest defined as power, we think as he does, and as disinterested observers we understand his thoughts and actions perhaps better than he, the actor on the political scene, does himself.

The concept of interest defined as power imposes intellectual discipline upon the observer, infuses rational order into the subject matter of politics, and thus makes the theoretical understanding of politics possible. On the side of the actor, it provides for rational discipline in action and creates that astounding continuity in foreign policy which makes American, British, or Russian foreign policy appear as an intelligible, rational continuum, by and large consistent within itself, regardless of the different motives, preferences, and intellectual and moral qualities of successive statesmen. A realist theory of international politics, then, will guard against two popular fallacies: the concern with motives and the concern with ideological preferences.

Motives

To search for the clue to foreign policy exclusively in the motives of statesmen is both futile and deceptive. It is futile because motives are the most illusive of psychological data, distorted as they are, frequently beyond recognition, by the interests and emotions of actor and observer alike. Do we really know what our own motives are? And what do we know of the motives of others?

Yet even if we had access to the real motives of statesmen, that knowledge would help us little in understanding foreign policies, and might well lead us astray. It is true that the knowledge of the statesman's motives may give us one among many clues as to what the direction of his foreign policy might be. It cannot give us, however, the one clue by which to predict his foreign policies. History shows no exact and necessary correlation between the quality of motives and the quality of foreign policy. This is true in both moral and political terms.

We cannot conclude from the good intentions of a statesman that his foreign policies will be either morally praiseworthy or politically successful. Judging his motives, we can say that he will not intentionally pursue policies that are morally wrong, but we can say nothing about the probability of their success. If we want to know the moral and political qualities of his actions, we must know them, not his motives. How often have statesmen been motivated by the desire to improve the world, and ended by making it worse? And how often have they sought one goal, and ended by achieving something they neither expected nor desired?

Neville Chamberlain's politics of appeasement were, as far as we can judge, inspired by good motives; he was probably less motivated by considerations of personal power than were many other British prime ministers, and he sought to preserve peace and to assure the happiness of all concerned. Yet his policies helped to make the Second World War inevitable, and to bring untold miseries to millions of men. Sir Winston Churchill's motives, on the other hand, have been much less universal in scope and much more narrowly directed toward personal and national power, yet the foreign policies that sprang from these inferior motives were certainly superior in moral and political quality to those pursued by his predecessor. Judged by his motives, Robespierre was one of the most virtuous men who ever lived. Yet it was the utopian radicalism of that very virtue that made him kill those less virtuous than himself, brought him to the scaffold, and destroyed the revolution of which he was a leader.

Good motives give assurance against deliberately bad policies; they do not guarantee the moral goodness and political success of the policies they inspire. What is important to know, if one wants to understand foreign policy, is not primarily the motives of a statesman, but his intellectual ability to comprehend the essentials of foreign policy, as well as his political ability to translate what he has comprehended into successful political action. It follows that while ethics in the abstract judges the moral qualities of motives, political theory must judge the political qualities of intellect, will, and action.

Ideologies

A realist theory of international politics will also avoid the other popular fallacy of equating the foreign policies of a statesman with his philosophic or political sympathies, and of deducing the former from the latter. Statesmen, especially under contemporary conditions, may well make a habit of presenting their foreign policies in terms of their philosophic and political sympathies in order to gain popular support for them. Yet they will distinguish with Lincoln between their *"official* duty," which is to think and act in terms of the national interest, and their *"personal* wish," which is to see their own moral values and political principles realized throughout the world.[7] Political realism does not require, nor does it condone, indifference to political ideals and moral principles, but it requires indeed a sharp distinction between the desirable and the possible—between what is desirable everywhere and at all times and what is possible under the concrete circumstances of time and place. . . .

The difference, then, between political realism and other schools of thought is real, and it is profound. However much the theory of political realism may have been misunderstood and misinterpreted, there is no gainsaying its distinctive intellectual and moral attitude to matters political.

Intellectually, the political realist maintains the autonomy of the political sphere, as the economist, the lawyer, the moralist maintain theirs. He thinks in terms of interest defined as power, as the economist thinks in terms of interest defined as wealth; the lawyer, of the conformity of action with legal rules; the moralist, of the conformity of action with moral principles. The economist asks: "How does this policy affect the wealth of society, or a segment of it?" The lawyer asks: "Is this policy in accord with the rules of law?" The moralist asks: "Is this policy in accord with moral principles?" And the political realist asks: "How does this policy affect the power of the nation?" (Or of the federal government, of Congress, of the party, of agriculture, as the case may be.)

The political realist is not unaware of the existence and relevance of standards of thought other than political ones. As political realist, he cannot but subordinate these other standards to those of politics. And he parts

---

[7] Ed. note: The reference to Lincoln's admission of a conflict between personal opinions a leader may have and his official duty is a quote from an answer given by President Lincoln to Horace Greeley (according to Morgenthau, "a spokesman for the utopian moralists"):

If there be those who would not save the Union unless they could at the same time save slavery, I do not agree with them. If there be those who would not save the Union unless they could at the same time destroy slavery, I do not agree with them. My paramount object in this struggle *is* to save the Union, and is *not* either to save or to destroy slavery. If I could save the Union without freeing *any* slave I would do it, and if I could save it by freeing *all* the slaves, I would do it; and if I could save it by freeing some and leaving others alone I would also do that. What I do about slavery, and the colored race, I do because I believe it helps to save the Union; and what I forbear, I forbear because I do *not* believe it would help to save the Union. I shall do *less* whenever I shall believe what I am doing hurts the cause, and I shall do *more* whenever I shall believe doing more will help the cause. I shall try to correct errors when shown to be errors; and I shall adopt new views so fast as they appear to be true views.

I have here stated my purpose according to my view of *official* duty; and I intend no modification of my oft-expressed *personal* wish that all men everywhere could be free. . . .

company with other schools when they impose standards of thought appropriate to other spheres upon the political sphere. It is here that political realism takes issue with the "legalistic-moralistic approach" to international politics. . . .

It stands to reason that not all foreign policies have always followed so rational, objective, and unemotional a course. The contingent elements of personality, prejudice, and subjective preference, and of all the weaknesses of intellect and will which flesh is heir to, are bound to deflect foreign policies from their rational course. Especially where foreign policy is conducted under the conditions of democratic control, the need to marshal popular emotions to the support of foreign policy cannot fail to impair the rationality of foreign policy itself. . . .

The difference between international politics as it actually is and a rational theory derived from it is like the difference between a photograph and a painted portrait. The photograph shows everything that can be seen by the naked eye; the painted portrait does not show everything that can be seen by the naked eye, but it shows, or at least seeks to show, one thing that the naked eye cannot see: the human essence of the person portrayed.

Political realism contains not only a theoretical but also a normative element. It knows that political reality is replete with contingencies and points to the typical influences they exert upon foreign policy. Yet it shares with all social theory the need, for the sake of theoretical understanding, to stress the rational elements of political reality; for it is these rational elements that make reality intelligible for theory. Political realism presents the theoretical construct of a rational foreign policy which experience can never completely achieve.

At the same time political realism considers a rational foreign policy to be good foreign policy; for only a rational foreign policy minimizes risks and maximizes benefits and, hence, complies both with the moral precept of prudence and the political requirement of success. Political realism wants the photographic picture of the political world to resemble as much as possible its painted portrait. Aware of the inevitable gap between good— that is, rational—foreign policy and foreign policy as it actually is, political realism maintains not only that theory must focus upon the rational elements of political reality, but also that foreign policy ought to be rational in view of its own moral and practical purposes.

Hence, it is no argument against the theory here presented that actual foreign policy does not or cannot live up to it. . . . Far from being invalidated by the fact that, for instance, a perfect balance of power policy will scarcely be found in reality, it assumes that reality, being deficient in this respect, must be understood and evaluated as an approximation to an ideal system of balance of power.

Realism does not endow its key concept of interest defined as power with a meaning that is fixed once and for all. The idea of interest is indeed of the essence of politics and is unaffected by the circumstances of time and place. Thucydides' statement, born of the experiences of ancient Greece, that "identity of interests is the surest of bonds whether between states or individuals" was taken up in the nineteenth century by Lord Salisbury's remark that "the only bond of union that endures" among nations is "the absence of all clashing interests." It was erected into a general principle of government by George Washington:

> A small knowledge of human nature will convince us, that, with far the greatest part of mankind, interest is the governing principle; and that almost every man is more or less, under its influence. Motives of public virtue may for a time, or in particular instances, actuate men to the observance of a conduct purely disinterested; but they are not of themselves sufficient to produce persevering conformity to the refined dictates and obligations of social duty. Few men are capable of making a continual sacrifice of all views of private interest, or advantage, to the common good. It is vain to exclaim against the depravity of human nature on this account; the fact is so, the experience of every age and nation has proved it and we must in a great measure, change the constitution of man, before we can make it otherwise. No institution, not built on the presumptive truth of these maxims can succeed.

Yet the kind of interest determining political action in a particular period of history depends upon the political and cultural context within which foreign policy is formulated. The goals that might be pursued by nations in their foreign policy can run the whole gamut of objectives any nation has ever pursued or might possibly pursue.

The same observations apply to the concept of power. Its content and the manner of its use are determined by the political and cultural environment. Power may comprise anything that establishes and maintains the control of man over man. Thus power covers all social relationships which serve that end, from physical violence to the most subtle psychological ties by which one mind controls another. Power covers the domination of man by man, both when it is disciplined by moral ends and controlled by constitutional safeguards, as in Western democracies, and when it is that untamed and barbaric force which finds its laws in nothing but its own strength and its sole justification in its aggrandizement.

Political realism does not assume that the contemporary conditions under which foreign policy operates, with their extreme instability and the ever present threat of large-scale violence, cannot be changed. The balance of power, for instance, is indeed a perennial element of all pluralistic societies, as the authors of *The Federalist* papers well knew; yet it is capable of operating, as it does in the United States, under the conditions of relative stability and peaceful conflict. If the factors that have given rise to these conditions can be duplicated on the international scene, similar conditions of stability and peace will then prevail there, as they have over long stretches of history among certain nations.

What is true of the general character of international relations is also true of the nation state as the ultimate point of reference of contemporary foreign policy. While the realist indeed believes that interest is the perennial standard by which political action must be judged and directed, the contemporary connection between interest and the national state is a product of history, and is therefore bound to disappear in the course of history. Nothing in the realist position militates against the assumption that the present division of the political world into nation states will be replaced by larger units of a quite different character, more in keeping with the technical potentialities and the moral requirements of the contemporary world.

The realist parts company with other schools of thought before the all-important question of how the comtemporary world is to be transformed. The realist is persuaded that this transformation can be achieved only through the workmanlike manipulation of the perennial forces that have shaped the past as they will the future. The realist cannot be persuaded that we can bring about that transformation by confronting a political reality that has its own laws with an abstract ideal that refuses to take those laws into account.

Politics and Morality

Political realism is aware of the moral significance of political action. It is also aware of the ineluctable tension between the moral command and the requirements of successful political action. And it is unwilling to gloss over and obliterate that tension and thus to obfuscate both the moral and the political issue by making it appear as though the stark facts of politics were morally more satisfying than they actually are, and the moral law less exacting than it actually is.

Realism maintains that universal moral principles cannot be applied to the actions of states in their abstract universal formulation, but that they must be filtered through the concrete circumstances of time and place. The individual may say for himself: *"Fiat justitia, pereat mundus* (Let justice be done, even if the world perish)," but the state has no right to say so in the name of those who are in its care. Both individual and state must judge political action by universal moral principles, such as that of liberty. Yet while the individual has a moral right to sacrifice himself in defense of such a moral principle, the state has no right to let its moral disapprobation of the infringement of liberty get in the way of successful political action, itself inspired by the moral principle of national survival. There can be no political morality without prudence; that is, without consideration of the political consequences of seemingly moral action. Realism, then, considers prudence—the weighing of the consequences of alternative political actions—to be the supreme virtue in politics. Ethics in the abstract judges action by its conformity with the moral law; political ethics judges action by its political consequences. Classical and medieval philosophy knew this, and so did Lincoln when he said:

> I do the very best I know how, the very best I can, and I mean to keep doing so until the end. If the end brings me out all right, what is said against me won't amount to anything. If the end brings me out wrong, ten angels swearing I was right would make no difference.

Power as a Means
to the Nation's Ends

International politics, like all politics, is a struggle for power. Whatever the ultimate aims of international politics, power is always the immediate aim. Statesmen and peoples may ultimately seek freedom, security, prosperity, or power itself. They may define their goals in terms of a religious, philosophic, economic, or social ideal. They may hope that this ideal will materialize through its own inner force, through divine intervention, or through the natural development of human affairs. They may also try to further its realization through nonpolitical means, such as technical co-operation with other nations or international organizations. But whenever they strive to realize their goal by means of international politics, they do so by striving for power. The Crusaders wanted to free the holy places from domination by the Infidels; Woodrow Wilson wanted to make the world safe for democracy; the Nazis wanted to open Eastern Europe to German colonization, to dominate Europe, and to conquer the world. Since they all chose power to achieve these ends, they were actors on the scene of international politics.

Two conclusions follow from this concept of international politics. First, not every action that a nation performs with respect to another nation is of a political nature. Many such activities are normally undertaken without any consideration of power, nor do they normally affect the power of the nation undertaking them. Many legal, economic, humanitarian, and cultural activities are of this kind. Thus a nation is not normally engaged in international politics when it concludes an extradition treaty with another nation, when it exchanges goods and services with other nations, when it co-operates with other nations in providing relief from natural catastrophes, and when it promotes the distribution of cultural achievements throughout the world. In other words, the involvement of a nation in international politics is but one among many types of activities in which a nation can participate on the international scene.

Second, not all nations are at all times to the same extent involved in international politics. The degree of their involvement may run all the way from the maximum at present attained by the United States and the Soviet Union, through the minimum involvement of such countries as Switzerland, Luxembourg, or Venezuela, to the complete noninvolvement of Liechtenstein and Monaco. Similar extremes can be noticed in the history of particular countries. Spain in the sixteenth and seventeenth centuries was one of the main active participants in the struggle for power on the international scene, but plays today only a marginal role in it. The same is true of such countries as Austria, Sweden, and Switzerland. On the other hand, nations like the United States, the Soviet Union, and China are today much more deeply involved in international politics than they were fifty or even twenty years ago. In short, the relation of nations to international politics has a dynamic quality. It changes with the vicissitudes of power, which may push a nation into the forefront of the power struggle, or may deprive a nation of the ability to participate actively in it. . . .

The Nature of Political Power

The aspiration for power being the distinguishing element of international politics, as of all politics, international politics is of necessity power politics. While this fact is generally recognized in the practice of international affairs, it is frequently denied in the pronouncements of scholars, publicists, and even statesmen. . . . When we speak of power in the context of this book, we have in mind not man's power over nature, or over an artistic medium, such as language, speech, sound, or color, or over the means of production or consumption, or over himself in the sense of self-control. When we speak of power, we mean man's control over the minds and actions of other men. By political power we refer to the mutual relations of control among the holders of public authority and between the latter and the people at large.

Political power, however, must be distinguished from force in the sense of the actual exercise of physical violence. The threat of physical violence in the form of police action, imprisonment, capital punishment, or war is an intrinsic element of politics. When violence becomes an actuality, it signifies the abdication of political power in favor of military or pseudo-military power. In international politics in particular, armed strength as a threat or a potentiality is the most important material factor making for the political power of a nation. If it becomes an actuality in war, it signifies the substitution of military for political power. The actual exercise of physical violence substitutes for the psychological relation between two minds, which is of the essence of political power, the physical relation between two bodies, one of which is strong enough to dominate the other's movements. It is for this reason that in the exercise of physical violence the psychological element of the political relationship is lost, and that we must distinguish between military and political power.

Political power is a psychological relation between those who exercise it and those over whom it is exercised. It gives the former control over certain actions of the latter through the influence which the former exert over the latter's minds. That influence derives from three sources: the expectation of benefits, the fear of disadvantages, the respect or love for men or institutions. It may be exerted through orders, threats, persuasion, the authority or charisma of a man or of an office, or a combination of any of these. . . . Thus the statement that A has or wants political power over B signifies always that A is able, or wants to be able, to control certain actions of B through influencing B's mind.

Whatever the material objectives of a foreign policy, such as the acquisition of sources of raw materials, the control of sea lanes, or territorial changes, they always entail control of the actions of others through influence over their minds. The Rhine frontier as a century-old objective of French foreign policy points to the political objective to destroy the desire of Germany to attack France by making it physically difficult or impossible for Germany to do so. Great Britain owed its predominant position in world politics throughout the nineteenth century to the calculated policy of making it either too dangerous (because Great Britain was too strong) or unnecessary (because its strength was used with moderation) for other nations to oppose it.

The political objective of military preparations of any kind is to deter other nations from using military force by making it too risky for them to do so. The political aim of military preparations is, in other words, to make the actual application of military force unnecessary by inducing the prospective enemy to desist from the use of military force. The political objective of war itself is not per se the conquest of territory and the annihilation of enemy armies, but a change in the mind of the enemy which will make him yield to the will of the victor.

Therefore, whenever economic, financial, territorial, or military policies are under discussion in international affairs, it is necessary to distinguish between, say, economic policies that are undertaken for their own sake and economic policies that are the instruments of a political policy—a policy, that is, whose economic purpose is but the means to the end of controlling the policies of another nation. The export policy of Switzerland with regard to the United States falls into the first category. The economic policies of the Soviet Union with regard to the nations of Eastern Europe fall into the latter category. So do many economic policies of the United

States in Latin America, Asia, and Europe. The distinction is of great practical importance, and the failure to make it has led to much confusion in policy and public opinion.

An economic, financial, territorial, or military policy undertaken for its own sake is subject to evaluation in its own terms. Is it economically or financially advantageous? What effects has acquisition of territory upon the population and economy of the nation acquiring it? What are the consequences of a change in a military policy for education, population, and the domestic political system? The decisions with respect to these policies are made exclusively in terms of such intrinsic considerations.

When, however, the objectives of these policies serve to increase the power of the nation pursuing them with regard to other nations, these policies and their objectives must be judged primarily from the point of view of their contribution to national power. An economic policy that cannot be justified in purely economic terms might nevertheless be undertaken in view of the political policy pursued. The insecure and unprofitable character of a loan to a foreign nation may be a valid argument against it on purely financial grounds. But the argument is irrelevant if the loan, however unwise it may be from a banker's point of view, serves the political policies of the nation. It may of course be that the economic or financial losses involved in such policies will weaken the nation in its international position to such an extent as to outweigh the political advantages to be expected. On these grounds such policies might be rejected. In such a case, what decides the issue is not purely economic and financial considerations but a comparison of the political chances and risks involved; that is, the probable effect of these policies upon the power of the nation.

17 / A Critique of Political Realism

Stanley Hoffmann

The following essay analyzes the theory of political realism and its central concepts of interest and power. Hoffmann objects to many aspects of the theory—mostly because it puts power, rather narrowly defined, in a key position as both the purpose and the tool of foreign policy. Hoffmann also finds that

From pp. 30–38 of Stanley H. Hoffmann, Ed., *Contemporary Theory in International Relations,* © 1960. By permission of Prentice Hall, Inc., Englewood Cliffs, New Jersey. Applicable footnotes are reprinted, but they are renumbered.

Morgenthau's idea that national interest carries its own morality makes sense only in a period of relative international stability and consensus, as was perhaps the case in the eighteenth and nineteenth centuries. But the concept does not hold today, in an era of competing international ideologies and moralities. Furthermore, according to Hoffmann, the rational model of foreign policy based on interest defined in terms of power brushes aside the irrational and pathological aspects of diplomacy; and the rationality itself is then measured by success or failure. Unfortunately, the standards of success and failure of foreign policy are not clear. Many a past failure may appear to some as a success after all, and vice versa. (See the questions on the nature and durability of Kennedy's success in the Cuban missile crisis in Chapter 8.)

The "realist" theory of international politics . . . . is an attempt at providing us with a reliable "map" of the landscape of world affairs; an effort at catching the essence of world politics. The master key is the concept of interest defined in terms of power. To what extent does the theory accomplish its mission? It succeeds in focusing attention on the units which remain the principal actors in world affairs: the States. The theory also stresses the factors that account for the large degree of autonomy of International Relations: the differences between domestic and world politics which thwart the operation in the latter of ideas and institutions that flourish in the former, the drastic imperatives of survival, self-preservation and self-help which are both the causes and the products of such differences.

However, as a general theory, the "realist" analysis fails because it sees the world as a static field in which power relations reproduce themselves in timeless monotony. The map is inadequate for two main reasons. First, the "realist" analysis of power is a very debatable one. The cornerstone of the realist theory is the statement that the political sphere is just as autonomous as the respective spheres of the economist, or the lawyer, or the moralist. This we can certainly accept. But what kind of an autonomy are we talking about? There are two possible versions: a sphere can be autonomous either because it is concerned with a specialized and limited set of variables, or because it is concerned with *all* the variables with which the various specialized spheres deal—it then differs from these spheres by its own generality and by the way in which all these different variables are combined here. When Mr. Morgenthau discusses the need for theory and for a hierarchical integration of the various disciplines which contribute to the study of international relations, he rightly says that politics must play the role of the common, integrating core and thus adopts the second version.[8] But in the bulk of his writings, and particularly in his statement of the realist theory . . . he interprets autonomy in the first sense: the political

[8] Hans J. Morgenthau, *Dilemmas of Politics,* Chicago, 1958, pp. 98–100.

realist "thinks in terms of interest defined as power, as the economist thinks in terms of utility; the lawyer, of conformity of action with legal rules; the moralist, of conformity of action with moral principles."

Now, the decision to equate politics and power would be acceptable only if power were analyzed, not as a limited and specific set of variables, but as a complex and diffuse balance between all the variables with which the social sciences are concerned.[9] Political man should properly be seen as the "integrator" of moral man, economic man, religious man, and so on—not as a creature reduced to one special facet of human nature. Unfortunately such an Aristotelian position is not adopted here: the decision to equate politics and the effects of man's "lust for power" is combined with a tendency to equate power and evil or violence—a combination which mutilates reality. A "power monism" does not account for all politics, when power is so somberly defined; even in world affairs, the drive for participation and community plays a part, and the image of political man interested exclusively in the control of the actions of others for the sake of control, is simply not acceptable as a basis for theory.

Furthermore, the extent to which power as a carrier of evil and violence expresses a basic human instinct is questionable. Much of the international (or domestic) evil of power is rooted not in the sinfulness of man but in a context, a constellation, a situation, in which even good men are forced to act selfishly or immorally. Discrimination between the inherent or instinctive aspects of the "power drive," and the situational or accidental ones, is an important task. However, reactions to shifting situations are scarcely considered by the theory.

Also, it is dangerous to put in a key position a concept which is merely instrumental. Power is a means toward any of a large number of ends (including power itself). The quality and quantity of power used by men are determined by men's purposes. It would have been more logical to begin with a theory of ends rather than with the notion of power, which is here both ambiguous and abstracted from its ends. The "realist" theory neglects all the factors that influence or define purposes. Why statesmen choose at times to use national power in a certain way (say a policy of "imperialism") rather than in another is not made clear. The domestic considerations that affect national power: the nature of the regime, the structure of power, beliefs and values which account in great measure for the nation's goals and for the statesmen's motivations, are either left out or brushed aside. For instance it is not enough to say that "the political cohesion of a federal system is the result of superior power located in some part of it,"[10] for what remains to be explained is how such superior power

[9] See Talcott Parsons, *The Social System*, Glencoe, 1951, pp. 551 ff.

[10] Hans J. Morgenthau, "Another 'Great Debate': The National Interest of the United States," *American Political Science Review*, Vol. XLVI, No. 4 (December 1952), p. 968.

got to be located there, what convergence of interests or what community of values led to its establishment and underlies its authority. Similarly, internationally shared beliefs and purposes are left out. Reality comes out oversimplified, for we get a somewhat mechanistic view of international affairs in which the statesmen's role consists of adjusting national power to an almost immutable set of external "givens." Professor Morgenthau's metaphor about theory which, like a portrait, and unlike a photograph, should try to show "one thing that the naked eye cannot see: the human essence of the person portrayed" is most revealing. It is quite possible that there is a human essence of the person; but even if we had been able to discover it, we would still have to account for all the twists and vagaries of the person's existence and we cannot assume that they would be easily deducible from the "human essence" discovered. The same is true in world politics. Unfortunately, the "realist" world is a frozen universe of separate essences.

Even if the role of power were as determining as the theory postulates, the question arises whether any scheme can put so much methodological weight upon one concept, even a crucial one; for it seems to me that the concept of power collapses under the burden. It is impossible to subsume under one word variables as different as: power as a condition of policy and power as a criterion of policy; power as a potential and power in use; power as a sum of resources and power as a set of processes. Power is a most complex product of other variables, which should be allowed to see the light of the theory instead of remaining hidden in the shadow of power. Otherwise the theory is bound either to mean different things at different steps of the analysis (or when dealing with different periods), or else to end by selecting for emphasis only one aspect of power: either military force or economic strength. Thus, instead of a map which simplifies the landscape so that we can understand it, we are left with a distortion.

There is a second reason for the inadequacy of the map. The rigidity that comes from the timeless concept of power is compounded by the confusing use of other concepts that are dated in more ways than one, and which the theory applies to situations in which they do not fit. The model of the "realists" is a highly embellished ideal-type of eighteenth and nineteenth century international relations. This vision of the golden age is taken as a norm, both for empirical analysis and for evaluation. A number of oddities of the theory are explained thereby. First, the lack of an adequate discussion of ends; for when all the actors have almost the same credo, as they did during most of that period, it becomes easy to forget the effects of the common credo on the actors' behavior, and to omit from among the main variables of the theory a factor whose role seems constant. It is nevertheless an optical illusion to mistake a particular historical pattern for the norm of a scientific system. When we deal with a period such as twentieth century world politics, whose main characteristic may well be the division of an international society which had previously been rather coherent into rival groups devoted to mutually exclusive purposes and values, the neglect of ends is a fatal mistake.

good point

Second, the analysis of power apart from the processes and pressures of domestic politics follows from the same optical illusion. It is easy to understand why public philosophers should bemoan the days when no visible and organized groups challenged the primacy of foreign affairs, the continuity of diplomatic action, unsentimental equilibrium calculations, and privacy. But these principles are not eternal; the Greek city-states did not observe them—at their own peril, of course, but then the world restored in 1815 balanced its power and played its cards into the abyss of 1914; and no one has yet found a way of reversing the trend and of insulating the experts on Olympus from the germs carried by the common men in the swamps below.

Third, the conception of an objective and easily recognizable national interest, the reliable guide and criterion of rational policy, is one which makes sense only in a stable period in which the participants play for limited ends, with limited means, and without domestic kibitzers to disrupt the players' moves. In such a period, the survival of the main units is rarely at stake in the game, and a hierarchy can rather easily be established among the other more stable and far less vital interests that are at stake. In such a period, the influence on foreign policies of factors such as geography, natural resources, industrial capacity, and inherited traditions of national principles is particularly strong and relatively constant. Today, however, survival is almost always at stake, and technological leaps have upset the hierarchy of "stable" factors. The most divergent courses of action can be recommended as valid choices for survival. Ordinarily less compelling objectives, such as prestige, or an increment of power in a limited area, or the protection of private citizens abroad, all become tied up with the issue of survival, and the most frequent argument against even attempting to redefine a hierarchy of national objectives so as to separate at least some of them from survival, is the familiar fear of a "chain of events" or a "row of dominoes falling." In such circumstances of mutual fear and technological turmoil, interpretations of the national interest become almost totally subjective and the relative weight of "objective" factors which affect the states' capabilities and thereby influence state policies is almost impossible to evaluate. Consequently, a scholar attempting to use the theory as a key to the understanding of, or successful influence upon, contemporary realities risks being in the unhappy position of a Tiresias who recognizes interests which the parties concerned refuse to see, who diagnoses permanence where the parties find confusing change and whose ex post facto omniscience is both irritating and irrelevant.

Fourth, the idea that the national interest carries its own morality is *wrong*
also one which makes sense almost only in a stable period. For it is a
period in which an international consensus assures at least the possibility
of accommodation of national objectives; the conflicts of interests which are
involved are not struggles between competing international moralities. The
philosophical pluralism implicit in the "realist" theory (which purports to
be both normative and empirical) is not sufficiently thought through. For
in periods of stability and moderation, which bloom only because of a basic
agreement on values, the national interest can be said to be moral and
legitimate only because it expresses aspirations of a community which do
not rule out those of another group. What is moral is not the national
interest as such but its reasonableness, which insures its compatibility with
the interests of other states and with the common values of international
society; and what is legitimate is the possibility for each group to have such
temperate aspirations recognized. This is, at best, the kind of pluralism
which is implied by *one* particular set of values—those of liberalism. As
for periods of "nationalistic universalism," of secular religions and incompatible ideologies—here the tolerance characteristic of liberal pluralism
makes no sense whatsoever. It is one thing to say that ideological differences
do not justify crusades which would push the world into the chaos of total
war; it is quite another to suggest that *all* national interests (as they are
defined by statesmen) are to be given free play and recognition, in a period
when one state's interest all too often resides in eliminating another state.
A difference must be made between the pluralism of harmony, and the
pluralism of the jungle.

Fifth, the emphasis on the "rationality" of foreign policy and the desire
to brush aside the irrational elements as irrelevant intrusions or pathological
deviations are understandable only in terms of cabinet diplomacy, where
such deviations appear (especially with the benefit of hindsight) to have
been rare. There, rationality seemed like the simple adjustment of means
to stable and generally recognized ends. These concepts are far less applicable to a period in which the political struggles involve primarily the
determination of ends. In such a period, a conception of rationality adequate only for the selection of means cannot help us evaluate and classify
the ends of states (the narrowness of the theory's conception of rationality
makes it even more easy to understand why ends are insufficiently examined). Also, revolutionary periods are often characterized by the selection
of means which are perfectly irrational from any point of view, *including* that of the adequacy of those means to the previously selected ends.
Forgetting these two facts can entail serious mistakes. Thus, on the one
hand, to apply a rationality of means to the selection of ends can have
disastrous consequences in areas such as contemporary strategic doctrines.
For instance, it can lead us to advocate limited nuclear war as the most

rational way of employing the military resources of the West in the case of a conflict, without however having faced the previous question: whether such a strategy fits entirely the purposes the West has set for its relations both with the Communist camp and with the uncommitted nations, or, to put it somewhat differently, whether the purpose of this strategy— economy of force—is the highest end the West pursues. On the other hand, to forget that a nation might at some point select totally irrational means and be pushed by the dark logic of mutual fears into the very abyss of war that it wanted to avoid, is to assume too lightly that cool calculations of interest necessarily guide a nation's policy, or that mistaken calculations do not occur. Now, as the reader will see, debates among sociologists about the nature of war are not conclusive enough to allow us to assume that nations make war only because, and when, their leaders see in war a rational instrument of policy. In other words, a theory of world politics should certainly be rational but there is no need to suppose that reality is generally rational too.

Finally, the exclusion from the pale of world politics of those activities which were not undertaken by the states as such (i.e., by their governments), or which do not represent an obvious attempt to gain control over other nations (such as the signing of extradition treaties, or exchanges of goods and services, to use Mr. Morgenthau's own examples), is also understandable in certain periods only. It makes sense when a considerable range of activities which do, if only indirectly, affect the political power of the state, is left to private citizens (as was the case in the century of the liberal states). It makes sense when these activities are carried out unobtrusively within the common framework in which "power politics" operate, instead of serving as counters in the struggle for the establishment of a new framework. Nevertheless, even in the study of stable periods, the total exclusion of these acts is a mistake, because their temporary removal from the range of issues that involve directly the states' power is precisely the underpinning and one of the defining features of international relations in these periods—the submerged part of the iceberg. Behind the claim to realism, we thus find a reactionary utopia.

The consequence of this inadequacy of the map is that the theory's usefulness as a general theory for the discipline is limited. In the first place, from the point of view of systematic empirical analysis, it is too static. The price one has to pay for identifying the "timeless features" of the political landscape is the sacrifice of understanding the processes of change in world affairs. The theory stresses the autonomy of international relations to the point of leaving outside its pale the forces which work for change and which, cutting across the states, affect the states' behavior. Consequently the study of international relations tends to be reduced to a formalized ballet, where the steps fall into the same pattern over and over again, and which has no story to tell. To be sure, we are informed that the dancers do not have to remain the same: there might someday be other units than the nation states; but we cannot deal with the problem of knowing how the dancers will change. . . . [I]n other words, new dancers might well appear but there is no intermission in which the turnover could happen and while they are on stage their duty is to stay on the job. To change the metaphor, we are presented both with a single key to the closed room of politics among nations, and with a warning that the room is in a house whose key we cannot have, or whose opening must be left to the "workmanlike manipulation of perennial forces." We are not told what they are, or how they operate. Consequently, when they disturb the model, the model's builders are reduced to imprecations against these forces, or to devil explanations.

We reach at this point one of the most fundamental ambiguities of the theory. Realism quite correctly denounces the utopian's mistake of swinging from the goal of a universal harmony to the assumption that in the world as it is the conditions for such harmony already exist. Realism commits exactly the opposite mistake. The postulate of the permanence of power politics among nations as the core of international relations, tends to become a goal. The static qualities of the theory lead to confusion between the phenomenon of power conflicts and the transitory forms and institutions in which such conflicts have been taking place in recent centuries. Why should the sound reminder that power is here to stay mean that the present system of nation states will continue, or change only through forces that are of no concern to us? Such an attitude evades both the empirical duty of accounting for change, and the normative task of assessing whether the present system should indeed continue. It is one thing to say that change will have to be sifted through the slow procedures of present world politics, and meet with the states' consent. It is quite another thing to suggest diplomacy as the only effective procedure and the only meaningful restraint. I cannot help but feel that in spite of Mr. Morgenthau's qualifying statements, there is behind his theory the old position that whatever has been, must continue.

This brings us to a second limitation. A theory which stresses necessity in policy-making rather than choice, and adjustment to the environment or to the existing element of national power, rather than value objectives and the adjustment of the "givens" to such purposes, a theory concerned with the preservation of the present units rather than with change, has disturbing normative implications. It is something of a success philosophy. The criterion of a good foreign policy is its rationality, but the touchstone of rationality is success. Unfortunately the standards of success and failure are not made clear. First, how will we distinguish between the follies of straight utopianism and the fallacies of wrong realism—realism that did not work? Secondly, from what viewpoint shall we decide whether a statesman has succeeded or failed? Shall we turn to history alone? But at what stage? Metternich had succeeded by 1825, and failed by 1848, and writers disagree whether he had succeeded or failed by 1914. If we want an answer from history alone, we will be driven either to pure irrationalism ("it is a tale full of sound and fury . . ."), or to passive contemplation, or to elementary Machiavellianism: "within itself, history has no standard of value but success, and no measure of success but the attainment of power, or survival for a little longer than rival individuals or institutions have survived." [11] If, as we must, we set our standards outside and above history, then we must avoid trying to prove that history will inevitably recompense policies that meet our standards. Otherwise, we become salesmen for a philosophical stand, who travel the roads of history in search of a clientele of confirmations; we are no longer either scholars testing a hypothesis, or philosophers interested in an ideal which history cannot promise to bless at all times.

The former position we wish to avoid. It is particularly uncomfortable when one's basic postulate about human nature is such that history cannot be anything but a tale full of sound and fury, signifying nothing. For it is a postulate which stresses the inevitability and universality of evil, and which assumes that reason, "far from following its own inherent impulses, is driven toward its goal by the irrational forces the ends of which it serves." [12] Now, this view makes it almost impossible to understand how there could be a rational theory of rational human behavior. This is not the last contradiction: the "realist" theory combines a Hobbesian image of naked power politics with an attempt to show that states are nevertheless not condemned to a life that is "nasty, brutish, and short"; "realism" thus puts its faith in voluntary restraints, moderation, and the underlying assumption of possible harmony among national interests—points scarcely admitted by the original postulate, and justified only by a view of power and politics that makes some place for, let us say, a reasonable view of reason. The key to this riddle is to be found in another contradiction which our previous discussion should have suggested: the sharp contrast between the original postulate, whose logic is a permanent clash of forces of evil, and the norm of eighteenth and nineteenth century international relations— the period in which the world's state of nature was most Lockian or Humean, and Mr. Morgenthau's view of human nature most unjustified.

With such flaws and contradictions, the policy guidance the realist theory is able to afford is limited. "Realism" allows us to eliminate those policies that would foolishly forget the prerequisite of power; but it does not go much further. Too often, it is possible to build alternative and conflicting

[11] Alfred Cobban, "The Decline of Political Theory," *Political Science Quarterly,* Vol. LXVIII, No. 3 (September 1953), p. 333.

[12] Hans J. Morgenthau, *Scientific Man vs. Power Politics,* Chicago, 1946, p. 154.

cases of "realist" policies, or to justify in "realist" terms a policy that can also be defended on "utopian" grounds. Too many factors are left out for "realist" policy advice to avoid the dilemma of homilies and admonishments, or suggestions inappropriate for revolutionary periods, such as the advocacy of "peace through accommodation," diplomacy and compromise— a policy which runs against some of the facts of present international life, in particular against the unwillingness of the Soviet side to accept such rules and to seek such deals. The light that illuminated the landscape in the quiet obscurity of nineteenth century politics, is blown out by today's tempest.

7

Certainty
of Uncertainty[1]

Like all politics, international politics may be basically viewed as a communication process. National leaders constantly seek, obtain, evaluate, and act upon information and data received. Such data arrive in the form of action, declaration, diplomatic message, symbolic gesture, or nonaction, and the response of national leaders becomes, in turn, information fed into the global international communication grid to be, in a continuous circular process, received, evaluated, and reacted to by other national leaders.

Diplomatic and intelligence officers, stationed in all sensitive areas, try constantly to supplement the information available through public channels. They utilize ciphered messages that add confidential background and interpretation to public statements, declarations, or events, or they supply the national leaders with information on subjects that foreign nations try to conceal or distort. The validity of the communication depends, to a large degree, on the quality of the reporting diplomatic and intelligence officers as well as on the procedures by

[1] In the first century of our era a Roman scholar, Pliny, wrote: "There is nothing certain except uncertainty and nothing more miserable and more proud than man."

which their data are interpreted and channeled to the decision-makers. Evaluating information has always been a problem from ancient times of spies and royal messengers to the present telecommunications era. In the eighteenth century, a French writer gave the following advice to the writers of secret dispatches:

> The best despatches are those written in a clear and concise manner; unadorned by useless epithets, or by anything which may becloud the clarity of the argument. . . . A despatch which merely recited facts, without discussing them in light of the motives and policy of persons in authority, is nothing more than an empty court chronicle.[2]

Reliable and timely information is the first and fundamental requirement in the foreign policy-making process. Determination of national interest—however controversial the concept may be—is impossible without adequate information about the actors and their intentions and power on the international scene. If a policy-maker wants to base his decisions on facts rather than educated guesses or outright stargazing he will have to seek information and data dealing with the following six areas of concern to him and his nation:

1. What is the nature of the international system whose one component is his territorial state?
2. What, in a given situation, are his nation's vital, major, and minor interests?
3. What are the foreign nations' vital, major, and minor interests?
4. Are his nation's and foreign nations' interests in harmony or in conflict?
5. How does his nation's capability to attain its objectives compare with other nations' capabilities?
6. What is the foreign nations' perception of his own nation's goals and capabilities and, in a complex never-ending process, what is the foreign nations' perception of his own perception of their goals and capabilities?

Policy should be always based on realities, not on dreams, wild guesses, or wishful thinking. But what is reality? What is fact? What are the correct answers to the preceding complex and mutually intertwined six questions?

As the following case study of the Cuban Bay of Pigs will illustrate, even when in possession of some hard information, rarely if ever do national leaders have *all* the data that they should have to make a correct decision. Great uncertain-

---

[2] François de Callières, *On the Manner of Negotiating with Princes.* Trans. by A. F. Whyte (Notre Dame, Ind.: University of Notre Dame Press, 1963), p. 138. Chapter 9 of the present text contains actual texts of secret diplomatic messages exchanged between the German Embassy in Moscow and the Ministry of Foreign Affairs in Berlin. A reader may determine whether the Nazi diplomats had adhered to the eighteenth-century requirement of clear, concise, "unadorned" dispatches.

ties and very few certainties characterize the conduct of foreign policy of all nations. As real events in international politics, described by participant-observers of the crisis, the case studies on the Bay of Pigs (Selection 18) and on the Cuban missile crisis (Selections 19 and 20) will confirm what has long been asserted in theory, namely, "the permanent liability of the decision-making process that pertinent information is almost never complete and information which is available is rarely completely testable."[3] Guessing, logical deduction, or simple intuition seem inevitable in a situation characterized by a chronic dearth of hard facts.

18 / Bay of Pigs: A Case Study

Arthur M. Schlesinger, Jr.

In 1961 leaders of both the Democratic and Republican parties seemed generally to agree that Cuba under Fidel Castro was a direct threat to United States' national interests on two accounts: Cuba was a potential source of revolutionary intervention into the affairs of other Latin American states; and Cuba was a potential base for Soviet and/or Chinese military and intelligence actions dangerously close to the United States mainland. Since the logistics and the balance of military and economic power in the Caribbean was preponderantly in favor of the United States, it seemed obvious that the hostile Cuban government could be crushed easily if the United States chose to do so. However, American power was related to other spots in the world, such as Berlin, Turkey, Iran, Laos, and Vietnam, where the United States was far from immune to possible Soviet and Chinese counteraction over a Cuban offensive.

Therefore, a plan was developed to depose Castro's government without encouraging a reaction by Cuba's allies, China and the Soviet Union, against the United States' position in other parts of the world. The plan (based on

[3] Richard C. Snyder, R. W. Bruck, and Burton Sapin, "Decision Making as an Approach to the Study of International Politics," Monograph No. 3 of the *Foreign Policy Analysis Series* (Princeton, N.J.: Princeton University Press, 1954), p. 43.

Nixon's suggestion to use Cuban exiles against Castro) was first given official sanction by President Eisenhower on March 17, 1960, and was later endorsed by his successor, President John F. Kennedy. The object of the operations to be conducted by the Central Intelligence Agency (CIA) on April 17, 1961, was to dislodge Castro by triggering a general movement against him within his own country. To trigger this general uprising, a small force of anti-Castro Cuban exiles was organized, trained, armed, and landed by the CIA at the Bay of Pigs.

President Kennedy approved of the invasion scheme believing that it would be clandestine and, on the basis of estimates given to him, successful. Therefore, the United States government was prepared to present a false explanation that the invasion was a purely Cuban affair. However, the operation proved to be too large to be clandestine and too small to be successful. As President Kennedy's Special Assistant Theodore Sorenson later noted, "Ten or twenty thousand exiles might have done it but not 1,400, as bravely and as brilliantly as they fought." Castro's timely imprisonment of about 200,000 dissidents reduced the likelihood of a general uprising even if the invasion force had succeeded. As it was, the small invasion force was crushed by a superior Castro force in less than three days. Later, both publicly and privately, President Kennedy asserted his sole responsibility for the disaster. "He was aghast at the enormity of his error and angry at having been badly advised by some and let down by others," writes Sorenson, who adds: "Many wondered, nevertheless, how he could have approved such a plan."

A major foreign policy failure is usually a rich source of useful lessons. Unfortunately, participant-observers, when analyzing foreign policy failures in which they took part, sometimes ascribe all the faults to their own side, and give no credit to sheer accident or the successful opponent's vigilance or effectiveness. The same one-sided analysis often happens with foreign policy successes. In the euphoria of victory, the merits and cleverness of the participant-observer's side are often overplayed while the errors or stupidity and bad luck of the opponent are kept in the background. Schlesinger, a Special Assistant to President Kennedy, avoids these pitfalls and offers a balanced, fascinating account of the complex decision-making that produced the Bay of Pigs operation.

As a case study, Schlesinger's account adds practical illustration to the preceding theoretical controversy on the subject of national interest (Selections 16 and 17); it also raises several questions concerning the role of ideology and/or morals in politics that will be analyzed in Chapters 9 and 10. In particular, the reader may note the following for possible future reference:

1. The extent to which a new administration may become captive of decisions and commitments made by the preceding administration;
2. The importance of the experts who brief the policy-makers then tend to become policy-makers as a project is being implemented (the project, as it were, acquires a life and a momentum of its own);
3. The problem of disposing of the anti-Castro brigade should the plan for invasion be cancelled;
4. President Kennedy's unhesitating endorsement of methods of deceit for the sake of national interest;

5. President Kennedy's cancellation of the second air strike to support the invasion after he had authorized the first;
6. The absence of the Congress from any role in this scheme, except for a futile attempt by Fulbright to stop the project by his secret memorandum;
7. The feelings of impotence and guilt that Schlesinger himself experienced since he did not dare, when confronted with the nation's highest brass and experts, press his opposition to the project.

... The Eisenhower administration ... bequeathed the new President a force of Cuban exiles under American training in Guatemala, a committee of Cuban politicians under American control in Florida and a plan to employ the exiles in an invasion of their homeland and to install the committee on Cuban soil as the provisional government of a free Cuba. . . .

Late in February the Chiefs [4] sent an inspection team to the Guatemala base. In a new report in early March, they ... hinged victory on the capacity of the assault to produce anti-Castro action behind the lines. From the viewpoint of the Joint Chiefs, then, the Cuban resistance was indispensable to success. They could see no other way—short of United States intervention—by which an invasion force of a thousand Cubans, no matter how well trained and equipped nor how stout their morale, could conceivably overcome the 200,000 men of Castro's army and militia. . . .

On March 11, about a week after my return from Latin America, I was summoned to a meeting with the President in the Cabinet Room. An intimidating group sat around the table—the Secretary of State, the Secretary of Defense, the director of the Central Intelligence Agency, three Joint Chiefs resplendent in uniforms and decorations, the Assistant Secretary of State for Inter-American Affairs, the chairman of the Latin American Task Force and appropriate assistants and bottle-washers. I shrank into a chair at the far end of the table and listened in silence. . . . It fell to Allen Dulles and Richard M. Bissell, Jr.,[5] as the originators of the project to make the main arguments for action. . . .

Both Dulles and Bissell were at a disadvantage in having to persuade a skeptical new administration about the virtues of a proposal nurtured in the hospitable bosom of a previous government—a proposal on which they had personally worked for a long time and in which their organization had a heavy vested interest. This cast them in the role less of analysts than of advocates, and it led them to accept progressive modifications so long as

[4] Joint Chiefs of Staff is the highest military agency of the United States. It is composed of the Army Chief of Staff, Chief of Naval Operations, Air Force Chief of Staff, and Commandant of the Marine Corps.——Ed.

[5] Director and Deputy Director of the Central Intelligence Agency.——Ed.

the expedition in some form remained; perhaps they too unconsciously supposed that, once the operation began to unfold, it would not be permitted to fail.

The determination to keep the scheme alive sprang in part, I believe, from the embarrassments of calling it off. As Dulles said at the March 11 meeting, "Don't forget that we have a disposal problem. If we have to take these men out of Guatemala, we will have to transfer them to the United States, and we can't have them wandering around the country telling everyone what they have been doing." What could one do with "this asset" if not send it on to Cuba? If transfer to the United States was out, demobilization on the spot would create even greater difficulties. The Cubans themselves were determined to go back to their homeland, and they might well forcibly resist efforts to take away their arms and equipment. Moreover, even if the Brigade were successfully disbanded, its members would disperse, disappointed and resentful all over Latin America. They would tell where they had been and what they had been doing, thereby exposing CIA operations. And they would explain how the United States, having prepared an expedition against Castro, had then lost its nerve. . . .

The contingency had thus become a reality: having created the Brigade as an option, the CIA now presented its use against Cuba as a necessity. Nor did Dulles's arguments lack force. Confronted by them, Kennedy tentatively agreed that the simplest thing, after all, might be to let the Cubans go where they yearned to go—to Cuba. Then he tried to turn the meeting toward a consideration of how this could be done with the least political risk. The first step was to form a more liberal and representative exile organization, and this the President directed should be done as soon as possible.

Bissell then renewed the case for the Trinidad plan.[6] Kennedy questioned it as "too spectacular." He did not want a big amphibious invasion in the manner of the Second World War; he wanted a "quiet" landing, preferably at night. And he insisted that the plans be drawn on the basis of *no United States military intervention*—a stipulation to which no one at the table made objection. . . .

We all in the White House considered uprisings behind the lines essential to the success of the operation; so too did the Joint Chiefs of Staff; and so,

[6] The original CIA plan selected the town of Trinidad as the point of invasion. It had the advantages of a harbor, a defensible beachhead, remoteness from Castro's main army, and easy access to the Escambray Mountains in case of a failure. Trinidad was to be taken by a heavy and concentrated amphibious assault at dawn and to be supported by paratroop drops on the hills behind the town and by simultaneous strikes against the Cuban air force. Following the tactics familiar from World War II the CIA planners envisioned a continuous buildup and enlargement of the beachhead, which as a "liberated" territory would attract the allegiance and support of the Cubans. Because this operation at dawn would be too "visible" and noisy, the CIA planners, urged by Kennedy, chose another spot for night landing in the Zapata area around Cochinos Bay, the Bay of Pigs.——Ed.

we thought, did the CIA. It was only . . . . much later that Allen Dulles wrote: "Much of the American press assumed at the time that this action was predicated on a mistaken intelligence estimate to the effect that a landing would touch off a widespread and successful popular revolt in Cuba. . . . I know of no estimate that a spontaneous uprising of the unarmed population of Cuba would be touched off by the landing." This statement plainly reflected the CIA notion that the invasion would win by attrition rather than by rebellion. It also, strictly construed, was accurate enough in itself—if due attention is paid to such key words as "spontaneous," "unarmed" and "landing." Obviously no one expected the invasion to galvanize the unarmed and unorganized into rising against Castro at the moment of disembarkation. But the invasion plan, as understood by the President and the Joint Chiefs, did assume that the successful *occupation* of an enlarged beachhead area would rather soon incite *organized* uprising by *armed* members of the Cuban resistance. . . .

Approach to a Decision

The meetings in the Cabinet Room were now taking place every three or four days. The President, it seemed to me, was growing steadily more skeptical as his hard questioning exposed one problem after another in the plans. Moreover, the situation in Laos was at a point of crisis. Kennedy feared that, if the Cuban invasion went forward, it might prejudice chances of agreement with the Soviet Union over Laos; Ambassador Thompson's cables from Moscow reported Khrushchev's unusual preoccupation with Cuba. On the other hand, if we did in the end have to send American troops to Laos to fight communism on the other side of the world, we could hardly ignore communism ninety miles off Florida. Laos and Cuba were tied up with each other, though it was hard to know how one would affect the other. But after the March 29 meeting I noted: "The final decision will have to be made on April 4. I have the impression that the tide is flowing against the project."

Dulles and Bissell, convinced that if the Cubans were ever to be sent against Castro they had to go now, sure that the Brigade could accomplish its mission and nagged by the disposal problem, now redoubled their efforts at persuasion. Dulles told Kennedy that he felt much more confident about success than he had ever been in the case of Guatemala. CIA concentrated particularly in the meetings on trying to show that, even if the expedition failed, the cost would not be excessive. Obviously no one could believe any longer that the adventure would not be attributed to the United States— news stories described the recruitment effort in Miami every day—but somehow the idea took hold around the cabinet table that this would not much matter so long as United States soldiers did not take part in the actual fighting. If the operation were truly 'Cubanized,' it would hopefully appear as part of the traditional ebb and flow of revolution and counter-revolution in the Caribbean.

Moreover, if worst came to worst and the invaders were beaten on the beaches, then, Dulles and Bissell said, they could easily "melt away" into the mountains. This might have been true at Trinidad, which lay near the foothills of the Escambray, and it was more true of the Bay of Pigs than of the other two alternative sites proposed in mid-March. But the CIA exposition was less than candid both in implying that the Brigade had undergone guerrilla training (which had substantially ended five months earlier, before most of the Cubans had arrived in Guatemala) and in suggesting the existence of an easy escape hatch. I don't think we fully realized that the Escambray Mountains lay eighty miles from the Bay of Pigs, across a hopeless tangle of swamps and jungles. And no one knew (until Haynes Johnson interviewed the survivors) that the CIA agents in Guatemala were saying nothing to the Cubans about this last resort of flight to the hills, apparently fearing to lower their morale. "We were never told about this," San Román said later. "What we were told was, 'If you fail *we* will go in.' " . . .

In the meantime, Senator Fulbright had grown increasingly concerned over the newspaper stories forecasting an invasion. The President was planning to spend Easter weekend in Palm Beach and, learning that Fulbright also was going to Florida, invited him to travel on the plane. On March 29 Fulbright, with the assistance of Pat Holt, a member of the Foreign Relations Committee staff, wrote a memorandum which he gave Kennedy the next day.

There were two posible policies toward Cuba, Fulbright argued: overthrow, or toleration and isolation. The first would violate the spirit and probably the letter of the OAS charter, hemisphere treaties and our own federal legislation. If successful, it "would be denounced from the Rio Grande to Patagonia as an example of imperialism." It would cause trouble in the United Nations. It would commit us to the heavy responsibility of making a success of post-Castro Cuba. If it seemed to be failing, we might be tempted to use our own armed force; and if we did this, "even under the paper cover of legitimacy, we would have undone the work of thirty years in trying to live down earlier interventions."

> To give this activity even covert support is of a piece with the hypocrisy and cynicism for which the United States is constantly denouncing the Soviet Union in the United Nations and elsewhere. This point will not be lost on the rest of the world—nor on our own consciences.

Instead, Fulbright urged a policy of containment. The Alliance for Progress provided a solid basis for insulating the rest of the hemisphere from Castro.

As for the Cuban exiles, an imaginative approach could find a more productive use of their talents than invading their homeland. Remember always, Fulbright concluded, "The Castro regime is a thorn in the flesh; but it is not a dagger in the heart."

It was a brilliant memorandum. Yet the President returned from Palm Beach more militant than when he had left. But he did ask Fulbright to attend the climactic meeting on April 4. This meeting was held at the State Department in a small conference room beside Rusk's office. After the usual routine—persuasive expositions by the CIA, mild disclaimers by Rusk and penetrating questions by the President—Kennedy started asking people around the table what they thought. Fulbright, speaking in an emphatic and incredulous way, denounced the whole idea. The operation, he said, was wildly out of proportion to the threat. It would compromise our moral position in the world and make it impossible for us to protest treaty violations by the Communists. He gave a brave, old-fashioned American speech, honorable, sensible and strong; and he left everyone in the room, except me and perhaps the President, wholly unmoved. . . .

A Personal Note

As we were leaving the room, the President called me back and asked for my opinion. I said that I was against the operation and tried to explain why. Listening, he nodded his head once or twice but said little. My explanation seemed to me hurried and disorderly, so the next morning I went to the office at six-thirty and wrote down my views in time to put them on the President's desk before his day began.

I had been thinking about little else for weeks and was clear in my mind that the invasion was a terrible idea. This was not because the notion of sponsoring an exile attempt to overthrow Castro seemed intolerable in itself. As my memorandum said, "If we could achieve this by a swift, surgical stroke, I would be for it." The rigid nonintervention argument had never deeply impressed me. The United States had a proud tradition of supporting refugees against tyranny in their homelands; a student of American history could not easily forget Louis Kossuth nor the fact that revolutions in Ireland, Italy, Russia, China and Palestine had all been nourished in the United States. Few of those who expressed indignation at aid to the opponents of Castro would have expressed equal indignation if in 1958 the American government had given identical aid to Castro against Batista; nor would they have objected in April 1961 to aid for the democratic Dominicans against Trujillo. . . .

Nor did I object to the operation because of its possible impact on Moscow. My guess was that the Soviet Union regarded Cuba as our special domain and was surprised that we had not taken action long since to rid ourselves of Castro on the model of their own intervention in Hungary. (I was probably wrong here in not allowing for the possibility of Soviet reprisals against West Berlin.) . . .

My opposition (expressed in this memorandum of April 5 and a second one five days later) was founded rather on the implausibility of its two political premises: that, if only Cubans took part, the United States could dissociate itself from the consequence; and that, if the beachhead could be held for a few days and enlarged, there would be defections from the militia and uprisings behind the lines. The memorandum proposed two counter-considerations as fundamental:

> a) No matter how "Cuban" the equipment and personnel, the U.S. will be held accountable for the operation, and our prestige will be committed to its success.

And, because there was no convincing evidence that the invasion would touch off a mass insurrection:

> b) Since the Castro regime is presumably too strong to be toppled by a single landing, the operation will turn into a protracted civil conflict.

If the military estimate was correct that the Brigade could secure its foothold in Cuba, the danger would be "that, if the rebellion appears to be failing, the rebels will call for U.S. armed help; that members of Congress will take up the cry; and that pressure will build up which will make it politically hard to resist the demand to send in the Marines." . . .

. . . [Kennedy's] response to my first memorandum was oblique. He said, "You know, I'v reserved the right to stop this thing up to 24 hours before the landing. In the meantime, I'm trying to make some sense out of it. We'll just have to see." But he too began to become a prisoner of events. . . .

These memoranda look nice on the record, but they represented, of course, the easy way out. In the months after the Bay of Pigs I bitterly reproached myself for having kept so silent during those crucial discussions in the Cabinet Room, though my feelings of guilt were tempered by the knowledge that a course of objection would have accomplished little save to gain me a name as a nuisance. I can only explain my failure to do more than raise a few timid questions by reporting that one's impulse to blow the whistle on this nonsense was simply undone by the circumstances of the discussion.

It is one thing for a Special Assistant to talk frankly in private to a President at his request and another for a college professor, fresh to the government, to interpose his unassisted judgment in open meeting against that of such august figures as the Secretaries of State and Defense and the Joint Chiefs of Staff, each speaking with the full weight of his institution behind him. Moreover, the advocates of the adventure had a rhetorical advantage. They could strike virile poses and talk of tangible things—fire power, air strikes, landing craft and so on. To oppose the plan, one had to invoke intangibles—the moral position of the United States, the reputation of the President, the response of the United Nations, 'world public opinion' and other such odious concepts. These matters were as much the institutional concern of the State Department as military hardware was of Defense. But, just as the members of the White House staff who sat in the Cabinet Room failed in their job of protecting the President, so the representatives of the State Department failed in defending the diplomatic interests of the nation. I could not help feeling that the desire to prove to the CIA and the Joint Chiefs that they were not soft-headed idealists but were really tough guys, too, influenced State's representatives at the cabinet table. . . .

Go Ahead Signal

Why had [Kennedy] decided to go ahead? So far as the operation itself was concerned, he felt, as he told me that afternoon, that he had successfully pared it down from a grandiose amphibious assault to a mass infiltration. Accepting the CIA assurances about the escape hatch, he supposed that the cost, both military and political, of failure was now reduced to a tolerable level. He added, "If we have to get rid of these 800 men, it is much better to dump them in Cuba than in the United States, especially if that is where they want to go"—a remark which suggested how much Dulles's insistence on the disposal problem had influenced the decision, as well as how greatly Kennedy was himself moved by the commitment of the Cuban patriots. He was particularly impressed by the fact that three members of the Cuban Revolutionary Council had sons in the Brigade; the exile leaders themselves obviously believed that the expedition would succeed. As the decision presented itself to him, he had to choose whether to disband a group of brave and idealistic Cubans, already trained and equipped, who wanted very much to return to Cuba on their own, or to permit them to go ahead. The President saw no obligation to protect the Castro regime from democratic Cubans and decided that, if the Cubans wished to make the try on the categorical understanding that there would be no direct United States military support, he would help them to do so. If the expedition succeeded, the overthrow of Castro would greatly strengthen democratic prospects in the hemisphere; if he called it off, he would forever be haunted by the feeling that his scruples had preserved Castro in power.

More generally, the decision resulted from the fact that he had been in office only seventy-seven days. He had not had the time or opportunity to test the inherited instrumentalities of government. He could not know which of his advisers were competent and which were not. For their part, they did not know him or each other well enough to raise hard questions with force and candor. Moreover, the massed and caparisoned authority of his senior officials in the realm of foreign policy and defense was unanimous for going ahead. The director of the Central Intelligence Agency advocated the adventure; the Joint Chiefs of Staff and the Secretary of Defense approved its military aspects, the Secretary of State its political aspects. They all spoke with the sacerdotal prerogative of men vested with a unique understanding of arcane matters. "If someone comes in to tell me this or that about the minimum wage bill," Kennedy said to me later, "I have no hesitation in overruling them. But you always assume that the military and intelligence people have some secret skill not available to ordinary mortals." The only opposition came from Fulbright and myself . . . . and this did not bulk large against the united voice of institutional authority. Had one senior adviser opposed the adventure, I believe that Kennedy would have canceled it. No one spoke against it.

One further factor no doubt influenced him: the enormous confidence in his own luck. Everything had broken right for him since 1956. He had won the nomination and the election against all the odds in the book. Everyone around him thought he had the Midas touch and could not lose. Despite himself, even this dispassionate and skeptical man may have been affected by the soaring euphoria of the new day. . . .

Ordeal by Fire

As for the Cubans themselves, their spirit was high. Many of the new recruits, however, had been at the base only a few days. Some had not even fired a gun. Of the 1400 men, only about 135 were soldiers. Of the rest, 240 students made up the largest single group. In addition, there were businessmen, lawyers, doctors, landowners and their sons, along with fishermen and peasants. At least fifty were Negroes. The average age was about twenty-nine, though one man was as old as sixty-one and some were no more than sixteen. . . . The rank and file were politically heterogeneous. The only common purpose was to return home and get rid of Castro.

On April 10 the Brigade began to move by truck from the Guatemalan base to the point of embarkation at Puerto Cabezas in Nicaragua. By April 13 the men were beginning to board the boats. On April 14 the United States advisers finally disclosed the invasion plan—the seizure of three beaches along forty miles of the Cuban shore in the Bay of Pigs area, with paratroops dropping inland to control the roads crossing the swamps to the sea. Castro's air force, the advisers said, would be neutralized in advance, and five hundred guerrillas were waiting nearby to join the fight. The Brigade's mission was to hold the beach for three days, after which, as the chief American adviser put it, "you will be so strong, you will be getting so many people to your side, that you won't want to wait for us. You will go straight ahead. You will put your hands out, turn left, and go straight into Havana." The Cubans, still regarding the Americans with veneration and not used to locker-room pep talks, left the briefing in a state of exaltation.

As the flotilla of seven small ships waited off Puerto Cabezas on the late afternoon of April 14, Luis Somoza, the dictator of Nicaragua, appeared at the dock, his face powdered, bodyguards in his wake. He shouted boldly, "Bring me a couple of hairs from Castro's beard," and waved the patriots farewell. The members of the Brigade trailed their vivid battalion scarves in the wind, and the boats, tinted by the red light of the dying sun, set out for Cuba.

The neutralization of Castro's air force was to be brought about by air strikes from Nicaraguan bases before the landings. This question of air attack had been under debate since January. The State Department had opposed pre-invasion strikes as incompatible with the ground rule against showing the American hand. In the Department's view, there should be no air activity until the invaders secured an airstrip of their own in Cuba and their air power could appear to be something they were mounting out of their own resources. The Pentagon, on the other hand, had contended that pre-invasion strikes were essential to knock out the Cuban air force and protect the disembarkation.

The Trinidad plan had contained no provision for advance strikes; but with the Bay of Pigs plan there had come a compromise—a strike against Cuban airfields two days before the landings, to be carried out, in order to meet State's objections, by Cuban pilots pretending to be defectors from Castro's air force. After an interval to permit U-2 overflights and photographic assessment of the damage, a second strike would follow at dawn on D-day morning. No one supposed that the cover story would hold up for very long; Castro, for example, would obviously know in short order that he was not being attacked by deserters from his own air force. But the planners expected that it would hold at least until the invaders hit the beaches—long enough to mask the second strike. It was also recognized that the pre-invasion strikes would probably cause Castro to move against the underground. . . .

As the ships made their slow way toward Cuba, eight B-26s took off from Puerto Cabezas in the night. At dawn on Saturday morning they zoomed down on three main Cuban airfields. CIA had estimated Castro's air strength at about fifteen B-26s and ten Sea Furies; there were also four T-33 jet trainers, but these did not figure significantly in either CIA's or, what is worse, the Joint Chiefs' calculations. The Cuban air force, according to the CIA estimate, was "entirely disorganized," its planes "for the most part obsolete and inoperative," its combat efficiency "almost nonexistent."

The pilots returned to Nicaragua with optimistic claims of widespread damage. The overflights the next day, however, showed only five aircraft definitely destroyed. And not all the attacking planes made it back to the base. One developed engine trouble, and its pilot headed for Florida, finally making an emergency landing in Key West. In the meantime, a ninth B-26 had flown straight from Nicaragua to Miami to put the cover plan into operation. The pilot on landing announced himself as a Castro defector who had just bombed the airfields. The unscheduled arrival of the second plane at Key West complicated things somewhat; and the appearance at Jacksonville the day before of a perfectly genuine Castro defector in a Cuban plane compounded the confusion. . . .

The President had meanwhile gone off to his Virginia retreat at Glen Ora early Saturday afternoon; had he remained, contrary to custom, in Washington, the press would have presumed that something was up. At Sunday noon, the last 'no-go' point, he authorized the expedition to proceed to the beaches. But in Washington newspapermen were starting to call the State Department and ask penetrating questions about the fugitive B-26s in Key West and Miami. It was evident that the CIA cover story was cracking. . . .

In particular, the collapse of the cover story brought the question of the second air strike into new focus. The President and the Secretary understood this strike as one which would take place simultaneously with the landings and have the appearance of coming from the airstrip on the beach. It had slid by in the briefings, everyone assuming that it would be masked by the cover story. But there could be no easy attribution to defectors now. Nor did the fact that the planes were B-26s flown by Cuban pilots save the situation; despite the great to-do about 'Cubanizing' the operation, they would still be United States planes in the eyes of the UN. Rusk, after his talks with Stevenson, concluded that a second Nicaraguan strike would put the United States in an untenable position internationally and that no further strikes should be launched until the planes could fly (or appear to fly) from the beachhead. Bundy agreed, and they called the President at Glen Ora.

It was now late Sunday afternoon. When Rusk said that the projected strike was one which could only appear to come from Nicaragua, Kennedy said, "I'm not signed on to this"; the strike he knew about was the one coming ostensibly from the beachhead. After a long conversation, the President directed that the strike be canceled. When he put down the phone, he sat on in silence for a moment, shook his head and began to pace the room in evident concern, worried perhaps less about this decision than about the

confusion in the planning; what would go wrong next? Those with him at
Glen Ora had rarely seen him so low. . . .

. . . CIA . . . dejectedly sent out the stop order, which arrived in Nicaragua
as the pilots were waiting in their cockpits for take-off.

At four-thirty the next morning . . . . the expeditionary force was at its
stations off the Bay of Pigs, and frogmen were beginning to mark the invasion points on shore. The first frogman on each beach was, in spite of
Kennedy's order, an American.

Fiasco

The frogmen almost immediately encountered a militia patrol, rifle
fire shattered the silence, and hope of tactical surprise was gone. On the
ships the Cubans watched wild flashes of lights on the shore and then
began with uncertain hearts to clamber into landing craft. Some of the
small boats, as they made their way through black waters, ran against coral
reefs, not mentioned in the briefing, and foundered, the men swimming to
other boats or toward land. Gradually the invaders gathered on the beaches
and pushed inland. After daybreak paratroops dropped from the skies and
seized interior points.

Castro's air force, alterted by the first clash, reacted with unexpected
vigor against both the ships and the men on the beaches. At nine-thirty in
the morning, a Sea Fury sank the ships carrying the ammunition reserve for
the next ten days and most of the communications equipment: an inexplicable concentration of treasure in a single hull. Other ships suffered damage,
and the rest of the flotilla put out to sea. The Brigade's slow-moving B-26s
flew defensive missions over the beachhead, but Castro's forgotten T-33s,
fast jet trainers armed with 50-calibre machine guns, shot four of them
down. The fighting went on through a hot, clear day, the invaders digging in
behind their tanks, bazookas and mortars, while Castro's forces, unable to
cross the swamps, massed to move down the highways toward the beaches.

In Havana Castro's police arrested two hundred thousand people, herding
them into theaters and auditoriums. Through the island anyone suspected
of underground connections was taken into custody. . . .

By early Tuesday it was clear that the invasion was in trouble. An attempt
to knock out Castro's planes by a B-26 raid that morning had been
frustrated by heavy haze over the airfield. I noted later that day: "The
T-33s turned out to be far more effective than any of us had been led to
suppose. This created havoc. . . . In addition, Castro tanks reached the
beachhead sooner than had been expected. And the landings failed to set off
mass uprisings behind the lines." . . .

Could anything be done about the invasion? Kennedy seemed deeply
concerned about the members of the Brigade. They were brave men and

patriots; he had put them on the beachhead; and wanted to save as many as he could. But he did not propose to send in the Marines. Some people, he noted, were arguing that failure would cause irreparable harm, that we had no choice now but to commit United States forces. Kennedy disagreed. Defeat, he said, would be an incident, not a disaster. The test had always been whether the Cuban people would back a revolt against Castro. If they wouldn't, the United States could not by invasion impose a new regime on them. But would not United States prestige suffer if we let the rebellion flicker out? "What is prestige?" Kennedy asked. "Is it the shadow of power or the substance of power? We are going to work on the substance of power. No doubt we will be kicked in the can for the next couple of weeks, but that won't affect the main business." . . .

It was a long and grim day—the longest and grimmest the New Frontier had known. The reports from Cuba continued sketchy, but whatever news there was was bad. . . .

The routine of Washington life is implacable. The prime minister of Greece was visiting the capital that week, and the Kennedys had to go to a dinner at the Greek Embassy. Once again, the President concealed anguish under a mask of courtesy and composure. So many regrets must have flowed through his mind during these bitter hours—the advice so authoritatively rendered and so respectfully accepted, the unexamined assumptions and the misconceived plans, the blow to the bright hopes of the new administration, the problems at home and abroad; but most of all, I think, it was the vision of the men on the beaches, who had gone off with such splendid expectations, who had fought so bravely and who now would be shot down like dogs or carted off to Castro's prisons. This vision haunted him that week and many weeks and months to come. . . .

. . . United States destroyers, with air cover and orders to fire if fired upon, were already searching the waters off the coast; Kennedy was prepared to run more risks to take the men off the beaches than to put them there.

The Last Act

Thursday, April 20, was the ninetieth day of the Kennedy administration. The gay expectations of the Hundred Days were irrevocably over, the hour of euphoria past. Through the country and the world the debacle was producing astonishment and disillusion.

At home the shock of defeat somewhat muted the voices of criticism. Some on the right, though fewer than one might have expected, were talking about sending in the Marines. But some on the left, more than one might have thought, now saw full vindication of their pre-election doubts about

Kennedy. A telegram from Cambridge put the matter to me with sarcastic brevity: NIXON OR KENNEDY: DOES IT MAKE ANY DIFFERENCE? It was signed: GRADUATE STUDENTS. . . .

. . . Afterward Kennedy would sometimes recur incredulously to the Bay of Pigs, wondering how a rational and responsible government could ever have become involved in so ill-starred an adventure. . . .

What caused the disaster? Too much comment on the Bay of Pigs has fallen into the fallacy of Douglas Southall Freeman, who once wrote a long chapter analyzing the reasons for Lee's defeat at Gettysburg without mentioning the interesting fact that the Union Army was there too. For the reality was that Fidel Castro turned out to be a far more formidable foe and in command of a far better organized regime than anyone had supposed. His patrols spotted the invasion at almost the first possible moment. His planes reacted with speed and vigor. His police eliminated any chance of sabotage or rebellion behind the lines. His soldiers stayed loyal and fought hard. He himself never panicked; and, if faults were chargeable to him, they were his overestimate of the strength of the invasion and undue caution in pressing the ground attack against the beachhead. His performance was impressive.

One reason Washington miscalculated Castro, of course, was a series of failures in our own intelligence. We regarded him as an hysteric. We dismissed his air force and forgot his T-33s. We thought that his troops would defect. We supposed that, although warned by advance air strikes, he would do nothing to neutralize the Cuban underground (either that, or we supposed that the underground, without alert or assistance from us, would find means to protect itself and eventually rise against the regime). And there were tactical errors. We chose an invasion site without a way of escape, and we did not in any case tell the Brigade of the guerrilla option. We put too much precious ammunition and communications equipment in a single ship. We did not give the Brigade enough pilots to keep its planes in continuous action. On the other hand, if one renounced the fall-back plan of flight to the hills, the invasion site was well chosen and easily defensible. The men of the Brigade fought with great bravery against superior force and inflicted far more casualties than they received.

Subsequent controversy has settled on the cancellation of the second air strike as the turning point. In retrospect, there clearly was excessive apprehension that Sunday evening; it is hard now to see why, the first strike already having taken place, a second would have made things so much worse at the United Nations or elsewhere. Kennedy came later to feel that the cancellation of the second strike was an error. But he did not regard it as a decisive error, for, even on the most unlikely assumption that the second strike achieved total success and wiped out Castro's air force, it would still have left 1200 men against 200,000. The Brigade's air power was already in decline because of the scarcity of pilots; and, once the mass arrests had taken place, there was no hope of uprising behind the lines. The second air strike might have protracted the stand on the beachhead from three days to ten; it might have permitted the establishment of the provisional government; it might have made possible the eventual evacuation of the invading force. There is certainly nothing to suggest that it could possibly have led to the overthrow of the regime on the terms which Kennedy laid down from the start—that is without United States armed intervention. . . .

The expedition was not only misconceived politically. It was also misconceived technically. If it was to be a covert operation for which we could plausibly disclaim responsibility, it should have been, at most, a guerrilla infiltration. Once it grew into a conventional amphibious invasion, it was clearly beyond the limits of disownability. Unless we were prepared to back it to the hilt, it should have been abandoned. When the President made it clear time after time that for the most cogent reasons we would not back it to the hilt, the planners should not have deluded themselves into thinking that events would reverse this decision or that the adventure would succeed on its own. Instead of trying to compromise between the claims of clandestinity and the claims of military impact, we should have chosen one or the other. The President had insisted that the political and military risks be brought into balance: given the nature of the operation, this was impossible, and someone should have said so.

All of us, the President most of all, went through this sequence of thoughts again and again in the months to come. And yet, and yet: for all the utter irrationality with which retrospect endowed the project, it had a certain queer logic at the time as it emerged from the bowels of government. The men were there; they had been armed and trained; something had to be done with them; this was what they wanted to do themselves; and, if the worst happened, they could always turn into guerrillas and melt away in the hills. This sequence spun about in our minds for a long time too.

8

Perceptions:
Springs of Action[1]

Common experience confirms that different persons view, interpret, and therefore react to the same event or information in different, often conflicting ways. Objective "reality"[2] is perceived subjectively; both acquisition and interpretation of information reflects the variety of human experiences, skills, and foibles.

When, for instance, two persons witness a car accident, they often reach conflicting conclusions as to what actually happened. Their different perceptions of a collision will reflect the difference in their respective distance from the

[1] Stanley Hoffmann, "Perception, Reality and the Franco-American Conflict," in John C. Farrell and Asa P. Smith (Eds.), *Image and Reality in World Politics* (New York: Columbia University Press, 1967), pp. 13–14, writes: "The distinction between perception and reality is always arbitrary. Here as elsewhere, perceptions are part of the reality . . . [and] more than part of reality: they mold it, insofar they are springs and fuel of action. Moreover, they are themselves shaped by reality. . . . Thus reality is in considerable part the product of conflict of wills, of a contest of active perceptions competing for the privilege of defining reality."

[2] Kenneth E. Boulding, "The Learning and Reality-Testing Process in the International System," *Journal of International Affairs*, 21:1 (1967), 2, writes: "The problem of what constitutes realism in our image of the world has bothered philosophers from the very beginnings of human thought, and it is certainly far from being resolved. Indeed [the English philosopher] Hume may well have demonstrated that it cannot be resolved, simply because images can only be compared with other images and never with reality. Nevertheless, common sense leads us to reject Humean skepticism in practice; we must live and act for the most part as if our images of the world were true."

scene as well as the difference in their respective personality structures and their own skill in driving or the lack of it, the number of past convictions for hazardous driving, and their previous experience with insurance companies.

Similarly when two nations are on a collision course or actually collide, the national leaders will differently perceive and react to the event, depending on their distance from the scene, their own political skill or lack of it, the impact of past commitments and national history, and their experience with alliances and collective security. Ideally, scanning the world horizon, national leaders should be able reliably to distinguish a threat from a conciliatory move, a mortal danger from a minor irritation, and an irreconcilable foe from a potential partner or neutral. In fact, their perception of the event is often partly or totally false; yet their image, however false it may be, will trigger action that, in turn, will affect the reality. At the same time, the objective reality will condition the consequences of an action based on a false image. Or, as Harold and Margaret Sprout put it:

> With respect to policy-making and the content of policy-decision what matters is how the policy-maker imagines the milieu to be, not how it actually is. With respect to the operational results of decisions, what matters is how things are, not how the policy-maker imagines them to be.[3]

The difference in perception of international events is quite common not only between the leaders of two rival nations but also, within a nation, between the leadership and the public. Two reasons for the difference may be noted:

1. Generally speaking, the leaders possess more complete information, including secret data, than does the public. An uninformed and usually uninterested man-in-the-street[4] is bound to react to international events emotionally rather than rationally, and, at any rate, differently from a scholar, an area specialist, a military expert, or a political leader.

The contradistinction between the leader, on the one hand, and the public, on the other, needs to be further qualified since there are many different publics—the opposition, pressure groups, mass media, party militants, protesters, and the mass of voters—all these segments reciprocally influencing each other. In the American context, for instance, a voter observes the world through his own very special type of bias or distortion, depending on what has shaped his

---

[3] Harold and Margaret Sprout, "Environmental Factors in the Study of International Politics," *The Journal of Conflict Resolution*, 1:4 (1957), 328.

[4] J. David Singer rightly notes in his "Man and World Politics: The Psycho-Cultural Interface," *Journal of Social Issues*, 25:3 (1968), p. 127: "It has become something of a ritual for political scientists to note how uninterested and/or uninformed the bulk of the world's citizens are in regard to politics, and while the evidence seems compelling, it may be somewhat beside the point for students of foreign policy.... The fact is that those members who are attentive and/or informed are generally those whose opinions do exercise some impact on the policy-making process."

approach to international events—reading *National Observer*, or *Black Panther*, or *Time*, or *Reader's Digest*, or *Chicago Daily Tribune*, or *The New York Times*.[5]

2. The second factor that causes the leaders and the public to perceive the world scene differently is their respective responsibility and lack of it for decision and action with reference to international events. The public, mass media, radio commentators, columnists, the opposition, the protesters, and the general public meditate, agitate, and above all *talk* while the policy-maker must also *act* and bear the consequences. Responsibility for action affects our perception: a fire means different things for a person trapped in a house afire, for a fireman, or for a curious spectator. Responsibility for reaction to an event necessarily creates a special type of bias in the decision-making capacity of a national leader.

19 / The First Nuclear Confrontation in History— The Cuban Missile Crisis of 1962: A Case Study

Theodore C. Sorensen

The Cuban missile crisis of 1962 is one of the most awe-inspiring events of recent history. It occurred during the Kennedy administration after the fiasco at the Bay of Pigs and at a time when Castro's Cuba was receiving military and economic aid from communist countries, primarily the Soviet Union. Cuba had already been under the watchful eyes of the United States intelligence network when information gathered by the U-2 high-altitude espionage aircraft revealed beyond any doubt the Soviet clandestine attempt to introduce

Abridgment of pp. 669, 671–676, 678–685, 687–694, 696–718 *(passim)*, in *Kennedy* by Theodore C. Sorensen. Copyright © 1965 by Theodore C. Sorensen. Reprinted by permission of Harper & Row, Publishers. Reprinted in the British Commonwealth (excluding Canada) and used by permission of the publishers, Hodder and Stoughton. Copyright. Some author's footnotes have been omitted; footnotes added by the editor are so marked.

[5] A study of biased informational input—liberal or conservative—into the formation of public opinion among the semi-elites in the United States has been undertaken by Dr. John H. Schultz at Fullerton College, California. It is planned to be published under the title *Liberals, Conservatives and the Cold War*.

medium- and intermediate-range ballistic missiles, capable of carrying nuclear warheads, into Cuba.

At the time they were first discovered, the estimate was that the missiles would become operational by October 1962. This date seemed deliberately to coincide with Soviet Premier Khrushchev's planned visit to the United Nations General Assembly in New York. The Soviet intention of deceipt and surprise emerged also from the emphatic assurances given by Soviet Ambassador Dobrynin to Theodore Sorensen, then a Special Assistant to President Kennedy and the author of the following excerpt, that "nothing will be undertaken before the American Congressional elections that could complicate the international situation or aggravate the tension in the relations between our two countries."

The case study demonstrates the primary importance of timely and reliable information; in this case it was an aerial photograph of the first rude beginnings of a Soviet medium-range missile base in the San Cristóbal area of Cuba. Reliable information is, however, only one element in the complex process of appropriate interpretation of, and reaction to, a new reality. On the basis of one hard fact many questions for which there was no ready answer had to be asked: Why did the Soviet leadership decide to build a secret Soviet nuclear missile base in Cuba? Were its intentions offensive or defensive? Should the American response be to alert the public or, on the contrary, explain the new fact as really not new? What would be the Soviet reaction to an American energetic or soft action then and in the future?

The movement of Soviet personnel and equipment into Cuba . . . had been the subject of a series of meetings and reports in the White House beginning in August. Naval ships and planes photographed every Soviet vessel bound for Cuba. Aerial reconnaissance flights covered the entire island twice monthly. A special daily intelligence report on Cuba began on August 27.

The intelligence picture was clouded by the constant rumors reported to the CIA, to the press and to some members of Congress by Cuban refugees that Soviet surface-to-surface missiles had been seen on the island. All these rumors and reports, numbering in the hundreds, were checked out. All proved to be unfounded, resulting from the inability of civilians to distinguish between offensive and defensive missiles or the wishful thinking of patriots hoping to goad the United States into an invasion of Cuba. . . .

Photographs taken [on August 29], and reported to the President on August 31, provided the first significant "hard intelligence": antiaircraft surface-to-air missiles (SAMs), missile-equipped torpedo boats for coastal defense and substantially more military personnel. But neither these pictures nor those taken on September 5 (which also revealed MIG-21 fighter aircraft) produced evidence of offensive ballistic missiles, for which in fact no recognizable equipment had yet arrived. In a public statement on September 4 revealing the August 31 findings, the President repeated that there

was as yet no proof of offensive ground-to-ground missiles or other significant offensive capability. He added, however: "Were it to be otherwise, the
gravest issues would arise."

With the exception of CIA Chief John McCone, who speculated that the
SAM sites might be intended to protect offensive missile installations, but
whose absence on a honeymoon prevented his views from reaching the
President, Kennedy's intelligence and Kremlinology experts stressed that
no offensive Soviet missiles had ever been stationed outside of Soviet
territory, not even in Eastern Europe, where they could be constantly
guarded and supplied; that the Soviets would in all likelihood continue to
limit their military assistance to Cuba to defensive weapons; and that they
evidently recognized that the development of an *offensive* military base
in Cuba might provoke U.S. military intervention. This distinction between
offensive and defensive capabilities, while not always clear-cut, was regarded
as crucial by all concerned. The presence in Cuba of Soviet weapons incapable of attacking the United States was obnoxious but not sufficiently
different from the situation which had long existed in Cuba and elsewhere
to justify a military response on our part.

Continued Soviet shipments and the belligerent Moscow statement of
September 11,[6] however, impelled the President to deliver an even more
explicit statement at his September 13 news conference. . . . [H]e underlined
once again the difference between offensive and defensive capabilities:

> If at any time the Communist build-up in Cuba were to endanger or
> interfere with our security in any way . . . or if Cuba should ever . . .
> become an offensive military base of significant capacity for the Soviet
> Union, then this country will do whatever must be done to protect its
> own security and that of its allies.

Answering a questioner's reference to the Moscow warning that any U.S.
military action against the build-up would mean "the unleashing of war,"
the President replied that, regardless of any threats, he would take whatever action the situation might require, no more and no less. . . .

Discovery

On October 9 the President—whose personal authorization was
required for every U-2 flight and who throughout this period had authorized
all flights requested of him—approved a mission over the western end of
Cuba. . . .

Delayed by bad weather until October 14, the U-2 flew in the early
morning hours of that cloudless Sunday high over western Cuba, moving

---

[6] In that statement Khrushchev threatened nuclear retaliation in case of a United
States military action against Cuba.——Ed.

from south to north. Processed that night, the long rolls of film were scrutinized, analyzed, compared with earlier photos, and reanalyzed throughout Monday by the extraordinarily talented photo interpreters of the U.S. Government's intelligence network; and late that afternoon they spotted in the San Cristóbal area the first rude beginnings of a Soviet medium-range missile base.

By Monday evening, October 15, the analysts were fairly certain of their findings. Between 8 and 10 P.M., the top CIA officials were notified and they notified in turn the Defense and State intelligence chiefs and, at his home, McGeorge Bundy. Bundy immediately recognized that this was no unconfirmed refugee report or minor incident. He decided, however—and quite rightly, I believe—not to call the President but to brief him in person and in detail the next morning. . . .

Around 9 A.M. Tuesday morning, October 16, having first received a detailed briefing from top CIA officials, Bundy broke the news to the President as he scanned the morning papers in his bedroom. Kennedy, though angry at Khrushchev's efforts to deceive him and immediately aware of their significance, took the news calmly but with an expression of surprise. He had not expected the Soviets to attempt so reckless and risky an action in a place like Cuba, and had accepted—perhaps too readily, in retrospect—the judgment of the experts that such a deployment of nuclear weapons would be wholly inconsistent with Soviet policy. Even John Mc-Cone had assumed that no missiles would be moved in until an operational network of SAMs would make their detection from the air difficult. (Why the Soviets failed to coordinate this timing is still inexplicable.). . . .

. . . [A]t 11 A.M., as CIA Deputy Director Marshall Carter spread the enlarged U-2 photographs before him with comments by a photo interpreter, all doubts were gone. The Soviet missiles were there; their range and purpose were offensive; and they would soon be operative. . . .

. . . Soviet medium-range ballistic missiles, said Carter, could reach targets eleven hundred nautical miles away. That covered Washington, Dallas, Cape Canaveral, St. Louis and all SAC bases and cities in between; and it was estimated that the whole complex of sixteen to twenty-four missiles could be operational in two weeks. The photographs revealed no signs of nuclear warheads stored in the area, but no one doubted that they were there or soon would be.

The President was somber but crisp. His first directive was for more photography. He expressed the nation's gratitude to the entire photo collection and analysis team for a remarkable job. . . . American reconnaissance and intelligence had done well to spot them before they were operational. But now more photographs were needed immediately, said the President. We had to be sure—we had to have the most convincing possible evidence —and we had to know what else was taking place throughout the island.

Even a gigantic hoax had to be guarded against, someone said. Daily flights were ordered covering all of Cuba.

Kennedy's second directive was to request that those present set aside all other tasks to make a prompt and intensive survey of the dangers and all possible courses of action—because action was imperative. . . .

The President's third directive enjoined us all to strictest secrecy until both the facts and our response could be announced. Any premature disclosure, he stressed, could precipitate a Soviet move or panic the American public before we were ready to act. A full public statement later would be essential, he said, talking in the same vein about briefing former President Eisenhower. There was discussion about declaring a national emergency and calling up Reserves. But for the present secrecy was vital; and for that reason advance consultations with the Allies were impossible. He had already given the surface impression that morning that all was well, keeping his scheduled appointments. . . .

But even as he went about his other duties, the President meditated not only on what action he would take but why the Soviets had made so drastic and dangerous a departure from their usual practice. Evidently they had hoped, with the help of the SAMs and an American preoccupation with elections, to surprise the United States in November with a completed, operational missile chain. But why—and what next? The answer could not then—or perhaps ever—be known by Americans with any certainty. . . .

. . . To be sure, these Cuban missiles alone, in view of all the other megatonnage the Soviets were capable of unleashing upon us, did not substantially alter the strategic balance *in fact*—unless these first installations were followed by so many more that Soviet military planners would have an increased temptation to launch a pre-emptive first strike. But that balance would have been substantially altered *in appearance;* and in matters of national will and world leadership, as the President said later, such appearances contribute to reality.

. . . [I]t was clear that the Soviet move, if successful, would "materially . . . and politically change the balance of power" in the entire cold war, as he would later comment. Undertaken in secrecy, accompanied by duplicity, the whole effort was based on confronting Kennedy and the world in November with a threatening *fait accompli,* designed perhaps to be revealed by Khrushchev personally, we speculated, in a bristling UN speech, to be followed by a cocky demand for a summit on Berlin and other matters. . . .

Planning a Response

My recollection of the ninety-six hours that followed is a blur of meetings and discussions, mornings, afternoons, evenings. The proposals varied, their proponents varied, our progress varied. . . . [I]n the Pentagon

... McNamara and the Joint Chiefs executed the President's instructions to alert our forces for any contingency and to be ready in a week for any military action against Cuba. . . .

At 6:30 P.M. we met again with the President in the Cabinet Room, as we would regularly for the next several weeks. That Tuesday was the first of thirteen days of decision unlike any other in the Kennedy years—or, indeed, inasmuch as this was the first direct nuclear confrontation, unlike any in the history of our planet.

Much misinformation has been written about this series of meetings, about who said what, and about such terms as "hawks and doves," "think tank," "Ex Comm" and "Trollope ploy" which I never heard used at the time. With all due respect to those Cabinet and other officers sometimes credited in these accounts with shaping our deliberations when the President was absent, the best performer in this respect was the Attorney General [Robert F. Kennedy]—not because of any particular idea he advanced, not because he presided (no one did), but because of his constant prodding, questioning, eliciting arguments and alternatives and keeping the discussions concrete and moving ahead, a difficult task as different participants came in and out. Bundy and I sought to assist in this role. Indeed, one of the remarkable aspects of those meetings was a sense of complete equality. Protocol mattered little when the nation's life was at stake. Experience mattered little in a crisis which had no precedent. Even rank mattered little when secrecy prevented staff support. We were fifteen individuals on our own, representing the President and not different departments. Assistant Secretaries differed vigorously with their Secretaries; I participated much more freely than I ever had in an NSC meeting; and the absence of the President encouraged everyone to speak his mind.

It was after noting these tendencies in a Wednesday afternoon meeting, held while the President fulfilled a campaign commitment in Connecticut, that I recommended he authorize more such preparatory meetings without his presence. He agreed, and these meetings continued in George Ball's conference room on the State Department's seventh floor. But inasmuch as some or all of us met daily with the President, those meetings over which he did not preside—held chiefly while he maintained his normal schedule for the sake of appearances and to carry out other duties—were not formulating policy or even alternatives without his knowledge. And when he did preside, recognizing that lower-ranking advisers such as Thompson would not voluntarily contradict their superiors in front of the President, and that persuasive advisers such as McNamara unintentionally silenced less articulate men, he took pains to seek everyone's individual views. In sharp contrast with his first Cuban crisis, when he had conferred with a somewhat different group, he knew his men, we knew each other, and all weighed the consequences of failure.

As the week wore on, the tireless work of the aerial photographers and photo interpreters gave an even greater sense of urgency to our deliberations. More MRBM sites were discovered, for a total of six. They were no longer recognizable only, in the President's words, "to the most sophisticated expert." Their construction had proceeded at such a pace in those few days that there could be no mistaking the Soviet intention to have them operational much earlier than we had anticipated on Tuesday. The literally miles of film taken of the island—which was blanketed daily with six or seven flights—now revealed excavations for three IRBM sites as well. The 2,200-mile IRBMs, when readied in December, would be capable of reaching virtually any part of the continental United States. At these locations, too, the fields and wooded areas photographed in earlier coverage had suddenly been transformed into networks of roads, tents, equipment and construction, all completely manned and closely guarded by Soviet personnel only.

The knowledge that time was running out dominated our discussions and kept us meeting late into the night. The stepped-up U-2 flights had apparently not alerted the Soviets to our discovery. But we had to formulate and declare our position, said the President, before they knew we knew, before the matter leaked out to the public and before the missiles became operational.

Despite the fatiguing hours and initially sharp divisions, our meetings avoided any loss of temper and frequently were lightened by a grim humor. Each of us changed his mind more than once that week on the best course of action to take—not only because new facts and arguments were adduced but because, in the President's words, "whatever action we took had so many disadvantages to it and each . . . raised the prospect that it might escalate the Soviet Union into a nuclear war."

It was an agonizing prospect. In no other period during my service in the White House did I wake up in the middle of the night, reviewing the deliberations of that evening and trying to puzzle out a course of action. Not one of us at any time believed that any of the choices before us could bring anything but either prolonged danger or fighting, very possibly leading to the kind of deepening commitment of prestige and power from which neither side could withdraw without resort to nuclear weapons.

The Soviet statement of September 11 had warned that any U.S. military action against Cuba would unleash nuclear war. What would Khrushchev actually do if we bombed the missile sites—or blockaded the island—or invaded? What would we do in return, and what would his reaction be then? These were the questions we asked that week. Among the locations listed as possible targets for Soviet retaliation were West Berlin (first on everyone's list, and therefore the subject of a special subcommittee of our group established by the President); Turkey (because our exposed Jupiter missiles there were most likely to be equated with the Soviet missiles in Cuba); Iran (where the Soviets had a tactical advantage comparable to ours in the Caribbean and a longstanding desire for control); Pakistan, Scandinavia and Italy. Nor could we worry only about Soviet retaliation. Castro, not known for his steady reactions, might order an attack on Guantánamo, on Florida or on whatever planes or ships we employed. He might also order the execution of the Bay of Pigs prisoners. The news that week that Red China had attacked India made us wonder whether this was a coincidence or whether a whole round of conflagrations would include Formosa, Korea and the Indochinese peninsula. The most dire possibility of all was that the Soviets might conclude—from a similar analysis of measures and countermeasures, as seen from their point of view—that all-out war was inevitable and thereupon launch a pre-emptive nuclear strike on the United States to make certain they hit us first.

The fact that Khrushchev had already made one major miscalculation—in thinking he could get away with missiles in Cuba—increased the danger that he would make more. . . .

The President asked Rusk to prepare an analysis of possible Allied reactions; and the Secretary summarized it for our Wednesday afternoon meeting in his department. He emphasized that our evidence and reasoning would have to be convincing, and that our response would have to offer the Soviets a way out, but that the above problems would still remain. When he concluded, I asked, "Are you saying in effect that if we take a strong action the Allies and Latin Americans will turn against us and if we take a weak action they will turn away from us?" "That's about it," replied Rusk. There was a moment of gloomy silence until General Taylor interjected: "And a Merry Christmas to you, too!"

The bulk of our time Tuesday through Friday was spent in George Ball's conference room canvassing all the possible courses as the President had requested, and preparing the back-up material for them: suggested time schedules or scenarios, draft messages, military estimates and predictions of Soviet and Cuban responses. Initially the possibilities seemed to divide into six categories, some of which could be combined:

1. Do nothing.

2. Bring diplomatic pressures and warnings to bear upon the Soviets. Possible forms included an appeal to the UN or OAS for an inspection team, or a direct approach to Khrushchev, possibly at a summit conference. The removal of our missile bases in Turkey in exchange for the removal of the Cuban missiles was also listed in our later discussions as a possibility which Khrushchev was likely to suggest if we didn't.

3. Undertake a secret approach to Castro, to use this means of

splitting him off from the Soviets, to warn him that the alternative was his island's downfall and that the Soviets were selling him out.

4. Initiate indirect military action by means of a blockade, possibly accompanied by increased aerial surveillance and warnings. Many types of blockades were considered.

5. Conduct an air strike—pinpointed against the missiles only or against other military targets, with or without advance warning. (Other military means of directly removing the missiles were raised—bombarding them with pellets that would cause their malfunctioning without fatalities, or suddenly landing paratroopers or guerrillas—but none of these was deemed feasible.)

6. Launch an invasion—or, as one chief advocate of this course put it: "Go in there and take Cuba away from Castro."

Other related moves were considered—such as declaring a national emergency, sending a special envoy to Khrushchev or asking Congress for a declaration of war against Cuba (suggested as a means of building both Allied support and a legal basis for blockade, but deemed not essential to either). But these six choices were the center of our deliberations.

Choice No. 1—doing nothing—and choice No. 2—limiting our response to diplomatic action only—were both seriously considered. As some (but not all) Pentagon advisers pointed out to the President, we had long lived within range of Soviet missiles, we expected Khrushchev to live with our missiles nearby, and by taking this addition calmly we could prevent him from inflating its importance. All the other courses raised so many risks and drawbacks that choice No. 2 had its appeal. All of us came back to it at one discouraged moment or another; and it was advocated to the President as a preferable alternative to blockade by one of the regular members of our group in the key Thursday night meeting discussed below.

But the President had rejected this course from the outset. He was concerned less about the missiles' military implications than with their effect on the global political balance. The Soviet move had been undertaken so swiftly, so secretly and with so much deliberate deception—it was so sudden a departure from Soviet practice—that it represented a provocative change in the delicate status quo. Missiles on Soviet territory or submarines were very different from missiles in the Western Hemisphere, particularly in their political and psychological effect on Latin America. . . .

Various approaches to Castro (choice No. 3)—either instead of or as well as to Khrushchev—were also considered many times during the week. This course was set aside rather than dropped. The President increasingly felt that we should not avoid the fact that this was a confrontation of the great powers—that the missiles had been placed there by the Soviets, were manned and guarded by the Soviets, and would have to be removed by the Soviets in response to direct American action.

The invasion course (choice No. 6) had surprisingly few supporters. One leader outside our group whose views were conveyed to us felt that the missiles could not be tolerated, that the Soviet motivation was baffling, that a limited military action such as a blockade would seem indecisive and irritating to the world, and that an American airborne seizure of Havana and the government was the best bet. But with one possible exception, the conferees shared the President's view that invasion was a last step, not the first; that it should be prepared but held back; that an invasion—more than any other course—risked a world war, a Soviet retaliation at Berlin or elsewhere, a wreckage of our Latin-American policy and the indictment of history for our aggression.

Thus our attention soon centered on two alternatives—an air strike and a blockade—and initially more on the former. The idea of American planes suddenly and swiftly eliminating the missile complex with conventional bombs in a matter of minutes—a so-called "surgical" strike—had appeal to almost everyone first considering the matter, including President Kennedy on Tuesday and Wednesday. It would be over quickly and cleanly, remove the missiles effectively and serve as a warning to the Communists. It could be accompanied by an explanatory address to the nation and by a blockade or increased aerial surveillance to guard against future installations. The air-strike advocates in our group prepared an elaborate scenario, which provided for a Presidential announcement of the missiles' presence Saturday, calling Congress back into emergency session, and then knocking the missiles out early Sunday morning, simultaneously notifying Khrushchev of our action and recommending a summit. Cuba was to be notified at the UN shortly in advance. Leaflet warnings to Russians at the sites were also considered.

But there were grave difficulties to the air-strike alternative, which became clearer each day.

1. The "surgical" strike, like the April, 1961, overthrow of Castro by a small exile brigade, was merely a hopeful illusion—and this time it was so recognized. It could not be accomplished by a few sorties in a few minutes, as hoped, nor could it be limited to the missile sites alone. To so limit the strike, declared the Joint Chiefs firmly, would be an unacceptable risk. Castro's planes—and newly arrived Soviet MIGs and IL-28 bombers, if operative—might respond with an attack on our planes, on Guantánamo or even on the Southeastern United States. The SAMs would surely fire at our planes. Cuban batteries opposite Guantánamo might open fire. The nuclear warhead storage sites, if identified, should not remain. All or most of these targets would have to be taken out in a massive bombardment.

Even then, admitted the Air Force—and this in particular influenced the President—there could be no assurance that all the missiles would have been removed or that some of them would not fire first, unleashing their nuclear warheads on American soil. The more we looked at the air strike, the clearer it became that the resultant chaos and political collapse would ultimately necessitate a U.S. invasion. Most of the air-strike advocates, openly agreed that their route took us back to the invasion course, and they added Cuban military installations and invasion support targets to the list of sites to be bombed. But invasion with all its consequences was still opposed by the President.

2. The problem of advance warning was unsolvable. A sudden air strike at dawn Sunday without warning, said the Attorney General [Robert F. Kennedy] in rather impassioned tones, would be "a Pearl Harbor in reverse, and it would blacken the name of the United States in the pages of history" as a great power who attacked a small neighbor. The Suez fiasco was also cited as comparable. Latin Americans would produce new Castros in their bitterness; the Cuban people would not forgive us for decades; and the Soviets would entertain the very dangerous notion that the United States, as they had feared all these years, was indeed capable of launching a pre-emptive first strike. But to provide advance warning raised as many difficulties as no warning at all. It would enable the Soviets to conceal the missiles and make their elimination less certain. It would invite Khrushchev to commit himself to bombing us if we carried out our attack, give him time to take the propaganda and diplomatic initiative, and stir up a host of UN, Latin-American and Allied objections which we would have to defy or let the missiles stand. Many of those originally attracted to the air-strike course had favored it in the hope that a warning would suffice, and that the Soviets would then withdraw their missiles. But no one could devise any method of warning that would not enable Khrushchev either to tie us into knots or force us into obloquy. I tried my hand, for example, at an airtight letter to be carried from the President to the Soviet Chairman by a high-level personal envoy. The letter would inform Khrushchev that only if he agreed in his conference with that courier (and such others as he called in) to order the missiles dismantled would U.S. military action be withheld while our surveillance oversaw their removal. But no matter how many references I put in to a summit, to peaceful intentions and to previous warnings and pledges, the letter still constituted the kind of ultimatum which no great power could accept, and a justification for either a pre-emptive strike against this country or our indictment in the court of history. From that point on, I veered away from the air-strike course.

3. The air strike, unlike the blockade, would directly and definitely attack Soviet military might, kill Russians as well as Cubans and thus more likely provoke a Soviet military response. Not to respond at all would be

too great a humiliation for Khrushchev to bear, affecting his relations not only at home and with the Chinese but with all the Communist parties in the developing world. Any Cuban missiles operational by the time of our strike might be ordered by Khrushchev to fire their nuclear salvos into the United States before they were wiped out—or, we speculated, the local Soviet commander, under attack, might order the missiles fired on the assumption that war was on. The air-strike advocates did not shrink from the fact that a Soviet military riposte was likely. "What will the Soviets do in response?" one consultant favoring this course was asked. "I know the Soviets pretty well," he replied. "I think they'll knock out our missile bases in Turkey." "What do we do then?" "Under our NATO Treaty, we'd be obligated to knock out a base inside the Soviet Union." "What will they do them?" "Why, then we hope everyone will cool down and want to talk." It seemed rather cool in the conference room as he spoke. . . .

. . . As the consensus shifted away from any notion of trying political or diplomatic pressure before resorting to military action, and away from the "surgical" air strike as an impossibility, it shifted on Thursday toward the notion of blockade. It was by no means unanimous—the advocates of a broad air strike were still strong—but the blockade alternative was picking up important backers.

At first there had been very little support of a blockade. . . . It appeared almost irrelevant to the problem of the missiles, neither getting them out nor seeming justifiable to our many maritime allies who were sensitive to freedom of the seas. Blockade was a word so closely associated with Berlin that it almost guaranteed a new Berlin blockade in response. Both our allies and world opinion would then blame the U.S. and impose as a "solution" the lifting of both blockades simultaneously, thus accomplishing nothing.

Moreover, blockade had many of the drawbacks of the airstrike plan. If Soviet ships ignored it, U.S. forces would have to fire the first shot, provoking Soviet action elsewhere—by their submarines against our ships there or in other waters, by a blockade of our overseas bases or by a more serious military move against Berlin, Turkey, Iran or the other trouble spots mentioned. One view held that Khrushchev and the U.S. could both pretend that an air strike on Cuba was no affair of the Soviet Union but a blockade of Soviet ships was a direct challenge from which he could not retreat. And if Castro thought a blockade was effectively cutting him off, he might in desperation—or to involve Soviet help—attack our ships, Guantánamo or Florida. . . .

But the greatest single drawback to the blockade, in comparison with the air strike, was time. Instead of presenting Khrushchev and the world with a *fait accompli,* it offered a prolonged and agonizing approach, uncertain in its effect, indefinite in its duration, enabling the missiles to become operational, subjecting us to counterthreats from Khrushchev, giving him a propaganda advantage, stirring fears and protests and pickets all over the world, causing Latin-American governments to fall, permitting Castro to announce that he would execute two Bay of Pigs prisoners for each day it continued, encouraging the UN or the OAS or our allies to bring pressure for talks, and in all these ways making more difficult a subsequent air strike if the missiles remained. Our own people would be frustrated and divided as tensions built. . . .

Despite all these disadvantages, the blockade route gained strength on Thursday as other choices faded. It was a more limited, low-key military action than the air strike. It offered Khrushchev the choice of avoiding a direct military clash by keeping his ships away. It could at least be initiated without a shot being fired or a single Soviet or Cuban citizen being killed. Thus it seemed slightly less likely to precipitate an immediate military riposte. Moreover, a naval engagement in the Caribbean, just off our own shores, was the most advantageous military confrontation the United States could have, if one were necessary. Whatever the balance of strategic and ground forces may have been, the superiority of the American Navy was unquestioned; and this superiority was world-wide, should Soviet submarines retaliate elsewhere. To avoid a military defeat, Khrushchev might well turn his ships back, causing U.S. allies to have increased confidence in our credibility and Cuba's Communists to feel they were being abandoned.

Precisely because it was a limited, low-level action, the argument ran, the blockade had the advantage of permitting a more controlled escalation on our part, gradual or rapid as the situation required. It could serve as an unmistakable but not sudden or humiliating warning to Khrushchev of what we expected from him. Its prudence, its avoidance of casualties and its avoidance of attacking Cuban soil would make it more appealing to other nations than an air strike, permitting OAS and Allied support for our initial position, and making that support more likely for whatever air-strike or other action was later necessary.

On Thursday afternoon subcommittees were set up to plot each of the major courses in detail. The blockade subcommittee first had to decide what kind of blockade it recommended. We chose to begin with the lowest level of action—also the level least likely to anger allies engaged in the Cuban trade—a blockade against offensive weapons only. Inasmuch as the President had made clear that defensive weapons were not intolerable, and inasmuch as the exclusion of all food and supplies would affect innocent Cubans most of all, this delineation helped relate the blockade route more closely to the specific problem of missiles and made the punishment more nearly fit the crime. It also avoided the difficulty of stopping submarines and planes (which would have difficulty bringing in missiles and bombers even in sections). . . .

Our next consideration was the likely Soviet response. The probability of Soviet acquiescence in the blockade itself—turning their ships back or permitting their inspection—was "high, but not certain," in the words of one Kremlinologist; but it was predicted that they might choose to force us to fire at them first. Retaliatory action elsewhere in the world seemed almost certain. . . .

We then suggested possible U.S. responses to these Communist responses, advocating that Berlin be treated on the basis of its own previously prepared contingency plans without regard to actions elsewhere. These studies completed, we rejoined the air-strike subcommittee and the others in the conference room to compare notes.

Meanwhile, the President—with whom some of us had met both in the morning and afternoon of that Thursday—was holding a long-scheduled two-hour meeting with Soviet Foreign Minister Gromyko prior to the latter's return to Moscow from the UN. While all of us wondered whether this could possibly be the moment planned by the Soviets to confront Kennedy with their new threat, all agreed that the President should not tell Gromyko what we knew. . . .

Gromyko, seated on the sofa next to the President's rocker, not only failed to mention the offensive weapons but carried on the deception that there were none. In a sense, Kennedy had hoped for this, believing it would strengthen our case with world opinion. The chief topic of conversation was Berlin, and on this Gromyko was tougher and more insistent than ever. After the U.S. election, he said, if no settlement were in sight, the Soviets would go ahead with their treaty. ("It all seemed to fit a pattern," the President said to me later, "everything coming to a head at once—the completion of the missile bases, Khrushchev coming to New York, a new drive on West Berlin. If that move is coming anyway, I'm not going to feel that a Cuban blockade provoked it.") Then the Soviet Minister turned to Cuba, not with apologies but complaints. He cited the Congressional resolution, the Reservists call-up authority, various statements to the press and other U.S. interference with what he regarded as a small nation that posed no threat. He called our restrictions on Allied shipping a blockade against trade and a violation of international law. All this could only lead to great misfortunes for mankind, he said, for his government could not sit by and observe this situation idly when aggression was planned and a threat of war was looming.

The President made no response, and Gromyko then read from his notes:

> As to Soviet assistance to Cuba, I have been instructed to make it clear, as the Soviet Government has already done, that such assistance pursued solely the purpose of contributing to the defense capabilities of Cuba and to the development of its peaceful economy . . . training by Soviet specialists of Cuban nationals in handling defensive armaments

was by no means offensive. If it were otherwise, the Soviet Government would have never become involved in rendering such assistance.

Kennedy remained impassive, neither agreeing nor disagreeing with Gromyko's claim. He gave no sign of tension or anger. But to avoid misleading his adversary, he sent for and read aloud his September warning against offensive missiles in Cuba. Gromyko "must have wondered why I was reading it," he said later. "But he did not respond." . . .

In our earlier sessions that day the President had requested a 9 P.M. conference at the White House. While we had been meeting for only three days (that seemed like thirty), time was running out. Massive U.S. military movements had thus far been explained by long-planned Naval exercises in the Caribbean and an earlier announced build-up in Castro's air force. But the secret would soon be out, said the President, and the missiles would soon be operational.

The blockade course was now advocated by a majority. We were prepared to present the full range of choices and questions to the President. . . .

In the Oval Room on the second floor of the Mansion, the alternatives were discussed. Both the case for the blockade and the case for simply living with this threat were presented. The President had already moved from the air-strike to the blockade camp. He liked the idea of leaving Khrushchev a way out, of beginning at a low level that could then be stepped up; and the other choices had too many insuperable difficulties. Blockade, he indicated, was his tentative decision. . . .

. . . Yet it was true that the blockade approach remained somewhat nebulous, and I agreed to write the first rough draft of a blockade speech as a means of focusing on specifics.

But back in my office, the original difficulties with the blockade route stared me in the face: How should we relate it to the missiles? How would it help get them out? What would we do if they became operational? What should we say about our surveillance, about communicating with Khrushchev? I returned to the group late that afternoon with these questions instead of a speech; and as the concrete answers were provided in our discussions, the final shape of the President's policy began to take form. It was in a sense an amalgam of the blockade—air-strike routes; and a much stronger, more satisfied consensus formed behind it. Originally I was to have drafted an air-strike speech as well, but that was now abandoned.

Friday night—fortified by my first hot meal in days, sent in a covered dish by a Washington matron to whom I appealed for help—I worked until 3 A.M. on the draft speech. Among the texts I read for background were the speeches of Wilson and Roosevelt declaring World Wars I and II. At 9 A.M. Saturday morning my draft was reviewed, amended and generally approved—and, a little after 10 A.M. our time, the President was called back to Washington. . . .

The President's helicopter landed on the South Lawn a little after 1:30. After he had read the draft speech, we chatted in a relaxed fashion in his office before the decisive meeting scheduled for 2:30. I gave him my view of the key arguments: air strike no—because it could not be surgical but would lead to invasion, because the world would neither understand nor forget an attack without warning and because Khrushchev could out-maneuver any form of warning; and blockade yes—because it was a flexible, less aggressive beginning, least likely to precipitate war and most likely to cause the Soviets to back down.

Our meeting at 2:30 P.M. was held once again in the Oval Room up-stairs. For the first time we were convened formally as the 505th meeting of the National Security Council. We arrived at different gates at different times to dampen the now growing suspicion among the press. The President asked John McCone to lead off with the latest photographic and other intelligence. Then the full ramifications of the two basic tracks were set before the President: either to begin with a blockade and move up from there as necessary or to begin with a full air strike moving in all likelihood to an invasion. The spokesman for the blockade emphasized that a "cost" would be incurred for whatever action we took, a cost in terms of Com-munist retaliation. The blockade route, he said, appeared most likely to secure our limited objective—the removal of the missiles—at the lowest cost. Another member presented the case for an air strike leading to Castro's overthrow as the most direct and effective means of removing the problem.

At the conclusion of the presentations there was a brief, awkward silence. It was the most difficult and dangerous decision any President could make, and only he could make it. No one else bore his burdens or had his perspec-tive. Then Gilpatric, who was normally a man of few words in meetings with the President when the Defense Secretary was present, spoke up. "Essentially, Mr. President," he said, "this is a choice between limited action and unlimited action; and most of us think that it's better to start with limited action."

The President nodded his agreement. Before his decision became final, he wanted to talk directly with the Air Force Tactical Bombing Command to make certain that the truly limited air strike was not feasible. But he wanted to start with limited action, he said, and a blockade was the place to start. . . .

On Sunday morning . . . the President met with Tactical Air Command Chief Walter Sweeney, Jr. and a few others (the Attorney General driving in directly from Virginia still in his riding togs). Told there was no way of making certain all the missiles would be removed by an air attack, Kennedy confirmed that the air strike was out and the blockade was on. . . .

News leaks and inquiries for the first time were a growing problem, as crisis was in the air. The movement of troops, planes and ships to Florida and the Caribbean, the unavailability of high officials, the summoning of Congressional leaders, the Saturday night and Sunday activity, the cancellation of the Presidential and Vice Presidential campaign trips and the necessity of informing a much larger circle of officials meant that our cherished hours of secrecy were numbered. Washington and New York newspapers were already speculating. Publishers were asked not to disclose anything without checking. . . . The direct questions of other reporters were avoided, evaded or answered incorrectly by officials who did not know the correct answers; and a few outright falsehoods were told to keep our knowledge from the Communists.

It was "the best kept secret in government history," said the President, amazed as well as pleased. . . .

At 2:30 that Sunday afternoon, October 21, the President met with the NSC once again. He reviewed the State Department's drafts of instructions to embassies and Presidential letters to allies, all to be sent out in code that night and held for delivery. He reviewed the approaches to the OAS and UN, and agreed that UN supervision and inspection of the missiles' removal would be requested. He asked Navy Chief of Staff George W. Anderson, Jr., to describe plans and procedures for the blockade. First, said the Admiral, each approaching ship would be signaled to stop for boarding and inspection. Then, if no satisfactory response was forthcoming, a shot would be fired across her bow. Finally, if there was still no satisfactory response, a shot would be fired into her rudder to cripple but not to sink. "You're certain that can be done?" asked the President with a wry smile. "Yes, sir!" responded the Admiral. . . .

Most of that meeting was spent in a page-by-page review of the latest speech draft. Among the issues raised at that meeting, and in my earlier and later meetings with the President, were the following:

1. Should the latest enlarged photographs be shown by the President on TV? No, he decided—both because the average viewer could discern too little for it to be intelligible and because the mere presence of pictures might contribute to panic. The desire to avoid panic also caused the President to delete all references to the missiles' megatonnage as compared with Hiroshima, and to speak of their capability of "striking," instead of "wiping out," certain cities. But to increase hemispheric unity, he did include a reference to the Canadian and Latin-American areas within their target range.

2. Should the speech admit our secret surveillance by U-2 planes, internationally sensitive since 1960 and an illegal violation of Cuban air space? Yes—deciding to make a virtue out of necessity, the President listed increased surveillance as an announced part of his response, justifying it on the basis of an earlier OAS communiqué against secret military prepara-

tions in the hemisphere, adding that "further action will be justified" if the missiles remain, and hinting at the nature of that action by urging a consideration of the hazards "in the interest of both the Cuban people and the Soviet technicians *at the sites.*"

3. Would he institute the blockade without OAS approval? Yes, if we could not get it, because our national security was directly involved. But hoping to obtain OAS endorsement, he deliberately obscured this question in the speech by a call for unspecified OAS action and an announcement of the blockade and other steps "in the defense of our own security and of the entire Western Hemisphere."

4. Should his speech anticipate, and try to forestall, a retaliatory blockade around Berlin? Yes—both by emphasizing that we were not "denying the necessities of life as the Soviets attempted to do in their Berlin blockade of 1948" and by warning that we would resist "any hostile move anywhere in the world against the safety and freedom of peoples to whom we are committed—including in particular the brave people of West Berlin."

5. What should he say about diplomatic action? Nothing that would tie our hands, anything that would strengthen our stand. Saturday's discussion, which obtained some additional State Department support and refinement over the weekend, was a major help here. The President deleted from my original draft a call for a summit meeting, preferring to state simply that we were prepared to present our case.

> and our own proposals for a peaceful world at any time ... in the United Nations or in any other meeting that could be useful, without limiting our freedom of action.... I call upon Chairman Khrushchev ... to join in an historic effort to end the perilous arms race and to transform the history of man.... We have in the past ... proposed the elimination of all arms and military bases.... We are prepared to discuss ... the possibilities of a genuinely independent Cuba.

... Kennedy struck from the speech any hint that the removal of Castro was his true aim. He did not talk of total victory or unconditional surrender, simply of the precisely defined objective of removing a specific provocation. In the same vein, he deleted references to his notification of the Soviets, to the treatment awaiting any ships attempting to run the blockade and to predictions of the blockade's effect on Castro, believing that making these matters public was inconsistent with his desire not to force Khrushchev's hand. Lesser action items proposed by the State Department—specifically, a Caribbean Security Conference and further shipping restrictions—he deleted as too weak-sounding and insignificant for a speech about nuclear war. There was no mistaking that central subject, underlined most specifically in the words: *"It shall be the policy of this nation to regard any nuclear missile launched from Cuba against any nation in the Western Hemisphere*

*as an attack by the Soviet Union on the United States, requiring a full re-
taliatory response upon the Soviet Union."*

Throughout Sunday evening and most of Monday, minor changes in the
text were made, each one being rushed to USIA translators and to the State
Department for transmission to our embassies. The whole nation knew on
Monday that a crisis was at hand—particularly after Salinger's announcement at noon that the President had obtained 7 P.M. network time for a
speech of the "highest national urgency." Crowds and pickets gathered outside the White House, reporters inside. I refused all calls from newsmen,
answering the telephoned questions of only one powerful Congressman
("Is it serious?" "Yes") and Ted Kennedy ("Should I give my campaign
dinner speech on Cuba?" "No"). I informed Mike Feldman and Lee
White in my office by giving them copies of the speech. "It's a shame,"
cracked White with heavy irony, gazing out the window. "They've just
finished sanding that Executive Office Building." . . .

The President's speech, now completed, served as the basic briefing document in all capitals of the world and in a series of ambassadorial meetings
in the State Department. Photographs were provided as well. Soviet Ambassador Dobrynin was invited to Rusk's office at 6 P.M. Ambassador
Kohler delivered the same message in Moscow a little later. U.S. custodians
of nuclear weapons in Turkey and Italy were instructed to take extraordinary precautions to make certain that such weapons were fired only upon
Presidential authorization. Latin-American governments were told of possible disorders and the availability of riot control equipment. Our own missions were instructed to tape their windows. Many State, Defense and
White House officers went on a twenty-four-hour watch, with cots in offices
and personnel working in shifts. . . .

. . . [At 7 P.M.] the most serious speech in his life was on the air:

> Good evening, my fellow citizens:
> This government, as promised, has maintained the closest surveillance
> of the Soviet military build-up on the island of Cuba. Within the past
> week, unmistakable evidence has established the fact that a series of
> offensive missile sites is now in preparation on that imprisoned island.
> The purpose of these bases can be none other than to provide a nuclear
> strike capability against the Western Hemisphere. . . .
> This urgent transformation of Cuba into an important strategic base,
> by the presence of these large, long-range and clearly offensive weapons
> of sudden mass destruction, constitutes an explicit threat to the peace
> and security of all the Americas. . . .
> We will not prematurely or unnecessarily risk the costs of world-wide
> nuclear war in which even the fruits of victory would be ashes in our
> mouth, but neither will we shrink from that risk at any time it must be
> faced.

He went on to outline—in careful language which would guide us all week—the initial steps to be taken, emphasizing the word "initial": quarantine, surveillance of the build-up, action if it continued, our response to any use of these missiles, the reinforcement of Guantánamo, OAS and UN action and an appeal to Khrushchev and the Cuban people. . . .

The crisis had officially begun. Some Americans reacted with panic, most with pride. . . .

The Presidency was never lonelier than when faced with its first nuclear confrontation. John Kennedy never lost sight of what either war or surrender would do to the whole human race. His UN mission was preparing for a negotiated peace and his Joint Chiefs of Staff were preparing for war, and he intended to keep both on rein. He was determined, despite divided counsel and conflicting pressures, to take all necessary action and no unnecessary action. He could not afford to be hasty or hesitant, reckless or afraid. The odds that the Soviets would go all the way to war, he later said, seemed to him then "somewhere between one out of three and even." . . .

Quarantine

The Alliance held. Macmillan phoned his support, although expressing his interest in a summit talk on disarmament and an interim suspension of activity on both sides. Adenauer, Brandt and the people of West Berlin did not flinch or complain. Despite some wavering by Canada, the NATO Council and De Gaulle pledged their backing after Acheson's briefings, attaching neither reservations nor complaints on grounds of no advance consultation, and ignoring the pickets and protests flooding London and other capitals. The British press, even more than that of the French and some neutrals, was largely negative. Some questioned whether missiles were really there, and at the suggestion of Ambassador Ormsby-Gore, with whom he reviewed the pictures after Tuesday's dinner, the President released the best photographs of the evidence. Pacifist complaints, interestingly enough, were all directed at the American quarantine, with no word about the Soviet missile deception. Philosopher Bertrand Russell, for example, wired Kennedy: "Your action desperate . . . no conceivable justification," while wiring Khrushchev: "Your continued forbearance is our great hope."

But of far greater importance to Kennedy than Lord Russell was the action taken by the twenty members of the OAS in immediately and unanimously adopting a broad authorizing resolution. . . .

In the UN, in Washington and in the foreign embassies, support for the U.S. position was surprisingly strong. This was due in part to the shock of Soviet perfidy, and their futile attempts to deny the photographic evidence of attempted nuclear blackmail. It was due in part to world-wide recognition that this was an East-West nuclear confrontation, not a U.S. quarrel with

Cuba. It was due in part to the President's choice of a low level of force at the outset and to his forceful but restrained approach. It was due, finally, to the excellent presentations made in the UN by Ambassador Stevenson, with Schlesinger as an emergency aide and John McCloy to lend bipartisan stature.

At 4 P.M. Tuesday, October 23, and again on Thursday, October 25, flanked by photo interpreters and intelligence analysts, Stevenson made a forceful presentation to the UN Security Council. Zorin had charged that the CIA had manufactured the evidence. Then let a UN team inspect the sites, said Stevenson.

> STEVENSON: All right, sir, let me ask you one simple question: Do you, Ambassador Zorin, deny that the U.S.S.R. has placed and is placing medium—and intermediate—range missiles and sites in Cuba? Yes or no. Don't wait for the translation. Yes or no.
>
> ZORIN: I am not in an American courtroom, sir . . .
>
> STEVENSON: You are in the court of world opinion right now!
>
> ZORIN: . . . and therefore I do not wish to answer a question that is put to me in the fashion that a prosecutor does. In due course, sir, you will have your reply.
>
> STEVENSON: I am prepared to wait for my answer until Hell freezes over, if that's your decision.

. . . [In the meantime President Kennedy's] attention was focused on the Navy as never before. The "quarantine" was a new form of reprisal under international law, an act of national and collective self-defense against an act of aggression under the UN and OAS charters and under the Rio Treaty of 1947. Its legality, much strengthened by the OAS endorsement, had been carefully worked out. A "Proclamation of Interdiction of the Delivery of Offensive Weapons to Cuba" was discussed in our two Executive Committee meetings on the first day after the President's speech—at 10 A.M. and 6 P.M. Tuesday—and it was then immediately issued, effective the next day. The proclamation stressed that

> force shall not be used except in case of failure or refusal to comply with directions . . . after reasonable efforts have been made to communicate them to the vessel or craft, or in case of self-defense. In any case force shall be used only to the extent necessary.

Behind this "disable, don't sink" order, its graduated timing, its exclusion for the time of POL[7] (which automatically let all tankers pass) and the President's personal direction of the quarantine's operation, was his determination not to let needless incidents or reckless subordinates escalate so

---

[7] POL means a blockade directed against all tankers that would carry Petroleum-Oil-Lubricants to Cuba. Such a blockade could cause a collapse of the Cuban economy.——Ed.

dangerous and delicate a crisis beyond control. He had learned at the Bay of Pigs that the momentum of events and enthusiasts could take issues of peace and war out of his own hands. Naval communications permitted this operation, unlike the Bay of Pigs situation, to be run directly out of his office and the Pentagon. . . .

The big question was the big ocean. To us, Khrushchev appeared—in a harsh but rambling Soviet Government statement Tuesday morning rejecting the quarantine as "piracy," in two private letters to Kennedy Tuesday morning and Wednesday evening (both answered within hours after their receipt with firm restatements of our position) and in his answers to appeals from Bertrand Russell and Acting Secretary General U Thant—to have been caught off balance, to be maneuvering, to be seeking a consensus among the top Kremlin rulers, uncertain whether to admit that the missiles were there in view of the widespread denunciations of that action. The Soviets, it seemed, had counted on surprising us, on disunity in the West and on a sufficient fear of war in the United States to prevent any military response. Having proven them wrong on those counts, we wondered whether their inconsistent positions reflected a possible internal struggle. . . .

. . . [E]ighteen Soviet dry cargo ships [were now] heading toward the quarantine . . . Five of these ships with large hatches were being watched with special care. The Executive Committee, in session most of each day, soon knew every Soviet ship by name and which of them were suspected of carrying armaments. Tuesday night, as the ships came on, the tension built. Robert Kennedy was dispatched that night to find out from the Soviet Ambassador whether any instructions had been issued to the Soviet ship captains. He learned nothing. "You fellows who thought the blockade was the most peaceful answer may find out differently pretty soon," said the President. At our Wednesday morning meeting, held just as the quarantine went into effect, some half-dozen Soviet submarines were reported to have joined these ships. Orders were prepared to sink any subs interfering with the quarantine. In the midst of the same meeting, more news arrived. The Soviet ships nearest Cuba had apparently stopped or altered their course. A feeling of relief went round the table.

The prospects of confrontation at sea were not, however, by any means over. Soviet intentions were not yet clear. The quarantine had not yet been tested. . . . Khrushchev summoned a visiting American businessman to tell him that Kennedy should agree to a summit, that conflict in the Caribbean could lead to nuclear war (including the use of the offensive missiles he now admitted were in Cuba) and that Soviet submarines would sink any American vessel forcing a Soviet ship to stop.

At dawn Thursday a Soviet tanker was hailed and, on the instructions of the President—who thought it possible that the tanker had not yet received its instructions from Moscow—passed through the barrier like all non-suspicious tankers after merely identifying itself. So was an East German passenger ship. At dawn Friday an American-made, Panama-owned, Greek-manned, Lebanese-registered freighter under charter to the Soviet Union was halted and boarded—after the Navy obtained the President's authorization. His preference had been not to intercept any Soviet ships until necessary, but to have a nonbloc ship under Soviet charter boarded to show we meant business. Inspected by an unarmed boarding party and found to be carrying only trucks and truck parts, the freighter was allowed to pass through.[8]

The real problem was not Lebanese freighters and Soviet tankers but the Soviet cargo ships and their submarine escorts. They would have to be stopped Friday, said the President, if U Thant's proposals had not altered their course by then. The Navy was eager to go far out into the ocean to intercept the key Soviet ships. The President, backed by McNamara and Ormsby-Gore and watching the tracking of each ship on a large board in the White House "Situation Room," insisted that Khrushchev be given all possible time to make and communicate an uncomfortable decision to his ships. In a sharp clash with the Navy, he made certain his will prevailed.

Gradually, rather than dramatically, the good news came in, mixed, in fact, with the "bad" news recounted above. Sixteen of the eighteen Russian ships, including all five with large hatches, were reported Wednesday to have stopped—then to be lying dead in the water or moving in uncertain circles— and, finally, Thursday and Friday to have turned around. "That's nice," observed one member of our group. "The Soviets are reacting to us for a change." U.S. planes followed them all the way back to Soviet ports. A minimum of force had obtained a maximum gain. The value of conventional strength in the nuclear age had been underlined as never before. The quarantine, speculated the President later, "had much more power than we first thought it did because, I think, the Soviet Union was very reluctant to have us stop ships which carried . . . highly secret and sensitive material." The Soviet military, he reasoned, long obsessed with secrecy, could not risk letting their missiles, warheads and electronic equipment fall into our hands.

Peril Point

The dangers of a naval confrontation had not ended, but at least they had temporarily eased. The dangers posed by the missiles in Cuba,

---

[8] One of the boarding ships, the President learned afterward, was the U.S. destroyer *Joseph P. Kennedy, Jr.* About the same time, a replica of the PT-109—then in Florida for a film story—was commandeered in a side incident involving Cuban exiles, and the President felt these coincidences would never be believed.

however, were increasing. More of the MRBMs—now hastily camouflaged —were becoming operational, reported McCone at the briefings which began each of our morning meetings. Work was going ahead full speed. All the MRBMs would be operational by the end of the week, with the IRBMs to be ready a month or so later. Throughout Thursday and Friday the President and Executive Committee pondered new ways of stepping up the political, economic and military pressure on the Soviets, including:

1. Tightening the blockade. The addition of missile fuel to the proscribed list already provided a reason to stop tankers, if desired. The next step would be POL, then all commodities other than food and medicine.

2. Increased low-level flights. These would provide not only improved reconnaissance but also a means of harassing the Soviets and humiliating Castro, particularly if nighttime flights with flares were added. The fear of more serious reprisal had stopped Cuban as well as Soviet attempts to down these planes. Their daily operations, moreover, would make more feasible a surprise air strike.

3. Action inside Cuba. The President authorized a leaflet drop directed at the people of Cuba, asked the USIA to prepare it, personally cleared its text and pictures (low-level photographs of the missile sites), ordered it to go ahead and then held it up temporarily. Meanwhile ways of reaching Castro directly were explored once again.

4. Air strike.

5. Invasion. Those who had favored the last two courses the previous week now renewed their advocacy.

The President refused to rush. Preparations for an invasion as well as other military contingencies were still under way. Soviet ships had turned back. Talks were going on at the U.N. But in a message to U Thant, in a White House statement and in a State Department announcement, the continued work on the missile sites was noted in the gravest tones.

The State Department press officer, in making this announcement Friday noon, went beyond the White House position by referring reporters to that passage in the President's Monday night speech which had said "further action will be justified" if work on the missiles continued. This remark, accompanied by some imprecise Congressional and press speculation, immediately touched off headlines that an invasion or air strike was imminent. For the first time, the President lost his temper. He called the Secretary of State, then the Assistant Secretary, then the press officer, Lincoln White, his voice rising and his language intensifying with each call. This was going to be a prolonged struggle, he argued, requiring caution, patience and as little public pressure on him as possible.

But in the next twenty-four hours he was to joke that White's error might have had a helpful effect. A new Khrushchev-to-Kennedy letter was received at the State Department Friday evening, October 26—long, meandering, full of polemics but in essence appearing to contain the germ of a reasonable settlement: inasmuch as his missiles were there only to defend Cuba against invasion, he would withdraw the missiles under UN inspection if the U.S. agreed not to invade. Similar talk came the same day in the UN from Zorin to U Thant and, through a highly informal channel, from Counselor of the Soviet Embassy in Washington Aleksander Fomin to the ABC-TV correspondent covering the State Department, John Scali. In Khrushchev's letter the offer was a bit vague. It seemed to vary from one paragraph to the next, and was accompanied by the usual threats and denunciations. Nevertheless it was with high hopes that the Executive Committee convened Saturday morning, October 27, to draft a reply.

In the course of that meeting our hopes quickly faded. A new Khrushchev letter came in, this time public, making no mention of the private correspondence but raising the ante: the Jupiter missiles in Turkey must be removed in exchange. In addition, we learned, Fomin and Zorin were talking about extending the UN inspection to U.S. bases. Had Khrushchev's hard-liners once again taken the lead, we speculated, or had the appearance of this same swap proposal in Washington and London newspapers encouraged the Soviets to believe we would weaken under pressure? Many Western as well as neutral leaders were, in fact, quick to endorse the new Soviet position. Still another possibility was that the second, public proposal had actually been written first.[9]

More bad news followed. A new Soviet ship was reported approaching the quarantine zone. The latest photographs showed no indications that missile site work was being held up awaiting our reply to the Friday letter. On the contrary, permanent and expensive installations of nuclear warhead storage bunkers and troop barracks were going ahead rapidly. Khrushchev's letter, said some, was designed merely to delay and deceive us until the missile installations were complete. Then came the worst news: the first shooting and fatality of the crisis, ground fire on two low-flying reconnaissance planes and the downing of a high-flying U-2 by a Soviet-operated SAM. The dead pilot, Major Rudolf Anderson, Jr., had flown the mission thirteen days earlier which first discovered the missiles.

We had talked earlier in the week of what response this nation would make should an unarmed U.S. plane—on a publicly announced mission of surveillance—be shot down, and had decided tentatively on a single retaliatory strike against a SAM site, then knocking them all out if attacks

---

[9] While the answer to this and all other questions about internal Soviet thinking and actions will probably never be known with any certainty, the far greater length of time required to send a private, coded message made this possibility highly doubtful.

continued. Now the time had come to implement that policy, killing Soviets in the process, probably flushing Castro's planes, possibly leading to a full air strike, an invasion or further Soviet ripostes. But the President had been careful not to give blanket authority to carry out this decision to the Air Force in advance; and he preferred not to give it now. He wanted to wait one more day—for more information on what happened to our planes and for Khrushchev's final negotiating position. He called off the flare-drop flight scheduled for that night (each reconnaissance flight had to be approved individually by the President each day), because of the danger that the flares might be taken for air-to-ground fire from the planes. But he approved an announcement that all necessary measures would be taken "to insure that such missions are effective and protected," authorized fighter escorts, and ordered the fighters to respond to any MIG attack. He also urged State and Defense officials to prepare for the worst in Berlin, Turkey and Iran, where, in the face of unexpected Allied unity, the expected Soviet counterthrust had not yet occurred.

That same day, to make matters worse, an American U-2 plane over Alaska had encountered navigational difficulties and flown deep into Soviet territory, bringing up a bevy of Soviet fighters but no fire, before regaining its course. The President decided to ignore this incident unless the Soviets publicized it; but he wondered if Khrushchev would speculate that we were surveying targets for a pre-emptive nuclear strike. (Khrushchev did, in fact, write later of the danger of such a plane, "which might have been taken for a nuclear bomber . . . intruding when everything has been put into combat readiness.")

Everything was in combat readiness on both sides. The conventional and the nuclear forces of the United States were alerted world-wide. Both air-strike planes and the largest invasion force mounted since World War II were massed in Florida. Our little group seated around the Cabinet table in continuous session that Saturday felt nuclear war to be closer on that day than at any time in the nuclear age. If the Soviet ship continued coming, if the SAMs continued firing, if the missile crews continued working and if Khrushchev continued insisting on concessions with a gun at our head, then —we all believed—the Soviets must want a war and war would be unavoidable.

The President had no intention of destroying the Alliance by backing down, but he thought it all the more imperative that our position be absolutely clear. He decided to treat the latest Khrushchev message as propaganda and to concentrate on the Friday night letter. . . .

The most attention was given to Khrushchev's letter of the previous night. Under the President's direction, our group worked all day on draft replies. Fatigue and disagreement over the right course caused more wrangling and irritability than usual. Finally the President asked the Attorney General and me to serve as a drafting committee of two to pull together a final version. He also asked me to clear the text with Stevenson, who had skillfully advanced parallel talks at the UN. The final draft of his reply—which confined itself to the proposals made in Khrushchev's Friday letter, ignoring the Fomin and Zorin talks and any specific reference to Turkish bases—read into the Chairman's letter everything we wanted. Stevenson feared it might be too stiff. But with two minor amendments acceptable to the President, I obtained Stevenson's clearance; and the President, in the interests of both speed and psychology, released the letter publicly as it was being transmitted to Moscow shortly after 8 P.M.

> The first thing that needs to be done . . . is for work to cease on offensive missile bases in Cuba and for all weapons systems in Cuba capable of offensive use to be rendered inoperable, under effective United Nations arrangements. [Note that, instead of arguing with Mr. K. over whether his missiles and planes were intended to be offensive, he insisted on action against those "capable of offensive use."]
> As I read your letter, the key elements of your proposals—which seem generally acceptable as I understand them—are as follows:
> 1. You would agree to remove these weapons systems from Cuba under appropriate United Nations observation and supervision; and undertake, with suitable safeguards, to halt the further introduction of such weapons systems into Cuba.
> 2. We, on our part, would agree—upon the establishment of adequate arrangements through the United Nations to ensure the carrying out and continuation of these commitments—(a) to remove promptly the quarantine measures now in effect and (b) to give assurances against an invasion of Cuba. [Note that, unlike the action to be undertaken by Khrushchev, ours was conditional upon UN arrangements.]
> . . . the first ingredient, let me emphasize . . . is the cessation of work on missile sites in Cuba and measures to render such weapons inoperable, under effective international guarantees. The continuation of this threat, or a prolonging of this discussion concerning Cuba by linking these problems to the broader questions of European and world security, would surely lead to an intensification of the Cuban crisis and a grave risk to the peace of the world.

At the private request of the President, a copy of the letter was delivered to the Soviet Ambassador by Robert Kennedy with a strong verbal message: The point of escalation was at hand; the United States could proceed toward peace and disarmament, or, as the Attorney General later described it, we could take "strong and overwhelming retaliatory action . . . unless [the President] received immediate notice that the missiles would be withdrawn." That message was conveyed to Moscow.

Meanwhile the Executive Committee was somewhat heatedly discussing plans for the next step. Twenty-four Air Force Reserve troop carrier squadrons were called up. Special messages to NATO, De Gaulle and Adenauer outlined the critical stage we had reached. The POL blockade, air-strike and invasion advocates differed over what to do when. An invasion, it was observed, might turn out differently than planned if the overground rockets (FROGs) spotted by our planes in the Soviet armored division now in Cuba were already equipped with nuclear warheads. In front of the White House, more than a thousand pickets mustered, some pleading for peace, some for war, one simply calling JFK a traitor.

The President would not, in my judgment, have moved immediately to either an air strike or an invasion; but the pressures for such a move on the following Tuesday were rapidly and irresistibly growing, strongly supported by a minority in our group and increasingly necessitated by a deterioration in the situation. The downing of our plane could not be ignored. Neither could the approaching ship, or the continuing work on the missile sites, or the Soviet SAMs. We stayed in session all day Saturday, and finally, shortly after 8 P.M., noting rising tempers and irritability, the President recessed the meeting for a one-hour dinner break. Pressure and fatigue, he later noted privately, might have broken the group's steady demeanor in another twenty-four or forty-eight hours. At dinner in the White House staff "mess," the Vice President, Treasury Secretary Dillon and I talked of entirely different subjects. The meeting at 9 P.M. was shorter, cooler and quieter; and with the knowledge that our meeting the next morning at 10 A.M. could be decisive—one way or the other—we adjourned for the night.

Success

Upon awakening Sunday morning, October 28, I turned on the news on my bedside radio, as I had each morning during the week. In the course of the 9 A.M. newscast a special bulletin came in from Moscow. It was a new letter from Khrushchev, his fifth since Tuesday, sent publicly in the interest of speed. Kennedy's terms were being accepted. The missiles were being withdrawn. Inspection would be permitted. The confrontation was over.

Hardly able to believe it, I reached Bundy at the White House. It was true. He had just called the President, who took the news with "tremendous satisfaction" and asked to see the message on his way to Mass. Our meeting was postponed from 10 to 11 A.M. It was a beautiful Sunday morning in Washington in every way.

With deep feelings of relief and exhilaration, we gathered in the Cabinet Room at eleven, our thirteenth consecutive day of close collaboration. Just as missiles are incomparably faster than all their predecessors, so this world-wide crisis had ended incredibly faster than all its predecessors. The talk preceding the meeting was boisterous. "What is Castro saying now?" chortled someone. Robert McNamara said he had risen early that morning to draw up a list of "steps to take short of invasion." When he heard the news, said John McCone, "I could hardly believe my ears." Waiting for the President to come in, we speculated about what would have happened

- if Kennedy had chosen the air strike over the blockade . . .
- if the OAS and other Allies had not supported us . . .
- if both our conventional and our nuclear forces had not been strengthened over the past twenty-one months . . .
- if it were not for the combined genius and courage that produced U-2 photographs and their interpretations . . .
- if a blockade had been instituted before we could prove Soviet duplicity and offensive weapons . . .
- if Kennedy and Khrushchev had not been accustomed to communicating directly with each other and had not left that channel open . . .
- if the President's speech of October 22 had not taken Khrushchev by surprise . . .
- if John F. Kennedy had not been President of the United States.

John F. Kennedy entered and we all stood up. He had, as Harold Macmillan would later say, earned his place in history by this one act alone. He had been engaged in a personal as well as national contest for world leadership and he had won. He had reassured those nations fearing we would use too much strength and those fearing we would use none at all. Cuba had been the site of his greatest failure and now of his greatest success. The hard lessons of the first Cuban crisis were applied in his steady handling of the second with a carefully measured combination of defense, diplomacy and dialogue. Yet he walked in and began the meeting without a trace of excitement or even exultation.

Earlier in his office—told by Bundy and Kaysen that his simultaneous plea to India and Pakistan to resolve their differences over Kashmir in view of the Chinese attack would surely be heeded, now that he looked "ten feet tall"—he had evenly replied: "That will wear off in about a week, and everyone will be back to thinking only of their own interests."

Displaying the same caution and precision with which he had determined for thirteen days exactly how much pressure to apply, he quickly and quietly organized the machinery to work for a UN inspection and reconnaissance effort. He called off the Sunday overflights and ordered the Navy to avoid halting any ships on that day. (The one ship previously approaching had stopped.) He asked that precautions be taken to prevent Cuban exile units from upsetting the agreement through one of their publicity-seeking raids. He laid down the line we were all to follow—no boasting, no gloating, not even a claim of victory. We had won by enabling Khrushchev to avoid complete humiliation—we should not humiliate him now. If Khrushchev wanted to boast that he had won a major concession and proved his peaceful manner, that was the loser's prerogative.

20 / Missiles in the Caribbean: A Postscript

Nikita S. Khrushchev
Charles Burton Marshall
Peking Review
The New York Times
Robert F. Kennedy

The preceding analysis (Section 19), written by a participant-observer, close to President Kennedy, was primarily included to illustrate the need and value of accurate information for the purpose of appropriate response and action; the essay concluded with the question of what would have been the fate of the world had not the U-2 photographs been illegally taken and had they not provided an irrefutable proof of duplicity of the Soviet leadership beyond any doubt to the whole world. The second reason for inclusion was to demonstrate the prevalence of uncertainty in a situation when Kennedy and his advisers tried to answer not only the question: What would we do if we were the Soviet policy-makers? but also "What would we do if we were they wondering what they would do if they were we wondering. . . . ?"[10] As the essay indicated all the top advisers at the White House constantly changed their views as to what was the best way to protect the United States' national interest in the light of the assumed Soviet interests and possible actions. We may assume that similar uncertainties prevailed at the Kremlin at the time when both superpowers stood at the nuclear threshold.

Sorensen's essay (Selection 19) represents also a rich source of lessons and questions relevant to practically all the problems and dilemmas raised in this book. In particular the following points are worthy of consideration:

[10] This is a paraphrase of an example given by Thomas C. Schelling in his article on the possibility to coordinate behavior among nations without communication (Selection 45).

1. *Impact of the past:* Kennedy disbelieved, at first, the reports on the Soviet installation of missiles in Cuba partly because these reports came from Cuban exile groups. Kennedy's cautiousness was an evident remnant of the Bay of Pigs disaster, based to some extent on some wishful thinking on the part of the Cuban exiles. Yet, in the missile crisis, their reports were correct. Did the past failure in Cuba make Kennedy more cautious first but then more inclined to gamble in an effort to compensate for the Bay of Pigs?

2. *The probability of nuclear war* was considered by some advisers to be one-to-one, three-to-one, or nine-to-one. Even the nine-to-one chance is terrifying.

3. *The role of personalities* and their particular reactions to events and information: Khrushchev might have made his first mistake by introducing offensive weapons into Cuba in a period that he deemed was marked by the American preoccupation with internal politics (November elections); would he make a second mistake by believing that Kennedy would be again "quarter-hearted" as he had been at the Bay of Pigs? When the aged American poet Robert Frost visited Khrushchev in September, he was told by the Soviet Premier that democracies (Kennedy?) were "too liberal to fight." Sorensen concluded his analysis with a question: What would have been the fate of the world had not John F. Kennedy been President of the United States? A Russian Sorensen might have asked a similar question with reference to Khrushchev.

4. *Art of diplomacy and deceit:* Kennedy made the extraordinary move to disregard a harsh Soviet note that followed a more conciliatory one and replied in a matching tone to the first one, although seemingly rescinded by the second one. Both sides also withheld information from each other since each planned to catch the other by surprise.

5. *The role of chance:* the CIA Director John McCone made a very early and correct estimate that the defensive Soviet missiles in Cuba were preparatory for the introduction of the offensive long-range ones *but* "his absence prevented his views from reaching the President"—the CIA Director was away on his honeymoon.

6. *The nature and durability of Kennedy's success:* Should the President's achievement be measured in terms of an improved *image* of the American power, determination, and diplomatic skill (certainly not a minor point in the international contest of perceptions) or in terms of a *materially improved security* which the Soviet missiles in Cuba were allegedly about to jeopardize? According to Sorensen, Kennedy was less concerned with the missiles' military implications than with their political impact on the delicate balance between Russia and the United States. In view of all the other missiles with their megaton warheads the Soviets were capable of unleashing upon the United States, the Cuban missiles alone did not substantially alter the strategic balance *in fact;* but, as Sorensen noted, "that balance would have been substantially altered *in appearance;* and in matters of national will and world leadership," as the President said later, "such appearances contribute to reality." This seems to be a practical confirmation of the basic theorem according to which situations defined as real are real in their consequences.

In 1970s the Soviet decision to build a submarine base on the southern coast of Cuba at Cienfuegos reopened most of the issues that had been present in the 1962 crisis and seemed to have been successfully settled by Kennedy. In the fall of 1970 Washington issued several public and diplomatic warnings that the new Soviet base and its link with nuclear submarines submerged in the Caribbean would be viewed with "utmost seriousness" by the United States as a violation of the 1962 agreement by which land-based missiles were withdrawn from Cuba. One of the 1970 warnings cited President Kennedy's statement that peace would be assured only "if all offensive missiles were removed from Cuba and kept out of the Hemisphere in the future." The self-evident purpose of the new Soviet base at Cienfuegos was to repair and refuel the missile-firing submarines of the Soviet Navy (each of these submarines carries 16 ballistic missiles that are equipped with atomic warheads and can be launched from under the water at targets about 1500 miles away). Furthermore, Cienfuegos became also the base for seagoing tenders which carried much of the supporting systems for missile-firing;[11] they had been observed as being on constant move from Cienfuegos to mid-Atlantic and back. In the light of the advanced missile technology, the submarine-based missiles could be seen as fully replacing the previous Soviet plan for land-based missiles on the Cuban soil.

A few possible answers to the question on the nature and durability of Kennedy's achievement in 1962 follow.

IRBMs: Defensive, Not Offensive, Weapons

Nikita S. Khrushchev

Seeking to justify its aggressive actions, American reaction is repeating that the crisis in the Carribbean was created by Cuba herself, adding that blame rests also with the Soviet Union which shipped there rockets and IL-28 bombers.

But is this so? It is true that we carried weapons there at the request of the Cuban Government. But what motives guided us in doing that? Exclusively humanitarian motives—Cuba needed weapons as a means of containing the aggressors, and not as a means of attack. For Cuba was under a real threat of invasion. Piratical attacks were repeatedly made on her coasts, Havana was shelled, and airborne groups were dropped from planes to carry out sabotage.

A large-scale military invasion of Cuba by counterrevolutionary mer-

From a speech delivered by the former Soviet Premier before the Supreme Soviet on December 12, 1962.

[11] George H. Quester, "Missiles in Cuba, 1970," *Foreign Affairs,* 49:3 (April 1971), 493.

cenaries was launched in Cuba in April of last year. This invasion was prepared and carried out with full support on the part of the United States.

Further events have shown that the failure of the invasion did not discourage the United States imperialists in their desire to strangle Cuba. They began preparing another attack. . . .

Revolutionary Cuba was compelled to take all measures to strengthen her defense. . . .

Agreement was reached on a number of new measures, including the stationing of several score Soviet IRBM's in Cuba. These weapons were to be in the hands of Soviet military.

Indeed, had there been no threat of an invasion and had we had assurances that the United States would not invade Cuba, and would restrain its allies from this, had the United States guided itself by this course, there would have been no need for the stationing of our rockets in Cuba.

Some people pretend that the rockets were supplied by us for an attack on the United States. This, of course, is not wise reasoning. Why should we station rockets in Cuba for this purpose when we were and are able to strike from our own territory, possessing as we do the necessary number of intercontinental missiles of the required range and power?

The developments in the Caribbean confirmed that there was a threat of such aggression. By the third week of October, a large-scale buildup of U.S. naval and air forces, paratroopers and marines began in the South of the U.S., on the approaches to Cuba. The U.S. Government sent reinforcements to its naval base at Guantanamo lying on Cuban territory. Big military maneuvers were announced in the Caribbean. In the course of these "maneuvers," a landing was to be made on Vieques Island. On October 22, Kennedy's Administration announced a quarantine of Cuba. The word "quarantine" by the way, was merely a figleaf in this case. Actually it was a blockade, piracy on the high seas.

The events developed rapidly. The American command alerted all its armed forces, including the troops in Europe, and also the Sixth Fleet in the Mediterranean and the Seventh Fleet based in the area of Taiwan.

Several airborne, infantry, and armored divisions, numbering some 100,-000 men, were set aside for an attack on Cuba alone. Moreover, 183 warships with 85,000 naval personnel were moved to the shores of Cuba. The landing on Cuba was to be covered by several thousand military planes. Close to 20 per cent of all planes of the U.S. Strategic Air Command were kept in the air around the clock with atomic and hydrogen bombs on board. Reservists were called up. . . .

. . . United States militarist forces were pushing developments towards an attack on Cuba. On the morning of October 27, we received information from the Cuban comrades and from other sources which bluntly said that the invasion would be effected within the next two or three days. We assessed the messages received as a signal of utmost alarm. And this was a well founded alarm.

Immediate actions were needed to prevent an invasion of Cuba and to maintain peace. A message prompting a mutually acceptable solution was sent to the United States President. At that moment, it was not yet too late to put out the fuse of war which had already been lighted. Forwarding this message we took into consideration that the messages of the President himself expressed anxiety and the desire to find a way out of the obtaining situation. We declared that if the United States undertook not to invade Cuba and also would restrain other states allied with it from aggression against Cuba, the Soviet Union would be willing to remove from Cuba the weapons which the United States call "offensive."

The United States President replied by declaring that if the Soviet Government agreed to remove these weapons from Cuba the American Government would lift the quarantine, i.e., the blockade, and would give an assurance on renunciation of the invasion of Cuba both by the United States itself and other countries of the Western Hemisphere. The President declared quite definitely, and this is known to the whole world, that the United States will not attack Cuba and will restrain also its allies from such actions.

But we shipped our weapons to Cuba precisely for the prevention of aggression against her! That is why the Soviet Government reaffirmed its agreement to the removal of the ballistic rockets from Cuba. . . .

Which side triumphed, who won? In this respect one may say that it was sanity, the cause of peace and security of peoples, that won. Both sides displayed a sober approach and took into account that unless such steps are taken as could help overcome the dangerous development of events, a World War III might break out.

As a result of mutual concessions and compromise, an understanding was reached which made it possible to remove dangerous tension, to normalize the situation. . . .

Both sides made concessions. We withdrew ballistic rockets and agreed to withdraw IL-28 planes. This gives satisfaction to Americans. But both Cuba and the Soviet Union received satisfaction too: The American invasion of Cuba has been averted, the naval blockade lifted, the situation in the Caribbean area is returning to normalcy. People's Cuba exists, gains strength and develops under the leadership of its Revolutionary Government, its dauntless leader Fidel Castro.

A Pyrrhic Victory

Charles Burton Marshall

. . . The results could have been worse. They provide that small measure of comfort. The Government at least desisted from retracting missiles from Turkey to balance withdrawal of missiles from Cuba—a course urged by commentators and bishops out of what seemed an esthetic hankering for symmetry. Perhaps, indeed, the outcome was the best achievable in view of the lag in drawing an issue. No one will ever know for sure. [In August 1971, a Soviet journal, *Voprosy Istorii,* asserted that in 1962 Premier Khrushchev agreed to withdraw the Soviet missiles from Cuba after receiving private assurances from Robert F. Kennedy that the United States would pull its rockets out of Turkey.——Ed.]

The paeans occasioned by Soviet agreement to dismantle baffle me. Only by focusing narrowly on the issue of missile deployment can one call this a retraction on the part of the Soviet Union. Our President's avowal, on April 20 last year [1961] of resolve never to abandon Cuba to Communism has been publicly put aside—no mean feat of word-swallowing. By contrast, the Soviet pledge to shelter the Cuban regime is now redeemed. Cuba is now unmistakably a Soviet protectorate. We have negotiated on this basis with the Soviet Union. Communist power is ensconced in this hemisphere. We have in effect legitimized this. We have joined in invoking UN blessings on the arrangement.

One must await what events may disclose as to the power of precedent in the pattern—what other positions may go in a sequence of seeing a Communist regime put into power by whatever means, having the stakes raised, then guaranteeing the position in return for having the stakes lowered. As a gain, Cuba is somewhat akin to that victory at Ausculum: a few more such could be our undoing.

Soviet Appeasement

Peking Review (January 4, 1963)

. . . What we did strongly oppose, still strongly oppose, and will strongly oppose in the future is the sacrifice of another country's sovereignty in Kennedy-Khrushchev deal over Cuba without consulting Castro as a means of reaching a compromise with imperialism. A compromise of this sort can only be regarded as one hundred percent appeasement, a "Munich" pure and simple.

From p. 20 of Charles Burton Marshall, "Afterthoughts on the Cuban Blockade," *The New Republic* (November 10, 1962).

1970s: Soviet Submarines in the Caribbean

The New York Times (October 4, 1970)

For more than six months the Russians have been operating new Polaris-type ballistic-missiles submarines off the eastern coast of the United States. . . . This fact alone would have been enough to nullify whatever President John F. Kennedy gained in military strategy by going to the brink of thermonuclear war eight years ago to force the removal of land-based Russian missiles from Cuba. . . .

And aside from the questions of whether the Russians are building what amounts to a naval base at the Cuban port of Cienfuegos and whether the Nixon Administration should have made an international issue of the matter at this time, the military analysts believe the pattern of Soviet naval activity in the Caribbean clearly indicates that the Russians intend to use Cuba to serve the submarines and to keep them on station off the United States for extended periods.

Each of these nuclear submarines, termed the Yankee class by the United States Navy, carries 16 ballistic missiles whose atomic warheads can be launched from under the water at targets about 1,500 miles away.

If these submarines moved in close from their normal cruising range, far out in the Atlantic, the missiles could cover every city from the East Coast to the Kansas-Colorado line and all the population centers of eastern Canada.

From the Caribbean their range covers an expanse of cities and industry from El Paso, Texas, the Southwest, to Topeka, in the Midwest, to Pittsburgh and Washington.

Closer in, from the Gulf of Mexico, the missiles encompass most of the United States heartland in a fan that swings from the southeastern corner of California to North Dakota and to New York.

The New York Times (November 15, 1970)

The Cuban affair came to the attention of American intelligence when agents and Cuban refugees last August reported Soviet construction activity around Cienfuegos. With the visit by a Soviet naval flotilla on Sept. 9-12, United States interest sharpened.

U-2 reconnaissance planes, which have been photographing Cuba about every fortnight, took pictures about Sept. 14.

The rolls of film were processed at the U-2 base in Texas and the negatives were flown to the National Photo Interpretation Center in Washington. There positives were ready about six hours after the actual photographing of the base.

The photo interpretation center is operated jointly by the Central Intelligence Agency and the Defense Department in a former Navy building in southeast Washington. Photo analysts work in shifts around the clock, studying film. They use optical equipment for detecting camouflage and eliminating distortion. Military experts are at hand to analyze the pictures.

The Final Lesson

Robert F. Kennedy

The final lesson of the Cuban missile crisis is the importance of placing ourselves in the other country's shoes. During the crisis, President Kennedy spent more time trying to determine the effect of a particular course of action on Khrushchev or the Russians than on any other phase of what he was doing. What guided all his deliberations was an effort not to disgrace Khrushchev, not to humiliate the Soviet Union, not to have them feel they would have to escalate their response because their national security or national interests so committed them. . . .

Later, he was to say in his spech at American University in June of 1963: "Above all, while defending our own vital interests, nuclear powers must avert those confrontations which bring an adversary to the choice of either a humiliating defeat or a nuclear war." . . .

. . . The President believed from the start that the Soviet Chairman was a rational, intelligent man who, if given sufficient time and shown our determination, would alter his position. But there was always the chance of error, of mistake, miscalculation, or misunderstanding, and President Kennedy was committed to doing everything possible to lessen that chance on our side. . . .

After it was finished, he made no statement attempting to take credit for himself or for the Administration for what had occurred. He instructed all members of the Ex Comm and government that no interview should be given, no statement made, which would claim any kind of victory. He respected Khrushchev for properly determining what was in his own country's interest and what was in the interest of mankind. If it was a triumph, it was a triumph for the next generation and not for any particular government or people.

From p. 124 of Robert F. Kennedy, *Thirteen Days* (New York: W. W. Norton & Company, Inc., 1969).

9

The Role
of Ideology

If a national leader proclaims his full commitment to a particular ideology whose contents are well known, what does an observer really know about the leader's future policy initiatives and about his reactions to the actions of others?

In the 1930s many Western statesmen read and studied Hitler's book *Mein Kampf*, which spelled out his program of action and his racial theory. Some statesmen concluded that this was a work of a crackpot; others consoled themselves with the thought that Hitler could not possibly try to implement as chancellor of Germany what he had written as a militant protester in jail. But Hitler did mean every word and acted accordingly. The West was tragically wrong in its underestimate of Hitler's commitment to his dogmas as guides for action.

After World War II communist literature full of aggressive rhetorics and forecasts of the inevitable destruction of the capitalist world was subject to a similar international scrutiny and controversy. Was the communist ideology, as explained by Lenin and then by Stalin, to be a guide for postwar Soviet foreign policy? After having carefully studied Marxist-Leninist classics, and Stalin in particular, John Foster Dulles, the United States Secretary of State in the 1950s, concluded that he was "uniquely qualified to assess the meaning of Soviet policy." Citing Stalin's *Problems of Leninism* Dulles equated its importance with Hitler's *Mein Kampf* and viewed Stalin's ideological pronouncements as the best guide to Soviet foreign policy—its goals, strategy, and tactics. Selection 21 deals with Dulles' belief system and its consequences for United States policy; it should be compared with Selection 22, which contains Lenin's original analysis of imperialism as an inevitable phase and foreign policy of capitalism, and with Selection 23, which illustrates that Leninism can be interpreted by the Leninists to hold diametrically opposite meanings and so lead to inter-Leninist conflicts such as the Sino-Soviet political and ideological enmity.

In the context of this chapter we are not concerned with the question of whether a given ideology or creed—communism, nazism, socialism, fascism, Islam, Christianity, Buddhism, and so on—contains a correct or false analysis of life, history, nations, and men. Our concern is whether a national leader *believes* in his proclaimed creed or whether he only invokes it to deceive credulous masses, and in what way his interpretation of the creed will reflect his personality and/or his national environment, and to what extent he will remain guided by his dogmas when confronted with a new situation that his creed did not or could not anticipate. In particular it should be noted that no ideology, however supranational or universal it may claim to be, can escape the territorial imperatives of the present division of mankind into national compartments. Universal ideologies are implemented nationally; and they are implemented by men whose different temperament, previous experience, health, or age may lead to conflicting conclusions as to what is to be done in a concrete situation.

In the 1960s Communist China, with its leader Mao, and Communist Russia, with its leaders Brezhnev and Kosygin, accused each other of so reinterpreting and twisting their common creed that Soviet communism appeared to Peking as "social imperialism," secretly allied with American capitalist imperialism, and Chinese communism appeared to Moscow as "adventurist Trotskyism." Each invoked Lenin's authority against the other; and both might have been right and wrong in their respective incantations (Selection 23).

The preceding cautions concerning ideology as a decisive guide for political action do not suggest that ideology is an unimportant factor in politics. When a policy-maker receives and evaluates information about the international scene and relates it to his concept of his state's interests, a portion of his concept of national interest may indeed be the preservation of a creed and the political system based upon the assumptions of that creed.

Four points about the importance of ideology in the conduct of foreign policy may be noted:

1. A leader may be a "true believer" and may be inclined to place his ideological commitment above everything else. Earlier in this chapter we merely suggested that nobody can be certain whether a leader really believes in what he publicly proclaims. Thus, although he may lie, he may also tell the truth.

2. In an ideology-impregnated political system (fascist or communist)

the creed is bound to act as a screen through which the leader sifts all information about the external world. As Selection 22 illustrates, all men tend to resist contrary evidence to some extent and willingly deny much of reality in order to call their ideologically prejudiced souls their own.

3. Even if a given creed is used cynically by the leaders as "grass for the mass," it acquires some degree of reality since the leaders have to act or appear to act consistently with ideological precepts. Adhering to an official creed, in acts or appearances may sometimes simply be good politics, regardless of the leader's belief, since it assures the leader of continuing support from party zealots and the masses. A circular ideological feedback may thus develop.

4. An ideology that is not the decisive guide for political action at its home base may become a trigger of action on the part of the adversary. It is not unusual that an ideology is taken at its full face value and therefore much more seriously by its opponents than by its pragmatic promoters. Some such implications will be found in the case study on John Foster Dulles in Selection 21. It is a basic theorem in the social sciences (the so-called Thomas theorem) that "if men define situations as real, they are real in their consequences."[1] Applying this theorem to the problem of ideology in foreign policy, we may say that an ideology which its adversary defines as a real guide for action for the other side may become real in its international consequences, that is, first, in the adversary's reaction, and, second, in the ideological camp's counterreaction.

The following selections focus on the theory and practice of communist ideology. There are several reasons for this choice. First, the communist ideology is referred to by its adherents as the only reliable, scientific guide for political and social action. No other ideology seems to match this claim. Second, no other ideology has proved so successful in its organized growth over nations and continents in terms of square miles. It is now a creed that allegedly shapes the views and life of well over one billion people from East Berlin to Peking, Hanoi, and Havana. Third, the exact meaning of communist ideology has been the subject of many disputes among its modern adherents and practitioners. The Sino-Soviet dispute, the conflicts between the Soviet party and Yugoslavia (1948), Hungary (1956), Rumania (1963), Albania (1963), and Czechoslovakia (1968), and finally the purges of the individual leaders within national communist parties are dramatic illustrations of the never-ending conflict. Communists argue over what the theory actually says, and, more importantly, what concrete steps the theory calls for in a given situation. Finally, communist ideology, like no other, has been credited by its enemies with a decisive influence on the policies and action of the creed's leading adherents. To a great extent, the communist doctrine has frequently shaped foreign policies and action

[1] International Encyclopedia of Social Science, Vol. 16 (New York: Crowell-Collier and Macmillan, Inc., 1968), pp. 1–6 on William Isaac Thomas.

of anticommunist nations more profoundly than it determined the policies and action of the communist national leaders.

21 / Enemies Are Those Whom We Define as Such: A Case Study

Ole R. Holsti

The following is an excerpt from a study of the former U.S. Secretary of State John Foster Dulles and his attitude toward a single enemy, the Soviet Union. Primary data for the study were obtained from all publicly available statements made by Dulles during the years 1953–1959, including 122 press conferences, 70 addresses, 67 appearances at Congressional hearings, and 166 other documents. This documentation was supplemented by contemporary newspapers, secondary source questionnaires sent to a number of Dulles' closest associates, and memoirs written by those who worked closely with him. The purpose of Holsti's study was to prove or disprove that, at least in part, Dulles' attitudes about the Soviet Union can be traced to personal factors. It seems that his belief system contained a number of preconceptions that could only be altered slowly or imperfectly by hard facts. The author's hypothesis is that "an individual responds not only to the 'objective' characteristics of a situation, but also to the meaning the situation has for him." The person's subsequent behavior and the results of that behavior are determined by the meaning ascribed to a situation. Applied to international situations, it may be said, as Holsti argues, that "enemies are those who are defined as such, and if one acts upon that interpretation, it is more than likely that the original definition will be confirmed."

If the concept of the enemy is considered from the perspective of attitudes, one interesting problem is the manner in which attitudes about the enemy are maintained or changed. The history of international relations

From Ole R. Holsti, "Cognitive Dynamics and Images of the Enemy." Copyright by the Board of Editors of the *Journal of International Affairs,* reprinted from Volume XXI, No. 1, pp. 16–39 *(passim),* 1967. Permission to reprint is gratefully acknowledged to the Editors of the *Journal.* Some author's footnotes have been omitted; those remaining have been renumbered.

suggests two contradictory tendencies. On the one hand, just as there are no permanent allies in international relations, there appear to be no permanent enemies. During its history, the United States has fought wars against Britain, France, Mexico, Spain, Germany, Italy, and Japan, all of which are currently allies to some degree. Even the most enduring international antagonisms—for example, between France and Germany—have eventually dissolved. Thus, it is clear that attitudes toward enemies do change.

Although hostile relationships at the international level are not eternal, it is also evident that they tend to endure well past the first conciliatory gestures. This resistance to changes in attitudes may be attributed to a number of factors, not the least of which is an apparently universal tendency to judge the actions of others—and particularly of those defined as enemies —according to different standards from those applied to oneself. Because friends are expected to be friendly and enemies to be hostile, there is a tendency to view their behavior in line with these expectations. When the other party is viewed within the framework of an "inherent bad faith"[2] model the image of the enemy is clearly self-perpetuating, for the model itself denies the existence of data that could disconfirm it. At the interpersonal level such behavior is characterized as abnormal—paranoia. Different standards seem to apply at the international level; inherent-bad-faith models are not considered abnormal, and even their underlying assumptions often escape serious questioning.

This paper reports a case study of the cognitive dynamics associated with images of the enemy. The basic hypothesis—that there exist cognitive processes that tend to sustain such images—will be examined through study of a single individual, former Secretary of State John Foster Dulles, and his attitude toward a single "enemy," the Soviet Union. One point should be made explicit at the outset: there is no intent here to indicate that Secretary Dulles' attitudes or behavior were in any way "abnormal." It is precisely because of the assumption that his attitudes and behavior were within the normal range of high-ranking policy-makers that he was selected for intensive study. Thus, though Dulles was a unique personality in many respects, this research was undertaken on the premise that the findings may have implications for foreign-policy decision-making in general. . . .

The theoretical framework for this study has been developed from two

---

[2] This term, derived from Henry A. Kissinger, *The Necessity for Choice* (Garden City: Doubleday & Co., 1962), p. 201, is used here to denote a conception of the other nation by which it is defined as evil *whatever* the nature of its actions—"damned if it does, and damned if it doesn't." The reverse model is that of appeasement; all actions of the other party, regardless of their character, are interpreted as non-hostile. Despite some notable examples of appeasement, such as the Munich settlement prior to World War II, misinterpretation deriving from the appeasement model seems to be relatively rare at the international level.

major sources. The first and more general of these is the literature on the relationship of an individual's "belief system" to perception and action. The belief system, composed of a number of "images" of the past, present, and future, includes "all the accumulated, organized knowledge that the organism has about itself and the world." It may be thought of as the set of lenses through which information concerning the physical and social environment is received. It orients the individual to his environment, defining it for him and identifying for him its salient characteristics. National images may be considered as subparts of the belief system. Like the belief system itself, these are models that order for the observer what would otherwise be an unmanageable amount of information.

All images are stereotyped in the trivial sense that they oversimplify reality. It is this characteristic that makes images functional—and can render them dysfunctional. Unless the *content* of the image coincides in some way with what is commonly perceived as reality, decisions based on these images are not likely to fulfill the actor's expectations. Erroneous images may also prove to have a distorting effect by encouraging reinterpretation of information that does not fit the image; this is most probable with such inherent-bad-faith models as "totalitarian communism" or "monopolistic capitalism," which exclude the very types of information that might lead to a modification or clarification of the models themselves. Equally important is the *structure* of the belief system, which, along with its component images, is in continual interaction with new information. In general, the impact of this information depends upon the degree to which the structure of the belief system is "open" or "closed."

Further insight and more specific propositions concerning the relationship between the belief system and new information can be derived from the theoretical and experimental literature on the cognitive dynamics associated with attitude change, and more specifically, from those theories that have been described as "homeostatic" or "balance theories." Among the most prominent of these are theories that postulate a "tendency toward balance," a "stress toward symmetry," a "tendency toward increased congruity," and a "reduction of cognitive dissonance." Despite terminological differences, common to all these theories is the premise that imbalance between various components of attitude is psychologically uncomfortable.

Attitudes, which can be defined as "predispositions to respond in a particular way toward a specified class of objects," consist of both cognitive (beliefs) and affective (feelings) components. Beliefs and feelings are mutually interdependent. A person with strong positive or negative affect toward an object is also likely to maintain a cognitive structure consistent with that affect. The reverse relationship is also true. Thus new information that challenges the pre-existing balance between feelings and beliefs generates intrapersonal tension and a concomitant pressure to restore an internally consistent belief system by reducing the discrepancy in some manner, *but not necessarily through a change in attitude.*

A stable attitude about the enemy is one in which feelings and beliefs are congruent and reinforce each other. An interesting problem results when information incongruent with pre-existing attitudes is received. What happens, for example, when the other party is perceived to be acting in a conciliatory manner, a cognition that is inconsistent with the definition of the enemy as evil? According to the various balance theories, a number of strategies may be used to reduce this discrepancy between affect and cognition. The source of discrepant information may be *discredited,* thereby denying its truth or relevance. However, denial may be difficult if it involves too great a distortion of reality; denial is perhaps most likely to occur when the discrepant information is ambiguous, or when its source is not considered credible. Receipt of information not consistent with one's attitudes may lead to a *search for other information* that supports the pre-existing balance. The challenge to pre-existing attitudes about an object may lead a person to *stop thinking* about it, or at least to reduce its salience to a point where it is no longer uncomfortable to live with the incongruity. This strategy seems most likely if the attitude object has low ego-relevance for the person. It has been pointed out, for example, that the remoteness of international relations for most individuals places them under very little pressure to resolve incongruities in their attitudes. The person whose beliefs are challenged by new information may engage in *wishful thinking* by changing his beliefs to accord with his desires. The new information may be *reinterpreted* in a manner that will conform with and substantiate pre-existing attitudes rather than contradict them. The process of reinterpreting new and favorable information about a disliked person is illustrated in the following dialogue:

> MR. X: The trouble with Jews is that they only take care of their own group.
>
> MR. Y: But the records of the Community Chest show that they give more generously than non-Jews.
>
> MR. X: That shows that they are always trying to buy favor and intrude in Christian affairs. They think of nothing but money; that is why there are so many Jewish bankers.
>
> MR. Y: But a recent study shows that the per cent of Jews in banking is proportionally much smaller than the per cent of non-Jews.
>
> MR. X: That's just it. They don't go in for respectable business. They would rather run night clubs.

Discrepant information may also be *differentiated* into two or more subcategories, with a strong dissociative relationship between them. Whereas strategies such as discrediting discrepant information appear to be most germane for situations of limited and ambiguous information, differentiation is likely to occur in the opposite situation. Abundant information "equips the individual to make minor (and hair-splitting) adjustments which minimize the degree of change in generalized affect toward the object. . . . Upon receipt of new information, a person is more agile in producing 'yes, but . . . ' responses when he is well informed about an object than when he is poorly informed."

Finally, the new and incongruent information may be accepted, leading one to *modify or change his pre-existing attitudes* so as to establish a new, balanced attitude-structure.

One difficulty with balance theories as described to this point is that any and all data—attitude change or resistance to attitude change through a variety of strategies—appear to support them. If the theories are to be meaningful, they should enable the investigator to predict which of the outcomes discussed above is likely to take place under specified circumstances. At least four factors related to persuasibility have been identified: the *content* and *source* of the discrepant information, the *situation,* and the *personality* of the recipient. A further discussion of these four factors in conjunction with their relevance to John Foster Dulles will permit the development of specific propositions about his attitudes toward the Soviet Union and the effects of new information on these attitudes.

Content Factors

All discrepant information does not create an equal pressure to reduce dissonance. Attitudes about central values will be more resistant to change because of the introduction of discrepant information than those at the periphery of the belief system. Tolerance for incongruity is lowest and, therefore, the pressure for dissonance reduction is highest if the attitude object is highly salient for goal attainment. Attitudes that support important values, such as self-acceptance, tend to remain unchanged even in a high dissonance situation. Thus predictions concerning the effects of incongruent information about an attitude object presuppose some knowledge of the person's belief system and the relationship of the attitude object to central values in the belief system.

In his memoirs, Anthony Eden describes Dulles as "a preacher in a world of politics." Of the many attributes in Dulles' belief system it is perhaps this "theological" world view that was most germane to his conception of the enemy. It is clear that the Soviet Union represented the antithesis of the values that were at the core of his belief system. An associate recalled that "the Secretary's profound and fervent opposition to the doctrine and ambitions of communism was heightened by the fact that communism was atheistic." The distinction between moral and political bases for evaluating the Soviet Union was blurred, if not totally obliterated. The more Dulles' image of the Soviet Union was dominated by moral rather than political criteria, the more likely it would be that new information at odds with this model would be reinterpreted to conform with the image, leaving his basic views intact.

Situational Factors

An individual may hold inconsistent attitudes without discomfort if he is not compelled to attend to the discrepancy. But he may find himself in a situation that continually forces him to examine both information at odds with his attitudes and any inconsistency arising therefrom.

That Dulles' position as Secretary of State constantly forced him to examine every aspect of Soviet foreign policy is a point requiring no further elaboration. As a result, any discrepancies in his attitudes toward the Soviet Union were continually brought to his attention, presumably creating some pressure to reduce the dissonance created by incongruent information. Persons who are required to express their attitudes in public may be under greater constraint to maintain or restore a balance between components of attitudes; the pressure may be heightened if the situation is one in which a high social value is placed on consistency. Again it is clear that the office of Secretary of State required frequent public interpretations of Soviet policy. These statements were in turn scrutinized and evaluated for consistency by the press, Congress, interested publics, and allies. Thus situational factors would have made it difficult for Dulles to withdraw his attention from any discrepancies in those attitudes.

Source Factors

Responses to new information are related to the perceived credibility of the communicator; the higher the credibility of the source and the more he is esteemed, the more likely is the audience to be persuaded.

Dulles considered Soviet communicators to be generally unreliable, an opinion sustained both by the record of Soviet propaganda and by his judgment that "atheists can hardly be expected to conform to an ideal so high" as truth. The fact that much of the information which might be at odds with Dulles' image of the U.S.S.R. originated with the Soviets themselves tended to diminish rather than enhance the probability of attitude change; unless the truth of the information was beyond question, it was likely to be discredited owing to its source.

Personality Factors

Persuasibility exists as a factor independent of content. That is, certain personality types can be more easily persuaded than others to change their attitudes. Individuals also appear to differ in their tolerance for dissonance and tend to use different means to re-establish stable attitudes. There is also evidence that persons with low self-esteem and general passivity are more easily persuaded to alter their attitudes. . . . On the other hand, persons with high self-esteem are inclined to decrease their search for information under stress.

Data on attributes of Dulles' personality that might be relevant to the problem of attitude change are necessarily fragmentary and anecdotal rather than systematic. The problem is perhaps compounded by the controversy that surrounded him. Both critics and admirers seem to agree, however, that Dulles placed almost absolute reliance on his own abilities to conduct American foreign policy. He felt, with considerable justification, that his family background and his own career had provided him with exceptional training for the position of Secretary of State. Intensive study of the Marxist-Leninist classics added to his belief that he was uniquely qualified to assess the meaning of Soviet policy. This sense of indispensability carried over into the day-to-day operations of policy formulation, and during his tenure as Secretary of State he showed a marked lack of receptivity to advice. One of his associates wrote:

> He was a man of supreme confidence within himself. . . . He simply did not pay any attention to staff or to experts or anything else. Maybe in a very subconscious way he did catalog some of the information given him but he did not, as was characteristic of Acheson and several others of the Secretaries of State with whom I have worked, take the very best he could get out of his staff. . . .

Using this summary of content, situational, source, and personality factors as a base, a number of specific predictions about Dulles' attitudes toward the Soviet Union can be derived. It seems clear that Dulles' role was one that placed a high premium on consistency between elements of his attitudes toward the Soviet Union. At the same time, despite information that might challenge his beliefs, any fundamental change in attitude would appear unlikely. As long as the Soviet Union remained a closed society ruled by Communists, it represented the antithesis of values at the core of Dulles' belief system. Furthermore, information that might challenge the inherent-bad-faith model of the Soviet Union generally came from the Soviets themselves—a low-credibility source—and was often ambiguous enough to accommodate more than one interpretation. Finally, the sparse evidence available is at least consistent with the theory that Dulles had a low-persuasibility personality.

Thus, on the basis of the theoretical framework developed earlier, three strategies for restoring a balance between his belief system and discrepant information appear most likely to have been used by Dulles: discrediting the source of the new information so as to be consistent with the belief system; searching for other information consistent with pre-existing attitudes; and differentiating between various elements in the Soviet Union.

Dulles' views concerning the sources of Soviet foreign policy provide an almost classic example of differentiating the concept of the enemy into its good and bad components to maintain cognitive balance. His numerous statements indicate that he considered Soviet policy within a framework of three conflicting pairs of concepts: ideology vs. national interest; party vs. state; and rulers vs. people.

After Dulles had been temporarily retired to private life by his defeat in the New York senatorial election in 1949, he undertook his most extensive analysis of Soviet foreign policy in his book *War or Peace*. The source of that policy, he stated repeatedly, was to be found in the Stalinist and Leninist exegeses of Marx's works. In particular, he cited Stalin's *Problems of Leninism,* which he equated with Hitler's *Mein Kampf* as a master plan of goals, strategy, and tactics, as the best contemporary guide to Soviet foreign policy. From a careful reading of that book, he concluded, one could understand both the character of Soviet leaders and the blueprint of Soviet policy. Characteristically, he placed special emphasis on the materialistic and atheistic aspects of the Communist creed, attributes that he felt ensured the absolute ruthlessness of Soviet leaders in their quest for world domination. By the time Dulles took office as Secretary of State in 1953 he had clearly adopted the theory that Soviet policy was the manifestation of ideology. His six years in office appear to have confirmed for him the validity of that view; it changed only in that it became stronger with the passing of time.

The second dichotomy in Dulles' thinking concerning the sources of Soviet foreign policy—the Russian state vs. the Communist Party—paralleled the concepts of national interest and Marxist ideology. He often pointed to the existence of a conflict of interests and, therefore, of policies between party and state. It was to the Communist Party rather than to the Russian state that he attributed Soviet aggressiveness, asserting that the state was simply the tool of the party. During his testimony at the hearings in early 1957 on the Eisenhower Doctrine for the Middle East, the following dialogue took place. . . .

> SENATOR JACKSON: Would you not agree on this: that international communism has been used as an instrument of Russian foreign policy since 1918?

SECRETARY DULLES: I would put it the other way around. Russian foreign policy is an instrument of international communism.

From the distinction between party and state Dulles deduced that Soviet hostility toward the United States existed only on the top level of the party hierarchy and that, but for the party, friendly relations between Russia and the United States could be achieved.

The third dichotomy in Dulles' theory of Soviet foreign policy was that of the Russian people vs. the Soviet leaders. As in the case of the distinction between party and state, in which he equated the former with hostility toward the United States, he believed that the enmity of the Soviet leadership was in no way shared by the Russian people. At no time did he suggest anything but the highest degree of friendship between the Russian people and the free world. Typical of his view was the statement that: "There is no dispute at all between the United States and the peoples of Russia. If only the Government of Russia was interested in looking out for the welfare of Russia, the people of Russia, we would have a state of non-tension right away." By asserting that the rulers of the Soviet Union, as Communists, enjoyed little public support, Dulles laid the groundwork for the further assumption that, were Soviet leaders responsive to Russian public opinion, Soviet-American differences would be negligible. . . .

A theory such as Dulles', which postulated a divergence of interests between party and state and between elites and masses, is pessimistic for short-term resolution of conflict. At the same time, the theory is optimistic for the long-term, for it suggests that competing national interests are virtually nonexistent. It assumes that, but for the intransigence of the Communist elite, Russia and the United States would coexist in harmony . . . . In this respect, his theory was in accord with what has been described as "the traditional American assumption that only a few evil leaders stood in the way of a worldwide acceptance of American values and hence of peace." . . .

At the beginning of this paper it was asserted that "enemies are those whom we define as such." This is not to say, however, that images of the enemy are necessarily unrealistic or that they can be attributed solely to an individual's belief system.[3] Soviet policy itself was clearly an important source of Dulles' images, and his definition of the Soviet Union as an enemy was in many respects a realistic one. During his tenure of office, from 1953 to 1959, the Soviet Union did represent a potential threat to the United States; the cold war was not merely a product of Dulles' imagination, nor can the development of Soviet-American relations during the period be explained solely by reference to his belief system.

Another question also arises: To what extent do policy decisions reflect

[3] Except, of course, in abnormal cases such as paranoia. These are, however, outside the scope of this paper.

attributes of those who made them? The assertion that personal character-istics are crucial to politics because political decisions are made by in-dividuals is as trivial as it is true. If it were demonstrated that other factors (role, organization, culture, and the like) account for an overwhelming proportion of the variance in the formulation of foreign-policy decisions, then findings about individual behavior would be peripheral to international politics.

Although a decision-maker carries with him into office a complex of personal values, beliefs, and attitudes, even a high-ranking official such as the Secretary of State is subject to bureaucratic constraints. These range from constitutional and legal requirements to informal, but nevertheless real, limitations rooted in the expectations of his associates. The organiza-tional context may influence the premises and information upon which the incumbent makes his decisions in a number of ways: organizational goals tend to endure beyond the tenure of a single individual; pressures for policy continuity can affect the interpretation of new information; colleagues and subordinates can serve as important sources of values and information; and the tendency of groups to impose conformity on its members is well docu-mented. These constraints establish boundaries that restrict to a greater or lesser degree the scope of the incumbent's decisions and the criteria used to make them. . . .

The manner in which each decision-maker interprets his sphere of com-petence and perceives constraints upon it is also important. If he defines his role in narrow terms—for example, if he perceives his primary respon-sibility to be that of administering the Department of State rather than the formulation of policy—his influence on many issues will be concomitantly decreased. On the other hand, by defining his sphere of competence in broad terms, the decision-maker can increase his authority.

Dulles' admirers and critics agree that his impact on American foreign policy was second to none. Richard Rovere's judgment that "Mr. Dulles has exercised powers over American foreign policy similar to those exer-cised by Franklin D. Roosevelt during the war" is supported by most stu-dents of the Eisenhower Administration. His brilliant mind and forceful personality, combined with an almost total reliance upon his own abilities and the strong support of the President, served to magnify his influence. . . .

The decision-maker also operates within the somewhat broader and less clearly defined limits delineated by public opinion. In many respects Dulles' attitudes toward the Soviet Union resembled those of the public; opinion surveys have consistently revealed a tendency to view the Soviet Union in black-and-white terms not dissimilar to aspects of Dulles' views. This is not to say, however, that his attitudes merely reflected public opinion. Although public opinion may set broad limits on policy beyond which the decision-maker cannot move, it is also true that public attitudes are in large part shaped by decision-makers. . . .

If, as the evidence appears to suggest, at least part of Dulles' attitudes about the Soviet Union can be traced to personal factors, how far can one generalize from these findings? It seems reasonable to suppose that his manner of perceiving and interpreting the environment is not unique among decision-makers. Like Dulles, many Soviet officials have interpreted their adversaries' actions within a rigid inherent-bad-faith model, that of "monopoly capitalism." Many other examples could be cited. If this premise is correct, the implications for international politics are somewhat sobering.

When decision-makers for both parties to a conflict adhere to rigid images of each other, there is little likelihood that even genuine attempts to resolve the issues will have the desired effect. Such a frame of reference renders meaningful communication with adversaries, much less resolution of the conflict, almost impossible. . . . To the extent that each side undeviatingly interprets new information, even conciliatory gestures, in a manner calculated to preserve the original image of the adversary, they are caught up in a closed system with little prospect of changing the relations between them.

Because every decision-maker is in part a prisoner of beliefs and expectations that inevitably shape his definition of reality, to judge Dulles or any individual against a standard of omniscience or total rationality is neither fair nor instructive. Decisions based on less-than-perfect knowledge are unavoidable and will continue to be a source of potential danger as long as foreign policies are formulated by human beings. The avoidable hazards are those that arise from reducing complexities to simplicities, ruling out alternative sources of information and evaluation, and closing off to scrutiny and consideration competing views of reality. On these counts Dulles is open to legitimate criticism.

Modern technology has created an international system in which the potential costs of a foreign policy based on miscalculation have become prohibitive; one of the cruel paradoxes of international politics is that those decisions that require the most serious consideration of alternative interpretations of reality often carry with them the greatest pressures for conformity to stereotyped images. Wisdom in our world consists of maintaining an open mind under such pressures, for a realistic asssessment of opportunities and risks in one's relations with adversaries appears to be at least a necessary, if not a sufficient, condition for survival.

22 / Capitalism = Imperialism = War

Vladimir I. Lenin

The spiritual leader and organizer of the Bolshevik Revolution (November 7, 1917), Vladimir Ilyich Lenin, defined imperialism as an inevitable, final stage of monopoly capitalism. He engaged in a violent argument over the definition with another socialist leader, Karl Kautsky, who held that imperialism was a preferred but not inevitable policy of capitalism. Most probably Lenin believed in the blind and incurable urge of the capitalist system to engage in wars, exploitation, and imperialist conquests, thus speeding up its own inevitable doom. But even if he did not fully believe so, it was a good revolutionary tactic to say so and keep on depicting the adversary as an undiluted evil. Had Lenin admitted that the capitalist enemy might be rational and perhaps even reasonable, the implied possibility of a compromise might have reduced the intensity of revolutionary zeal and class hatred that he, as a revolutionary leader, needed to succeed. As will be noted, Lenin accused Kautsky of faulty logic and of "consoling the masses with hopes of peace under capitalism," an accusation reminiscent of the critique of the thesis of peaceful coexistence between capitalism and socialism leveled in the 1960s and 1970s by Peking against Moscow. Among other things, the current Russian thesis credits capitalism with sufficient rationality to dread a nuclear war.

Peking republished Lenin's polemic with Kautsky in a mass edition in 1965, from which this excerpt is taken. One wonders whether Lenin's references to European events appear outdated or incomprehensible to current Chinese readers. Even the excerpt that follows bears signs of the passage of time, particularly in the following four areas:

1. The main target of Lenin's ire, the social democrats, came to power in many European countries without war and without revolution.
2. The United States replaced Britain as the target of communist critique. The planet is no longer divided among a few colonial European powers; anticolonialism has won yet only in a few exceptional cases was its victory revolutionary and communist.
3. The nuclear dimension must be added to Lenin's conviction of constant intercapitalist wars, which the communists hoped to transform into socialist revolutions.
4. At the time of his writing, Lenin anticipated the world to be *either* capitalist *or* communist. However, after World War I, communism established itself in only one national state while the rest of the

From pp. 105–112, 133–134, 142–145 of Vladimir I. Lenin, *Imperialism, the Highest Stage of Capitalism* (Peking: Foreign Languages Press, 1965). Footnotes omitted.

world remained capitalist. Lenin's theory was forced to include a new probability: In a world divided between communist and capitalist nations, the most plausible type of war might well be one between the two opposing systems. A forecast of terrible wars between communism and capitalism to the bitter end became the dominant thesis under Stalin. It is no wonder that Stalin's favorite quote from Lenin was:

We live not only in a state but in a system of states, and the existence of the Soviet Republic side by side with the imperialist states is unthinkable. In the end either one or the other will conquer. And until that end comes, a series of most terrible collisions between the Soviet Republic and the bourgeois states is inevitable.

Stalin added a succinct, "Clear, one would think." [4]

If it were necessary to give the briefest possible definition of imperialism we should have to say that imperialism is the monopoly stage of capitalism. Such a definition would include what is most important, for, on the one hand, finance capital is the bank capital of a few very big monopolist banks, merged with the capital of the monopolist combines of industrialists; and, on the other hand, the division of the world is the transition from a colonial policy which has extended without hindrance to territories unseized by any capitalist power, to a colonial policy of monopolistic possession of the territory of the world which has been completely divided up.

But very brief definitions, although convenient, for they sum up the main points, are nevertheless inadequate, since very important features of the phenomenon that has to be defined have to be especially deduced. And so, without forgetting the conditional and relative value of all definitions in general, which can never embrace all the concatenations of a phenomenon in its complete development, we must give a definition of imperialism that will include the following five of its basic features: 1) the concentration of production and capital has developed to such a high stage that it has created nonopolies which play a decisive role in economic life; 2) the merging of bank capital with industrial capital, and the creation, on the basis of this "finance capital," of a financial oligarchy; 3) the export of capital as distinguished from the export of commodities acquires exceptional importance; 4) the formation of international monopolist capitalist combines which share the world among themselves, and 5) the territorial division of the whole world among the biggest capitalist powers is completed. Imperialism is capitalism in that stage of development in which the dominance of monopolies and finance capital has established itself; in which the export of capital has acquired pronounced importance; in which the division of the

[4] *Pravda* (February 14, 1938).

world among the international trusts has begun; in which the division of all territories of the globe among the biggest capitalist powers has been completed. . . .

In the matter of defining imperialism, however, we have to enter into controversy, primarily, with K. Kautsky, the principal Marxian theoretician of the epoch of the so-called Second International—that is, of the twenty-five years between 1889 and 1914. The fundamental ideas expressed in our definition of imperialism were very resolutely attacked by Kautsky in 1915, and even in November 1914, when he said that imperialism must not be regarded as a "phase" or stage of economy, but as a policy, a definite policy "preferred" by finance capital. . . . The best way to present Kautsky's idea is to quote his own definition of imperialism, which is diametrically opposed to the substance of the ideas which we have set forth.

Kautsky's definition is as follows:

> Imperialism is a product of highly developed industrial capitalism. It consists in the striving of every industrial capitalist nation to bring under its control or to annex larger and larger areas of *agrarian* [Kautsky's italics] territory, irrespective of what nations inhabit those regions.

This definition is utterly worthless because it one-sidedly, i.e., arbitrarily, singles out only the national question (although the latter is extremely important in itself as well as in its relation to imperialism), it arbitrarily and *inaccurately* connects this question *only* with industrial capital in the countries which annex other nations, and in an equally arbitrary and inaccurate manner pushes into the forefront the annexation of agrarian regions. . . .

The characteristic feature of imperialism is precisely that it strives to annex *not only* agrarian territories, but even most highly industrialized regions (German appetite for Belgium; French appetite for Lorraine), because 1) the fact that the world is already divided up obliges those contemplating a *redivision* to reach out for *every kind* of territory, and 2) an essential feature of imperialism is the rivalry between several Great Powers in the striving for hegemony, i.e., for the conquest of territory, not so much directly for themselves as to weaken the adversary and undermine *his* hegemony. . . .

The essence of the matter is that Kautsky detaches the politics of imperialism from its economics, speaks of annexations as being a policy "preferred" by finance capital, and opposes to it another bourgeois policy which, he alleges, is possible on this very same basis of finance capital. It follows, then, that monopolies in economics are compatible with non-monopolistic, non-violent, non-annexationist methods in politics. It follows, then, that the territorial division of the world, which was completed precisely during the epoch of finance capital, and which constitutes the basis of the present peculiar forms of rivalry between the biggest capitalist states, is compatible with a non-imperialist policy. The result is a slurring-over and a blunting of the most profound contradictions of the latest stage of capitalism, instead of an exposure of their depth; the result is bourgeois reformism instead of Marxism. . . .

"From the purely economic point of view," writes Kautsky, "it is not impossible that capitalism will yet go through a new phase, that of the extension of the policy of the cartels to foreign policy, the phase of ultra-imperialism," i.e., of a superimperialism, of a union of the imperialisms of the whole world and not struggles among them, a phase when wars shall cease under capitalism, a phase of "the joint exploitation of the world by internationally united finance capital."

We shall have to deal with this "theory of ultraimperialism" later on in order to show in detail how definitely and utterly it breaks with Marxism. At present, in keeping with the general plan of the present work, we must examine the exact economic data on this question. "From the purely economic point of view," is "ultraimperialism" possible, or is it ultra-nonsense? . . .

Kautsky called ultraimperialism or superimperialism what Hobson, thirteen years earlier, described as interimperialism. Except for coining a new and clever catchword, replacing one Latin prefix by another, the only progress Kautsky has made in the sphere of "scientific" thought is that he gave out as Marxism what Hobson, in effect, described as the cant of English parsons. After the Anglo-Boer War it was quite natural for this highly honourable caste to exert their main efforts to *console* the British middle class and the workers who had lost many of their relatives on the battlefields of South Africa and who were obliged to pay higher taxes in order to guarantee still higher profits for the British financiers. And what better consolation could there be than the theory that imperialism is not so bad; that it stands close to inter- (or ultra-) imperialism, which can ensure permanent peace? No matter what the good intentions of the English parsons, or of sentimental Kautsky, may have been, the only objective, i.e., real, social significance Kautsky's "theory" can have, is: a most reactionary method of consoling the masses with hopes of permanent peace being possible under capitalism, by distracting their attention from the sharp antagonisms and acute problems of the present times, and directing it towards illusory prospects of an imaginary "ultraimperialism" of the future. Deception of the masses—there is nothing but this in Kautsky's "Marxian" theory.

. . . [I]n the realities of the capitalist system, and not in the banal philistine fantasies of English parsons, or of the German "Marxist," Kautsky, "interimperialist" or "ultraimperialist" alliances, no matter what form they may assume, whether of one imperialist coalition against another, or of a general alliance embracing *all* the imperialist powers, are inevitably nothing more than a "truce" in periods between wars. Peaceful alliances prepare the ground for wars, and in their turn grow out of wars; the one conditions the other, giving rise to alternating forms of peaceful and non-peaceful struggle out of *one and the same* basis of imperialist connections and relations within world economics and world politics. But in order to pacify the workers and to reconcile them with the social-chauvinists who have deserted to the side of the bourgeoisie, wise Kautsky *separates* one link of a single chain from the other, separates the present peaceful (and ultraimperialist, nay, ultra-ultraimperialist) alliance of *all* the powers for the "pacification" of China (remember the suppression of the Boxer Rebellion) from the non-peaceful conflict of tomorrow, which will prepare the ground for another "peaceful" general alliance for the partition, say, of Turkey, on the day after tomorrow, *etc., etc.* Instead of showing the living connection between periods of imperialist peace and periods of imperialist war, Kautsky presents the workers with a lifeless abstraction in order to reconcile them to their lifeless leaders.

23 / Leninism or Social Imperialism?

Jen-min Jih Pao
Hung Chi
Chie-fang Chun Pao
Pravda

Lenin's theory of inevitable capitalist imperialism crystallized in the framework of a controversy between the two most prominent leaders of the

From pp. 5–15 of *Peking Review* (April 24, 1970). The three principal Chinese Communist newspapers—*Jen-min Jih Pao, Hung Chi,* and *Chie-fang Chun Pao*—prepared a long collective article under the title "Leninism or Social Imperialism." The occasion was the centenary of the birth of Lenin (April 22, 1870–1970). The purpose was to depict Soviet Russia as having betrayed—since Stalin's death—Lenin's legacy on both the domestic and international fronts. It was given a worldwide circulation in many languages. This exceprt is from the official translation as reproduced in *Peking Review.* The reader will note that *Peking Review* generally uses British rather than American spelling; it also spells Khrushchov with an "o," which is phonetically more accurate than the spelling adopted in the United States. Original footnotes have been omitted; footnotes added by the editor are so marked.

international socialist movement during World War I. The subject seemed to be a correct interpretation and a correct practical application of Karl Marx. Subsequently, a correct interpretation and a correct practical application of Lenin's theory became a matter a controversy among the communists. And the general validity of Lenin's concepts was challenged by both socialist and nonsocialist scholars and statesmen.

As the following excerpt from the Chinese Communist sources will show, much of the rhetorics in the current Sino-Soviet dispute rely heavily on verbatim quotes from Lenin. Lenin's words are used, of course, in order to prove the other side wrong. The contrast in the way in which the different communist leaders read different things into Lenin's analysis as a guide for action mirrors the contrasts in (1) their personality structures (Khrushchev versus Mao versus Castro versus Tito), (2) their personal experiences and respective positions of responsibility or irresponsibility (whether they are in power in their own nations, or in the opposition, or in the guerilla movement, or in jail), and (3) the nature and power of their national states (large or small, rich or poor, developed or underdeveloped, relatively secure like Yugoslavia or highly vulnerable like Mongolia, sandwiched between the two Communist superpowers). Furthermore, more than half a century has elapsed since Lenin wrote his study of imperialism. This time is a nuclear age, not World War I. During World War I Lenin could agree with the revolutionary socialists (Zimmerwald faction) that, given the choice between international peace but no revolution and some more years of war then revolution, the socialist choice should be for more years of war. (See also Max Weber on this point in Selection 25.) In disagreement with Mao and Lenin, the Russian successors to Lenin seem to suggest that such a choice does not exist in an era of nuclear missiles. After all, Lenin wrote his pamphlet on capitalist imperialism in the spring of 1916 during his exile in Zurich, Switzerland, long before the atomic era.

The attack on Lenin's oversimplification and economic determinism comes from different noncommunist sources. In Selection 24, for instance, Richard J. Barnet condemns the expansionist and interventionist trend in United States foreign policy, but argues that Lenin's theory of economically determined imperialism is inadequate to explain the trend. Barnet finds a more plausible explanation of expansionism in the bureaucratic compulsion (especially on the part of "national security managers" who are not primarily motivated by economic considerations) "to control as much of the world political environment as possible." Of course, bureaucratic security managers are also present in socialist countries.

In his essay on "The Leninist Myth of Imperialism," the famous French sociologist and political writer Raymond Aron challenges Lenin's equation (capitalist economy = imperialist expansion = intercapitalist wars) as a propagandistic oversimplification of a complex issue.[5] While some wars may have been caused by purely economic motivations, others have been caused by the will to power, the passion of the masses and/or their leaders, or simply miscal-

---

[5] Raymond Aron, *The Century of Total War* (Boston: The Beacon Press, 1968), pp. 56–73. The whole paperback is highly recommended.

culation. Wars that are possible under capitalism and its search for profit are also possible under socialism and its search for ideological, security, or territorial "profit." The Soviet armed invasion and occupation of Czechoslovakia in 1968 is a good example of a search for such profit, as was the Soviet invasion of Hungary in 1956. The Chinese vitriolic tone in the following article suggests a possibility of an armed collision between two Leninist superpowers.

Raymond Aron also noted other challengeable points in Lenin's thesis:

1. Capitalist rivalries have not led and do not necessarily lead to wars; "trade rivalries between nations are one thing, and life-and-death struggles another."

2. While it is true that capitalism in crisis may try to seek a remedy in war, the economic crisis in the 1930s led the United States to Roosevelt and the New Deal; in contrast, the 1930 crisis led Germany to Hitler and rearmament.

3. Was it really capitalism that had caused Nazi imperialism? "We maintain," writes Aron, "that the Third Reich was not driven to imperialism by residues of capitalism in its structure. If the private entrepreneurs or managers had been replaced by government-appointed managers, if the Ruhr had been nationalized, if the planning had been total, the imperialist temptation would not have been mitigated."[6]

4. Finally, as Norman Angell maintained in his book *The Great Illusion,* modern war does not pay and the annexation of provinces does not increase the wealth of the inhabitants of the conquering country.[7] This is perhaps why the capitalist countries could get rid of their colonies and be better off. Along this line of reasoning, then, a nuclear war would pay off even less than any other war Lenin could have visualized.

Original Lenin seemed to view capitalist imperialism as a blind beast rushing toward its own destruction. In his polemic with Kautsky, Lenin seemed to rule out not only an internal reform of capitalism but also any rational foreign policy and consideration of unbearable risks on the part of capitalist leaders.

The current polemic between Moscow and Peking returns, to some extent, to the old Lenin-Kautsky controversy. Peking seems to see the socialist-democratic shadow of Karl Kautsky hanging over Khrushchev's famous statement made at the Twentieth Congress of the Soviet Communist Party in 1956. Khrushchev then admitted the possibility of peaceful coexistence among the capitalist powers and even between the socialist and capitalist states. The assumption of a *rational* capitalist fear of the consequences of a nuclear collision underlined the new Khrushchev-Lenin thesis. As Khrushchev put it in 1956:

> There is a Marxist-Leninist premise which says that while imperialism exists, wars are inevitable. While capitalism remains on earth the reactionary forces representing the interests of the capitalist monopolies will continue to strive for war gambles and aggression, and may try to let loose war. *There is no fatal inevitability of war.* Now there

[6] *Ibid.,* p. 72.

[7] Norman Angell, *The Great Illusion* (New York: G. P. Putnam's Sons, 1933).

are powerful political and social forces, commanding serious means capable of preventing the unleashing of war.

This should be compared with Stalin's and the current Chinese thesis. Stalin's statement at the Fifteenth Congress of the Soviet Communist Party in 1927:

> We cannot forget the saying of Lenin to the effect that a great deal in the matter of our construction depends on whether we succeed in delaying war with the capitalist countries, *which is inevitable* but which may be delayed either until proletarian revolution ripens in Europe, or until the colonial revolutions come fully to a head, or, finally, until the capitalists fight among themselves over division of the colonies. Therefore the maintenance of peaceful relations with capitalist countries is an obligatory task for use. The basis of our relations with capitalist countries consists in admitting the coexistence of two opposed systems.

Comrade Mao Tsetung points out: "The rise to power of revisionism means the rise to power of the bourgeoisie." "The Soviet Union today is under the dictatorship of the bourgeoisie, a dictatorship of the big bourgeoisie, a dictatorship of the German fascist type, a dictatorship of the Hitler type."

This brilliant thesis of Comrade Mao Tsetung's most penetratingly reveals the class essence and social roots of Soviet revisionist social-imperialism and its fascist nature.

Since the Soviet revisionist renegade clique usurped Party and government power in the Soviet Union, the Soviet bourgeois privileged stratum has greatly expanded its political and economic power and has occupied the ruling position in the Party, the government, and the army as well as in the economic and cultural fields. And from this stratum there has emerged a bureaucrat monopoly capitalist class, namely, a new type of big bourgeoisie which dominates the whole state machine and controls all the social wealth. . . .

This new-type bureaucrat monopoly capitalist class constitutes the class basis of Soviet revisionist social-imperialism. At present the general representative of this class is Brezhnev. He has frantically pushed and developed Khrushchov revisionism and is completing the evolution from capitalist restoration to social-imperialism, which was already begun when Khrushchov was in power.

In staging the counter-revolutionary coup d'etat, the Khrushchov-Brezhnev renegade clique played a role which no imperialist or reactionary was in a position to play. As Stalin said, "The easiest way to capture a fortress is from within." The fortress of socialism, which had withstood the 14-nation armed intervention, the Whiteguard rebellion, the attack by several million

Hitlerite troops and imperialist sabotage, subversion, blockade and encircle-
ment of every kind, was finally captured from within by this handful of
renegades. The Khrushchov-Brezhnev clique are the biggest renegades in
the history of the international communist movement. They are criminals
indicted by history for their towering crimes.

Lenin denounced the renegades of the Second International as "socialism
in words, imperialism in deeds, the growth of opportunism into imperialism."

The Soviet revisionist renegade clique, too, has grown from revisionism
into social-imperialism. The difference lies in the fact that the social-imperialists of the Second International such as Kautsky did not hold state
power; they only served the imperialists of their own countries to earn a few
crumbs from the superprofits plundered from the people of other countries.
The Soviet revisionist social-imperialists, however, directly plunder and enslave the people of other countries by means of the state power they have
usurped. . . .

The Soviet revisionist renegade clique talks glibly about Leninism, socialism and proletarian internationalism, but it acts in an out-and-out imperialist way.

It talks glibly about practising "internationalism" towards its so-called
fraternal countries, but in fact it imposes fetter upon fetter, such as the
"Warsaw Treaty Organization" and the "Council for Mutual Economic
Assistance," on a number of East European countries and the Mongolian
People's Republic, thereby confining them within its barbed-wire "socialist
community" and freely ransacking them. . . .

It has adopted the most despotic and vicious methods to keep these
countries under strict control and stationed massive numbers of troops there,
and it has even openly dispatched hundreds of thousands of troops to
trample Czechoslovakia underfoot and install a puppet regime at bayonet
point. Like the old tsars denounced by Lenin, this gang of renegades bases
its relations with its neighbours entirely "on the feudal principle of
privilege." . . .

In order to press on with its social-imperialist policy of expansion and
aggression, the Brezhnev renegade clique has developed Khrushchov revisionism and concocted an assortment of fascist "theories" called the
"Brezhnev doctrine."　　　'

Now let us examine what stuff this "Brezhnev doctrine" is made of.[8]

[8] The reference to the Brezhnev Doctrine is, in fact, a reference to a long article
published by *Pravda,* the official organ of the Soviet Communist Party on September
25, 1968 in the wake of the Soviet armed intervention in Czechoslovakia and the
subsequent imposition of the Soviet concept of communism upon the liberal Czechoslovak Communists. The article entitled "Sovereignty and International Duties of
the Socialist Camp" contained the following key passages: "The sovereignty of each
socialist country cannot be opposed to the world of socialism, of the world revolution-

First, the theory of "limited sovereignty." Brezhnev and company say that safeguarding their so-called interests of socialism means safeguarding "supreme sovereignty." They flagrantly declare that Soviet revisionism has the right to determine the destiny of another country "including the destiny of its sovereignty."

What "interests of socialism"! It is you who have subverted the socialist system in the Soviet Union and pushed your revisionist line of restoring capitalism in a number of East European countries and the Mongolian People's Republic. What you call the "interests of socialism" are actually the interests of Soviet revisionist social-imperialism, the interests of colonialism. You have imposed your all-highest "supreme sovereignty" on the people of other countries, which means that the sovereignty of other countries is "limited," whereas your own power of dominating other countries is "unlimited." In other words, you have the right to order other countries about, whereas they have no right to oppose you; you have the right to ravage other countries, but they have no right to resist you. . . . So it is clear that Brezhnev's theory of "limited sovereignty" is nothing but an echo of imperialist ravings.

Secondly, the theory of "international dictatorship." Brezhnev and company assert that they have the right to "render military aid to a fraternal country to do away with the threat to the socialist system." . . .

. . . Do you think that by putting up the signboard of "aid to a fraternal country" you are entitled to use your military force to bully another country, or send your troops to overrun another country as you please? Flying the flag of "unified armed forces," you invaded Czechoslovakia. What difference is there between this and the invasion of China by the allied forces of eight powers in 1900, the 14-nation armed intervention in the Soviet Union and the "16-nation" aggression organized by U.S. imperialism against Korea!

Thirdly, the theory of "socialist community." Brezhnev and company shout that "the community of socialist states is an inseparable whole" and that the "united action" of "the socialist community" must be strengthened.

A "socialist community" indeed! It is nothing but a synonym for a colonial empire with you as the metropolitan state. . . .

Fourthly, the theory of "international division of labour." Brezhnev and company have greatly developed this nonsense spread by Khrushchov long ago. They have not only applied "international division of labour" to a

---

ary movement. . . . The weakening of any link in the world socialist system has a direct effect on all the socialist countries, which cannot be indifferent. . . . The Soviet Union and other socialist states (Poland, Hungary, and East Germany), in fulfilling their internationalist duty to the fraternal peoples of Czechoslovakia and defending their own socialist gains, had to act and did act in resolute opposition to the antisocialist forces in Czechoslovakia."——Ed.

number of East European countries and the Mongolian People's Republic as mentioned above, but have extended it to other countries in Asia, Africa and Latin America. They allege that the Asian, African and Latin American countries cannot "secure the establishment of an independent national economy," unless they "cooperate" with Soviet revisionism. "This co-operation enables the Soviet Union to make better use of the international division of labour. We shall be able to purchase in these countries increasing quantities of their traditional export commodities—cotton, wool, skins and hides, dressed non-ferrous ores, vegetable oil, fruit, coffee, cocoa beans, tea and other raw materials, and a variety of manufactured goods."[9]

What a list of "traditional export commodities"!

It is a pity that this list is not complete. To it must be added petroleum, rubber, meat, vegetables, rice, jute, cane sugar, etc.

In the eyes of the handful of Soviet revisionist oligarchs, the people of the Asian, African and Latin American countries are destined to provide them with these "traditional export commodities" from generation to generation. What kind of "theory" is this? The colonialists and imperialists have long advocated that it is they who are to determine what each country is to produce in the light of its natural conditions, and they have forcibly turned Asian, African and Latin American countries into sources of raw materials and kept them in a state of backwardness so that industrial capitalist countries can carry on the most savage colonial exploitation at their convenience. The Soviet revisionist clique has taken over this colonial policy from imperialism. Its theory of "international division of labour" boils down to "industrial Soviet Union, agricultural Asia, Africa and Latin America" or "industrial Soviet Union, subsidiary processing workshop Asia, Africa and Latin America."

The Soviet revisionist renegade clique has occupied Czechoslovakia by surprise attack, encroached upon Chinese territories such as Chenpao Island and the Tiehliekti area and made nuclear threats against our country. All this fully reveals the aggressive and adventurous nature of Soviet revisionist social-imperialism. Like the U.S. imperialists, the handful of oligarchs of Soviet revisionist social-imperialism have become another arch-criminal preparing to start a world war. . . .

. . . They have been increasing military expenditures still more frantically, stepping up their mobilization and preparation for wars of aggression and plotting to unleash a blitzkrieg of the Hitler type. . . .

In exposing tsarist Russia's policy of aggression a hundred years ago, Marx pointed out: "Its methods, its tactics, its manoeuvres may change, but the guiding star of this policy — world hegemony — will never change."

[9] A verbatim quote from the Soviet Premier A. N. Kosygin's report to the Twenty-third Congress of the Soviet Communist Party.——Ed.

Tsar Nicholas I once arrogantly shouted: "The Russian flag should not be taken down wherever it is hoisted." Tsars of several generations cherished the fond dream, as Engels said, of setting up a vast "Slav empire" extending from the Elbe to China, from the Adriatic Sea to the Arctic Ocean. They even intended to extend the boundaries of this vast empire to India and Hawaii. . . .

The Soviet revisionist new tsars have completely taken over the old tsars' expansionist tradition, branding their faces with the indelible stigma of the Romanov dynasty. They are dreaming the very dream the old tsars failed to make true and they are far more ambitious than their predecessors in their designs for aggression. . . .

The "Slav empire" of the old tsars vanished like a bubble long ago and tsardom itself was toppled by the Great October Revolution led by Lenin in 1917. The reign of the old tsars ended in thin air. Today too, in the era when imperialism is heading for total collapse, the new tsars' mad attempt to build a bigger empire dominating the whole world is nothing but a dream. . . .

Comrade Mao Tsetung points out: "The United States is a paper tiger. Don't believe in the United States. One thrust and it's punctured. Revisionist Soviet Union is a paper tiger too."

Chinese Imperialism: Moscow's Answer

Pravda (May 18, 1970)

Imperialist propagandists are echoed in Peking, which repeats their concoctions about the "aggressiveness" of the U.S.S.R., about the "crisis" of Soviet economy. It galvanizes Trotskyite ideas about some sort of "a bourgeois degeneration of Soviet power" and puts a sign of equality between United States imperialism and the Soviet Union, which is labeled "social imperialism." . . .

. . . [W]e cannot turn a blind eye on the fact that a militaristic psychosis is being stubbornly fanned in Peking and demands are made of the people "to prepare for hunger, to prepare for war." Even the recent launching of a satellite[10] is being used to whip up nationalistic passions and for threats against our country. . . .

Matters have gone so far that Hitler's ravings about the need to "save" the people from the "Slav threat" have been taken out of the mothballs. The people in Peking emulate the ringleaders of the Nazi Reich in attempting

[10] This is a reference to April 24, 1970, when China entered the superpowers' missile race by launching its first earth satellite (over 350 pounds), broadcasting the music of *Dongfanghong* ("The East Is Red") while orbiting.——Ed.

to portray the Soviet Union as a "colossus with feet of clay," clamoring about the Soviet "paper tiger" and threatening to "pierce it on the first attempt." ...

By their actions the Peking leaders leave no doubt that they strive to use the heroic freedom struggle of the peoples in their global intrigues that stem from the Great Han dreams of becoming new emperors of "the Great China" that would rule at least Asia, if not the whole world.

24 / The Third World: Why Do We Interfere?

Richard J. Barnet

The following is an excerpt from Richard J. Barnet's book on American policies toward the revolutionary ferment in the "Third World." The term, coined by the French (*Tiers Monde*), refers to what remains of the world after subtracting North America, Western Europe, and the Soviet Union. Barnet severely criticizes the United States' commitment to oppose internal violence and radical political change in such places as Greece, Lebanon, Vietnam, Cambodia, Laos, the Dominican Republic, Guatemala, British Guiana, Iran, and the Congo.

The American attempts to maintain sympathetic foreign elites in power or, on the contrary, to topple the hostile ones, are not new, of course. Nor is the United States the only power that engages in such attempts, either offensively or defensively. Before World War II, for instance, the frequent United States interventions in Latin America could be explained at least partly as a response to the European practices of interference and intrigue. After World War II, to meet the perceived threat of an expansion of communism under Soviet direction (and thus an expansion of the Soviet power itself), and also in view of continuing failure to settle conflicts with the Soviet Union at the conference table, the policy of the United States has been to try to stop further communist advances by strengthening noncommunist nations. The United States has offered its strength through economic and military aid (Truman Doctrine and Marshall Plan), alliances (OAS, NATO, SEATO, and others), and direct military involvement (Korea and Vietnam). "In carrying out these objectives," noted D. A.

Reprinted by permission of The World Publishing Company from pp. 3–19 *(passim)* of *Intervention and Revolution: The United States in the Third World* by Richard J. Barnet. An NAL book. Copyright © 1968 by Richard J. Barnet. Author's footnotes have been omitted; footnotes added by the editor are so marked. Headings have been added by the editor.

Graber, "the United States has found it advisable, on many occasions, to intervene in the domestic and foreign affairs of other nations." [11] Governments and leaders willing to cooperate with the United States policy have been more or less openly supported by the United States. This group includes Third World countries as well as "First" and "Second" worlds for example, Germany, Italy, and France in Western Europe, and Yugoslavia in communist Eastern Europe.

In this context many American leaders began to speak of the American "responsibility of power" or American "responsibility of peace" that has been thrust upon, not chosen by, the United States. President Johnson, for instance, asserted: "We did not choose to be the guardians at the gate." In Kennedy's words, America has become "the watchman on the walls of world freedom."

Barnet examines the rhetorics and the assumptions connected with the role of world guardian or policeman. Dismissing to some extent as simplistic the Marx-Leninist explanation of American interventionism by the categoric imperatives of capitalist economy, the author focuses on the fundamental clash of perceptions of modern political development between the Third World revolutionaries who guide insurgent movements and the "national security managers"— that is, officials in the State Department, Pentagon, CIA, and the White House— who manage United States foreign relations. The author seems also to imply the existence of Soviet counterparts to American security-bureaucrats; he denies, for instance, that the cold war has ever really been about the ideological conflict between communism and capitalism. He finds that the basic perspectives of Soviet and American leaders have always been remarkably similar; their bitter conflicts have been over their respective power positions in eastern Europe, Germany, and the Middle East. In Barnet's words, the two powers "have had quite different ideas about how to run their internal societies but they have shared the same general view of the proper role of a Great Power in the modern world."

Consequently, the United States is not alone in the interventionist role. The Soviet Union openly justifies its military interventions in socialist states (Hungary in 1956 and Czechoslovakia in 1968) and its assistance to communist revolutionaries sympathetic to the Russion view all over the world. China, Cuba, and several African nations are openly committed to intervention for the sake of their respective "good causes." The different techniques and methods by which the agents or instruments (money, weapons, propaganda) of one country gain access to the population, organized groups, or processes of another country have been appropriately called "informal access" or "informal penetration" in distinction to the conventional types of international contacts. One interesting study on this subject concludes that "informal penetration" has become the central feature of international politics in the period of nuclear stalemate and revolutionary ferment.[12] Chapter 13 will discuss interventions again in the framework of the balancing process.

---

[11] D. A. Graber, *Crisis Diplomacy: A History of U.S. Intervention Policies and Practices* (Washington, D.C.: Public Affairs Press, 1959), p. ix.

[12] Andrew M. Scott, *The Revolution in Statecraft: Informal Penetration* (New York: Random House, Inc., 1965), p. 4.

Since World War II the continents of Asia, Africa, and South America have been continually swept with violence. There have been a few old-fashioned wars between states where armies cross frontiers in strength to enforce demands against another government. In their border disputes India and Pakistan have behaved much like their European teachers. Israel and Egypt too have used political violence according to the conventional pattern and fought the sort of war which the nuclear powers now no longer dare to fight.

Most of the political violence that has inflamed human society since 1945, however, has been of a special character. Its source has not been conflict between states, but conflict within societies. The wars of our time have not been primarily fights for territory, raw materials, colonies, or the preservation of the king's honor, although all of these have at some point been involved. Essentially, contemporary wars have been fights for the rights of various political groups within the former colonial appendages of Europe to take political power and to exercise it on their own terms.

. . . The principal issue is not national security but making a nation. Unlike the leaders of developed nations, the enemies which revolutionary leaders see are not at the gate but already inside. Their country is occupied either by a foreign colonial power or by local landlords, generals, or self-serving politicians. As they see it, the issue is liberation. The goal is a radical redistribution of political and economic power to overcome centuries of political oppression and crushing poverty. The means is seizure of political power. . . .

. . . Most of these insurgent movements . . . . accept a Leninist or Marxist analysis of world politics and social change and they seek the solidarity and support of the established communist parties and governments. Some have received money, arms, and advice from Cuba, Russia, or China. But the indigenous revolutionary refuses to give allegiance to any brand of ortho-doxy, be it Russian, Chinese, or Cuban. Whatever his personal psychological motivations may be, his overriding concern is to change brutal conditions in his own land. Increasingly in recent years . . . one revolutionary leader after another has declared that armed struggle is the only path to radical social change.

Revolutionary movements grow in the soil of exploitation and injustice. The colonial conception is a total reproach to Western civilization and its professed ideals, for its essence is to treat man exactly as every prophet and moral philosopher from Christ to Kant warned us not to treat him—as a means, not an end. Whatever ancillary benefits colonists may have received from foreign masters, the economic well-being of the home country, not the health of the colony, defined the relationship. But the moral depravity of the colonialist does not mean that revolution is pure heroism or that its leaders are saints. Revolution is ugly and violent. It devours its children and innocent people along with it. The revolutionary always starts from a position of weakness, and he resorts to terrorism, the weapon of the weak—the derailed train, the bomb in the officers' club, or the cut throat of the colonialist collaborator (real or suspected). The revolutionary, even when he is fired by a righteous cause, often marks his success by reverting to the political type he supplants. He becomes a political intriguer, a persecutor of critics, a lover of luxury, or an addict of personal adulation.

A recurring tragedy of the past two hundred years is the betrayal of revolution, often by the men who made it. The historic aim of revolution, as Hannah Arendt has pointed out, is freedom, the opportunity to participate in the political process. Yet the Russian Revolution, which was fought in the name of freedom, degenerated into the bloody despotism of Stalin. China, Yugoslavia, the radical African regimes, Cuba, and North Vietnam have all promised far more freedom than they have delivered. The revolutionary regimes have largely eliminated starvation, spread education, and made dramatic progress toward industrialization. But, as Barrington Moore puts it:

> . . . communists cannot claim that the mass of the population has shouldered a lesser share of the burden of suffering under their form of industrialization than they did under the preceding forms of capitalism. . . . there is no evidence that the mass of the population anywhere has wanted an industrial society, and plenty of evidence that they did not. At bottom all forms of industrialization so far have been revolutions from above, the work of a ruthless minority.

U.S. Antirevolutionary Commitment

The United States government has seized upon the moral ambiguity of revolution to justify a global campaign to contain it, to channel it into acceptable paths, or to crush it. . . . [In 1947 President Truman] secured broad congressional support for use of American military power to put down violent revolution abroad. "We cannot allow changes in the status quo," the President declared, "by such methods as coercion, or by such subterfuges as political infiltration," making clear that it didn't matter whether revolutionaries were natives of the country they wished to change or not. Since violence is the engine of political change over most of the globe, President Truman committed the United States to a prodigious task. . . .

. . . [F]rom the Truman Doctrine on, the suppression of insurgent movements has remained a principal goal of U.S. foreign policy. It has been the prime target of the U.S. foreign-assistance program, most of the funds for which have gone for civic-action teams, pacification programs, support for local police, and, above all, military aid to the local army. . . .

Counterinsurgency is now the major preoccupation of U.S. military planners. They have mounted large programs to train local armies in counterguerrilla tactics, but these have been unequal to the task. Consequently, during the postwar period, on the average of once every eighteen months, U.S. military forces or covert paramilitary forces have intervened in strength in Asia, Africa, and Latin America to prevent an insurgent group from seizing power or to subvert a revolutionary government.

In recent years the pace of both insurgent activity and U.S. intervention has been stepped up sharply. In 1965 an American expeditionary force was sent to Vietnam and Marine divisions landed in the Dominican Republic to prevent insurgents from taking power. . . . Insurgent movements with radical programs, Marxist rhetoric, communist connections of any kind, or an anti-American bias are simply assumed to be the product of conspiracy by the "forces of international communism." The presence of a communist element —even the possibility of subsequent communist takeover—justifies U.S. intervention. . . .

There is the official ideology, which holds that the United States, having come to manhood, was tapped by history for a global mission of peacemaking and reform. "History and our own achievements have thrust upon us the principal responsibility for the protection of freedom on earth," President Johnson declared at a Lincoln Day dinner in 1965, a trace of sadness mixed with pride in his voice. "For the next ten or twenty years," his predecessor observed three years earlier, "the burden will be placed completely on our country for the preservation of freedom." The world community, at least those members of it with decent motives, look to the United States to lead the world and to keep order. For there is no one else. . . . The United States, uniquely blessed with surpassing riches and an exceptional history, stands above the international system, not within it. Alone among nations, she stands ready to be the bearer of the Law.

Guardian at the Gate

A few years ago the secretary of defense called in a group of foreign-newspaper correspondents to a special briefing at which he explained at great length that the United States is not and cannot be "the policeman of the world." . . . For a variety of reasons the image of the neighborhood policeman is more tarnished than it was a generation ago. In the age of big-city riots, police review boards, and the police state, the neutrality and responsibility of police are no longer taken for granted.

But the police idea is strongly entrenched in official ideology. It is merely expressed in other words, like "guardian" or "watchman," or, as in the Congo and Dominican operations, "rescuer of women and children." The world looks to Washington for protection against the insurgent band as well as the foreign invader. The American Responsibility is to provide it, whatever the cost, wherever it can. Intervention, with all its paraphernalia—the aid missions, the CIA operations, the roaming fleets bristling with nuclear weapons, the Green Berets, the pacification teams, and ultimately the expeditionary forces—is the inevitable consequence of greatness. It is the burden and the glory of the Republic.

Critics of American foreign policy tend to doubt the necessity or the wisdom of this self-appointed mission. Some with a sense of history are well aware that the United States is not the first powerful nation to explain the great role it has claimed for itself in terms of burden and sacrifice. For Cicero too the fledgling empire of the first century B.C. was a "guardianship," a domain over which the Roman people, whether by force or persuasion, could enforce the law of Rome and secure justice for primitive peoples. The British Empire was the "White Man's Burden," imposed by the stern hand of History. . . . In every century, powerful nations have reluctantly "come of age," playing out their imperial destiny by carrying on a *mission civilisatrice* on the land of some weaker neighbor.[13]

Inadvertent Imperialism

Yet many critics cling to the view that like everything else about America, her imperialism is exceptional. It springs from the purest motives. Senator J. William Fulbright, for example, while totally hostile to the policy, stresses American idealism as the furious energy which has prompted the United States to stand guard around the world against revolutions. Such critics do not doubt the sincerity, only the wisdom, of official statements such as Under Secretary Ball's remark that the United States has "a role of world responsibility divorced from territorial or narrow national interests." America's leaders may be guilty of the "arrogance of power," a bit quixotic in attempting to remake the world in our own image, naïve in thinking that a new liberal order can be ushered in so quickly, but they do not act from the base motives of the older empires. "Unlike Rome, we have not exploited our empire. On the contrary, our emprie has exploited us, making enormous drains on our resources and our energies," concludes Ronald Steel in his analysis of what he calls "the accidental empire."

Generations of British schoolboys have been delighted by Sir John Seeley's famous phrase that England conquered half the world in a fit of absence of mind. Such a self-image set them apart from the gross plunderers of the past. The Victorian imperialists were decent, civilized men who stum-

[13] Compare with the Soviet man's burden implied in the Brezhnev Doctrine that justifies the Soviet right and duty *(mission civilisatrice)* to intervene in the domestic affairs of socialist states.——Ed.

bled into a global domain. Indeed, as a historian of the time, G. P. Gooch, pointed out, taking over backward nations such as India did not increase England's power, only her responsibilities. Like these British critics, the small group of U.S. commentators who criticize the American empire at all see it as a consequence of bumbling, misguided benevolence, and "the politics of inadvertence."

For all the pride Americans have in Yankee shrewdness at home, there is a folklore tradition that the United States is continually duped abroad. Wily European statesmen from Clemenceau to Stalin have lured our Presidents beyond our shores and tricked them into underwriting their empires. Where the United States finds itself involved in a foreign adventure, it is because she has nobly, if foolishly, agreed to pull someone else's chestnuts out of the fire. If she has managed to turn burdens into opportunities and responsibilities into assets, this has been a happy accident. But quixotic idealism that requires the spending of billions to maintain overseas armies and to finance corrupt regimes is a luxury, these critics assert, when U.S. cities are falling apart and the money could be spent so much better here. . . .

The Imperialistic Stage of American Capitalism

Other critics of U.S. policy toward insurgent movements look for more familiar and more sinister motives. Drawing on the theories of Hilferding, Hobson, and Lenin of fifty years ago, they ascribe the development of America's self-proclaimed guardianship not to exceptional idealism but to economic imperialism. They see America not as a bumbler but as a country that has adroitly used its power and good fortune to consume sixty percent of the world's raw materials, to manipulate the global money market, and to control much of world trade. Those who hold these views include not only official communist propagandists, orthodox Marxist critics, a few remaining American populists of the tradition of Robert La Follette and Charles Beard, but also most politicians of the Third World, not only the revolutionaries in the hills but also many of the presidents, premiers, and generals in the palaces.

"With only one-fifteenth of the world's population and about the same proportion of the world's area and natural resources," the Advertising Council of America, Inc., has observed in its brochure *The Miracle of America,* "the United States—has more than half the world's telephone, telegraph, and radio networks—more than three quarters of the world's automobiles—almost half the world's radios—and consumes more than half the world's copper and rubber, two-thirds of the silk, a quarter of the coal, and nearly two-thirds of the crude oil."

These figures cause the Advertising Council to glow with pride and self-congratulation, but for critics they offer a sinister explanation of America's global role. America, like Britian before her, they say, is now the great defender of the Status Quo. She has committed herself against revolution and radical change in the underdeveloped world because independent governments would destroy the world economic and political system, which assures the United States its disproportionate share of economic and political power. Such critics . . . . conclude that America's preeminent wealth depends upon keeping things in the underdeveloped world much as they are, allowing change and modernization to proceed only in a controlled, orderly, and nonthreatening way. . . .

The United States supports right-wing dictatorships in Latin America, Southeast Asia, and the Middle East, they argue, not because it is confused but because these are the rulers who have tied their personal political destiny to the fortunes of the American corporations in their countries. . . .

This view of reality is an updated version of the traditional model of economic imperialism. Government protects the foreign investment of its businessmen through military intervention and political control. There is a strong element of truth to it, enough to satisfy America's enemies and some of her friends that it is an adequate explanation of U.S. policy toward the former colonial world. But just as "inadvertence" or misplaced idealism is not sufficient to explain a highly consistent policy of opposing revolution, neither is "the pursuit of profits" nor the search for stable markets and raw material sources. No doubt U.S. investments abroad have been an important factor in strengthening American commitments to oppose radical movements in the underdeveloped world. It is true that U.S. military and political activity in the Third World has expanded as foreign investment has increased. Foreign sales by U.S. companies based abroad increased five times in the years 1950 to 1964. Profits from foreign investment, particularly in extractive industries, are unusually high. . . .

Bureaucratic Management of National Security

Yet when all the evidence is marshaled, something is missing. To argue, as Lenin did, that the interventionist drive of the nation-state is attributable primarily to the basic needs of capitalism to export capital and to gain access to markets and raw materials is to ignore remarkably similar patterns of behavior in noncapitalist states. The drive to project power and influence, the will to dominate, and the frenetic search for security are characteristic of the large industrialized state, whatever its economic system. It is not hard to find instances where the machinery of government in the United States is used to promote and protect private investment. The activities of the State Department, the CIA, and the Pentagon in the Guatemalan invasion of 1954, the Bay of Pigs episode of 1961, and the Dominican intervention of 1965 are plausible cases where the protection or recovery of economic interests was a paramount consideration. But the intervention in Vietnam cannot be explained in these terms; there was virtually no American investment there to protect. Indeed, by 1968 the prosecution of the war aroused increasing opposition in the business community because of its unfavorable economic effects.

Classic theories of economic imperialism, which view the state as an agent of the most powerful domestic economic interests, underestimate the independent role of the national-security bureaucracy, which in the United States has taken on a life and movement of its own. It has the money and power at its disposal to develop within very broad limits its own conception of the national interest. To a great extent interventionist policy is the result of the development of the technology of intervention. Thus, for example, once counter-insurgency forces or spy ships are available the bureaucracy quickly finds that their use is essential. The principal justification is the drive for security which is so open-ended a concept that it permits the accumulation and projection of military power and political influence to become ends in themselves. The urge to achieve stability and control over the world environment by taming and cooling independent political forces in other countries is probably inherent in the hierarchical character of the foreign-policy bureaucracy.[14]

Behind the bureaucratic compulsion to control as much of the world political environment as possible there lies a host of real human fears and drives that are not adequately dealt with in traditional models of economic imperialism: the fear of attack, the fear of losing influence and respect, the fear of falling from the pinnacle of power, the urge to make other societies conform to a preconceived design, and the rationalized faith that the national interest and the welfare of mankind coincide. Even where the efforts to dominate appear to run counter to rational economic interests, the will to dominate persists. To argue that these fears and drives are ultimately rooted in economic relations may or may not be true, but if economic causation is defined so broadly, it does not seem to be a sufficiently incisive tool for either explaining or predicting the interventionist behavior of the modern state. In short, while the ideology of official altruism that four administrations have offered as the explanation of America's role in the postwar world requires us to believe that our government is different from all others and, indeed, from all other human institutions, neither the politics of inadvertence nor the traditional analyses of the politics of capitalism provide an adequate alternative.

[14] A different estimate of the United States and Soviet interventionist impulses will be found in Herz's article on the consequences of nuclear stalemate and in Morgenthau's conclusion that both the Soviet Union and the United States tend to downgrade the Third World as a major arena for their competition (Chapter 13, footnote 6).—Ed.

10

On Noble Ends and Ignoble Means

Does the end justify any means, only some, or none? Most individuals are familiar with the moral as well as practical dilemma of ends and means. It takes many forms and penetrates many aspects of the national and international scene. Revolutionaries justify their acts of violence or tyrannicide in moral terms; they judge the rulers to be immoral in their actions and policies toward the people. National leaders must decide whether the preservation of national territory, population, political institutions, and culture justify arms race or arms use; often, the nation's survival may be obtained by a defensive war against an aggressor—life may be preserved by killing.

The following selections will deal with the disturbing dilemma of noble ends and ignoble means. They will contrast pragmatic realists and cynics with those who argue that the end, however noble, cannot and should never ennoble violent, inhumane, or dishonest means. Those who claim that life should never be saved by killing or truth by lying, whatever the circumstances or provocation, are called "ethical perfectionists"; according to Arnold Wolfers, they

> ... will deny that any action that would be evil under one set of conditions could be morally justified under another. If men are held to be morally bound to act in accordance with an absolute ethic of love such as the Sermon on the Mount, obviously no set of circumstances, even circumstances in which the survival of a nation were at stake, could justify acts such as a resort to violence, untruthfulness, or treaty violation. The concern for self-preservation and power

itself would have to be condemned as evil. This being the case, the ethical perfectionist can offer no advice to statesmen other than that they give up public office and turn their backs on politics ... only a saintliness could come close to satisfying perfectionist moral commands.[1]

Gandhi and the Quakers disagree and suggest absolute moral imperatives as practical guides for individual and collective actions in the sphere of international politics (see Selection 27). (Nuclear deterrence and moral values are examined in depth by Philip Green in another context in Selection 37.)

In the selections that follow, it will be obvious that powerful moral arguments and persuasive *words* are unfortunately not matched by similarly unblemished *acts* or actual policy decisions. The reason is simple enough: There was not one concrete example of a moral perfectionist in the position of president, prime minister, or foreign policy-maker. The case of Gandhi, as Selection 27 suggests, is, at best, controversial. Following the liberation of India it was pragmatic Nehru, not saintly Gandhi, who became the first foreign policy-maker of free India. Was then Morgenthau right in his assertion that in politics "the very act of acting destroys our moral integrity"?[2]

In his essay on the primacy of national interest (Selection 16), Morgenthau called universal moral principles "moral abstractions." They are often invoked by national leaders hypocritically or out of some real form of self-deception but universal moral principles can hardly serve as realistic guidelines for the conduct of national policy. Furthermore, as we have already observed in examining political ideologies as guides for action (Chapter 9), the existence of several often-conflicting ethical codes tends to strengthen those very personal or very national interpretations, and often encourages deliberate distortion. In his critique of Morgenthau's political realism, Robert W. Tucker attacked his underestimate of the role of moral principles in international politics and defended the notion that moral principles have a concrete meaning.

> A foreign policy may be based upon universal moral principles which do have a definite content—the moral principles faithfully to observe promises made to others, not to resort to aggressive war, and many others. There is empirical proof that an awareness of the existence of universal moral principles having a definite content exists. It can be seen in the almost daily protestations of foreign offices that their conduct, but not that of their opponents, is in conformity with recognized principles of international morality. That these principles are not very effective in regulating the conduct of states is still another question.[3]

[1] Arnold Wolfers, "Statesmanship and Moral Choice," *World Politics*, 1:2 (January 1949), 177–178.

[2] Hans J. Morgenthau, *Scientific Man vs. Power Politics* (Chicago: University of Chicago Press, 1946) p. 189.

[3] Robert W. Tucker, "Professor Morgenthau's Theory of Political 'Realism,'" *The American Political Review*, 46:2 (March 1952), 222.

The last qualifying sentence has necessarily a chilling effect on the hope of many for a greater role of morality in the conduct of foreign policy.

Therefore, by necessity the case studies used throughout this book concentrate on leaders who have tried to make the best moral choice permitted by the circumstances; that is, in Wolfers' words, "moral nonperfectionists" rather than moral cynics. Instead of discussing absolute moral imperatives we find ourselves examining questions such as whether the circumstances were so severe or the cause so worthy as to justify such extreme measures, whether other means were avaliable that could have achieved the same results with a lesser cost in humane values, and whether the decision was based on a correct or false perception of the facts. Such a shift from absolute to very relative moral standards will be found also in the controversy concerning the decision to drop the atomic bombs on Hiroshima and Nagasaki in 1945 (Selection 29). The decision to use the bomb could not have been made by leaders who opposed violence under any circumstances. Instead, this perilous decision was made by those who, in 1941 in the wake of the unprovoked Japanese attack on Pearl Harbor, concluded that the most effective means of violence should be used by the United States for the purposes of self-defense, punishment of the aggressor, and prevention of another Pearl Harbor. Once a path of violence has been chosen, the difference between more or less advanced and more or less effective weapons—arrows, guns, gas, or nuclear explosion—may appear to be a difference in degree rather than in kind.

Many writers, statesmen, and revolutionaries also argue that the leaders of collectivities of men have been placed beyond the normal morality that is said to prevail among individuals in their mutual relations.[4] The collective interest of a revolutionary movement or the national interest of a territorial state is seen as endowed with its own superior morality which justifies any appropriate means should the good or honest ones be of no avail. This is, at least, what Kautilya, Machiavelli, and Trotsky maintained (see Selection 26).

[4] Joseph C. McKenna, S.J., "Ethics and War: A Catholic View," *American Political Science Review*, 54:3 (September 1960), 648, writes that the Sermon on the Mount, often cited as condemning all resort to violence, "in all literalness was addressed to individual persons in their individual capacities, not social collectivities or social leaders as such. Its admonitions ... do not necessarily imply, therefore, that the statesman and his nation are morally obliged to sacrifice every other consideration for the sake of peace."

25 / Ethical Paradoxes of Politics

Max Weber

Can any ethic establish commandments of identical content for politi-cal, erotic, or business relations? The famous German sociologist Max Weber suggests that this cannot be expected since by definition politics operates with very special means; namely, power backed up by threat or use of coercion. In his analysis, Weber distinguishes between an "ethic of political responsibility" (that is, for the foreseeable results of one's action) and an "ethic of ultimate ends" based on the assumption that from good comes only good but from evil only evil follows. Max Weber points out that the whole course of world history indicates the opposite. Good sometimes came from evil means, and evil was often the consequence of good intentions and method.

We must be clear about the fact that all ethically oriented conduct may be guided by one of two fundamentally differing and irreconcilably opposed maxims: conduct can be oriented to an 'ethic of ultimate ends' or to an 'ethic of responsibility.' This is not to say that an ethic of ultimate ends is identical with irresponsibility, or that an ethic of responsibility is identical with unprincipled opportunism. Naturally nobody says that. How-ever, there is an abysmal contrast between conduct that follows the maxim of an ethic of ultimate ends—that is, in religious terms, 'The Christian does rightly and leaves the results with the Lord'—and conduct that follows the maxim of an ethic of responsibility, in which case one has to give an ac-count of the foreseeable results of one's action. . . .

The decisive means for politics is violence. You may see the extent of the tension between means and ends, when viewed ethically, from the fol-lowing: as is generally known, even during the war the revolutionary soci-alists (Zimmerwald faction) professed a principle that one might strikingly formulate: 'If we face the choice either of some more years of war and then revolution, or peace now and no revolution, we choose—some more years of war!' Upon the further question: 'What can this revolution bring about?' every scientifically trained socialist would have had the answer: One cannot speak of a transition to an economy that in our sense could be called soci-alist; a bourgeois economy will re-emerge, merely stripped of the feudal

From pp. 120–122 *(passim)* of *From Max Weber: Essays in Sociology*, edited and translated by H. H. Gerth and C. Wright Mills. Copyright 1946 by Oxford University Press, Inc. Reprinted by permission.

elements and the dynastic vestiges. For this very modest result, they are willing to face 'some more years of war.' One may well say that even with a very robust socialist conviction one might reject a purpose that demands such means. With Bolshevism and Spartacism, and, in general, with any kind of revolutionary socialism, it is precisely the same thing. It is of course utterly ridiculous if the power politicians of the old regime are morally denounced for their use of the same means, however justified the rejection of their *aims* may be.

The ethic of ultimate ends apparently must go to pieces on the problem of the justification of means by ends. As a matter of fact, logically it has only the possibility of rejecting all action that employs morally dangerous means—in theory! In the world of realities, as a rule, we encounter the ever-renewed experience that the adherent of an ethic of ultimate ends suddenly turn into a chiliastic prophet. Those, for example, who have just preached 'love against violence' now call for the use of force for the last violent deed, which would then lead to a state of affairs in which *all* violence is annihilated. In the same manner, our officers told the soldiers before every offensive: 'This will be the last one; this one will bring victory and therewith peace.' The proponent of an ethic of absolute ends cannot stand up under the ethical irrationality of the world. He is a cosmic-ethical 'rationalist.' Those of you who know Dostoievski will remember the scene of the 'Grand Inquisitor,' where the problem is poignantly unfolded. If one makes any concessions at all to the principle that the end justifies the means, it is not possible to bring an ethic of ultimate ends and an ethic of responsibility under one roof or to decree ethically which end should justify which means.

You may demonstrate to a convinced syndicalist, believing in an ethic of ultimate ends, that his action will result in increasing the opportunities of reaction, in increasing the oppression of his class, and obstructing its ascent—and you will not make the slightest impression upon him. If an action of good intent leads to bad results, then, in the actor's eyes, not he but the world, or the stupidity of other men, or God's will who made them thus, is responsible for the evil. However a man who believes in an ethic of responsibility takes account of precisely the average deficiences of people; as Fichte has correctly said, he does not even have the right to presuppose their goodness and perfection. He does not feel in a position to burden others with the results of his own actions so far as he was able to foresee them; he will say: these results are ascribed to my action. The believer in an ethic of ultimate ends feels 'responsible' only for seeing to it that the flame of pure intentions is not quelched: for example, the flame of protesting against the injustice of the social order. To rekindle the flame ever anew is the purpose of his quite irrational deeds, judged in view of their possible success. They are acts that can and shall have only exemplary value.

But even herewith the problem is not yet exhausted. No ethics in the world can dodge the fact that in numerous instances the attainment of 'good' ends is bound to the fact that one must be willing to pay the price of using morally dubious means or at least dangerous ones—and facing the possibility or even the probability of evil ramifications. From no ethics in the world can it be concluded when and to what extent the ethically good purpose 'justifies' the ethically dangerous means and ramifications. . . .

26 / "Ends and Means" for a State, a Prince, and a Revolutionary

Kautilya
Niccolò Machiavelli
Leon Trotsky

The following three brief statements reaffirm a basic proposition: In Trotsky's words, "Organically the means are subordinated to the end."

Arthasāstra

Kautilya

The first statement is part of an Indian anthology of political and administrative wisdom and theory of statecraft, called *Arthasāstra*. It was prepared by a writer-politician Kautilya twenty-three centuries ago, in the period of the Indian Mauryan empire (300 B.C.).

A state should always observe such a policy as will help it strengthen its defensive fortifications and life-lines of communications, build plantations, construct villages, exploit mineral and forest wealth of the country, while at the same time preventing fulfilment of similar programmes in the rival state. . . . A state should build up its striking power through develop-

From pp. 56–57, 109, 132 *(passim)* of *Essentials of Indian Statecraft: Kautilya's Arthasāstra for Contemporary Readers* (Bombay: Asia Publishing House, 1962).

ment of the exchequer, the army and wise counsel; and till the proper time, should conduct himself as a weak power towards its neighbours, to evade conflict or envy from enemy or allied states. If the state is deficient in resources, it should acquire them from related or allied states. It should attract to itself capable men from corporations, from wild and ferocious tribes, foreigners, and organise espionage as will damage hostile powers. . . .

Reckless persons, fearless of life and who face elephants and tigers in fight, to earn a living, are termed sharp spies. Those who are devoid of affection and are cruel and lazy should be trained as poisoner-spies. . . .

Poisoners such as sauce makers, chefs, bathroom attendants, masseurs, bed-room attenders, toilet specialists, servants with bodily deformity, dwarfs, the dumb and the deaf, idiot and blind, professionals like actors, dancers, musicians, vocalists, comedians, poets as well as women, should spy on the private character of . . . officers. . . . A mendicant woman should carry such information to the bureau of espionage or intelligence. . . . Neither the bureau of espionage nor the wandering spies should know each other.

The Prince

Niccolò Machiavelli

This statement is a brief excerpt from one of twenty-six essays that comprise Machiavelli's book *The Prince*. Machiavelli (1469–1527) was a Florentine nobleman who, like Kautilya, was both a theoretician and a practitioner of politics.

. . . [T]here are two methods of fighting, the one by law, the other by force: the first method is that of men, the second of beasts; but as the first method is often insufficient, one must have recourse to the second. It is therefore necessary for a prince to know well how to use both the beast and the man. . . . Therefore, a prudent ruler ought not to keep faith when by so doing it would be against his interest, and when the reasons which made him bind himself no longer exist. If men were all good, this precept would not be a good one; but as they are bad, and would not observe their faith with you, so you are not bound to keep faith with them. Nor have legitimate grounds ever failed a prince who wished to show colourable excuse for the non-fulfilment of his promise. . . .

. . . Thus it is well to seem merciful, faithful, humane, sincere, religious, and also to be so; but you must have the mind so disposed that when it is

From pp. 64–66 of Niccolò Machiavelli, *The Prince and the Discourses* (New York: Random House, Inc., 1950).

needful to be otherwise you may be able to change to the opposite qualities. And it must be understood that a prince, and especially a new prince cannot observe all those things which are considered good in men, being often obliged, in order to maintain the state, to act against faith, against charity, against humanity, and against religion. And, therefore, he must have a mind disposed to adapt itself according to the wind, and as the variations of fortune dictate, and, as I said before, not deviate from what is good, if possible, but be able to do evil if constrained.

Proletarian Ends Justify Any Means

Leon Trotsky

The third statement is by Lenin's closest associate (and Stalin's enemy), Leon Trotsky (1877–1940). He maintains that in revolutionary politics "a means can be justified only by its end" which in turn must be justified. The problem is who does the justifying and according to what criteria. Trotsky added that lying and violence resulted from the class nature of the existing society and that, in the struggle against immoral society, the revolutionary use of lying and violence was morally justified: "The revolution itself is a product of class society and of necessity bears its traits." Only in a society without social contradictions, according to Trotsky, will there be no lies or violence. In 1940 Stalin sent an agent to murder Trotsky in his exile in Mexico. The murderer used a primitive axe for the purpose: the end justified the means.

A means can be justified only by its end. But the end in its turn needs to be justified. From the Marxist point of view, which expresses the historical interests of the proletariat, the end is justified if it leads to increasing the power of man over nature and to the abolition of the power of man over man. . . .

Dialectic materialism does not know dualism between means and end. The end flows naturally from the historical movement. Organically the means are subordinated to the end. The immediate end becomes the means for a further end. . . .

"We are to understand then that in achieving this end anything is permissible?" sarcastically demands the philistine, demonstrating that he understood nothing. That is permissible, we answer, which *really* leads to the liberation of mankind. Since this end can be achieved only through revolution, the liberating morality of the proletariat of necessity is endowed with a revolutionary character. It irreconcilably counteracts not only religious dogma but every kind of idealistic fetish, these philosophic gendarmes of

From pp. 395–396 of Irving Howe (Ed.), *The Basic Writings of Trotsky* (New York: Random House, Inc., 1965).

the ruling class. It deduces a rule of conduct from the laws of the development of society, thus primarily from the class struggle, this law of all laws.

"Just the same," the moralist continues to insist, "does it mean that in the class struggle against capitalists all means are permissible: lying, frame-up, betrayal, murder, and so on?" Permissible and obligatory are those and only those means, we answer, which unite the revolutionary proletariat, fill their hearts with irreconcilable hostility to oppression, teach them contempt for official morality and its democratic echoers, imbue them with consciousness of their own historic mission, raise their courage and spirit of self-sacrifice in the struggle.

27 / The Politics of Nonviolence

American Friends Service Committee

The following excerpt represents a protest against man's inhumanity to man. It also expresses a reaffirmation that nonviolence (in Gandhian terms *ahimsa,* as opposed to violence, *himsa*) resides in man's nature and can therefore be learned by all. Both Gandhi and the Quakers do not expect everyone to learn nonviolence quickly and practice it perfectly. "A personal commitment to practice peace begins with the effort to live affirmatively," says the Quaker pamphlet. "Here is no simple decision to say 'no' to military power and carry on business as usual in every other department of life."

Recognizing that it is impossible for the United States government to change its standard of values until a substantial number of its people first change theirs, the Quaker thesis reemphasizes the way of reaching the community through individual commitments. "If ever truth reaches power, if it ever speaks to the individual citizen, it will not be the argument that convinces. Rather it will be his own inner sense of integrity that impels him to say: 'Here I stand. Regardless of relevance or consequence,[5] I can do no other.' . . . It takes faith for an individual to live this way—faith in the 'impossible' ideal of world community."

From pp. 29–66 *(passim)* of *Speak Truth to Power: A Quaker Search for an Alternative to Violence* (Philadelphia: American Friends Service Committee, 1955). Reprinted by permission.

[5] Compare with Max Weber (Selection 25) and his concept of an "ethic of ultimate ends" according to which man does right by leaving the results with the Lord.

This emphasis on individual faith rather than argument is also typical of the Gandhian approach. "Nonviolence," says Gandhi, "which is a quality of heart, cannot come by an appeal to the brain." [6] This, in the opinion of some, including some integral though rational pacifists, is the basic weakness of the Gandhian or Quaker approach to international politics. In the opinion of others, this may be its main force.

Like Gandhi, the Quakers express the belief in the attainment of good ends only by good means; such belief is opposite to most of the following selections. The quaker way is clearly based on the Sermon on the Mount and related to the religious thought of the Dutch scholar Erasmus (1466–1536) who preached :"Try to help your enemy by overcoming him with kindness and meekness. If you can avoid evil by suffering it, do so." This corresponds to Gandhi's teaching: "In nonviolence the bravery consists in dying, not in killing." [7] According to the Quakers, practitioners of nonviolent politics must be ready to accept, but never cause, suffering: "To risk all may be to gain all. . . . We do fear death, but we want to live."

One important aspect of the Gandhian and Quaker creed is the firm hope for a contagious effect of a good example. The Quaker search for nonviolent alternatives to violent international politics aims at transforming relations among nations and men by gradually bringing about a peaceful transfer of power, effected freely and without compulsion by all concerned. The peaceful transfer of power from the British empire to Gandhian India is usually given as an example of the effectiveness of *ahimsa*. Gandhi's soul-force movement did aim at changing the British imperialistic attitudes and policies by nonviolent pressures. Gandhi's hope was to induce a compromise acceptable to all.

When Britain, exhausted by her involvements in two world wars, withdrew from India, her subsequent political behavior elsewhere, including her atomic armament and the rule over other colonies, gave little indication of a dramatic change of the British attitude. It should be recalled that this target of Gandhian nonviolent tactics, Great Britain, was a liberal and democractic community at home although an imperialistic conqueror abroad. How effective would have Gandhi been against Mao's China, Hitler's Germany, or Stalin's Russia? Furthermore, the massacres that the Hindu and Moslem communities inflicted upon each other in the wake of British withdrawal and the division of India into three segments (East Pakistan, India, and West Pakistan) questions the impact of Gandhian teaching even upon his own compatriots. "When we decided on partition of India and Pakistan," noted with sadness Gandhi's disciple Prime Minister Nehru in a press conference in February 1959, "I do not think any of us ever thought that there would be this terror of mutual killing after partition. It was in a sense to avoid that that we decided on partition. So we paid double price for it, first, you might say politically, ideologically; second, the actual thing happened that we tried to avoid." The estimate of the number of Hindus

---

[6] Mahatma Gandhi, *Non-Violence in Peace and War*, Vol. I (Ahmedabad: Navajivan Publishing House, 1948), p. 265.

[7] *Ibid.*, p. 276.

and Moslems killed in communal riots exceeds the number of the Japanese killed at Hiroshima five times.[8]

In view of the above facts and the evidence of continuing inhumanity of men the Quaker statement may appear naïve and impractical. And yet, nobody can deny the urgency of that appeal nor its honesty and readiness to self-sacrifice on the part of the initiators and authors of the pamphlet.

... The basic assumption upon which United States foreign policy rests is that our national interest can best be served by military preparedness against a Soviet threat on the one hand, and by constructive and world-wide economic, political, and social programs on the other. The most common image used to suggest an adequate American policy is that of a wall of military power as a shield against communism, behind which the work of democracy, in raising the level of life and educating the minds of men, can be carried on. Our material strength must provide the basis of security so that men may have a chance to grow and develop.

This is an appealing image, reflecting both our peaceful intentions and our high aspirations, but we believe it is false and illusory. We believe that whatever may have been true in the past, it is now impossible for a great nation to commit itself both to military preparedness and to carrying forward a constructive and positive program of peacemaking. We believe these two aims have become mutually exclusive, and that a willingness to resort to organized mass violence under any circumstances requires a commitment that condemns all other desires and considerations to relative ineffectiveness. . . .

The Devil Theory

If the United States has not been able to translate its desire for peace into policies that will actually achieve it, and if, as we have suggested, the underlying cause of the failure is our commitment to violence, is there any other policy that could be pursued which would offer more hope? A considerable number of our fellow Americans insist there is not. When it is suggested that reliance upon military might may well bring about our national ruin, they respond: "Perhaps you are right about that, but we have no other choice. The Soviet Union and communism are trying to impose

---

[8] That losses of human life in civil wars or riots may exceed those recorded at Dresden or Hiroshima is unfortunately not an uncommon experience. It is for instance officially admitted by the Indonesian government that in the wake of the anti-Communist coup in 1965 180,000 Communists were slaughtered (the majority of whom were members of the Chinese minority in Indonesia); unofficially it is estimated that the real total was 360,000 to 400,000. It is in this connection that Marcuse warned against placing an automatic equal sign between humanity and the student protesters: the anti-Communist riots were actually initiated by the Indonesian students.

upon us an evil so inhuman that under it life would not be worth living at all. To submit to this evil is to condemn our children to a degraded existence, and this is something which Americans cannot in honor accept. And since the Soviet Union will not be deterred by anything but force, we must be prepared to meet force with force, even though the process may end by destroying us."

We are not insensitive to this dilemma in which so many Americans find themselves. It arises at least in part from the conviction that for nations, as for individuals, there are values greater than physical survival. Moreover, we cannot brush aside the extent of evil within the Soviet orbit. The police state, government by terrorism and thought control, slave labor, mass deportations, and a monolithic party that demands unconditional obedience and denies the right of private conscience—all these are characteristics of any totalitarian system of government. In the face of such facts, it is understandable that most Americans have concluded that Soviet communism is the great evil abroad in the world, and that it is the prime responsibility of the United States to wield its vast power to protect mankind from its destructive influence.

This is the point where we believe many Americans misread the problem. Without overlooking the evils of communism, we must still reject the devil theory in history. It is an easy theory to accept, for men have made devils out of those they feared since the dawn of time. Indeed, in all the great conflicts of history, each belligerent has tended uniformly and insistently to attribute a monopoly of evil to the other. So in the struggles between Athens and Sparta, Rome and Carthage, Christian and Moslem, Catholic and Protestant. So in our own time in two world wars, and now finally in the growing conflict with the Soviet Union. . . .

Men tried to make the world safe for democracy by destroying Imperial Germany. But the devil reappeared in the Germany of Hitler, and so that Germany, too, was destroyed. Now once again the devil comes to life, and this time Americans are told his nationality is Russian, while Russians are told he is American. We think both are guilty of tragic oversimplification. We think the basic assumption of many of our fellow Americans as to the location of evil is wrong. We think, therefore, that the simple moral dilemma to which they point is false.

Our Real Enemy

The real evils that have driven the world to the present impasse, and which we must struggle to overcome, spring from the false values by which man has lived in East and West alike. Man's curse lies in his worship of the work of his hands, in his glorification of material things, in his failure to set any limit on his material needs. This idolatry leads him to lust for power, to disregard human personality, to ignore God, and to accept violence or any other means of achieving his ends. It is not an idolatry of which the communists alone are guilty. All men share it, and when it is examined, the global power struggle is given a new perspective. Let us be specific.

. . . One of the things that the United States fears most about the Soviet Union is its expansionism. The communist revolution proclaims itself as a global revolution, and in its seemingly insatiable lust for power has already brought much of the world within its orbit. Americans see this expansionism as something that must be halted at any cost and by whatever means.

But no less an historian than Arnold Toynbee has pointed out that a dominant factor in world history from about 1450 on was *the expansionism of the West*. It was the peoples of Western Europe, driven by their lust for power and possessions, who pushed out in all directions, subjugating or exterminating those who blocked the path, and resorting in their colonial operations to bloodshed and slavery and humiliation whenever it appeared necessary. Nor can the United States escape responsibility. Our history has also been marked by a dynamic, persistent, and seldom interrupted expansionism.

Less than two centuries ago the nation was a string of colonies along the Atlantic seaboard. Now it straddles the continent, and its military bastions are found in over half of all the nations in the world. Its navies cruise the coasts of Russia and China, and its bombers are based in Germany and Japan. It is easy for Americans to regard this as normal, though they would be outraged and terrified if Russian warships cruised our coasts and Russian bombers were based on Canada or Guatemala. It is also easy for Americans to forget that this expansionism was often as ruthless as that which we fear in others. The Indian was almost exterminated, the Negro and later the flood of European immigrants were cruelly exploited; violence was threatened or provoked with Mexico, with Spain, with Colombia, with Nicaragua—all in the name of expanding the power and influence of the United States.

To point out such things is not to justify either Russian or Western expansionism, nor is it to underestimate the human suffering and the social cost that are involved in new embodiments and contests of power. But it suggests that the disease is not geographical and that to build ever greater instruments of power is not to end the disease but to spread it until it destroys the whole organism of civilization. . . .

Finally, we come to the [Communist] acceptance of violence as the essential means of social revolution, and the corollary doctrine that the end justifies the means. Here again for many Americans are decisive reasons for citing Soviet communism as an absolute evil, which must at all costs be destroyed.

Violence has, indeed, reached unsurpassed proportions in our time. The outbreak of the first World War marked the beginning of this modern orgy of uncontrolled violence, and it has continued ever since. But no reputable historian has ventured the idea that either the first or the second World War was spawned by communism. Nor are the Russians responsible for the concept of blitzkrieg, or obliteration bombing, or for the first use of atomic weapons. These have all been loosed upon the world by the very nations which now profess outrage at the cynical Soviet concept of the role of violence and the validity of *any* means. Western theory is indeed outraged, but Western practice has in this area, too, belied Western theory. We have, in fact, been prepared to use any means to achieve *our* ends. Here again, as in so many other points in the exposure of the devil theory, we are reminded of the words Shakespeare put into the mouth of Shylock: "The villainy you teach me, I will execute, and it shall go hard, but I will better the instruction." . . .

It may be suggested that a way out is to attempt to coexist without war and without resolving the conflict. This course envisages an indefinite armed truce in the hope that time will produce changed conditions under which a more fundamental solution will be possible. To many thoughtful persons this is the most that can be hoped for, and certainly it is preferable to an attempt at violent resolution, but we believe no one should regard it as more than a temporary expedient. The dynamic nature of the principal contending powers and the basic conflict in their social philosophies promise continuing crises unless a more fundamental solution is found. . . .

A First Requirement for Solution

. . . We have insisted that violence is not the answer, but violence will persist until men rid themselves of the attitudes that justify it. As long as they remain blinded by self-righteousness, clinging to the dogmatic assumption that we-are-right-and-they-are-wrong or we-may-not-be-perfect-but-we're-better-than-they-are, so long will they justify a resort to violence. We believe, therefore, that any proposal to resolve the conflict without violence must begin with a recognition of the humbling fact of man's common guilt and common nobility. Without this recognition, the diplomatic representatives of the major contending powers, even if they can be persuaded to talk to one another, are bound when they negotiate to try to negotiate one another *out* of something which, ultimately, neither is willing to surrender. Negotiation on the assumption of moral superiority may succeed in marginal conflicts, but in central conflicts it is self-defeating. Self-righteousness is a rock on which negotiation always founders.

As the conflict between our country and the Soviet Union can in no case be resolved by might, so in no case can it be resolved by any method chained to self-righteousness. We who write this statement maintain that the only realistic hope left is to find a new basis for the resolution of the USA-USSR conflict, a basis that will free us for the truly creative action our times demand. The recognition that the evil is in Man is the basis and the only basis upon which efforts to reach a peaceful settlement can be saved from the fatal corruption of self-righteousness. . . .

To an attempt to explain and illustrate these non-violent ways of overcoming evil and dealing with human conflicts we now turn. We do so aware of the danger that those who profess non-violence may be tempted to self-righteousness. No one can be more wrong than those who are complacent about their own virtue or believe they have a simple and painless solution for the crisis of our age.

The Method of Non-Violence

What is this non-violent method that we suggest offers new hope? Its simplest and most obvious statement is found in the religious literature of many faiths, most familiarly to Christians in the Sermon on the Mount. At its heart, it is the effort to maintain unity among men. It seeks to knit the break in the sense of community whose fracture is both a cause and a result of human conflict. It relies upon love rather than hate, and though it involves a willingness to accept rather than inflict suffering, it is neither passive nor cowardly. It offers a way of meeting evil without relying on the ability to cause pain to the human being through whom evil is expressed. It seeks to change the attitude of the opponent rather than to force his submission through violence. It is, in short, the practical effort to overcome evil with good.

Most Americans reject as impractical the suggestion that it might offer a creative way out of our present international crisis. Much as they wish to end the scourge of war, and as ferquently as they have observed violence compounded by violence, they still cast aside as irrelevant the alternative which calls for renunciation of present methods in favor of the attempt to resolve conflict through the imaginative development of non-violence. "It's a nice idea," we are often told, "but it has no meaning in the brutal struggles of the present world. Men may dream of the day when nations will renounce violence, but in the meantime, international relations must be left to the realist."

They have been left to the "realist," and the results are written large and clear across the face of the world. The plain fact is that the "realists" have brought us to our greatest crisis. An arms race rages unchecked. Irrational hatred and massive retaliation are the established policies of great nations. Fear of atomic war grips the hearts of men, and paralyzes their intellect. Truly mankind stands at the edge of the precipice. Is the "realist" to be allowed to push us over? In his blind fury, is he now, like Samson, to pull the temple of civilization down upon himself and upon all men? Is it not time, while hope yet remains, to reconsider our easy rejection of the central perceptions of non-violence . . . point up the essential characteristics of the non-violent method . . . [and] the specific applications of this approach to the present world scene. . . .

The Context of a National Non-Violent Policy

1. *There would be revolutionary changes within the United States itself.* Since the non-violent insight underlines the necessity of first attacking our own evils, it is clear that the American people would be obligated to move farther in overcoming racial discrimination and religious intolerance. We would insist on maximum freedom of thought and expression, as demanded by our democratic philosophy, and would not tolerate tendencies toward transforming the nation into a police state. We would be more sensitive to the deadening impact of our industrial life. . . .

2. *The United States would give its support to the great social revolutions, which are both a major problem and a major hope of our time.* Regardless of whether men strive to overthrow domination from without or outworn feudalism from within, their determination is to achieve new dignity and status as human beings and to banish the physical poverty that has so long condemned them to misery. They deserve the support of every democratic society, and they would receive the support of this country if it were freed from its preoccupation with defense and the military power struggle. If this took place, men who seek freedom would no longer conclude, as many already have, that the only source of support is from communist nations, and they would cease to be available for communist armies. American support, moreover, would make it more possible for these revolutions themselves to be non-violent.

3. *The United States would devote its skills and resources to great programs of technical and economic assistance, carried on under United Nations auspices and with full participation in planning and administration by the receiving peoples.* The resources needed for these operations are so large that our own standard of living might be seriously affected, but the dividends would also be large. The mere fact of reducing the great economic imbalance between the United States and the poverty-stricken masses of Asia, Africa, and Latin America, would itself remove one of the major sources of embitterment and strife. Our willingness to share our material blessings, without ulterior motives and to an extent well beyond our unused

surpluses, would bring men to us as friends and cooperators, rather than alienate them as does present policy.

4. *The United States would get rid of its military establishment.* Various avenues might be taken to achieve this result. Many suggest that the most probable and most practical approach would be through the simple transfer of the security function to a world organization. The United Nations would assume the responsibility for defense, and might well be converted in the process into a federal instrument in much the same manner as the thirteen American colonies substituted a federal government for the unsatisfactory Articles of Confederation.

Others less insistent on the importance of world federation suggest that disarmament would occur as the result of multilateral agreement: universal in character, enforceable in practice, and complete down to the level needed for internal policing. Both of these approaches are valid, and both could be supported by the United States in the era about which we speculate, but in the last analysis a pacifist policy would require unilateral action if agreement could not be achieved. There is no escaping the necessity to be willing to act first ourselves if we are to have solid ground for getting others to act with us.

It will be said that for a nation to consider disarming alone in an armed world is madness; but the fact that obviously stares men in the face today is that *an armed world in this age is itself madness.* To refuse any longer to labor under the delusion that it is anything else is the beginning of common sense, as it is the counsel of divine wisdom. Moreover, it is quite possible that the Soviet Union, confronted with such a change in American behavior, might startle us with a new response. At the very least, the example of a people living without the burden of militarism and offering friendship to all, would call forth the impulses to freedom that exist in all men. . . .

Nor must it be forgotten how this whole non-violent era, about which we are speculating, would be brought about. Under our democratic philosophy, as we have already pointed out, it would not be created by fiat, but as the result of insistence on reconciling measures by a gradually growing pacifist minority. The writers are convinced that this process in itself would so change the climate of world opinion that no power on earth could oppose it effectively. . . .

Such is the program we would chart for the individual and for the state of which he is a part. We have not denied that it involves risk, but no policy can be formulated that does not involve risk. We have not suggested it will be easy, but only that no policy that aims at achieving peace can be easy. Finally, we have made no sweeping claims that it would work, but only that it appears to us more workable and more relevant than the barren doctrines of violence that now enslave us. We believe that it merits the consideration of thoughtful men.

28 / The Birth of the Atomic Age

Thomas F. Farrell

The following excerpt records the impression of an eyewitness of the first atomic explosion in a remote section of the Alamogordo Air Base, New Mexico at 5:30 A.M., July 16, 1945. The bomb was not dropped from a plane but was exploded on a platform on top of a 100-foot-high steel tower. General Farrell's observations were incorporated into a report, sent by General L. R. Groves to President Truman and Secretary Stimson, attending the Big Three Conference at Potsdam. Together with a group of atomic scientists, led by Dr. Oppenheimer, "the father of the atomic bomb," General Farrell observed the event from a control shelter, located 10,000 yards south of the point of explosion.

. . . The scene inside the shelter was dramatic beyond words. In and around the shelter were some 20-odd people concerned with last minute arrangements prior to firing the shot. Included were: Dr. Oppenheimer, the Director who had borne the great scientific burden of developing the weapon from the raw materials made in Tennessee and Washington and a dozen of his key assistants. . . . Everyone in that room knew the awful potentialities of the thing that they thought was about to happen. The scientists felt that their figuring must be right and that the bomb had to go off but there was in everyone's mind a strong measure of doubt. The feeling of many could be expressed by 'Lord, I believe; help Thou mine unbelief.' We were reaching into the unknown and we did not know what might come of it. It can be safely said that most of those present—Christian, Jew, and Atheist—were praying and praying harder than they had ever prayed before. If the shot were successful, it was a justification of the several years of intensive effort

From "Memorandum for the Secretary of War" (July 18, 1945), *Potsdam Papers,* Document 1305.

of tens of thousands of people—statesmen, scientists, engineers, manufacturers, soldiers, and many others in every walk of life.

In that brief instant in the remote. New Mexico desert the tremendous effort of the brains and brawn of all these people came suddenly and startlingly to the fullest fruition. Dr. Oppenheimer, on whom had rested a very heavy burden, grew tenser as the last seconds ticked off. He scarcely breathed. He held on to a post to steady himself. For the last few seconds, he stared directly ahead and then when the announcer shouted 'Now!' and there came this tremendous burst of light followed shortly thereafter by the deep growling roar of the explosion, his face relaxed into an expression of tremendous relief. Several of the observers standing back of the shelter to watch the lighting effects were knocked flat by the blast.

The tension in the room let up and all started congratulating each other. Everyone sensed 'This is it!' No matter what might happen now all knew that the impossible scientific job had been done. Atomic fission would no longer be hidden in the cloisters of the theoretical physicists' dreams. It was almost full grown at birth. It was a great new force to be used for good or for evil. There was a feeling in that shelter that those concerned with its nativity should dedicate their lives to the mission that it would always be used for good and never for evil.

Dr. Kistiakowsky, the impulsive Russian, threw his arms around Dr. Oppenheimer and embraced him with shouts of glee. Others were equally enthusiastic. All the pent-up emotions were released in those few minutes and all seemed to sense immediately that the explosion had far exceeded the most optimistic expectations and wildest hopes of the scientists. All seemed to feel that they had been present at the birth of a new age—The Age of Atomic Energy—and felt their profound responsibility to help in guiding into right channels the tremendous forces which had been unlocked for the first time in history.

As to the present war, there was a feeling that no matter what else might happen, we now had the means to insure its speedy conclusion and save thousands of American lives. As to the future, there had been brought into being something big and something new that would prove to be immeasurably more important than the discovery of electricity or any of the other great discoveries which have so affected our existence.

The effects could well be called unprecedented, magnificent, beautiful, stupendous and terrifying. No man-made phenomenon of such tremendous power had ever occurred before. The lighting effects beggared description. The whole country was lighted by a searing light with the intensity many times that of the midday sun. It was golden, purple, violet, gray and blue. It lighted every peak, crevasse and ridge of the nearby mountain range with a clarity and beauty that cannot be described but must be seen to be

imagined. It was that beauty the great poets dream about but describe most
poorly and inadequately.

29 / The Decision to Use the Atomic Bomb

Louis Morton

Why was the bomb dropped? However strange this may seem, the
official justification has humane overtones: It ended the war in the Pacific earlier
and at a lesser cost in human lives and suffering than would have been the case
if Japan had to be brought to unconditional surrender by conventional bombing
and subsequent invasion of the four main islands. The 1945 equation seemed
to be: 75,000 to 100,000 Japanese killed by the bomb as against the anticipated
total of one million dead and maimed for life on both sides.

This equation has been since attacked as false. One argument is that Japan
knew in the summer of 1945 that it was close to defeat; actually it began to sue
for peace, though not accepting yet the terms of unconditional surrender.
Conditional surrender was then one possible alternative—since, finally, even
after Hiroshima and Nagasaki, unconditional surrender was toned down and
the Japanese people were allowed by the victors to retain their imperial dynasty.
Another alternative was perhaps an experimental explosion of the atomic bomb
on a deserted atoll to be witnessed by the representatives of Japan and the
United Nations thus securing unconditional surrender by means of an atomic
demonstration, without destruction of human lives.

The foreign and domestic critics of the first use of nuclear weapons in history
have accused the United States of racial motivations, even suggesting that the
bomb would not have been dropped on the Germans had it been ready before
May 1945, since the Germans were a white people too, like the Americans.
While it cannot be denied that the anti-Japanese feeling after Pearl Harbor
contained racial overtones, in the same period the people and the leaders of
the United States, officially and nonofficially experienced a warm feeling toward
another nation of the yellow race, China. Furthermore, the fact is that the
initial decision to develop the bomb was based on the expectation that Nazi
Germany might develop it first and therefore the original hypothetical target
was Germany rather than Japan. If racial considerations were part of the deci-

From Louis Morton, "The Decision to Use the Atomic Bomb." Reprinted by special
permission from *Foreign Affairs,* January 1957. Copyright by the Council on Foreign
Relations, Inc., New York.

sion, the antisemitism of the Nazis was certainly much more a factor in Albert Einstein's famous letter to President Roosevelt suggesting the development of the bomb than any feeling of superiority toward an Oriental race.

Whatever the reader's final conclusion may be, he may find it both useful and disturbing to try, for himself, to answer the following hypothetical question (in the framework of our preceding discussion on the role of ethical considerations in political and military decisions): If no third alternative to either the atomic death of 75,000 Japanese or the conventional death of perhaps six or seven times that number was in July 1945 perceived as realistic, what would have been his own choice between the nuclear and the conventional ending of war?

The epic story of the development of the atomic bomb is by now well known. It began in 1939 when a small group of eminent scientists in this country called to the attention of the United States Government the vast potentialities of atomic energy for military purposes and warned that the Germans were already carrying on experiments in this field. The program initiated in October of that year with a very modest appropriation and later expanded into the two-billion-dollar Manhattan Project had only one purpose—to harness the energy of the atom in a chain reaction to produce a bomb that could be carried by aircraft if possible, and to produce it before the Germans could. That such a bomb, if produced, would be used, no responsible official even questioned. "At no time from 1941 to 1945," declared Mr. Stimson, "did I ever hear it suggested by the President, or by another responsible member of the Government, that atomic energy should not be used in the war." And Dr. J. Robert Oppenheimer recalled in 1954 that "we always assumed if they [atomic bombs] were neded, they would be used."

So long as the success of the project remained in doubt there seems to have been little or no discussion of the effects of an atomic weapon or the circumstances under which it would be used. "During the early days of the project," one scientist recalled, "we spent little time thinking about the possible effects of the bomb we were trying to make." It was a "neck-and-neck race with the Germans," the outcome of which might well determine who would be the victor in World War II. But as Germany approached defeat and as the effort to produce an atomic bomb offered increasing promise of success, those few men who knew what was being done and who appreciated the enormous implications of atomic energy became more and more concerned. Most of this concern came from the scientists in the Metallurgical Laboratory at Chicago, where by early 1945 small groups began to question the advisability of using the weapon they were trying to hard to build. It was almost as if they hoped the bomb would not work after it was completed.

On the military side, the realization that a bomb would probably be ready for testing in the summer of 1945 led to concrete planning for the use of the new weapon, on the assumption that the bomb when completed would work. By the end of 1944 a list of possible targets in Japan had been selected, and a B-29 squadron was trained for the specific job of delivering the bomb. . . .

It was not until March 1945 that it became possible to predict with certainty that the bomb would be completed in time for testing in July. On March 15, Mr. Stimson discussed the project for the last time with President Roosevelt, but their conversation dealt mainly with the effects of the use of the bomb, not with the question of whether it ought to be used. Even at this late date, there does not seem to have been any doubt at the highest levels that the bomb would be used against Japan if it would help bring the war to an early end. But on lower levels, and especially among the scientists at the Chicago laboratory, there was considerable reservation about the advisability of using the bomb.

After President Roosevelt's death, it fell to Stimson to brief the new President about the atomic weapon. At a White House meeting on April 25, he outlined the history and status of the program and predicted that "within four months we shall in all probability have completed the most terrible weapon ever known in human history." This meeting, like Stimson's last meeting with Roosevelt, dealt largely with the political and diplomatic consequences of the use of such a weapon rather than with the timing and manner of employment, the circumstances under which it would be used, or whether it would be used at all. The answers to these questions depended on factors not yet known. But Stimson recommended, and the President approved, the appointment of a special committee to consider them.

This special committee, known as the Interim Committee, played a vital role in the decision to use the bomb. Secretary Stimson was chairman. . . . James F. Byrnes, who held no official position at the time, was President Truman's personal representative. . . .

The work of the Interim Committee, in Stimson's words, "ranged over the whole field of atomic energy, in its political, military, and scientific aspects." . . . Of particular concern to the committee was the question of how long it would take another country, particularly the Soviet Union, to produce an atomic bomb. "Much of the discussion," recalled Dr. Oppenheimer who attended the meeting of June 1 as a member of a scientific panel, "revolved around the question raised by Secretary Stimson as to whether there was any hope at all of using this development to get less barbarous [*sic*] relations with the Russians."

The work of the Interim Committee was completed June 1, 1945, when it submitted its report to the President, recommending unanimously that:

1. The bomb should be used against Japan as soon as possible.
2. It should be used against a military target surrounded by other buildings.
3. It should be used without prior warning of the nature of the weapon. . . .

"The conclusions of the Committee," wrote Stimson, "were similar to my own, although I reached mine independently. I felt that to extract a genuine surrender from the Emperor and his military advisers, they must be administered a tremendous shock which would carry convincing proof of our power to destroy the empire. Such an effective shock would save many times the number of lives, both American and Japanese, that it would cost."

Among the scientists working on the Manhattan Project were many who did not agree. To them, the "wave of horror and repulsion" that might follow the sudden use of an atomic bomb would more than outweigh its military advantages. "It may be very difficult," they declared, "to persuade the world that a nation which was capable of secretly preparing and suddenly releasing a new weapon, as indiscriminate as the rocket bomb and a thousand times more destructive, is to be trusted in its proclaimed desire of having such weapons abolished by international agreement." The procedure these scientists recommended was, first, to demonstrate the new weapon "before the eyes of representatives of all the United Nations on the desert or a barren island," and then to issue "a preliminary ultimatum" to Japan. If this ultimatum was rejected, and "if the sanction of the United Nations (and of public opinion at home) were obtained," then and only then, said the scientists, should the United States consider using the bomb. "This may sound fantastic," they said, "but in nuclear weapons we have something entirely new in order of magnitude of destructive power, and if we want to capitalize fully on the advantage their possession gives us, we must use new and imaginative methods."

These views, which were forwarded to the Secretary of War on June 11, 1945, were strongly supported by 64 of the scientists in the Chicago Metallurgical Laboratory in a petition sent directly to the President. At about the same time, at the request of Dr. Arthur H. Compton, a poll was taken of the views of more than 150 scientists at the Chicago Laboratory. Five alternatives ranging from all-out use of the bomb to "keeping the existence of the bomb a secret" were presented. Of those polled, about two-thirds voted for a preliminary demonstration, either on a military objective or an uninhabited locality; the rest were split on all-out use and no use at all.

These views, and presumably others, were referred by Secretary Stimson to a distinguished Scientific Panel consisting of Drs. Arthur H. Compton,

Enrico Fermi, E. O. Lawrence and J. Robert Oppenheimer, all nuclear physicists of the first rank. "We didn't know beans about the military situation," Oppenheimer later said. "We didn't know whether they [the Japanese] could be caused to surrender by other means or whether the invasion [of Japan] was really inevitable. . . . We thought the two overriding considerations were the saving of lives in the war and the effect of our actions on the stability of the postwar world." On June 16 the panel reported that it had studied carefully the proposals made by the scientists but could see no practical way of ending the war by a technical demonstration. Almost regretfully, it seemed, the four members of the panel concluded that there was "no acceptable alternative to direct military use." "Nothing would have been more damaging to our effort," wrote Stimson, " . . . than a warning or demonstration followed by a dud—and this was a real possibility." With this went the fear, expressed by Byrnes, that if the Japanese were warned that an atomic bomb would be exploded over a military target in Japan as a demonstration, "they might bring our boys who were prisoners of war to that area." Furthermore, only two bombs would be available by August, the number General Groves estimated would be needed to end the war; these two have to obtain the desired effect quickly. And no one yet knew, nor would the scheduled ground test in New Mexico prove, whether a bomb dropped from an airplane would explode.

Nor, for that matter, were all those concerned certain that the bomb would work at all, on the ground or in the air. Of these doubters, the greatest was Admiral Leahy, who until the end remained unconvinced. "This is the biggest fool thing we have ever done," he told Truman after Vannevar Bush had explained to the President how the bomb worked. "The bomb will never go off, and I speak as an expert in explosives."

Thus, by mid-June 1945, there was virtual unanimity among the President's civilian advisers on the use of the bomb. The arguments of the opponents had been considered and rejected. So far as is known, the President did not solicit the views of the military or naval staffs, nor were they offered.

Military Considerations

The military situation on June 1, 1945, when the Interim Committee submitted its recommendations on the use of the atomic bomb, was distinctly favorable to the Allied cause. Germany had surrendered in May and troops from Europe would soon be available for redeployment in the Pacific. Manila had fallen in February; Iwo Jima was in American hands; and the success of the Okinawa invasion was assured. Air and submarine attacks had virtually cut off Japan from the resources of the Indies, and

B-29s from the Marianas were pulverizing Japan's cities and factories. The Pacific Fleet had virtually driven the Imperial Navy from the ocean, and planes of the fast carrier forces were striking Japanese naval bases in the Inland Sea. Clearly, Japan was a defeated nation.

Though defeated in a military sense, Japan showed no disposition to surrender unconditionally. And Japanese troops had demonstrated time and again that they could fight hard and inflict heavy casualties even when the outlook was hopeless. Allied plans in the spring of 1945 took these facts into account and proceeded on the assumption that an invasion of the home islands would be required to achieve at the earliest possible date the unconditional surrender of Japan—the announced objective of the war and the basic assumption of all strategic planning. . . .

Though the Joint Chiefs had accepted the invasion concept as the basis for preparations, . . . it was well understood that the final decision was yet to be made. By mid-June the time had come for such a decision and during that period the Joint Chiefs reviewed the whole problem of Japanese strategy. Finally, on June 18, at a meeting in the White House, they presented the alternatives to President Truman. . . .

General Marshall presented the case for invasion. . . . After considerable discussion of casualties and of the difficulties ahead, President Truman made his decision. Kyushu would be invaded as planned and preparations for the landing were to be pushed through to completion. . . . The program thus approved by Truman called for:

1. Air bombardment and blockade of Japan from bases in Okinawa, Iwo Jima, the Marianas and the Philippines.
2. Assault of Kyushu on November 1, 1945, and intensification of blockade and air bombardment.
3. Invasion of the industrial heart of Japan through the Tokyo Plain in central Honshu, tentative target date March 1, 1946.

During the White House meeting of June 18, there was discussion of the possibility of ending the war by political means. The President displayed a deep interest in the subject and both Stimson and McCloy emphasized the importance of the "large submerged class in Japan who do not favor the present war and whose full opinion and influence had never yet been felt." There was discussion also of the atomic bomb, since everyone present knew about the bomb and the recommendations of the Interim Committee. The suggestion was made that before the bomb was dropped, the Japanese should be warned that the United States had such a weapon. "Not one of the Chiefs nor the Secretary," recalled Mr. McCloy, "thought well of a bomb warning, an effective argument being that no one could be certain, in spite of the assurances of the scientists, that the 'thing would go off.' "

Though the defeat of the enemy's armed forces in the Japanese homeland was considered a prerequisite to Japan's surrender, it did not follow that Japanese forces elsewhere, especially those on the Asiatic mainland, would surrender also. It was to provide for just this contingency, as well as as to pin down those forces during the invasion of the home islands, that the Joint Chiefs had recommended Soviet entry into the war against Japan.

Soviet participation was a goal long pursued by the Americans. Both political and military authorities seem to have been convinced from the start that Soviet assistance, conceived in various ways, would shorten the war and lessen the cost. In October 1943, Marshal Stalin had told Cordell Hull, then in Moscow for a conference, that the Soviet Union would eventually declare war on Japan. At the Tehran Conference in November of that year, Stalin had given the Allies formal notice of this intention and reaffirmed it in October 1944. In February 1945, at the Yalta Conference, Roosevelt and Stalin had agreed on the terms of Soviet participation in the Far Eastern war. Thus, by June 1945, the Americans could look forward to Soviet intervention at a date estimated as three months after the defeat of Germany.

But by the summer of 1945 the Americans had undergone a change of heart. Though the official position of the War Department still held that "Russian entry will have a profound military effect in that almost certainly it will materially shorten the war and thus save American lives," few responsible American officials were eager for Soviet intervention or as willing to make concessions as they had been at an earlier period. What had once appeared extremely desirable appeared less so now that the war in Europe was over and Japan was virtually defeated. President Truman, one official recalled, stated during a meeting devoted to the question of Soviet policy that agreements with Stalin had up to that time been "a one-way street" and that "he intended thereafter to be firm in his dealings with the Russians." . . .

The failure of the Soviets to abide by agreements made at Yalta had also done much to discourage the American desire for further coöperation with them. But after urging Stalin for three years to declare war on Japan, the United States Government could hardly ask him now to remain neutral. Moreover, there was no way of keeping the Rusians out even if there had been a will to do so. In Harriman's view, "Russia would come into the war regardless of what we might do."

A further difficulty was that Allied intelligence still indicated that Soviet intervention would be desirable, if not necessary, for the success of the invasion strategy. In Allied intelligence, Japan was portrayed as a defeated nation whose military leaders were blind to defeat. Though her industries had been seriously crippled by air bombardment and naval blockade and her armed forces were critically deficient in many of the resources of war, Japan was still far from surrender. She had ample reserves of weapons and ammunition and an army of 5,000,000 troops, 2,000,000 of them in the home islands. The latter could be expected to put up a strong resistance to invasion. In the opinion of the intelligence experts, neither blockade nor bombing alone would produce unconditional surrender before the date set for invasion. And the invasion itself, they believed, would be costly and possibly prolonged.

According to these intelligence reports, the Japanese leaders were fully aware of their desperate situation but would continue to fight in the hope of avoiding complete defeat by securing a better bargaining position. Allied warweariness and disunity, or some miracle, they hoped, would offer them a way out. "The Japanese believe," declared an intelligence estimate of June 30, " . . . that unconditional surrender would be the equivalent of national extinction, and there are as yet no indications that they are ready to accept such terms." It appeared also to the intelligence experts that Japan might surrender at any time "depending upon the conditions of surrender" the Allies might offer. Clearly these conditions, to have any chance of acceptance, would have to include retention of the imperial system.

How accurate were these estimates? Judging from postwar accounts of Japan, they were very close to the truth. Since the defeat at Saipan, when Tojo had been forced to resign, the strength of the "peace party" had been increasing. . . .

The Suzuki Cabinet that came into power in April 1945 had an unspoken mandate from the Emperor to end the war as quickly as possible. But it was faced immediately with another problem when the Soviet Government announced it would not renew the neutrality pact after April 1946. The German surrender in May produced another crisis in the Japanese Government and led, after considerable discussion, to a decision to seek Soviet mediation.

At the end of June, the Japanese finally approached the Soviet Government directly through Ambassador Sato in Moscow, asking that it mediate with the Allies to bring the Far Eastern war to an end. In a series of messages between Tokyo and Moscow, which the Americans intercepted and decoded, the Japanese Foreign Office outlined the position of the government and instructed Ambassador Sato to make arrangements for a special envoy from the Emperor who would be empowered to make terms for Soviet mediation. Unconditional surrender, he was told, was completely unacceptable, and time was of the essence. But the Russians, on one pretext and another, delayed their answer until mid-July when Stalin and Molotov left for Potsdam. Thus, the Japanese Government had by then accepted defeat and was seeking desperately for a way out; but it was not willing even at this late date to surrender unconditionally, and would accept no terms that did not include the preservation of the imperial system.

Allied intelligence thus had estimated the situation in Japan correctly. Allied invasion strategy had been reëxamined and confirmed in mid-June, and the date for the invasion fixed. The desirability of Soviet assistance had been confirmed also and plans for her entry into the war during August could now be made. No decision had been reached on the use of the atomic bomb, but the President's advisers had recommended it. The decision was the President's and he faced it squarely. But before he could make it he would want to know whether the measures already concerted would produce unconditional surrender at the earliest moment and at the lowest cost. If they could not, then he would have to decide whether circumstances warranted employment of a bomb that Stimson had already labeled as "the most terrible weapon ever known in human history."

The Decision

Though responsibility for the decision to use the atomic bomb was the President's, he exercised it only after careful study of the recommendations of his senior advisers. Chief among these was the Secretary of War, under whose broad supervision the Manhattan Project had been placed. Already deeply concerned over the cost of the projected invasion, the political effects of Soviet intervention and the potential consequences of the use of the atomic bomb, Stimson sought a course that would avoid all these evils. The difficulty, as he saw it, lay in the requirement for unconditional surrender. It was a phrase that might make the Japanese desperate and lead to a long and unnecessary campaign of attrition that would be extremely costly to both sides. But there was no way of getting around the term; it was firmly rooted in Allied war aims and its renunciation was certain to lead to charges of appeasement.

But if this difficulty could be overcome, would the Japanese respond if terms were offered? The intelligence experts thought so, and the radio intercepts from Tokyo to Moscow bore them out. So far as the Army was concerned there was much to be gained by such a course. Not only might it reduce the enormous cost of the war, but it would also make possible a settlement in the Western Pacific "before too many of our allies are committed there and have made substantial contributions towards the defeat of Japan." In the view of the War Department these aims justified "any concessions which might be attractive to the Japanese, so long as our realistic aims for peace in the Pacific are not adversely affected."

The problem was to formulate terms that would meet these conditions.

There was considerable discussion of this problem in Washington in the spring of 1945 by officials in the Department of State and in the War and Navy Departments. Joseph C. Grew, Acting Secretary of State, proposed to the President late in May that he issue a proclamation urging the Japanese to surrender and assuring them that they could keep the Emperor. Though Truman did not act on the suggestion, he thought it "a sound idea" and told Grew to discuss it with his cabinet colleagues and the Joint Chiefs. On June 18, Grew was back with the report that these groups favored the idea, but that there were differences on the timing.

Grew's ideas, as well as those of others concerned, were summarized by Stimson in a long and carefully considered memorandum to the President on July 2. Representing the most informed military and political estimate of the situation at this time, this memorandum constitutes a state paper of the first importance. If any one document can be said to provide the basis for the President's warning to Japan and his final decision to use the atomic bomb, this is it.

The gist of Stimson's argument was that the most promising alternative to the long and costly struggle certain to follow invasion was to warn the Japanese "of what is to come" and to give them an opportunity to surrender. There was, he thought, enough of a chance that such a course would work to make the effort worthwhile. Japan no longer had any allies, her navy was virtually destroyed and she was increasingly vulnerable to air attack and naval blockade. Against her were arrayed the increasingly powerful forces of the Allies, with their "inexhaustible and untouched industrial resources." In these circumstances, Stimson believed the Japanese people would be susceptible to reason if properly approached. "Japan," he pointed out, "is not a nation composed of mad fanatics of an entirely different mentality from ours. On the contrary, she has within the past century shown herself to possess extremely intelligent people. . . . " But any attempt, Stimson added, "to exterminate her armies and her population by gunfire or other means will tend to produce a fusion of race solidity and antipathy. . . . "

A warning to Japan, Stimson contended, should be carefully timed. It should come before the actual invasion, before destruction had reduced the Japanese "to fanatical despair" and, if the Soviet Union had already entered the war, before the Russian attack had progressed too far. It should also emphasize, Stimson believed, the inevitability and completeness of the destruction ahead and the determination of the Allies to strip Japan of her conquests and to destroy the influence of the military clique. It should be a strong warning and should leave no doubt in Japanese minds that they would have to surrender unconditionally and submit to Allied occupation.

The warning, as Stimson envisaged it, had a double character. While promising destruction and devastation, it was also to hold out hope to the

Japanese if they heeded its mesage. In his memorandum, therefore, Stimson stressed the positive features of the warning and recommended that it include a disavowal of any intention to destroy the Japanese nation or to occupy the country permanently. Once Japan's military clique had been removed from power and her capacity to wage war destroyed, it was Stimson's belief that the Allies should withdraw and resume normal trade relations with the new and peaceful Japanese Government. "I personally think," he declared, "that if in saying this we should add that we do not exclude a constitutional monarchy under her present dynasty, it would substantially add to the chance of acceptance."

Not once in the course of this lengthy memorandum was mention made of the atomic bomb. There was no need to do so. Everyone concerned understood clearly that the bomb was the instrument that would destroy Japan and impress on the Japanese Government the hopelessness of any course but surrender. As Stimson expressed it, the atomic bomb was "the best possible sanction," the single weapon that would convince the Japanese "of our power to destroy the empire."

Though Stimson considered a warning combined with an offer of terms and backed up by the sanction of the atomic bomb as the most promising means of inducing surrender at any early date, there were other courses that some thought might produce the same result. One was the continuation and intensification of air bombardment coupled with surface and underwater blockade. This course had already been considered and rejected as insufficient to produce surrender, though its advocates were by no means convinced that this decision was a wise one. And Stimson himself later justified the use of the bomb on the ground that by November 1 conventional bombardment would have caused greater destruction than the bomb. This apparent contradiction is explained by the fact that the atomic bomb was considered to have a psychological effect entirely apart from the damage wrought.

Nor did Stimson, in his memorandum, consider the effect of the Soviet Union's entry into the war. By itself, this action could not be counted on to force Japan to capitulate, but combined with bombardment and blockade it might do so. At least that was the view of Brigadier-General George A. Lincoln, one of the Army's top planners, who wrote in June that "probably it will take Russian entry into the war, coupled with a landing, or imminent threat of landing on Japan proper by us, to convince them [the Japanese] of the hopelessness of their position." Why, therefore, was it not possible to issue the warning prior to a Soviet declaration of war against Japan and rely on that event, together with an intensified air bombardment, to produce the desired result? If together they could not secure Japan's surrender, would there not still be time to use the bomb before the scheduled invasion of Kyushu in November?

No final answer to this question is possible with the evidence at hand. But one cannot ignore the fact that some responsible officials feared the political consequences of Soviet intervention and hoped that ultimately it would prove unnecessary. This feeling may unconsciously have made the atom bomb solution more attractive than it might otherwise have been. Some officials may have believed, too, that the bomb could be used as a powerful deterrent to Soviet expansion in Europe, where the Red tide had successively engulfed Rumania, Bulgaria, Jugoslavia, Czechoslovakia and Hungary. In an interview with three of the top scientists in the Manhattan Project early in June, Mr. Byrnes did not, according to Leo Szilard, argue that the bomb was needed to defeat Japan, but rather that it should be dropped to "make Russia more manageable in Europe." [9]

It has been asserted also that the desire to justify the expenditure of the two billion dollars spent on the Manhattan Project may have disposed some favorably toward the use of the bomb. Already questions had been asked in Congress, and the end of the war would almost certainly bring on a full-scale investigation. What more striking justification of the Manhattan Project than a new weapon that had ended the war in one sudden blow and saved countless American lives? "It was my reaction," wrote Admiral Leahy, "that the scientists and others wanted to make this test because of the vast sums that had been spent on the project. Truman knew that, and so did other people involved."

This explanation hardly does credit to those involved in the Manhattan Project and not even P. M. S. Blackett, one of the severest critics of the

[9] Ed. note: In his book *Atomic Diplomacy: Hiroshima and Potsdam: The Use of the Atomic Bomb and the American Confrontation with Soviet Power* (New York: Simon and Schuster, Inc., 1965), pp. 240–242, Gar Alperovitz argues that the demonstration of the United States atomic superiority and readiness to use it against an enemy
    ... was needed to convince the Russians to accept the American plan for a stable peace. And the crucial point of this effort was the need to force agreement on the main questions in dispute: the American proposals for Central and Eastern Europe. . . . Vannevar Bush, Stimson's chief aide for atomic matters, has been quite explicit: "That bomb was developed on time. . . ." Not only did it mean a quick end to the Japanese war, but "it was also delivered on time so that there was no necessity for any concession to Russia at the end of the war."

Alperovitz also records the change of mind of the Secretary of War, Stimson, one month after Hiroshima:

    By early September the Secretary of War had come full circle, concluding that "I was wrong" and that the attempt to use the atomic bomb to gain diplomatic objectives was "by far the more dangerous course." In a profoundly ironic, but unsuccessful, attempt to change the policy he had launched, shortly before leaving office Stimson urged an immediate and direct approach to Moscow to attempt to establish international control of atomic energy which might head off "an armament race of a rather desperate character." Apparently greatly disturbed by the bombing of Hiroshima, and now openly opposed to Secretary Byrnes, he advised: *"If we fail to approach them now and merely continue to negotiate with them, having this weapon rather ostentatiously on our hip, their suspicions and their distrust of our purposes and motives will increase."*

decision to use the bomb, accepted it. "The wit of man," he declared, "could hardly devise a theory of the dropping of the bomb, both more insulting to the American people, or more likely to lead to an energetically pursued Soviet defense policy."

But even if the need to justify these huge expenditures is discounted—and certainly by itself it could not have produced the decision—the question still remains whether those who held in their hands a weapon thought capable of ending the war in one stroke could justify withholding that weapon. Would they not be open to criticism for failing to use every means at their disposal to defeat the enemy as quickly as possible, thereby saving many American lives?

And even at that time there were some who believed that the new weapon would ultimately prove the most effective deterrent to war yet produced. How better to outlaw war forever than to demonstrate the tremendous destructive power of this weapon by using it against an actual target?

By early July 1945 the stage had been set for the final decision. Stimson's memorandum had been approved in principle and on July 4 the British had given their consent to the use of the bomb against Japan. It remained only to decide on the terms and timing of the warning. This was the situation when the Potsdam Conference opened on July 17, one day after the bomb had been successfully exploded in a spectacular demonstration at Alamogordo, New Mexico. The atomic bomb was a reality and when the news reached Potsdam there was great excitement among those who were let in on the secret. Instead of the prospect of long and bitter months of fighting the Japanese, there was now a vision, "fair and bright indeed it seemed" to Churchill, "of the end of the whole war in one or two violent shocks."

President Truman's first action was to call together his chief advisers—Byrnes, Stimson, Leahy, Marshall, King and Arnold. "I asked for their opinion whether the bomb should be used," he later wrote. The consensus was that it should. Here at last was the miracle to end the war and solve all the perplexing problems posed by the necessity for invasion. But because no one could tell what effect the bomb might have "physically or psychologically," it was decided to proceed with the military plans for the invasion.

No one at this time, or later in the conference, raised the question of whether the Japanese should be informed of the existence of the bomb. That question, it will be recalled, had been discussed by the Scientific Panel on June 16 and at the White House meeting with the JCS, the service Secretaries and Mr. McCloy on June 18. For a variety of reasons, including uncertainty as to whether the bomb would work, it had then been decided that the Japanese should not be warned of the existence of the new weapon. The successful explosion of the first bomb on July 17 did not apparently outweigh the reasons advanced earlier for keeping the bomb a secret, and evidently none of the men involved thought the question needed to be reviewed. The Japanese would learn of the atomic bomb only when it was dropped on them.

The secrecy that had shrouded the development of the atomic bomb was torn aside briefly at Potsdam, but with no visible effect. On July 24, on the advice of his chief advisers, Truman informed Marshal Stalin "casually" that the Americans had "a new weapon of unusual destructive force." "The Russian Premier," he recalled, "showed no special interest. All he said was that he was glad to hear it and hoped we would make 'good use of it against the Japanese.'" One cannot but wonder whether the Marshal was preoccupied at the moment or simulating a lack of interest.[10]

On the miiltary side, the Potsdam Conference developed nothing new. The plans already made were noted and approved. Even at this late stage the question of the bomb was divorced entirely from military plans and the final report of the conference accepted as the main effort the invasion of the Japanese home islands. November 15, 1946, was accepted as the planning date for the end of the war against Japan.

During the conference, Stalin told Truman about the Japanese overtures —information that the Americans already had. The Marshal spoke of the matter also to Churchill, who discussed it with Truman, suggesting cautiously that some offer be made to Japan. "Mr. Stimson, General Marshall, and the President," he later wrote, "were evidently searching their hearts, and we had no need to press them. We knew of course that the Japanese were ready to give up all conquests made in the war." That same night, after dining with Stalin and Truman, the Prime Minister wrote that the Russians intended to attack Japan soon after August 8—perhaps within two weeks of that date. Truman presumably received the same information, confirming Harry Hopkins' report of his conversation with Stalin in Moscow in May.

[10] Ed. note: In his book on the Potsdam Conference, *Between War and Peace* (Princeton, N. J.: Princeton University Press, 1960), p. 178, Herbert Feis commented on the apparent lack of interest demonstrated by Stalin at Potsdam:

> What had been feared had not come to pass. Stalin had not tried to find out what the nature of the new weapon was, or how was it made. . . . But was this only because he did not realize the significance of what Truman was telling him? Stalin was not dull in grasping the meaning of even the most passing remark, or incurious about any improvements in weapons. It did not occur to any of the American and British officials who were at Potsdam that Stalin might already have knowledge of the production and testing of the new weapon. Possibly he did not. But it would be curious if he had not, in view of the secret and illicit reports that had been sent by Soviet agents to Moscow about the problems solved in making the bomb, the engineering difficulties mastered, and the method of denotation.

Herbert Feis refers to the famous communist spies who had been working within the framework of the Manhattan Project—especially Klaus Fuchs, a member of the scientific team at Los Alamos, New Mexico—and who were later convicted for their espionage activities and transmissions of atomic secrets to the Soviet spy network.

All that remained now was to warn Japan and give her an opportunity to surrender. In this matter Stimson's and Grew's views, as outlined in the memorandum of July 2, were accepted, but apparently on the advice of the former Secretary of State Cordell Hull it was decided to omit any reference to the Emperor. Hull's view, solicited by Byrnes before his departure for Potsdam, was that the proposal smacked of appeasement and "seemed to guarantee continuance not only of the Emperor but also of the feudal privileges of a ruling caste." And should the Japanese reject the warning, the proposal to retain the imperial system might well encourage resistance and have "terrible political repercussions" in the United States. For these reasons he recommended that no statement about the Emperor be made until "the climax of Allied bombing and Russia's entry into the war." Thus, the final terms offered to the Japanese in the Potsdam Declaration on July 26 made no mention of the Emperor or of the imperial system. Neither did the declaration contain any reference to the atom bomb but simply warned the Japanese of the consequences of continued resistance. Only those already familiar with the weapon could have read the references to inevitable and complete destruction as a warning of atomic warfare.

The receipt of the Potsdam Declaration in Japan led to frantic meetings to decide what should be done. It was finally decided not to reject the note but to await the results of the Soviet overture. At this point, the military insisted that the government make some statement to the people, and on July 28 Premier Suzuki declared to the press that Japan would ignore the declaration, a statement that was interpreted by the Allies as a rejection.

To the Americans the rejection of the Potsdam Declaration confirmed the view that the military was still in control of Japan and that only a decisive act of violence could remove them. The instrument for such action lay at hand in the atomic bomb; events now seemed to justify its use. But in the hope that the Japanese might still change their minds, Truman held off orders on the use of the bomb for a few days. Only silence came from Tokyo, for the Japanese were waiting for a reply from the Soviet Government, which would not come until the return of Stalin and Molotov from Potsdam on August 6. Prophetically, Foreign Minister Tojo wrote Sato on August 2, the day the Potsdam Conference ended, that he could not afford to lose a single day in his efforts to conclude arrangements with the Russians "if we were to end the war before the assault on our mainland." By that time, President Truman had already decided on the use of the bomb.

Preparations for dropping the two atomic bombs produced thus far had been under way for some time. The components of the bombs had been sent by cruiser to Tinian in May and the fissionable material was flown out in mid-July. The B-29s and crews were ready and trained, standing by for orders, which would come through the Commanding General, U. S. Army Strategic Air Forces in the Pacific, General Spaatz. Detailed arrangements and schedules were completed and all that was necessary was to issue orders.

At General Arnold's insistence, the responsibility for selecting the particular target and fixing the exact date and hour of the attack was assigned to the field commander, General Spaatz. In orders issued on July 25 and approved by Stimson and Marshall, Spaatz was ordered to drop the "first special bomb as soon as weather will permit visual bombing after about 3 August 1945 on one of the targets: Hiroshima, Kokura, Niigata, and Nagasaki." He was instructed also to deliver a copy of this order personally to MacArthur and Nimitz. Weather was the critical factor because the bomb had to be dropped by visual means, and Spaatz delegated to his chief of staff, Major-General Curtis E. LeMay, the job of deciding when the weather was right for this most important mission.

From the dating of the order to General Spaatz it has been argued that President Truman was certain the warning would be rejected and had fixed the date for the bombing of Hiroshima even before the issuance of the Potsdam Declaration. But such an argument ignores the military necessities. For operational reasons, the orders had to be issued in sufficient time "to set the military wheels in motion." In a sense, therefore, the decision was made on July 25. It would stand unless the President changed his mind. "I had made the decision," wrote Truman in 1955. "I also instructed Stimson that the order would stand unless I notified him that the Japanese reply to our ultimatum was acceptable." The rejection by the Japanese of the Potsdam Declaration confirmed the orders Spaatz had already received.

The Japanese Surrender

On Tinian and Guam, preparations for dropping the bomb had been completed by August 3. The original plan was to carry out the operation on August 4, but General LeMay deferred the attack because of bad weather over the target. On August 5 the forecasts were favorable and he gave the word to proceed with the mission the following day. At 0245 on August 6, the bomb-carrying plane was airborne. Six and a half hours later the bomb was released over Hiroshima, Japan's eighth largest city, to explode 50 seconds later at a height of about 2,000 feet. The age of atomic warfare had opened.

Aboard the cruiser *Augusta* on his way back to the United States, President Truman received the news by radio. That same day a previously prepared release from Washington announced to the world that an atomic bomb had been dropped on Hiroshima and warned the Japanese that if they did not surrender they could expect "a rain of ruin from the air, the like of which has never been seen on this earth."

On August 7, Ambassador Sato in Moscow received word at last that Molotov would see him the next afternoon. At the appointed hour he arrived at the Kremlin, full of hope that he would receive a favorable reply to the Japanese proposal for Soviet mediation with the Allies to end the war. Instead, he was handed the Soviet declaration of war, effective on August 9. thus, three months to the day after Germany's surrender, Marshal Stalin had lived up to his promise to the Allies.

Meanwhile, President Truman had authorized the use of the second bomb —the last then available. The objective was Kokura, the date August 9. But the plane carrying the bomb failed to make it run over the primary target and hit the secondary target, Nagasaki, instead. The next day Japan sued for peace.

The close sequence of events between August 6 and 10, combined with the fact that the bomb was dropped almost three months before the scheduled invasion of Kyushu and while the Japanese were trying desperately to get out of the war, has suggested to some that the bombing of Hiroshima had a deeper purpose than the desire to end the war quickly. This purpose, it is claimed, was nothing less than a desire to forestall Soviet intervention into the Far Eastern war. Else why this necessity for speed? Certainly nothing in the military situation seemed to call for such hasty action. But if the purpose was to forestall Soviet intervention, then there was every reason for speed. And even if the Russians could not be kept out of the war, at least they would be prevented from making more than a token contribution to victory over Japan. In this sense it may be argued that the bomb proved a success, for the war ended with the United States in full control of Japan.

This theory leaves several matters unexplained. In the first place, the Americans did not know the exact date on which the Soviet Union would declare war but believed it would be within a week or two of August 8. If they had wished to forestall a Soviet declaration of war, then they could reasonably have been expected to act sooner than they did. Such close timing left little if any margin for error. Secondly, had the United States desired above everything else to keep the Russians out, it could have responded to one of the several unofficial Japanese overtures, or made the Potsdam Declaration more attractive to Japan. Certainly the failure to put a time limit on the declaration suggests that speed was not of the essence in American calculations. Finally, the date and time of the bombing were left to Generals Spaatz and LeMay, who certainly had no way of knowing Soviet intentions. Bad weather or any other untoward incident could have delayed the attack a week or more. . . .

Did the atomic bomb accomplish its purpose? Was it, in fact, as Stimson said, "the best possible sanction" after Japan rejected the Potsdam Declaration? The sequence of events argues strongly that it was, for bombs were dropped on the 6th and 9th, and on the 10th Japan surrendered. But in the excitement over the announcement of the first use of an atomic bomb and then of Japan's surrender, many overlooked the significance of the Soviet

Union's entry into the war on the 9th. The first bomb had produced conster-
nation and confusion among the leaders of Japan, but no disposition to surrender. The Soviet declaration of war, though not entirely unexpected, was
a devastating blow and, by removing all hope of Soviet mediation, gave the
advocates of peace their first opportunity of come boldly out into the open.
When Premier Suzuki arrived at the palace on the morning of the 9th, he
was told that the Emperor believed Japan's only course now was to accept
the Potsdam Declaration. The militarists could and did minimize the effects
of the bomb, but they could not evade the obvious consequences of Soviet
intervention, which ended all hope of dividing their enemies and securing
softer peace terms.

In this atmosphere, the leaders of Japan held a series of meetings on
August 9, but were unable to come to agreement. In the morning came word
of the fate of Nagasaki. This additional disaster failed to resolve the issues
between the military and those who advocated surrender. Finally the
Emperor took the unprecedented step of calling an Imperial Conference,
which lasted until 3 o'clock the next morning. When it, too, failed to produce
agreement the Emperor told his ministers that he wished the war brought to
an end. The constitutional significance of this action is difficult for West-
erners to comprehend, but it resolved the crisis and produced in the cabinet
a formal decision to accept the Potsdam Declaration, provided it did not
prejudice the position of the Emperor.

What finally forced the Japanese to surrender? Was it air bombardment,
naval power, the atomic bomb or Soviet entry? The United States Strategic
Bombing Survey concluded that Japan would have surrendered by the end
of the year, without invasion and without the atomic bomb. Other equally
informed opinion maintained that it was the atomic bomb that forced Japan
to surrender. "Without its use," Dr. Karl T. Compton asserted, "the war
would have continued for many months." Admiral Nimitz believed firmly
that the decisive factor was "the complete impunity with which the Pacific
Fleet pounded Japan," and General Arnold claimed it was air bombardment
that had brought Japan to the verge of collapse. But Major-General Claire
Chennault, wartime air commander in China, maintained that Soviet entry
into the Far Eastern war brought about the surrender of Japan and would
have done so "even if no atomic bombs had been dropped."

It would be a fruitless task to weigh accurately the relative importance
of all the factors leading to the Japanese surrender. There is no doubt that
Japan had been defeated by the summer of 1945, if not earlier. But defeat
did not mean that the military clique had given up; the Army intended to
fight on and had made elaborate preparations for the defense of the homeland. Whether air bombardment and naval blockade or the threat of invasion would have produced an early surrender and averted the heavy losses
almost certain to accompany the actual landings in Japan is a moot question.

Certainly they had a profound effect on the Japanese position. It is equally impossible to assert categorically that the atomic bomb alone or Soviet intervention alone was the decisive factor in bringing the war to an end. All that can be said on the available evidence is that Japan was defeated in the military sense by August 1945 and that the bombing of Hiroshima, followed by the Soviet Union's declaration of war and then the bombing of Nagasaki and the threat of still further bombing, acted as catalytic agents to produce the Japanese decision to surrender. Together they created so extreme a crisis that the Emperor himself, in an unprecedented move, took matters into his own hands and ordered his ministers to surrender. Whether any other set of circumstances would have resolved the crisis and produced the final decision to surrender is a question history cannot yet answer.[11]

30 / Ends and Means: A Continuing Debate

I cannot but esteem it as a favour that God hath granted us, that it is still in our power to die bravely, and in a state of freedom. . . . Let our wives die before they are abused, and our children before they have tasted of slavery; and after we have slain them, let us bestow that glorious benefit upon one another mutually and preserve ourselves in freedom, as an excellent funeral monument for us . . . a testimonial when we are dead . . . that, according to our original resolution, we have preferred death before slavery.

> —Eleazar Ben Yair in his address to the people of the Jewish fortress of Masada in the Roman-held Judea in A.D. 73
> (Flavius Josephus, *Wars of the Jews*)

[11] Ed. note: With justification a reader of the preceding analysis may wonder why the problem of nuclear fallout that was to affect nations other than Japan did not figure more prominently in the decision-making process. After the war, nuclear fallout at times was perhaps one of the most powerful arguments against further development of nuclear devices and their testing. In his memoirs (Clement Attlee, *Twilight of Empire,* New York: Barnes & Noble, Inc., 1961 p. 74), the British deputy premier and the leader of the Labour Party, Clement Attlee records his agreement with President Truman's decision to use the bomb and adds: "We knew nothing whatever at the time about the genetic effects of an atomic explosion. I knew nothing about fall-out and all the rest of what emerged after Hiroshima. As far as I know, President Truman and Winston Churchill knew nothing of those things either, nor did Sir John Anderson who coordinated research on our side. Whether the scientists directly concerned knew or guessed, I do not know. But if they did, then so far as I am aware, they said nothing of it to those who had to make the decision." With Churchill, Attlee was the leader of the wartime Conservative-Labour coalition. Attlee also attended the Potsdam Conference, replacing Churchill in the middle of it when in the British election the people voted Churchill out of power and the Labour in; Attlee became England's Prime Minister.

... The fires stormed. At the station entrances were mounds of dead children, and others were being piled up, as they were brought out of the station. There must have been a children's train at the station. More and more dead were stacked up, in layers, on top of each other, and covered with blankets.

> —David Irving (The Destruction of Dresden, an account of the U.S.-British raid on the German city of Dresden in February 1945)

I don't like to hit a village. You know you're hitting women and children, too. But you've got to decide that your cause is noble and that the work has to be done.

> —An American pilot in Vietnam (The New York Times, July 7, 1965)

I can see women and children in my sleep. Some days ... some nights, I can't even sleep. I just lay thinking about them.

> —Paul Meadlo on his personal experience in the My Lai massacre (CBS interview, November 27, 1969)

Imagine that you are creating a fabric of human destiny with the object of making men happy in the end, giving them peace and rest at last, but that it was essential and inevitable to torture to death only one tiny creature—that baby beating its breast with its fist, for instance—and to found that edifice on its unavenged tears, would you consent to be the architect on those conditions? ... And can you admit the idea that men for whom you are building it would agree to accept their happiness on the foundation of the unexpiated blood of a little victim, and accepting it would remain happy for ever? ... It's not God that I don't accept, Alyosha, only I most respectfully return Him the [entrance] ticket.

> —Fyodor Dostoevsky (The Brothers Karamazov)

I've never known a soldier nor did I ever myself ever wantonly kill a human being in my entire life. If I have committed a crime, the only crime I've committed is in judgment of my values. Apparently I valued my troops' lives more than I did that of the enemy. When my troops were getting massacred and mauled by an enemy, I couldn't see, I couldn't feel, and I couldn't touch—that nobody in the military system ever described them as anything other than Communism. They didn't give it a race, they didn't give it a sex, they didn't give it an age.

> —First Lieut. William L. Calley, Jr., addressing the jury at Fort Benning considering his sentence for his action at My Lai. On March 31, 1971, Calley was sentenced to life imprisonment for premeditated murder.

Man appears to be the missing link between anthropoid apes and human beings.

> —Konrad Lorenz (On Aggression)

Part III

War, Deterrence, and Diplomacy

11
Politics and Guns

When national leaders perceive a threat to their nations' security, they can choose between two fundamental policy alternatives: *submission* to a superior power or *preservation* of the nation's freedom of action.

Submission to a superior power is usually an outcome of an irresistible blackmail or a lost war. A striking example of submission was Czechoslovakia's involuntary surrender to blackmail by Nazi Germany at the time of the Munich Conference in 1938. Japan's surrender to the United States, following the Hiroshima and Nagasaki bomb and the Soviet attack on Manchuria, is an example of surrender as an outcome of a lost war.

History has also known a few cases of *voluntary* "submissions" in the form of a merger of separate sovereignties into a new sovereign federal pool for the purpose of common defense and promotion of common welfare. The origins of the United States and Swiss federations are good examples.

Methods of preserving or increasing a nation's freedom of action are the subject of this and the following chapters. In response to a *threat* to national security and well-being or in response to a new *opportunity* to promote national interest more vigorously, nations have traditionally used three basic techniques: diplomatic negotiations, deterrence, and war.

The purpose of *negotiations* is to discover and, if possible, agree on a compromise solution to a conflict between two or more national interests. A characteristic feature of diplomatic negotiation is communication between national leaders concerning (1) their respective estimates that the clash of interests is soluble without violence and (2) what the terms of a solution, based on mutual concessions, might be. If no concession whatsoever is deemed possible, no compromise between nations is likely to take place. Negotiations are the subject of the concluding Chapter 14.

Deterrence is another technique serving the goal of national preservation. Other terms used for this method of action vary from dissuasion to intimidation, to balance of power, to peace by mutual terror. Unlike diplomatic negotiations that aim at solving a conflict, the purpose of deterrence is for one nation to stop or redirect an undesirable policy or action of another. By signaling its own determination and capabilities, the deterring nation induces its adversary to believe that its contemplated action will represent an unbearable cost and unacceptable risk. The deterring nation tries to prevent the adversary's implementation of an undesirable design by a display of intimidatory power such as armaments, alliances, or collective security. Or, the rival nation can be weakened from within by various types of interference, ranging from psychological warfare to giving aid to guerrilla movements; rival alliances may be eroded by threats or lures addressed to a selected few, thus making neutralism or outright shift of alliance membership an attractive alternative. The hope—never a certainty—is that through intimidation, balancing processes, and interference peace and the nation's vital interests may be preserved. Chapters 12 and 13 will deal with the techniques and assumptions of nuclear deterrence and other balancing methods in more detail. Peace by overwhelming imbalance of power, called collective security, is subject to analysis by Kenneth W. Thompson in Selection 41.

War is still another possible response to either a threat (defensive war) or an opportunity (war of conquest). In our era war for self-preservation could more often than not lead to the opposite result: self-destruction. As Chapter 10 on ends and means of violence indicated, it is usually easier to condemn an aggressive war, initiated for the purpose of territorial expansion and conquest, than a clearly defensive war, waged in response to a direct and unprovoked aggression. Finland's defensive war against Russia in 1939 is a good example. Sometimes a timely initiation of military action is deemed defensive when its goal is to prevent an impending attack or frustrate a plan for expansion. The line between an offensive war and defensive action in anticipation of aggression is often quite blurred. The Russian-Finnish war in 1939 was subsequently explained by Moscow as having actually been defensive—that is, in anticipation of a future German-Russian conflict, approaches to Leningrad had to be secured for the purpose of a more effective defense. Ancient Greece offers another example of "defensive offensive" or "offensive defense." The tragic Peloponnesian War began when Sparta and her allies concluded that further growth of the power of Athens must be stopped by military action. The *History of the Peloponnesian War*, written by the Greek historian Thucydides (born 455 B.C.), describes the rivalry among Greek city-states; it contains perceptive insights into the problems of anxieties, uncertainties, errors, and passions that also mark modern relations among nations. At the then-meeting at Sparta, the leading power of the Peloponnesos (the peninsula constituting southern Greece) many of the present-day hawkish and dovish arguments were heard. Some arguments stressed the need to contain the expansionist power of Athens as early as possible by war; others advocated a long-term policy of containment by means of arms race and alliances; others still favored diplomacy. In spite of the advice that all the avenues of diplomatic negotiations should be explored before an irrevocable course of action be taken and in spite of many warnings as to the unpredictability of the outcome of any major war, the hawks prevailed, especially following the arguments of the delegate from Corinth (Sparta's ally):

> "Spartans . . . you can see yourselves how Athens has deprived some states of their freedom and is scheming to do the same thing for others . . . and that she herself has for a long time been preparing for the eventuality of war. . . . And it is you who are responsible for all this. It was you who in the first place allowed the Athenians to fortify their city and build the Long Walls after the Persian War. . . . The great trust and confidence which you have in your own constitution and in your own way of life is a quality which certainly makes you moderate in your judgments; it is also, perhaps, responsible for the kind of ignorance which you show when you are dealing with foreign affairs. . . . You will not see that the likeliest way of securing peace is this: only to use one's power in the case of justice, but to make it perfectly plain that one is resolved not to tolerate aggression. Your activity has done harm enough. Now let there be an end of it. Give your allies the help you promised and invade Attica at once.". . .
>
> The Spartans voted that the treaty had been broken and that war should be declared not so much because they were influenced by the speeches of their allies as because they were afraid of the further growth of Athenian power, seeing, as they did, that already the greater part of Hellas was under the control of Athens.[1]

The purpose of negotiations, deterrence, or war is political: to influence the behavior of the leaders and their nations. This common denominator of political purpose places all three preservation techniques in much less neat categories than they would otherwise suggest by being discussed in separate chapters or subheadings. These three methods of action form, in fact, a composite whole. National leaders not only alternate between various methods of action but they deliberately combine them in different admixtures such as arms race *and* proposals for disarmament, blackmail, lures, war, *and* diplomacy, and deterrence *and* diplomacy. The olive branch is often attached to a bayonet, and vice versa.

---

[1] Thucydides, *History of the Peloponnesian War*, Translated by Rex Warner (Baltimore: Penguin Books, Inc., 1954), p. 35.

A good example of the admixture is President Kennedy's choice of words for his 1961 inaugural address:

> Those nations who would make themselves our adversary . . . we dare not tempt them with weakness. For only when our arms are sufficient beyond doubt can we be certain beyond doubt that they will never be employed. . . . Let us never negotiate out of fear. But let us never fear to negotiate. Let both sides explore what problems unite us instead of belaboring the problems that divide us.

Never certain of the ultimate effects of any policy or action, national leaders find themselves between two abysses: war or submission. They try to avoid both of them.

In the nuclear and missile age a new problem was added to the political, military, economic, and moral ones that underscore the fatal political decision to engage in violence. It is a fact that a war fought with nuclear missiles could lead to the annihilation of mankind. It seems unthinkable that sensible, thinking men could rationally choose such a suicidal path. The real problem, however, is that nuclear war might be initiated by faulty logic, miscalculation, daredevil gamble, error, accident, or because men in command have lost control over their own senses. Thinking about the unthinkable is the subject of the essay by Herman Kahn (Selection 33).

31 / War as an Instrument of National Policy

Karl von Clausewitz

"War is only a continuation of state policy by other means," wrote Prussian General Karl von Clausewitz. His statement about the dominantly political context of any war is still valid today insofar as the fundamental choice between war and any other alternative is primarily determined by political leaders—not by generals—with or without the support of the people. As a rule, generals execute the decisions taken by political leaders; and, when a general has the power to determine the issue of war or peace, his authority is actually derived from his political position rather than his professional military expertise or career.

From Vol. I, pp. xxiii, 1–23 *(passim)*, and Vol. III, pp. 121–130 *(passim)*, of Karl von Clausewitz, *On War*. Reprinted by permission of Routledge & Kegan Paul Ltd., 1940, and Barnes & Noble, Inc.

Generals, statesmen, and revolutionary leaders have studied and invoked Clausewitz on many occasions. The reason is obvious: Like Clausewitz, the revolutionary leaders relate violence and use of weapons to political ends. Lenin studied Clausewitz in detail, and annotated many of his conclusions with approval. Quoting, for instance, a sentence by Clausewitz: "It may well be and happens very frequently that a military commander uses all his forces to defend his own country on enemy soil," Lenin added a note of approval: "Defend one's country on foreign soil." A similar approval was added to Clausewitz' conclusion that the more one gains insight into the true nature of war, the more the difference between an offensive and defense disappears. In his letter to Razin, published by *Pravda* (February 23, 1946), Stalin asked the question: "What interested Lenin in Clausewitz? For what did he praise him?" And after noting several examples Stalin added: "He further praised Clausewitz for the fact that Clausewitz confirmed in his work the proposition, correct from the Marxist point of view, to the effect that retreat under certain unfavorable conditions is just as lawful form of struggle as an offensive."

Mao's famous dictum "Political power grows out of a gun" can be traced directly to Clausewitz' manual on the use of force in politics. In the current Sino-Soviet conflict, the Chinese Communists invoked both Clausewitz and Lenin to ridicule the Soviet proposal for a complete and general disarmament in a world in which capitalism and imperialism still exist:

> As Marxist-Leninists see it, war is the continuation of policies by other means, and every war is inseparable from the political struggle which gave rise to it. . . . Lumping just wars and unjust wars together and opposing all of them indiscriminately is a bourgeois pacifist and not a Marxist-Leninist approach. . . . However, certain persons [Khrushchev was meant] now actually hold that it is possible to bring about a "world without weapons, without armed forces and without wars," through "general and complete disarmament" while the system of imperialism and of the exploitation of man by man still exists. This is sheer illusion.[2]

The following excerpt is from Clausewitz' classic treatise on the subject of war. It was written at the beginning of the nineteenth century, long before the nuclear awakening. In that period Clausewitz perhaps could view war as a *rational instrument of national policy*. As Rapoport rightly noted in his introduction to a discussion on Clausewitz:

> The three words "rational," "instrument," and "national" are the key concepts of his paradigm. In this view, the decision to wage war "ought" to be rational, in the sense that it ought to be based on estimated costs and gains of the war. Next, war "ought" to be instrumental, in the sense that it ought to be waged in order to achieve some goal, never for its own sake; and also in the sense that strategy and tactics ought to be directed towards just one end, namely towards victory. Finally,

[2] "A letter from the Central Committee of the Chinese Communist Party to the Soviet Communist Party," *Peking Review* (June 14, 1963).

war "ought" to be national, in the sense that its objective should be to advance the interests of a national state and that the entire effort of the nation ought to be mobilized in the service of the military objective.

We have paraphrased Clausewitz's philosophy in terms of what, according to its precepts, war *ought* to be. Actually, Clausewitz says what war *is*. At the same time he is well aware that actual decisions to wage war or to avoid it were often made without due considerations of relevant circumstances; that strategies and tactics were often determined by matters irrelevant to the objective of war; and that, until his own time, wars had not been national wars.[3]

The question could be asked what would be Clausewitz's view of war in the nuclear era. One possible answer to this question is suggested by Rapoport: "Had Clausewitz lived to our day, he might have observed that international politics has become the continuation of war by other means."[4]

War is nothing but a duel on an expensive scale. . . . War . . . is an act of violence intended to compel our opponent to fulfill our will. . . . Physical force . . . is therefore the means; the compulsory submission of our enemy to our will is the ultimate object. . . . Two motives lead men to War: instinctive hostility and hostile intention. . . . Even the most civilized nations may burn with passionate hatred of each other. . . . The disarming or the overthrow of the enemy, whichever we call it, must always be the aim of the Warfare. . . . If we desire to defeat the enemy, we must proportion our efforts to his powers of resistance. . . . The political object, as the original motive of the War, will be the standard for determining both the aim of the military force and also the amount of effort to be made. . . . War is no pastime; no mere passion for venturing and winning; no work of a free enthusiasm; it is a serious means for a serious object. The War of a community—of whole Nations and particularly of civilized Nations—always starts from a political condition and is called forth by a political motive. It is, therefore, a political act. . . . if we reflect that War has its root in a political object, then naturally this original motive which called it into existence should also continue the first and highest consideration in its conduct. Still, the political object is no despotic lawgiver on that account; it must accommodate itself to the nature of the means, and though changes in these means may involve modification in the political objective, the latter always retains the prior right to consideration. Policy, therefore, is interwoven with the whole action of War, and must exercise a continuous influence upon it as far as the nature of the forces liberated by it will permit; we see, therefore,

[3] Anatol Rapoport, "Introduction" to Karl von Clausewitz, *On War* (Baltimore: Penguin Books, Inc., 1968), p. 13.

[4] Anatol Rapoport, *Strategy and Conscience* (New York: Harper & Row, Publishers, Inc., 1964), p. xvii.

that war is not merely a political act, but also a real political instrument, a continuation of political commerce, a carrying out of the same by other means. The political view is the object, War is the means, and the means must always include the object in our conception. . . . *War is only a continuation of state policy by other means.*

War is only a part of political intercourse, therefore, by no means an independent thing itself. We know, certainly, that war is only called forth through the political intercourse of Governments and Nations; but in general, it is supposed that such intercourse is broken off by War, and that a totally different state of things ensues, subject to no laws but its own.

We maintain, on the contrary, that War is nothing but a continuation of political intercourse, with a mixture of other means. We say mixed with other means in order thereby to maintain at the same time that this political intercourse does not cease by the war itself, is not changed into something quite different, but that, in its essence, it continues to exist whatever may be the form or means which it uses and that the chief lines on which the events of the War progress, and to which they are attached, are only the general features of policy which run all through the War until peace takes place. And how can we conceive it to be otherwise? Does cessation of the diplomatic notes stop the political relations between different Nations and governments? Is not War merely another kind of writing and language for political thoughts? It has certainly a glamour of its own, but its logic is not peculiar to itself. Accordingly, War can never be separated from political intercourse, and if, in the consideration of the matter, this is done in any way, all the threads of different relations, are, to a certain extent, broken, and we have before us a senseless thing without an object. . . . That the political point of view should end completely when War begins is only conceivable in contests which are Wars of life and death from pure hatred: As Wars are in reality, they are, as we before said only the expressions or manifestations of policy itself. The subordination of the political point of view to the military would be contrary to common sense, for policy has declared the War; it is the intelligent faculty, War only the instrument, and not the reverse. The subordination of the military point of view to the political is, therefore, the only thing which is possible. . . . In one word, the Art of War, in its highest point of view is policy, but, no doubt, a policy which fights battles instead of writing notes.

According to this view, to leave a great military enterprise, or the plan for one, to *a purely military judgment and decision* is a distinction which cannot be allowed and is even prejudicial; indeed, it is an irrational proceeding to consult professional soldiers on a plan of a War, that they may give a *purely military opinion* upon what Cabinet ought to do. . . . Experience in general . . . teaches us that notwithstanding the . . . scientific character of military art in the present day, still the leading outlines of a War, are always determined by the Cabinet, that is, if we would use technical language, by a political, not a military, organ.

This is perfectly natural, none of the principal plans which are required for a War can be made without an insight into the political relations; and, in reality, when people speak, as they often do, of the prejudicial influence of policy on the conduct of a War, they say in reality something very different from what they intend. It is not this influence but the policy itself which should be found fault with. If policy is right, that is, if it succeeds in hitting the object, then it can only act with advantage on the War. If this influence of policy causes a divergence from the object, the cause is only to be looked for in a mistaken policy.

It is only when policy promises itself a wrong effect from certain military means and measures, an effect opposed to their nature, that it can exercise a prejudicial effect on War by the course it prescribes. Just as a person in a language with which he is not conversant, sometimes says what he does not intend, so policy, when intending right may often order things which do not tally with its own views.

This has happened times without end and it shows that a certain knowledge of the nature of War is essential to the management of political intercourse.

Once more: War is an instrument of policy; it must necessarily bear its character, it must measure with its scale: the conduct of War, in its great features, is therefore, policy itself, which takes up the sword in place of the pen, but does not on that account cease to think according to its own laws.

32 / How World War II Came: Nazi-Soviet Cooperation, 1939–1941

Archives of the German Foreign Office

At the end of World War II, the British and American forces in defeated Germany succeeded in capturing a major part of the German secret archives. Thus was gained a fascinating insight into the secret decision-making

From pp. 50–353 *(passim)* of the U.S. Department of State, *Nazi-Soviet Relations, 1939–1941, Documents from the Archives of the German Foreign Office* (Washington, D.C.: U.S. Government Printing Office, 1948).

processes of two great European powers, Nazi Germany and Communist Russia. In terms of both the number of documents and their political and military sensitivity, the publication of the Nazi top-secret archives has not been matched by the other three sensational revelations of government secrets in modern times: the first case, the Bolshevik publication of the secret treaties concluded by the preceding czarist government with its allies during World War I; the second, the Soviet and Yugoslav publication of their top-secret party correspondence concerning communist Yugoslavia's expulsion from the Cominform in 1948; and the third, the top-secret Pentagon study on the escalation of the war in Vietnam, published by the *New York Times* in 1971. In these three instances the published documents referred only to very limited periods of time and specific issues. This is in contrast to the completeness of the Nazi archives that contain almost all documents dealing with the totality of Germany's foreign policy, secret diplomatic dispatches, and military plans and operations. The German documents were microfilmed and are now stored in the national archives of the United States and Great Britain.

A study of confiscated German documents reveals that the outbreak of World War II on September 3, 1939, was largely caused by Hitler's overconfidence in his proficiency in the art of brinkmanship. In the light of his personal experience with the Western leaders at Munich (Neville Chamberlain and Edouard Daladier), he underestimated their subsequent determination to assist Poland if attacked. One document reveals that at a conference with the Nazi leadership on August 14—less than three weeks before the outbreak of World War II—Hitler assured his colleagues that Britain would, in the end, draw back: "The men I got to know in Munich are not the kind that start a new World War." Until the last moment Hitler hoped to isolate his war with Poland and postpone a world conflict until a later date when Germany would be fully prepared. His agreement with Stalin was meant as a device to frighten the Western democracies into passivity by a specter of a Nazi-Soviet axis. Hitler hoped to conquer Poland in a limited local *blitzkrieg*.

While Hitler underestimated the West, Stalin seemed to have overestimated, first, the possibility to harmonize his own and Hitler's territorial ambitions in eastern Europe, and, second, the capacity of France to offer a prolonged resistance to the Nazi onslaught. Probably bewitched by history as it happened in World War I, Stalin anticipated a very long period of reciprocal whitebleeding between Germany and France on the western front. Such a situation would have indeed given Russia a long period of immunity against involvement in war and therefore time to build up Soviet economic and military strength. By the end of a European war Russia could have emerged as the most powerful nation in Europe. The cooperation between the two dictators and the resulting Soviet immunity collapsed in 1941. Unable to defeat England and suspicious of Russia's growing strength and territorial appetite, Hitler decided to transform his partnership with Stalin into a bitter and fatal German-Russian war. Russia's lack of anticipation or readiness for Hitler's shift in war aims greatly facilitated the initial success and penetration by the Nazi armies deep into Russian territory.

The Nazi-Soviet rapprochement began one month after the Nazi forces had occupied (March 15, 1939) what was left of Czechoslovakia after the Munich conference in September 1938; at that time Czechoslovakia lost its Sudeten-German border territories that had also contained defensible mountain ridges, supplemented by modern fortifications. The Soviet embassy in Berlin was ordered by Moscow to explore the possibility of an improvement of Soviet-Nazi relations, taking as a pretext the problem of the outstanding Soviet contracts placed with the Czech industries prior to the Nazi takeover. The initial Nazi reaction was lukewarm. Only in August 1939, when the Nazi government realized the seriousness of the British and French commitments to Poland, did Hitler reply to the Soviet initiative with such interest and eagerness that Moscow was now able to demand from Germany more than it could have obtained the preceding spring: half of Poland which as a state was to be erased from the map of Europe, the Baltic states, and the Bessarabian province of Rumania. Dreading war on two fronts, Hitler granted Russia all the territories Stalin had requested.

The following excerpts from the then-diplomatic correspondence between Moscow and Berlin begin with a "most urgent" message sent by German Foreign Minister Ribbentrop to his ambassador in Moscow, Schulenburg. Hitler's order to initiate talks with the Soviet Communist leadership is symptomatic of diplomatic negotiating tactics. The order opens with a clear deemphasis of the communist and Nazi ideologies that, in the past, had so often been proclaimed by both sides as mutually exclusive.

Many of the Nazi top-secret documents have well captured the tone and flavor of the Soviet-Nazi summitry, including the jokes and toasts exchanged over the dead body of Poland and over the beginning of World War II. These documents, while unique in diplomatic history, would naturally be even more instructive if the corresponding Soviet documents were included. But Soviet secrets are well guarded behind the Kremlin walls. The Soviet-Nazi cooperation, while questioned to some extent in the Soviet press during and following the Khrushchev era, had never been subjected to nearly such negative criticism as were many other aspects of the Stalin area.

In 1969, on the thirtieth anniversary of the outbreak of World War II, Vladimir M. Khostov, the head of the Soviet History Institute of the Academy of Sciences, declared in an interview with a Soviet newspaper, *Sovetskaya Rossiya*,[5] that the Soviet government in summer 1939 "had to insure the national security of the U.S.S.R., to save the country and the people from the approaching danger." It also had to agree to the treaty of nonaggression with Germany, Khostov added, in order to "fulfill its sacred duty to the world working class, to save the first socialist state from the threat hanging over it." The Soviet evaluation of the merits of the Soviet-Nazi Pact in the 1939–1941 period, conveniently called an intercapitalist war, does not raise nor does it answer two fundamental questions:

1. Would world war have started if Hitler had not been given the Soviet assurance that during his attack on Poland and then on France he could

[5](August 31, 1969), 1.

assume that there would be no disturbance on the *eastern* front?

2. Was the extent of damage inflicted by Hitler on the "first socialist state" greater or smaller than it would have been had the Soviet leaders—ideology or not—adopted a different national policy on the eve of World War II?

THE REICH FOREIGN MINISTER TO THE GERMAN AMBASSADOR
IN THE SOVIET UNION (SCHULENBURG)—TELEGRAM

MOST URGENT   BERLIN, August 14, 1939—10:53 p.m.

Received Moscow, August 15, 1939—4:40 a.m.

No. 175 of August 14

For the Ambassador personally.

I request that you call upon Herr Molotov personally and communicate to him the following:

1. The ideological contradictions between National Socialist Germany and the Soviet Union were in past years the sole reason why Germany and the U.S.S.R. stood opposed to each other in two separate and hostile camps. The developments of the recent period seem to show that differing world outlooks do not prohibit a reasonable relationship between the two states, and the restoration of cooperation of a new and friendly type. The period of opposition in foreign policy can be brought to an end once and for all and the way lies open for a new sort of future for both countries.

2. There exist no real conflicts of interest between Germany and the U.S.S.R. The living spaces of Germany and the U.S.S.R. touch each other, but in the natural requirements they do not conflict. Thus there is lacking all cause for an aggressive attitude on the part of one country against the other. Germany has no aggressive intentions against the U.S.S.R. The Reich Government is of the opinion that there is no question between the Baltic and the Black Seas which cannot be settled to the complete satisfaction of both countries. Among these are such questions as: the Baltic Sea, the Baltic area, Poland, Southeastern questions, etc. In such matters political cooperation between the two countries can have only a beneficial effect. The same applies to German and Soviet economy, which can be expanded in any direction.

3. There is no doubt that German-Soviet policy today has come to an historic turning point. The decisions with respect to policy to be made in the immediate future in Berlin and Moscow will be of decisive importance for the aspect of relationships between the German people and the peoples of the U.S.S.R. for generations. On those decisions will depend whether the two peoples will some day again and without any compelling reason take up arms against each other or whether they pass again into a friendly relationship. It has gone well with both countries previously when they were friends and badly when they were enemies.

4. It is true that Germany and the U.S.S.R., as a result of years of hostility in their respective world outlooks, today look at each other in a distrustful fashion. A great deal of rubbish which has accumulated will have to be cleared away. It must be said, however, that even during this period the

natural sympathy of the Germans for the Russians never disappeared. The policy of both states can be built anew on that basis.

5. The Reich Government and the Soviet Government must, judging from all experience, count it as certain that the capitalistic Western democracies are the unforgiving enemies of both National Socialist Germany and of the U.S.S.R. They are today trying again, by the conclusion of a military alliance, to drive the U.S.S.R. into the war against Germany. In 1914 this policy had disastrous results for Russia. It is the compelling interest of both countries to avoid for all future time the destruction of Germany and of the U.S.S.R., which would profit only the Western democracies.

6. The crisis which has been produced in German-Polish relations by English policy, as well as English agitation for war and the attempts at an alliance which are bound up with that policy, make a speedy clarification of German-Russian relations desirable. Otherwise these matters, without any German initiative, might take a turn which would deprive both Governments of the possibility of restoring German-Soviet friendship and possibly of clearing up jointly the territorial questions of Eastern Europe. The leadership in both countries should, therefore, not allow the situation to drift, but should take action at the proper time. It would be fatal if, through mutual lack of knowledge of views and intentions, our peoples should be finally driven asunder.

As we have been informed, the Soviet Government also has the desire for a clarification of German-Russian relations. Since, however, according to previous experience this clarification can be achieved only slowly through the usual diplomatic channels, Reich Foreign Minister von Ribbentrop is prepared to make a short visit to Moscow in order, in the name of the Führer, to set forth the Führer's views to Herr Stalin. Only through such a direct discussion, in the view of Herr von Ribbentrop, can a change be brought about, and it should not be impossible thereby to lay the foundations for a definite improvement in German-Russian relations. . . .

MEMORANDUM BY THE GERMAN AMBASSADOR IN THE SOVIET UNION
(SCHULENBURG)
SECRET

I began the interview with Molotov on August 15 about 8:00 p.m. by stating that according to information which had reached us the Soviet Government was interested in continuing the political conversations, but that it preferred that they be carried on in Moscow.

Molotov replied that this was correct.

Then I read to Herr Molotov the contents of the instruction which had been sent to me and the German text was immediately translated into Russian, paragraph by paragraph. . . .

Molotov then declared that in view of the importance of my communication he could not give me an answer at once but he must first render a report to his Government. He could state at once, however, that the Soviet Government warmly [lebhaft] welcomed the intention expressed on the German side to bring about an improvement in relations with the Soviet Union. . . .

Molotov repeated that he was interested above everything alse in an answer to the question of whether on the German side there was the desire to make more concrete the points which had been [previously] outlined. So, for example, the Soviet Government would like to know whether Germany saw any real possibility of influencing Japan in the direction of a better relationship with the Soviet Union. "Also, how did things stand with the idea of the conclusion of a nonaggression pact? Was the German Government sympathetically inclined to the idea or would the matter have to be gone into more deeply?" were Molotov's exact words. . . .

Moscow, August 16, 1939   COUNT VON DER SCHULENBURG

Ribbentrop to Moscow

THE REICH FOREIGN MINISTER TO THE GERMAN AMBASSADOR
IN THE SOVIET UNION (SCHULENBURG)—TELEGRAM
URGENT   BERLIN, AUGUST 16, 1939—4:15 p.m.
                        Received Moscow, August 17, 1939—1 a.m.

No. 179 of August 16
   For the Ambassador personally.
   I request that you again call upon Herr Molotov with the statement that you have to communicate to him, in addition to yesterday's message for Herr Stalin, a supplementary instruction just received from Berlin, which relates to the questions raised by Herr Molotov. Please then state to Herr Molotov the following:

   1. The points brought up by Herr Molotov are in accordance with German desires. That is, Germany is ready [*bereit*] to conclude a nonaggression pact with the Soviet Union and, if the Soviet Government so desires, one which would be irrevocable [*unkündbar*] for a term of twenty-five years. Further, Germany is ready to guarantee the Baltic States jointly with the Soviet Union. Finally, it is thoroughly in accord with the German position, and Germany is ready, to exercise influence for an improvement and consolidation of Russian-Japanese relations.

   2. The Führer is of the opinion that, in view of the present situation, and of the possibility of the occurrence any day of serious incidents (please at this point explain to Herr Molotov that Germany is determined not to endure Polish provocation indefinitely), a basic and rapid clarification of German-Russian relations and the mutual adjustment of the pressing questions are desirable. For these reasons the Reich Foreign Minister declares that he is prepared to come by plane to Moscow at any time after Friday, August 18, to deal on the basis of full powers from the Führer with the entire complex of German-Russian questions and, if the occasion arises [*gegebenenfalls*], to sign the appropriate treaties.

   ANNEX: I request that you read these instructions to Herr Molotov and ask for the reaction of the Russian Government and Herr Stalin. Entirely confidentially, it is added for your guidance that it would be of very special interest to us if my Moscow trip could take place at the end of this week or the beginning of next week.

RIBBENTROP

THE GERMAN AMBASSADOR IN THE SOVIET UNION (SCHULENBURG)
TO THE GERMAN FOREIGN OFFICE—TELEGRAM
VERY URGENT   Moscow, August 21, 1939—7:30 p.m.
SECRET
No. 200 of August 21
Supplementing my telegram No. 199 of August 21.
Text of Stalin's reply:
"August 21, 1939. To the Chancellor of the German Reich, A. Hitler. I thank you for the letter. I hope that the German-Soviet nonagression pact will mark a decided turn for the better in the political relations between our countries.

The people of our countries need peaceful relations with each other. The assent of the German Government to the conclusion of a nonaggression pact provides the foundation for eliminating the political tension and for the establishment of peace and collaboration between our countries.

The Soviet Government has authorized me to inform you that its agrees to Herr von Ribbentrop's arriving in Moscow on August 23. J. Stalin."

SCHULENBURG

FULL POWERS—TO THE REICH FOREIGN MINISTER,
HERR JOACHIM VON RIBBENTROP
I hereby grant full power to negotiate, in the name of the German Reich, with authorized representatives of the Government of the Union of Soviet Socialist Republics, regarding a nonagression treaty, as well as all related questions, and if occasion arises, to sign both the nonaggression treaty and other agreements resulting from the negotiations, with the proviso that this treaty and these agreements shall enter into force as soon as they are signed.

Obersalzberg, August 22, 1939.   ADOLF HITLER

The Nazis and the Communists at the Kremlin

MEMORANDUM OF A CONVERSATION HELD ON THE NIGHT OF AUGUST 23D TO 24TH, BETWEEN THE REICH FOREIGN MINISTER, ON THE ONE HAND, AND HERR STALIN AND THE CHAIRMAN OF THE COUNCIL OF PEOPLE'S COMMISSARS MOLOTOV, ON THE OTHER HAND
VERY SECRET!
STATE SECRET

The following problems were discussed:

1. Japan:

The REICH FOREIGN MINISTER stated that the German-Japanese friendship was in no wise directed against the Soviet Union. We were, rather, in a position, owing to our good relations with Japan, to make an effective contribution to an adjustment of the differences between the Soviet Union and Japan. Should Herr Stalin and the Soviet Government desire it, the Reich Foreign Minister was prepared to work in this direction. He would use his influence with the Japanese Government accordingly and keep in touch with the Soviet representative in Berlin in this matter.

HERR STALIN replied that the Soviet Union indeed desired an improvement in its relations with Japan, but that there were limits to its patience with regard to Japanese provocations. If Japan desired war, it could have it. The Soviet Union was not afraid of it and was prepared for it. If Japan desired peace—so much the better! Herr Stalin considered the assistance of Germany in bringing about an improvement in Soviet-Japanese relations as useful, but he did not want the Japanese to get the impression that the initiative in this direction had been taken by the Soviet Union. . . .

2. Italy:

HERR STALIN inquired of the Reich Foreign Minister as to Italian aims. Did not Italy have aspirations beyond the annexation of Albania—perhaps for Greek territory? Small, mountainous, and thinly populated Albania was, in his estimation, of no particular use to Italy.

The REICH FOREIGN MINISTER replied that Albania was important to Italy for strategic reasons. Moreover, Mussolini was a strong man who could not be intimidated.

This he had demonstrated in the Abyssinian conflict, in which Italy had asserted its aims by its own strength against a hostile coalition. Even Germany was not yet in a position at that time to give Italy appreciable support.

Mussolini welcomed warmly the restoration of friendly relations between Germany and the Soviet Union. He had expressed himself as gratified with the conclusion of the Nonagression Pact. . . .

4. England:

HERREN STALIN and MOLOTOV commented adversely on the British Military Mission in Moscow, which had never told the Soviet Government what it really wanted.

The REICH FOREIGN MINISTER stated in this connection that England had always been trying and was still trying to disrupt the development of good relations between Germany and the Soviet Union. England was weak and wanted to let others fight for its presumptuous claim to world domination.

HERR STALIN eagerly concurred and observed as follows: the British Army was weak; the British Navy no longer deserved its previous reputation. England's air arm was being increased, to be sure, but there was a lack of pilots. If England dominates the world in spite of this, this was due to the stupidity of the other countries that always let themselves be bluffed. It was ridiculous, for example, that a few hundred British should dominate India.

THE REICH FOREIGN MINISTER concurred and informed Herr Stalin confidentially that England had recently put out a new feeler which was connected with certain allusions to 1914. It was a matter of a typically English, stupid maneuver. The Reich Foreign Minister had proposed to the Führer to inform the British that every hostile British act, in case of a German-Polish conflict, would be answered by a bombing attack on London.

HERR STALIN remarked that the feeler was evidently Chamberlain's letter to the Führer, which Ambassador Henderson delivered on August 23 at the Obersalzberg. Stalin further expressed the opinion that England, despite its weakness, would wage war craftily and stubbornly.

5. France:

HERR STALIN expressed the opinion that France, nevertheless, had an army worthy of consideration.

The REICH FOREIGN MINISTER, on his part, pointed out to Herren Stalin and Molotov the numerical inferiority of France. While Germany had available an annual class of more than 300,000 soldiers, France could muster only 150,000 recruits annually. The West Wall was five times as strong as the Maginot Line. If France attempted to wage war with Germany, she would certainly be conquered.

6. Anti-Comintern Pact:

The REICH FOREIGN MINISTER observed that the Anti-Comintern Pact was basically directed not against the Soviet Union but against the Western democracies. He knew, and was able to infer from the tone of the Russian press, that the Soviet Government fully recognized this fact.

HERR STALIN interposed that the Anti-Comintern Pact had in fact frightened principally the City of London and the small British merchants.

The REICH FOREIGN MINISTER concurred and remarked jokingly that Herr Stalin was surely less frightened by the Anti-Comintern Pact than the City of London and the small British merchants. What the German people thought of this matter is evident from a joke which had originated with the Berliners, well known for their wit and humor, and which had been going the rounds for several months, namely, "Stalin will yet join the Anti-Comintern Pact."

7. Attitude of the German people to the German-Russian Nonaggression Pact:

The REICH FOREIGN MINISTER stated that he had been able to determine that all strata of the German people, and especially the simple people, most warmly welcomed the understanding with the Soviet Union. The people felt instinctively that between Germany and the Soviet Union no natural conflicts of interests existed, and that the development of good relations had hitherto been disturbed only by foreign intrigue, in particular on the part of England.

HERR STALIN replied that he readily believed this. The Germans desired peace and therefore welcomed friendly relations between the Reich and the Soviet Union.

The REICH FOREIGN MINISTER interrupted here to say that it was certainly true that the German people desired peace, but, on the other hand, indignation against Poland was so great that every single man was ready to fight. The German people would no longer put up with Polish provocation.

    8. Toasts:

In the course of the conversation, HERR STALIN spontaneously proposed a toast to the Führer, as follows:

"I know how much the German nation loves its Führer; I should therefore like to drink to his health."

HERR MOLOTOV drank to the health of the Reich Foreign Minister and of the Ambassador, Count von der Schulenburg.

HERR MOLOTOV raised his glass to Stalin, remarking that it had been Stalin who—through his speech of March of this year, which had been well understood in Germany—had brought about the reversal in political relations.

HERREN MOLOTOV and STALIN drank repeatedly to the Nonaggression Pact, the new era of German-Russian relations, and to the German nation.

The REICH FOREIGN MINISTER in turn proposed a toast to Herr Stalin, toasts to the Soviet Government, and to a favorable development of relations between Germany and the Soviet Union.

    9. When they took their leave, HERR STALIN addressed to the Reich Foreign Minister words to this effect:

The Soviet Government takes the new Pact very seriously. He could guarantee on his word of honor that the Soviet Union would not betray its partner.

Moscow, August 24, 1939.   HENCKE

TREATY OF NONAGGRESSION BETWEEN GERMANY
AND THE UNION OF SOVIET SOCIALIST REPUBLICS

    The Government of the German Reich and
    the Government of the Union of Soviet Socialist Republics

desirous of strengthening the cause of peace between Germany and the U.S.S.R., and proceeding from the fundamental provisions of the Neutrality Agreement concluded in April 1926 between Germany and the U.S.S.R., have reached the following agreement:

Article I. Both High Contracting Parties obligate themselves to desist from any act of violence, any aggressive action, and any attack on each other, either individually or jointly with other powers.

Article II. Should one of the High Contracting Parties become the object of belligerent action by a third power, the other High Contracting Party shall in no manner lend its support to this third power.

Article IV. Neither of the two High Contracting Parties shall participate in any groupings of powers whatsoever that is directly or indirectly aimed at the other party.

Article VII. The present treaty shall be ratified within the shortest possible time. The ratifications shall be exchanged in Berlin. The agreement shall enter into force as soon as it is signed.

Done in duplicate, in the German and Russian languages.

Moscow, August 23, 1939.

For the Government
of the German Reich:
  v. RIBBENTROP

With full power of the
Government of the U.S.S.R.:
  V. MOLOTOV

SECRET ADDITIONAL PROTOCOL

On the occasion of the signature of the Nonaggression Pact between the German Reich and the Union of Socialist Soviet Republics the undersigned plenipotentiaries of each of the two parties discussed in strictly confidential conversations the question of the boundary of their respective spheres of influence in Eastern Europe. These conversations led to the following conclusions:

1. In the event of a territorial and political rearrangement in the areas belonging to the Baltic States (Finland, Estonia, Latvia, Lithuania), the northern boundary of Lithuania shall represent the boundary of the spheres of influence of Germany and the U.S.S.R. In this connection the interest of Lithuania in the Vilna area is recognized by each party.

2. In the event of a territorial and political rearrangement of the areas belonging to the Polish state the spheres of influence of Germany and the U.S.S.R. shall be bounded approximately by the line of the rivers Narew, Vistula, and San.

The question of whether the interests of both parties make desirable the maintenance of an independent Polish state and how such a state should be bounded can only be definitely determined in the course of further political developments.

In any event both Governments will resolve this question by means of a friendly agreement.

3. With regard to Southeastern Europe attention is called by the Soviet side to its interest in Bessarabia. The German side declares its complete political disinterestedness in these areas.

4. This protocol shall be treated by both parties as strictly secret.

Moscow, August 23, 1939.

For the Government
of the German Reich:
  v. RIBBENTROP

Plenipotentiary of the
Government of the U.S.S.R.:
  V. MOLOTOV

Russia Attacks Poland

THE REICH FOREIGN MINISTER TO THE GERMAN AMBASSADOR
IN THE SOVIET UNION (SCHULENBURG)—TELEGRAM

No. 253 of September 3   BERLIN, September 3, 1939—6:50 p.m.
                Received Moscow September 4, 1939—12:30 a.m.

Very Urgent! Exclusively for Ambassador. Strictly secret! For chief of Mission or his representative personally. Top secret. To be decoded by himself. Strictest secrecy!

We definitely expect to have beaten the Polish Army decisively in a few weeks. We would then keep the area that was established as German sphere of interest at Moscow under military occupation. We would naturally, however, for military reasons, also have to proceed further against such Polish military forces as are at that time located in the Polish area belonging to the Russian sphere of interest.

Please discuss this at once with Molotov and see if the Soviet Union does not consider it desirable for Russian forces to move at the proper time against Polish forces in the Russian sphere of interest and, for their part, to occupy this territory. In our estimation this would be not only a relief for us, but also, in the sense of the Moscow agreements, in the Soviet interest as well.

In this connection please determine whether we may discuss this matter with the officers who have just arrived here and what the Soviet Government intends their position to be.

RIBBENTROP

THE GERMAN AMBASSADOR IN THE SOVIET UNION (SCHULENBURG)
TO THE GERMAN FOREIGN OFFICE—TELEGRAM

Moscow, September 6, 1939—5:46 p.m.
Received September 6, 1939—8:15 p.m.

Pol V 8924

No. 279 of September 6

Reference your telegram No. 267 of the 5th.

Since anxiety over war, especially the fear of a German attack, has strongly influenced the attitude of the population here in the last few years, the conclusion of a nonaggression pact with Germany has been generally received with great relief and gratification. However, the sudden alteration in the policy of the Soviet Government, after years of propaganda directed expressly against German aggressors, is still not very well understood by the population. Especially the statements of official agitators to the effect that Germany is no longer an aggressor run up against considerable doubt. The Soviet Government is doing everything to change the attitude of the population here toward Germany. The press is as though it had been transformed. Attacks on the conduct of Germany have not only ceased completely, but the portrayal of events in the field of foreign politics is based to an outstanding degree on German reports and anti-German literature has been removed from the book trade, etc.

The beginning of the war between Germany and Poland has powerfully affected public opinion here, and aroused new fear in extensive groups that the Soviet Union may be drawn into the war. Mistrust sown for years against Germany, in spite of effective counterpropaganda which is being carried on in party and business gatherings, cannot be so quickly removed. The fear is expressed by the population that Germany, after she has defeated Poland, may turn against the Soviet Union. The recollection of German strength in the World War is everywhere still lively.

In a judgment of conditions here the realization is of importance that the Soviet Government has always previously been able in a masterly fashion to influence the attitude of the population in the direction which it has desired, and it is not being sparing this time either of the necessary propaganda.

SCHULENBURG

THE GERMAN AMBASSADOR IN THE SOVIET UNION (SCHULENBURG)
TO THE GERMAN FOREIGN OFFICE—TELEGRAM
VERY URGENT   Moscow, September 9, 1939—12:56 a.m.
                               Received September 9, 1939—5 a.m.

No. 300 of September 8

I have just received the following telephone message from Molotov:

"I have received your communication regarding the entry of German troops into Warsaw. Please convey my congratulations and greetings to the German Reich Government. Molotov."

SCHULENBURG

THE GERMAN AMBASSADOR IN THE SOVIET UNION (SCHULENBURG)
TO THE GERMAN FOREIGN OFFICE—TELEGRAM
VERY URGENT   Moscow, September 16, 1939.
STRICTLY SECRET

No. 371 of September 16

Reference your telegram No. 360 of September 15.

I saw Molotov at 6 o'clock today and carried out instructions. Molotov declared that military intervention by the Soviet Union was imminent—perhaps even tomorrow or the day after. Stalin was at present in consultation with the military leaders and he would this very night, in the presence of Molotov, give me the day and hour of the Soviet advance.

Molotov added that he would present my communication to his Government but he believed that a joint communiqué was no longer needed; the Soviet Government intended to motivate its procedure as follows: the Polish State had collapsed and no longer existed; therefore all agreements concluded with Poland were void; third powers might try to profit by the chaos which had arisen; the Soviet Union considered itself obligated to intervene to protect its Ukrainian and White Russian brothers and make it possible for these unfortunate people to work in peace.

The Soviet Government intended to publicize the above train of thought by the radio, press, etc., immediately after the Red Army had crossed the border, and at the same time communicate it in an official note to the Polish Ambassador here and to all the missions here.

Molotov conceded that the projected argument of the Soviet Government contained a note that was jarring to German sensibilities but asked that in view of the difficult situation of the Soviet Government we not let a trifle like this stand in our way. The Soviet Government unfortunately saw no possibility of any other motivation, since the Soviet Union had thus far not concerned itself about the plight of its minorities in Poland and had to justify abroad, in some way or other, its present intervention. . . .

SCHULENBURG

THE GERMAN AMBASSADOR IN THE SOVIET UNION (SCHULENBURG)
TO THE GERMAN FOREIGN OFFICE—TELEGRAM
VERY URGENT   Moscow, September 17, 1939.
SECRET
Reference my telegram No. 371 of September 16.

Stalin received me at 2 o'clock at night at the presence of Molotov and Voroshilov and declared that the Red Army would cross the Soviet border this morning at 6 o'clock along the whole line from Polozk to Kamenetz-Podolsk.

In order to avoid incidents, Stalin urgently requested that we see to it that German planes as of today do not fly east of the Bialystok-Brest-Litovsk-Lemberg Line. Soviet planes would begin today to bomb the district east of Lemberg.

I promised to do my best with regard to informing the German Air Force, but asked in view of the little time left that the Soviet planes do not approach the abovementioned line too closely today.

SCHULENBURG

THE GERMAN AMBASSADOR IN THE SOVIET UNION (SCHULENBURG)
TO THE GERMAN FOREIGN OFFICE—TELEGRAM
STRICTLY SECRET   Moscow, September 20, 1939—2:23 a.m.
                                    Received September 20, 1939—4:55 a.m.
No. 395 of September 19

Molotov stated to me today that the Soviet Government now considered the time ripe for it, jointly with the German Government, to establish definitively the structure of the Polish area. In this regard, Molotov hinted that the original inclination entertained by the Soviet Government and Stalin personally to permit the existence of a residual Poland had given way to the inclination to partition Poland along the Pissa-Narev-Vistula-San Line. . . .

SCHULENBURG

THE GERMAN AMBASSADOR IN THE SOVIET UNION (SCHULENBURG)
TO THE GERMAN FOREIGN OFFICE—TELEGRAM
VERY URGENT   Moscow, September 25, 1939—10:58 p.m.
STRICTLY SECRET   Received September 26, 1939—12:30 a.m.
No. 442 of September 25

Stalin and Molotov asked me to come to the Kremlin at 8 p.m. today. Stalin stated the following: In the final settlement of the Polish question anything that in the future might create friction between Germany and the Soviet Union must be avoided. From this point of view, he considered it wrong to leave an independent Polish rump state. He proposed the following: From the territory to the east of the demarcation line, all the Province of Lublin and that portion of the Province of Warsaw which extends to the Bug should be added to our share. In return, we should waive our claim to Lithuania.

Stalin designated this suggestion as a subject for the forthcoming negotiations with the Reich Foreign Minister and added that, if we consented, the Soviet Union would immediately take up the solution of the problem of the Baltic countries in accordance with the Protocol of August 23, and expected in this matter the unstinting support of the German Government. Stalin expressly indicated Estonia, Latvia, and Lithuania, but did not mention Finland.

I replied to Stalin that I would report to my Government.

SCHULENBURG

The Dictators Divide the World—Berlin 1940

MEMORANDUM OF THE FINAL CONVERSATION BETWEEN REICH FOREIGN MINISTER VON RIBBENTROP AND THE CHAIRMAN OF THE COUNCIL OF PEOPLE'S COMMISSARS OF THE U.S.S.R. AND PEOPLE'S COMMISSAR FOR FOREIGN AFFAIRS, HERR MOLOTOV, ON NOVEMBER 13, 1940

SECRET

RM 42/40

Duration of conversation: 9:45 p.m. until 12 midnight.

Because of the air raid alert that had been ordered, Reich Minister for Foreign Affairs von Ribbentrop and Herr Molotov went into the Reich Foreign Minister's air raid shelter after the supper at the Embassy of the U.S.S.R. at 9:40 p.m. on November 13, 1940, in order to conduct the final conversation.

The Reich Foreign Minister opened the conversation with the statement that he wanted to take the opportunity to supplement and give more specific form to what had been discussed thus far. . . . He had to stress explicitly, however, that this was merely a matter of ideas which were still rather rough, but which might perhaps be realized at some time in the future. By and large, it was a matter of achieving future collaboration between the countries of the Tripartite Pact—Germany, Italy, and Japan—and the Soviet Union, and he believed that first a way must be found to define in bold outlines the spheres of influence of these four countries and to reach an understanding on the problem of Turkey. . . . He conceived the future developments as follows: Herr Molotov would discuss with Herr Stalin the issues raised in Berlin; then, by means of further conversations, an agreement could be reached between the Soviet Union and Germany; thereupon the Reich Foreign Minister would approach Italy and Japan in order to find out how their interests with respect to the delimitation of spheres of influence could be reduced to a common formula. He had already approached Italy as to Turkey. The further *modus procedendi* between Italy, the Soviet Union, and Germany would be to exert influence upon Turkey in the spirit of the wishes of the three countries. If they succeeded in reducing the interests of the four countries concerned to a common denominator—which, given good will, was entirely possible—it would undoubtedly work to the advantage of all concerned. The next step would consist in attempting to record both sets of issues in confidential documents. If the Soviet Union entertained a similar view, that is, would be willing to work against the extension, and for the early termination of the war (the Reich Foreign Minister believed that Herr Molotov had indicated his willingness in the previous discussions), he had in mind as the ultimate objective an agreement for collaboration between the countries of the Tripartite Pact and the Soviet Union. He had drafted the contents of this agreement in outline form and he would like to inform Herr Molotov of them today, stressing in advance that he had not discussed these issues so concretely either with Japan or with Italy. He considered it necessary that Germany and the Soviet Union settle the issue first. This was not by any means a matter of a German proposal, but— as already mentioned—one of still rather rough ideas, which would have to be deliberated by both parties and discussed between Molotov and Stalin. It would be advisable to pursue the matter further, particularly in diplomatic negotiations with Italy and Japan, only if the question had been settled as between Germany and the Soviet Union.

Then the Reich Foreign Minister informed Herr Molotov of the contents of the agreement outlined by him in the following words:

> The Governments of the states of the Three Power Pact, Germany, Italy, and Japan, on the one side, and the Government of the U.S.S.R. on the other side, motivated by the desire to establish in their natural boundaries an order serving the welfare of all peoples concerned and to create a firm and enduring foundation for their common labors toward this goal, have agreed upon the following:
>
> *Article 1.* In the Three Power Pact of September 27, 1940, Germany, Italy, and Japan agreed to oppose the extension of the war into a world conflict with all possible means and to collaborate toward an early restoration of world peace. They expressed their willingness to extend their collaboration to nations in other parts of the world which are inclined to direct their efforts along the same course as theirs. The Soviet Union declares that it concurs in these aims and is on its part determined to cooperate politically in this course with the Three Powers.
>
> *Article 2.* Germany, Italy, Japan, and the Soviet Union undertake to respect each other's natural spheres of influence. In so far as these spheres of influence come into contact with each other, they will constantly consult each other in an amicable way with regard to the problems arising therefrom.
>
> *Article 3.* Germany, Italy, Japan, and the Soviet Union undertake to join no combination of powers and to support no combination of powers which is directed against one of the Four Powers.

> The Four Powers will assist each other in economic matters in every way and will supplement and extend the agreements existing among themselves.

The Reich Foreign Minister added that this agreement was intended for a period of ten years, with the provision that the Governments of the Four Powers, before the expiration of this term, were to reach an understanding regarding the matter of an extension of the agreement.

The agreement itself would be announced to the public. Beyond that, with reference to the above-mentioned agreement, a confidential (secret) agreement could be concluded—in a form still to be determined—establishing the focal points in the territorial aspirations of the Four Countries.

As to Germany, apart from the territorial revisions to be made in Europe at the conclusion of the peace, her territorial aspirations centered in the Central African region.

The territorial aspirations of Italy, apart from the European territorial revisions to be made at the conclusion of the peace, centered in North and Northeast Africa.

The aspirations of Japan would still have to be clarified through diplomatic channels. Here too, a delimitation could easily be found, possibly by fixing a line which would run south of the Japanese home islands and Manchukuo.

The focal points in the territorial aspirations of the Soviet Union would presumably be centered south of the territory of the Soviet Union in the direction of the Indian Ocean.

Such a confidential agreement could be supplemented by the statement that the Four Powers concerned, except for the settlement of individual issues, would respect each other's territorial aspirations and would not oppose their realization.

The above-mentioned agreements could be supplemented by a second secret protocol, to be concluded between Germany, Italy, and the Soviet Union. This second secret protocol could perhaps read that Germany, Italy, and the Soviet Union, on the occasion of the signing of the agreement between Germany, Italy, Japan, and the Soviet Union, were agreed that it was in their common interest to release Turkey from her previous ties and win her progressively to a political collaboration with them.

They declare that they would pursue this aim in close contact with each other, in accordance with a procedure to be established. . . .

[A thorough discussion of every aspect of Nazi propositions followed.]

. . . Molotov stated that the Germans were assuming that the war against England had already actually been won. If, therefore, as had been said in another connection, Germany was waging a life and death struggle against England, he could only construe this as meaning that Germany was fighting "for life" and England "for death." As to the question of collaboration, he quite approved of it, but he added that they had to come to a thorough understanding. This idea had also been expressed in Stalin's letter. A delimitation of the spheres of influence must also be sought. On the point, however, he

(Molotov) could not take a definitive stand at this time, since he did not know the opinion of Stalin and of his other friends in Moscow in the matter. However, he had to state that all these great issues of tomorrow could not be separated from the issues of today and the fulfillment of existing agreements. The things that were started must first be completed before they proceeded to new tasks. The conversations which he—Molotov—had had in Berlin had undoubtedly been very useful, and he considered it appropriate that the questions raised should now be further dealt with through diplomatic channels by way of the ambassadors on either side.

Thereupon Herr Molotov cordially bade farewell to the Reich Foreign Minister, stressing that he did not regret the air raid alarm, because he owed to it such an exhaustive conversation with the Reich Foreign Minister.

Moscow, November 18, 1940.   HILGER

Russia Asks for a Too Large Slice of the World

THE GERMAN AMBASSADOR IN THE SOVIET UNION (SCHULENBURG)
TO THE FOREIGN OFFICE—TELEGRAM

VERY URGENT   Moscow, November 26, 1940—5:34 a.m.
STRICTLY SECRET   Received November 26, 1940—8:50 a.m.
No. 2362 of November 25

For the Reich Minister in person.

Molotov asked me to call on him this evening and in the presence of Dekanosov stated the following:

The Soviet Government has studied the contents of the statements of the Reich Foreign Minister in the concluding conversation on November 13 and takes the following stand:

"The Soviet Government is prepared to accept the draft of the Four Power Pact which the Reich Foreign Minister outlined in the conversation of November 13, regarding political collaboration and reciprocal economic [support] subject to the following conditions:

"1. Provided that the German troops are immediately withdrawn from Finland, which under the compact of 1939, belongs to the Soviet Union's sphere of influence. At the same time the Soviet Union undertakes to ensure peaceful relations with Finland and to protect German economic interests in Finland (export of lumber and nickel).

"2. Provided that within the next few months the security of the Soviet Union in the Straits is assured by the conclusion of a mutual assistance pact between the Soviet Union and Bulgaria, which geographically is situated inside the security zone of the Black Sea boundaries of the Soviet Union, and by the establishment of a base for land and naval forces of the U.S.S.R. within range of the Bosporus and the Dardanelles by means of a long-term lease.

"3. Provided that the area south of Batum and Baku in the general direction of the Persian Gulf is recognized as the center of the aspirations of the Soviet Union.

"4. Provided that Japan [renounces] her rights to concessions for coal and oil in Northern Sakhalin.

"In accordance with the foregoing, the draft of the protocol concerning the delimitation of the spheres of influence as outlined by the Reich Foreign Minister would have to be amended so as to stipulate the focal point of the aspirations of the Soviet Union south of Batum and Baku in the general direction of the Persian Gulf.

"Likewise, the draft of the protocol or agreement between Germany, Italy, and the Soviet Union with respect to Turkey should be amended so as to guarantee a base for light naval and land forces of the U.S.S.R. on [am] the Bosporus and the Dardanelles by means of a long-term lease, including—in case Turkey declares herself willing to join the Four Power Pact—a guarantee of the independence and of the territory of Turkey by the three countries named. . . .

In conclusion Molotov stated that the Soviet proposal provided for five protocols instead of the two envisaged by the Reich Foreign Minister. He would appreciate a statement of the German view.

SCHULENBURG

Hitler Decides to Destroy Russia

THE FÜHRER AND COMMANDER-IN-CHIEF OF THE GERMAN ARMED FORCES

MILITARY SECRET

TOP SECRET   FÜHRER'S HEADQUARTERS
BY OFFICER ONLY   December 18, 1940.

Directive No. 21—Operation Barbarossa

The German Armed Forces must be prepared *to crush Soviet Russia in a quick campaign* (Operation Barbarossa) even before the conclusion of the war against England.

For this purpose the *Army* will have to employ all available units, with the reservation that the occupied territories must be secured against surprise attacks.

For the *Air Force* it will be a matter of releasing such strong forces for the eastern campaign in support of the Army that a quick completion of the ground operations may be expected and that damage to Eastern German territory by enemy air attacks will be as slight as possible. This concentration of the main effort in the East is limited by the requirement that the entire combat and armament area dominated by us must remain adequately protected against enemy air attacks and that the offensive operations against England, particularly her supply lines, must not be permitted to break down.

The main effort of the *Navy* will remain unequivocally directed against *England* even during an eastern campaign.

I shall order the *concentration* against Soviet Russia possibly eight weeks before the intended beginning of operations.

Preparations requiring more time to start are to be started now—if this has not yet been done—and are to be completed by May 15, 1941.

It is to be considered of decisive importance, however, that the intention to attack is not discovered. . . .

THE GERMAN AMBASSADOR IN THE SOVIET UNION (SCHULENBURG)
TO THE GERMAN FOREIGN OFFICE—TELEGRAM

Moscow, June 14, 1941—1:30 a.m.
Received June 14, 1941—8 a.m.

No. 1368 of June 13

People's Commissar Molotov has just given me the following text of a Tass despatch which will be broadcast tonight and published in the papers tomorrow:

Even before the return of the English Ambassador Cripps to London, but especially after his return, there have been widespread rumors of "an impending war between the U.S.S.R. and Germany" in the English and foreign press. These rumors allege:

1. That Germany supposedly has made various territorial and economic demands on the U.S.S.R. and that at present negotiations are impending between Germany and the U.S.S.R. for the conclusion of a new and closer agreement between them;

2. That the Soviet Union is supposed to have declined these demands and that as a result Germany has begun to concentrate her troops on the frontier of the Soviet Union in order to attack the Soviet Union;

3. That on its side the Soviet Union is supposed to have begun intensive preparations for war with Germany and to have concentrated its troops on the German border.

Despite the obvious absurdity of these rumors, responsible circles in Moscow have thought it necessary, in view of the persistent spread of these rumors, to authorize Tass to state that these rumors are a clumsy propaganda maneuver of the forces arrayed against the Soviet Union and Germany, which are interested in a spread and intensification of the war.

Tass declares that:

1. Germany has addressed no demands to the Soviet Union and has asked for no new closer agreement, and that therefore negotiations cannot be taking place;

2. According to the evidence in the possession of the Soviet Union, both Germany and the Soviet Union are fulfilling to the letter the terms of the Soviet-German Nonagression Pact, so that in the opinion of Soviet circles the rumors of the intention of Germany to break the Pact and to launch an attack against the Soviet Union are completely without foundation, while the recent movements of German troops which have completed their operations in the Balkans, to the eastern and northern parts of Germany, must be explained by other motives which have no connection with Soviet-German relations;

3. The Soviet Union, in accordance with its peace policy, has fulfilled and intends to fulfill the terms of the Soviet-German Nonagression Pact; as a result, all the rumors according to which the Soviet Union is preparing for a war with Germany are false and provocative;

4. The summer calling-up of the reserves of the Red Army which is now taking place and the impending maneuvers mean nothing but a training of the reservists and a check on the operations of the railroad system, which as is known takes place every year; consequently, it appears at least nonsensical to interpret these measures of the Red Army as an action hostile to Germany.

SCHULENBURG

THE REICH FOREIGN MINISTER TO THE GERMAN AMBASSADOR
IN THE SOVIET UNION (SCHULENBURG)—TELEGRAM
VERY URGENT   BERLIN, June 21, 1941.
STATE SECRET
By radio
  For the Ambassador personally.

1. Upon receipt of this telegram, all of the cipher material still there is to be destroyed. The radio set is to be put out of commission.

2. Please inform Herr Molotov at once that you have an urgent communication to make to him and would therefore like to call on him immediately. Then please make the following declaration to him.

"The Soviet Ambassador in Berlin is receiving at this hour from the Reich Minister for Foreign Affairs a memorandum giving in detail the facts which are briefly summarized as follows:

"I. In 1939 the Government of the Reich, putting aside grave objections arising out of the contradiction between National Socialism and Bolshevism, undertook to arrive at an understanding with Soviet Russia. Under the treaties of August 23 and September 28, 1939, the Government of the Reich effected a general reorientation of its policy toward the U.S.S.R. and thenceforth adopted a cordial attitude toward the Soviet Union. This policy of goodwill brought the Soviet Union great advantages in the field of foreign policy.

"The Government of the Reich therefore felt entitled to assume that thenceforth both nations, while respecting each other's regime and not interfering in the internal affairs of the other partner, would arrive at good, lasting, neighborly relations. Unfortunately it soon became evident that the Government of the Reich had been entirely mistaken in this assumption.

"II. Soon after the conclusion of the German-Russian treaties, the Comintern resumed its subversive activity against Germany, with the official Soviet-Russian representatives giving assistance. Sabotage, terrorism, and espionage in preparation for war were demonstrably carried out on a large scale. In all the countries bordering on Germany and in the territories occupied by German troops, anti-German feeling was aroused and the German attempt to set up a stable order in Europe was combated. Yugoslavia was gladly offered arms against Germany by the Soviet Russian Chief of Staff, as proved by documents found in Belgrade. The declarations made by the U.S.S.R. on conclusion of the treaties with Germany, regarding her intention to collaborate with Germany, thus stood revealed as deliberate misrepresentation and deceit and the conclusion of the treaties themselves as a tactical maneuver for obtaining arrangements favorable to Russia. The guiding principle remained the weakening of the non-Bolshevik countries in order the more easily to demoralize them and, at a given time, to crush them.

"III. In the diplomatic and military fields it became obvious that the U.S.S.R.—contrary to the declaration made at the conclusion of the treaties that she did not wish to Bolshevize and annex the countries falling within her sphere of influence—was intent on pushing her military might westward wherever it seemed possible and on carrying Bolshevism further into Europe. The action of the U.S.S.R. against the Baltic States, Finland, and Rumania, where Soviet claims even extended to Bucovina, showed this clearly. The occupation and Bolshevization by the Soviet Union of the sphere of influence granted to her clearly violated the Moscow agreements, even though the Government of the Reich for the time being accepted the facts.

"IV. When Germany, by the Vienna Award of August 30, 1940, settled the crisis in Southeastern Europe resulting from the action of the U.S.S.R. against Rumania, the Soviet Union protested and turned to making intensive military preparations in every field. Germany's renewed effort to achieve an understanding, as reflected in the exchange of letters between the Reich Foreign Minister and Herr Stalin and in the invitation to Herr Molotov to come to Berlin, brought demands from the Soviet Union which Germany could not accept, such as the guarantee of Bulgaria by the U.S.S.R., the establishment of a base for Soviet Russian land and naval forces at the Straits, and the complete abandonment of Finland. Subsequently, the policy of the U.S.S.R. directed against Germany became more and more obvious. The warning addressed to Germany regarding occupation of Bulgaria and the declaration made to Bulgaria after the entry of German troops, which was of a definitely hostile nature, were as significant in this connection as was the promise to protect the rear of Turkey in the event of a Turkish entry into the war in the Balkans, given in March 1941.

"V. With the conclusion of the Soviet-Yugoslav Treaty of Friendship of April 5 last, which was intended to stiffen the spines of the Yugoslav plotters, the U.S.S.R. joined the common Anglo-Yugoslav-Greek front against Germany. At the same time she tried *rapprochement* with Rumania, in order to induce that country to detach itself from Germany. It was only the rapid German victories that caused the failure of the Anglo-Russian plan for an attack against the German troops in Rumania and Bulgaria.

"VI. This policy was accompanied by a steadily growing concentration of all available Russian forces on a long front from the Baltic Sea to the Black Sea, against which countermeasures were taken by Germany only later. Since the beginning of the year this has been a steadily growing menace to the territory of the Reich. Reports received in the last few days eliminated the last remaining doubts as to the aggressive character of this Russian concentration, and completed the picture of an extremely tense military situation. In addition to this, there are the reports from England regarding the negotiations of Ambassador Cripps for still closer political and military collaboration between England and the Soviet Union.

"To sum up, the Government of the Reich declares, therefore, that the Soviet Government, contrary to the obligations it assumed,

1) has not only continued, but even intensified its attempts to under-mine Germany and Europe;
2) has adopted a more and more anti-German foreign policy;
3) has concentrated all its forces in readiness at the German border. Thereby the Soviet Government has broken its treaties with Germany and is about to attack Germany from the rear, in its struggle for life. The Führer has therefore ordered the German Armed Forces to oppose this threat with all the means at their disposal."

End of declaration.

Please do not enter into any discussion of this communication. It is incumbent upon the Government of Soviet Russia to safeguard the security of the Embassy personnel.

RIBBENTROP

33 / How Nuclear War Might Come

Herman Kahn

In 1960 Herman Kahn, a nuclear physicist and an expert in national security planning, published a book [6] that attempted to direct attention to the possibility of a thermonuclear war, to ways of reducing the likelihood of such a war, and to methods for coping with the consequences should war occur despite the national leaders' efforts to avoid it. The book was both acclaimed for its boldness to think about the unthinkable and sharply criticized for the same reasons. Two years later Herman Kahn tried to clarify his theses and theories in a second book, which also included fourteen possible alternative policies. These alternatives ranged from a pacifist act of renunciation of all violence to initiation of preventive nuclear war. The following excerpt is from Kahn's second book.

Reprinted from pp. 19–21, 41–60, 244–263 (*passim*) by permission of the publisher, Horizon Press, from *Thinking about the Unthinkable* by Herman Kahn, copyright © 1962. Some author's footnotes have been omitted; footnotes added by the editor are so marked.

[6] *On Thermonuclear War* (Princeton, N.J.: Princeton University Press, 1960).

Social inhibitions which reinforce natural tendencies to avoid thinking about unpleasant subjects are hardly uncommon. The psychological factors involved in ostrich-like behavior have parallels in communities and nations. . . .

In our times, thermonuclear war may seem unthinkable, immoral, insane, hideous, or highly unlikely, but it is not impossible. To act intelligently we must learn as much as we can about the risks. We may thereby be able better to avoid nuclear war. We may even be able to avoid the crises that bring us to the brink of war. But despite our efforts we may some day come face to face with a blunt choice between surrender or war. We may even have war thrust upon us without being given any kind of a choice. We must appreciate these possibilities. We cannot wish them away. Nor should we overestimate and assume the worst is inevitable. This leads only to defeatism, inadequate preparations (because they seem useless), and pressures toward either preventive war or undue accommodation. . . .

It is well to note at the outset a recurring tendency to underestimate the likelihood of war. Ever since the catastrophic and disillusioning experience of 1914–18, war has been unthinkable to most people in the West. Many illogically have tended to assume it was consequently also unlikely or even impossible. In December, 1938, only three months after Munich, Lloyd's of London gave odds of 32 to 1 that there would be no war in 1939. On August 7, 1939, *The London Daily Express* reported the results of a poll of its European reporters. Ten out of twelve said, "No war this year." Hitler invaded Poland three weeks later. It seems fair to suspect that a great deal of wishful thinking influenced these predictions.

How War Might Come

There are many ways in which a war might start today. In semi-technical jargon, these can be put into four rough categories: (1) Inadvertent War; (2) War as a Result of Miscalculation; (3) Calculated War; and (4) Catalytic War. These categories doubtless do not exhaust the ways in which a war might start, nor do they represent mutually exclusive possibilities. Our weapons systems are so new, and their impact upon each other and upon international relations are so little known, it would not be too surprising if a war started in some unanticipated manner.

Inadvertent War

At the top of the list I have put the unpremeditated war, the fearful possibility that war might occur almost unintentionally as a result of mechanical or human error, false alarm, self-fulfilling prophecy, or unauthorized behavior. I believe the current probability of inadvertent war is low. It is at the top of the list for two reasons: First, because I believe that the other ways in which a war might occur today are even less probable; and, second, because I believe that inadvertent war might well become a much more dangerous possibility in the not too distant future, partly as a result of the growing number of buttons that can be pressed accidentally, but chiefly as a result of the proliferation of independent nuclear capabilities in other countries, each with its own standards of safety and stability. . . .

Probably the major protection against inadvertent war is the widespread belief among almost all decision makers that only an insane man would go to war and that the other side is not insane. Therefore the cautious decision maker will discount any signals or events that might be construed as warning of an attack. (It should be noted that, as such, "caution" makes inadvertent war less probable; it makes a Pearl Harbor more feasible.) . . .

This type of situation might also set in motion a disastrous "self-fulfilling prophecy," in much the same way that hostility often breeds hostility. That is, one side's defensive action may be observed by the other which, mis-interpreting it as aggressive, may therefore make some defensive move. This, if misread in turn by the opposite side, confirms the original suspicions. Reactions and signals may thus be set into motion until a point of no re-turn is reached. This is one reason why it is necessary for each side not only to be cautious and responsible, but also to make sure that the other understands what is happening. If a temporizing measure involves doing things which raise apprehensions on the other side, it is important to allay those apprehensions. If either side fears that a surprise attack on its military forces could result in unacceptable damage then, unless there is some degree of co-operation between them, there is an ever-present possibility of a false preemption—a possibility that the apprehensive side may launch an attack simply because it fears one from the other side and thinks that only by preempting can its forces survive.

It is also conceivable that some pathological or irresponsible person might deliberately try to start a war. The Soviets have made much of the possibility that a deranged or irresponsible American pilot on airborne alert might take it into his head to attack Russia alone. Not only are there many safeguards against this, but it is most unlikely that a single-plane attack would touch off a war. . . .

War by Miscalculation

Nearly as worrisome as the possibility of inadvertent war is the more or less premeditated war which might result from a decision maker's miscalculation, misunderstanding, or failure to think adequately through the consequences of his actions. I would include in this category wars re-sulting from a committal strategy, escalation, or overconfidence.

Many people believe that war by miscalculation is most likely to arise through the use or misuse of a committal strategy. For example, one side may believe that if it makes it clear it is going to stand firm in some crisis then, "since neither side wants war," the other side will back down. It then makes whatever announcements and takes whatever actions may be necessary or appropriate to give the appearance, and perhaps the reality, of having committed itself irrevocably. If, then, the other side does not back down, war can result. A graphic if somewhat oversimplified example of such a situation is given by Bertrand Russell:

> This sport is called "Chicken!" It is played by choosing a long straight road with a white line down the middle and starting two very fast cars towards each other from opposite ends. Each car is expected to keep the wheels on one side of the white line. As they approach each other mutual destruction becomes more and more imminent. If one of them swerves from the white line before the other, the other, as he passes, shouts "Chicken!" and the one who has swerved becomes an object of contempt.[7]

To win this game one must try to convince the opponent that it is not worthwhile for him to be so reckless. One can do this by convincing him that one is totally reckless, oblivious to the danger, or out of control. These objectives can probably be met best by getting into the car dead drunk, wearing very dark glasses, and conspicuously throwing the steering wheel out of the window as soon as the car has gotten up to speed. If the opponent is watching, he will feel under some pressure to get out of the way. However, if the opponent refuses to back down after the "irrevocable" commitment has been made, it would be irrational to carry out this rationally made commitment. Since both sides may use the same strategy, it is obvious the game may end in disaster.

The game of chicken is an extreme example of the use of "rationality of irrationality" strategies, but it illustrates clearly a situation in which each side can demonstrate logically that by using a committal strategy it can force the other side to back down. Yet an observer might correctly conclude that neither side, or both sides, will back down. "Rationality of irrationality" strategies can be important in almost any bargaining situation. It can make sense to commit oneself irrevocably to do something in a particular eventuality, and at the same time it may not make sense to carry out the commitment if the eventuality occurs. For this reason, the success of such a strategy may well depend upon the taking of some action which in appearance to the other side, and perhaps in fact, removes the power to revoke the commitment. The success of such a strategy may also depend upon using it before the other side does.

[7] Bertrand Russell, *Common Sense and Nuclear Warfare* (New York: Simon and Schuster, 1959), p. 30.

According to Bertrand Russell, the game of chicken is played by youthful degenerates and by nations. Actually, it is played at one time or another by everyone (even in the raising of children), if in less potentially disastrous form. The analogy of the game of chicken to diplomacy is useful to illustrate a valid point but, as in the case of all analogies, it can be misleading if one ignores the significant differences between the game as played with cars by youthful degenerates and the game as played by diplomats. Most bargaining situations involve potential gains and losses for both sides.[8] The central issue is usually the division of these gains and losses and not the humiliation of one side or the other; a major purpose of diplomacy is to prevent a crisis which can only be settled by the total and humiliating defeat of one side or the other.

Nonetheless, the dangerous game of chicken can occur at the international level. Barring enforceable alternatives, the less one is willing to play, the more likely it is that one may have to end up playing the most dangerous form. Whether we like it or not, our life, liberty, and security may depend on being willing to play. As Russell states:

> Practical politicians may admit all this, but they argue that there is no alternative. If one side is unwilling to risk global war, while the other side is willing to risk it, the side which is willing to run the risk will be victorious in all negotiations and will ultimately reduce the other side to complete impotence. "Perhaps"—so the practical politician will argue—"it might be ideally wise for the sane party to yield to the insane party in view of the dreadful nature of the alternative, but, whether wise or not, no proud nation will long acquiesce in such an ignominious role." We are, therefore, faced, quite inevitably, with the choice between brinkmanship and surrender.[9]

War by miscalculation might also result from the process generally called "escalation." A limited move may appear safe, but set into motion a disastrous sequence of decisions and actions. One may readily imagine some intensifying crisis in which neither side really believes the issue is big enough to end in war, but in which both sides are willing to accept some small risk of war. Escalation might develop as a result of other parties becoming involved, as a consequence of the issues taking on new significance, or as a result of accident, miscalculation, unauthorized behavior, or other inadvertent cause. Escalation can also be deliberate—as in the game of chicken. . . .

The fact that the threat of escalation is used, perhaps effectively, to deter limited action presents a serious problem for arms controllers. To the extent that various types of arms control measures would reduce the possibility of

[8] Compare with Schelling, Selection 45.——Ed.
[9] Russell, *Common Sense*, pp. 30–31.

escalation, to that extent an important deterrent upon limited actions might also be decreased. Although I feel that this is not sufficient reason for refusing to adopt arms control measures, many Europeans are antagonistic to any reliable limits upon the use of nuclear weapons precisely because such limitations may indeed make it safer for the Soviets to use or threaten lesser kinds of violence. It may be that before arms control measures can or should be adopted, effective substitute deterrents, less violent in effect, will have to be devised. For this reason, a strengthened conventional force might be necessary were we to reach a nuclear arms control agreement.

A war by miscalculation might also result from simple overconfidence. Overconfidence, of course, can take many forms—ranging from ignorance, stupidity, and negligence, through a failure to realize that even the most closely calculated paper plans are still only paper plans with possibly no more than a tenuous relationship to the real world and the actual course of events. Overconfidence can be based on a mystical belief in the manifest destiny of the West or the historical imperative of ultimate victory for the East. It can consist of a mistaken belief by one side that its force and war plans are such that it can win without serious damage to itself if it initiates an attack. Lastly, war through overconfidence can come about because of a mistaken belief by one side that it has a sufficient preponderance of force or such clever war plans that the other side would not dare to initiate an attack, no matter what the provocation.

It is almost impossible to imagine a Western government initiating an attack on the basis of optimistic calculations unless the decision makers have had their judgment affected by desperation. I am less confident of the possible effect of underestimation, overestimation, ignorance, or recklessness in the Communist bloc.

War by Calculation

It is commonly believed that war could arise only as a result of inadvertence or miscalculation—a belief based partly on the view that war would automatically result in mutual annihilation, and partly on the assumption that no decision maker who is calculating correctly would ever knowingly take action that entailed an appreciable probability of war. The first view is demonstrably incorrect, at least today. The second assumption is not borne out by past or current history. After due study, a nation might decide that going to war would be the least undesirable of its choices, and it might be right in its calculation; we must therefore include this unpleasant prospect as one of the possible ways in which wars could start. The common statement, "There is no alternative to peace," may not look as convincing when it appears as—"No alternative to any kind of peace," or "Peace at any price."

To mention one often-used example: 15 to 30 million Soviet citizens were killed in World War II; in addition the Soviet Union lost about one-third of its wealth. It is sometimes pointed out that this was not the result of calculation, and that no alternatives were ever really offered to the Soviets. However, given the nature of the Nazis and their program, I believe that even the average Soviet citizen (not to mention the government), if presented with a choice, would have been willing to accept the cost of World War II in order to achieve the position they have since won, as an alternative to Nazi domination. They might feel themselves presented with a similar choice someday. Only now both the risks and the prize would be greater. It is also conceivable that the West, or the United States alone, could believe itself faced with a choice between domination and occupation by the Soviets or China, on the one hand, and substantial casualties and property damage, but survival and possibly even "victory," on the other. Faced with such a choice it is not inconceivable that we might choose to go to war. . . .

The so-called "preventive war" furnishes another example of possible war by calculation. A preventive war might be in the nature of a preemptive strike, or it might simply be an unprovoked attack, depending more upon the motivations of those initiating it than anything else. . . . Almost all authorities agree that at present the advantages of striking first are so great that, should there seem to be a high probability that the other side is actually attacking, it might be better to risk the certainty of a relatively small retaliatory strike, rather than the high probability of a much more destructive first blow. Calculated preemption is not unlikely in the event of a reciprocal fear of surprise attack,[10] a situation very similar to the self-fulfilling prophecy. Situations could arise in which each side felt there was a more or less symmetrical fear of attack by the other side. In such a situation each side may feel itself under pressure to preempt because it knows the other side is under similar pressure. Reciprocal fear itself may make it rational, indeed almost imperative, to strike, even though the fear may be based on a mutual misunderstanding. The danger of such a situation increases directly with the advantage to be gained by striking first, and with each side's estimate of the likelihood that the other will strike first. The advantage to an enemy of striking us first will depend on the difference between our striking power before and after he attacks, that is, on the vulnerability of our forces. Moreover, his estimate of the likelihood of our striking him will be influenced by the vulnerability of his forces to our first strike. As described, a preemptive strike resulting from reciprocal fear of surprise attack is not a case of miscalculation. It is a case of correct calculation; though each side has nothing to fear but fear, the knowledge that the other side is afraid fully justifies that fear. . . .

[10] Thomas C. Schelling, *The Strategy of Conflict* (Cambridge, Mass.: Harvard University Press). See Chapter 9, pp. 207–29. [See also Selection 45.——Ed.]

A preventive war need not be preemption. It might be a deliberate and calculated attack made without regard to the immediate likelihood of an attack by the other side, or even the likelihood that the other side is planning to attack eventually. One side has only to feel that a war is inevitable—or so likely that it might as well get the disaster over with as soon as it attains a sufficient lead, or before more destructive weapons are constructed. One side has only to believe it safer, either for itself or for the world, to seize the opportunity than to wait.

A preventive war might . . . . occur if an arms-control agreement broke down with the result that one side had a considerable lead, because of its previous success in undetected violations or greater ability to rearm. The side with a commanding lead might well feel that, rather than see the world subjected again to all the dangers of an arms race, it would be accomplishing an essential public service by stopping the race from starting anew. This could best be done by stopping the cause of the race—the government of its opponent. A nation might be willing to start the war soon after an arms-control agreement ended because the risks of such a war, even if things went awry, would not be so great as they might have been before the agreement had lowered the level of the balance of terror.

The likelihood of war breaking out soon after a renewed arms race, but before both sides have fully rearmed, is often ignored. Most writers focus their attention on the time of the breakdown, when the posture is more likely to be determined by the agreement, and on feasible violations of the agreement, and do not consider adequately the possible situation some months or a year or two later. A more dangerous situation, neglected by many unilateral disarmers, is what happens after a substantial degree of unilateral disarmament if we should change our minds or even if the Soviets or Chinese should fear that we were about to change our minds.

Finally, we must also consider the more remote possibility that one side or the other might deliberately go to war simply to achieve world domination. Most people (the author included) believe the risks involved in going to war are so great today that no matter how promising an attack might look on paper, the "imponderables" and other uncertainties are so large that not even a moderately irresponsible decision maker would go to war for positive gains, though one like Hitler might. . . .

I believe that the probability of war by calculation is low because I think this is the place where deterrence is most likely to work and—perhaps optimistically—that we are going to be competent about deterrence. If we weaken our deterrent prematurely, however, the possibility of war by calculation may move to the top of the list.

Many people interested in disarmament or arms control *at any cost* (not to speak of many professional planners) refuse to take seriously the potential effect of disarmament upon deterrence. There are, and in spite of anything we do there will remain, great pressures toward war. While the arms controllers are going to try to balance these effects by making the peaceful alternatives to war more attractive, there are practical limits to what they can accomplish, at least for some time. The pressures toward war are likely to be restrained effectively only if the fear of punishment is not diminished to the vanishing point.

These cautions as to arms control do not mean that arms control should not be pursued with vigor. . . . They do mean that an insistence on reasonable and workable arrangements is essential to prevent an even more unstable situation than we have today. A bad arms control agreement may be vastly worse than none at all.

Catalytic War

This last category is based on the notion that some third party or nation might for its own reasons deliberately start a war between the two major powers. There is a wide range of possible motivations and means for such an attempt. For example, some third, fourth, or fifth power in the international hierarchy might wish to improve its relative position by arranging for the two top nations to destroy each other. It might attack the United States under circumstances which would suggest a Soviet attack, counting on our retaliation to precipitate a full scale war. Some people fear the dissemination of nuclear weapons among "ambitious" powers because they feel that such weapons provide a particularly handy and dangerous means by which to precipitate the mutual destruction of the Soviet Union and the United States. . . . [The] risks of destruction would be [however] so great for the triggering power, if discovered, that it is difficult to believe any nation would take such a chance. . . .

Alternative National Policies

In thinking about the ways to prevent war, and in thinking about how to fight, survive, and terminate a war, should it occur. . . . my colleagues and I have sought answers to such questions as these:

How likely is accidental war? How can one make it less likely?

How dangerous is the arms race today? What will it be like in the future?

What would conditions be if a nuclear attack leveled fifty of America's largest cities? Would the survivors envy the dead?

How many million American lives would an American President risk by standing firm in differing types of crises? By starting a nuclear war? By continuing a nuclear war with the hope of avoiding surrender?

How many European and Soviet and other lives would he risk?

These questions can be put in a more concrete and hence more upsetting form. Consider, for example, the debate about the defense of Europe. . . . Our present doctrine seems to indicate that if the strengthened [nonnuclear] forces prove inadequate to repel a possible [Soviet conventional] attack, we will initiate the use of nuclear weapons.

The questions now become more unpleasant since we must acknowledge the likelihood that this use of nuclear weapons might not be limited. Whether we intend it or not, we may have obligated ourselves to go to an all-out central war. Attempts at restraint may turn out to be unreliable; passion, irrationality, and technical difficulties of control and discrimination might cause escalation into all-out war. In this context we must ask ourselves several questions. First, would we in fact initiate an all-out war if the Soviets attacked Europe? Would we even risk one by initiating a lesser response which could easily escalate into all-out war? What would be the European attitude toward fighting a "limited" nuclear (or even a large conventional) war on their territory?

In seeking the answers to these questions, the President must estimate the cohesion of the Alliance, and weigh the possibility of tens of millions, possibly hundreds of millions, of American and European casualties—not to speak of Russians and others. He must ask himself whether he is willing to sacrifice, or so much as risk, New York in order to defend Paris or London or revenge their destruction. If he concludes that he is not—and there are many who think that he would not willingly make the trade—then he must ask himself whether he wishes to change either his commitments or his preparations.

He may conclude that even if he is not willing to initiate a war or a limited reprisal that could easily develop into war, he must maintain a pretense of being willing. Perhaps the facade will work. After all, even if he is not willing to go to an all-out war, the Soviets cannot rely on this. The uncertainty regarding his response may deter them from testing his resolve.

The President may be unwilling to go to all-out war, and also unwilling to rely on the deterrent effect of Russian uncertainty about our response acting as a deterrent. In that case he has to have realistic contingency plans for lesser responses than all-out war, to be used in the event the Soviets are not deterred. He must then ask himself: Should he disclose these contingency plans to the Soviets so as to make credible the action we will take to make their aggression unprofitable? Should he keep these plans secret so that the Soviets will not be encouraged to expect a less than all-out response? How will our allies react to either policy? Will their attitude change in an intense crisis? Would we prefer an ally to be involved in a disastrous local war rather than see its resources added to the Communist bloc?

Perhaps, in addition to having a "wider choice than humiliation or holocaust," the President may wish to prepare for the possibility of holocaust, and for the problems involved in lessening the damage. Even if we are not willing to fight an all-out thermonuclear war, it may still be forced on us, or occur inadvertently.

The reader should have gathered by now that the Unthinkable, or at least the Hard to Think About, includes not only the unpleasant possibility of thermonuclear war but the kinds of crises which would force us to face up to hard choices, the long-term results of the arms race, and, finally, the new ways of organizing international relations to be more capable of meeting the problems that the next four decades will bring. . . .

In order to give some orientation as to the range of strategies which a nation like the United States might choose to follow, I will describe [several] possibilities here. These descriptions are simply a first attempt to suggest some reasonable examples for study and evaluation. I have deliberately included some extreme samples which have almost no chance of being followed in practice, even if a good case might be made for them. It is nevertheless valuable to study them, in order to shed light on the more practicable examples we are most likely in fact to follow, and to clarify the range of choices. . . .

Act of Renunciation

This is the course urged by some pacifists. It is one of the two most extreme strategies I will describe, the other being preventive war. It has an ancient history, from early Christian teachings through the *non-violent* resistance preached by Thoreau and Gandhi. It is advocated today by some proponents of nuclear disarmament. As an ethical proposition the issues were clearly enunciated in the original manifesto of the Society of Friends of King Charles the Second of England in 1660:

> We utterly deny all outward wars and strife, and fighting with outward weapons, for any end, or under any pretence whatever; this is our testimony to the world. The Spirit of Christ by which we are guided is not changeable, so as once to command us from a thing as evil, and again to move unto it; and we certainly know, and testify to the world, that the Spirit of Christ, which leads us into all truth, will never move us to fight and war against any man with outward weapons, neither for the kingdom of Christ, nor for the kingdom of the world.

It is important to note that the Friends would fight neither for the kingdom of Christ nor for the kingdoms of the earth. They hoped that their teachings would be universally adopted, but even if they were not, and the Friends (because of their ideas) were temporarily to lose everything or almost everything, or whole countries were to lose their liberties because they applied these ideas, they would not feel their policy to be a mistake. It is a strategy based on morality, not on effectiveness.[11]

The ranks of the moral pacifists have recently been enlarged by many who argue that some form of the act of renunciation is a better strategy, more practical, than reliance on nuclear weapons—that it is less risky and more effective in accomplishing our national goals. Many of these nuclear pacifists are willing to use such low levels of force as local guerrilla warfare, or even conventional high-explosive military operations to resist enemy occupation, but they would not use nuclear weapons even to resist a nuclear attack. Some hope that, by a single dramatic gesture, or a series of them, we could "reform" the Soviets (and the Chinese?) and then the rest of the world. Even if the program had a complete or partial failure, we would at least eliminate those international tensions and aspects of the arms race that result from self-fulfilling prophecies. Others have less faith in dramatic gestures but hope that, over a period of time, they can expose the uselessness and immorality of force by precept and example. Even more important we would renounce immoral activities such as holding tens of millions of innocent people as hostages to be killed if their government commits certain acts. This argument often concludes that at the worst the United States and Europe, and possibly the world, would suffer a relatively peaceful takeover; and the resultant tyranny would mellow with time. One of the basic comparisons to be made in considering this type of proposal would be to weigh the risk and horror of such an occupation (by the Soviets? the Chinese? others?) against the risk and horror of nuclear war.

Some other elements that might enter a renunciation strategy are the possible allocation of a really large per cent of the Gross National Product to foreign aid (as much as 50 to 100 billion dollars a year). There could be various types of "peace corps," going all the way from those occupied in the current technical aid program to missionaries and volunteer non-violent groups that could interpose themselves in various situations and risk their lives for the principles of peace and progress. . . .

Minimum Deterrence

There are many strategies which could come under this heading, but the one I outline here emphasizes actions directed toward immediately slowing down the arms race and minimizing the consequences of nuclear conflict. A nation pursuing this strategy might procure a small but reliable and relatively invulnerable force having as its sole objective the deterrence

[11] Compare with Max Weber's concept of ethics of ultimate ends and ethics of responsibility for foreseeable consequences (Selection 25). Compare also with Selection 27 that contains a sample of the Friends' creed as adapted to the twentieth century.——Ed.

of a direct attack upon the United States or its military forces. It would not procure any Counterforce capabilities. It might even go far to avoid the appearance of possessing any first-strike capability, or any willingness to threaten and risk all-out war over extreme provocation such as nuclear attacks upon allies. It would certainly not risk a war over lesser provocations. This minimum deterrence strategy would also avoid the offense-defense arms race that might be touched off by the procurement of an active defense against ballistic missiles or by extensive civil defense measures. . . .

In its non-military aspect, this strategy could include [the following elements]: willingness to negotiate, some accommodation, foreign aid, and similar measures. It presumably would place heavy emphasis on conventional forces for defense of "third areas" but not at the expense of encouraging an arms race even in this area. . . .

. . . [T]he inadequacy of the defense of the third areas may force these countries to procure their own weapons and thus this strategy could in the long run accelerate the arms race. . . .

[T]he above strategies involve the danger that they could well end up, even if the United States were successfully defended, in turning the rest of the world over to the Soviet bloc. In a sense, this result would not be surprising. It should almost be expected. One major aim of the first [two] strategies is control of the arms race. Many do not believe that either the Americans by themselves, or the Americans together with the Russians, can do this adequately. Therefore it might be argued, "Why don't we turn the job over to the Russians?" One way to do this effectively is for us to get out of their way. . . . Adherents also point out that a Soviet takeover of the rest of the world is not inevitable in any of the above strategies if for no other reason than that, once we removed ourselves as a threat, internal division might develop in the Communist camp—divisions likely to be increased by any attempt to absorb or conquer most of the world. Furthermore, by adopting a less aggressive and more constructive posture we increase our ability to wage psychological warfare for the minds and hearts of men. Lastly, by reducing the strategic military competition, we have removed some of the motivation for such a take-over. In any case the feasibility and possible consequences of such a "take-over" need to be studied. . . .

Rule of Law

One way in which the war system might wither away would be if nations got in the habit of resolving disputes through adjudication, arbitration, some sort of relatively peaceful ritual (for example, as by medieval jousts or the potlatch wars of the California Indians) [12] or by submission

[12] In Chapters 4 and 5 the hopes and doubts concerning this approach are discussed in some detail, especially the problem of *how* to induce nations to settle their disputes

to some sort of international court. While it is unlikely that, in the absence of international legislative and enforcement machinery, the process would go all the way, it is possible that some startling improvements could be made over the current international order. . . .

Preventive War

This strategy accepts the idea that we wish to win—and that we are prepared to win through a thermonuclear war because we are convinced there is no alternative. It prepares to fight that war, though it may not explicitly admit this. The execution of this policy presumably would take place during an intense crisis or as a result of the escalation of small war. A preventive attack would likely result in a controlled war, accompanied by an offer to the Soviets to call the war off under certain conditions. The offer would most likely be made not to the Presidium but to some other Soviet group, possibly the military.

The notion of preventive war is so abhorrent to almost everybody in the West that even those who feel some inclination toward this strategy have, so far as I know, never studied it. I suspect it deserves some study, again partly with the idea of showing how risky and difficult it is, and partly to fulfill an intellectual obligation. If we are attempting to look at the total range of choices, we should study both unilateral disarmament *and* preventive war.

It should be noted that both the unilateral disarmament and preventive war strategies tend to take the same cataclysmic view that any of the more moderate strategies would be disastrous. We must, these strategies hold, go to the limit; they simply go to different limits.

I would argue tentatively that both the act of renunciation (unilateral disarmament) and preventive war strategies are choices of despair. In this connection, it is interesting to note that Bertrand Russell in the late forties came perilously close to advocating preventive war [In his speech at Westminster School on November 20, 1948, Russell said: "Either we must have a war against Russia before she has the atom bomb or we will have to lie down and let them govern us."]. In a certain sense, his [subsequent] position [was] unchanged from the one he took then: It is simply clear now that we will not use our military power to force the Russians to give in to us; therefore, it follows that we must give in to them. It is, of course, true that Russell preaches this doctrine to both sides, but almost nobody believes that the Soviets will listen, or even be much affected by it. We may be less confident of deafness in the West.

I have already mentioned that the major objection to the first [two]

---

by an increased use of the United Nations machinery or the International Court of Justice.——Ed.

strategies is the possibility that they might result in the Soviets taking over much or all of the world. Alternatively, if the Soviets do not do so, we might have to rely on them to protect these areas and us from the Chinese. The major objection made to the [other] . . . strategies is that they do not pay enough attention to slowing down and controlling the arms race. Indeed, even their proponents often agree that these last strategies would lead, at least in the short run, to an acceleration of the arms race. The differences between the first set and the last set of strategies reflect the fact that those who worry a great deal about the arms race tend to deemphasize the challenges and threats presented by the Chinese and Soviet Communists, while those who worry about the Communists tend to deemphasize the most menacing characteristics of the arms race. Many of those who adopt the middle . . . strategies worry more or less equally and seriously about both problems. . . .

All three of the above views may, of course, turn out to have been excessively preoccupied with the possibility of disaster. It is not inconceivable that the balance of terror or other mechanism will deter or prevent attack, provocation, escalation, inadvertence and so on, and that we are now entering an era of unprecedented stability, marred only by "border" skirmishes and minor battles; that the major frontiers and power groupings may remain basically unchanged or change peacefully over the next century or two, while the war system withers or evolves away. While one can make this last view modestly persuasive, it is hard to believe that most of the persuasion does not come as much from wishful thinking as from realistic estimates of the likely degree of rationality, caution, flexibility, and good will that is going to be available. In the absence of luck, skill, and inspiration backed up by courage, energy, and intensity, the twentieth century may yet see: (1) Another name joining the company of Alexander the Great, Attila the Hun, Ghengis Khan, Tamerlane, Napoleon, and Hitler; (2) a war more mutually destructive and pointless than World War I; (3) a war in which is both destructive and yet perhaps "worthwhile" as I believe World War II was; (4) the total decline of our civilization, or some other unpleasant results of the use or threats of violence.

12

Nuclear Deterrence

Unlike war, which usually aims at weakening or destroying the capabilities and will of the adversary, deterrence aims at altering the policies and actions of other nations. One of the most frequent and often effective methods of deterrence is *armaments* whose purpose is dual: to be used *directly* in war, since no nation can ever exclude the ultimate test of force; and to be used *indirectly* to signalize the capacity and will to deter or coerce. Indirect use of armaments may obtain desired results through the threat of violence but without actually resorting to war. Nations have often been prevented from taking an undesirable course of action by credible intimidation: the deterring nation can make known its military capabilities as well as its determination to use them if a message of deterrence goes unheeded. "When they see that our actual strength is keeping pace with the language that we use," said Archidamus, a Spartan king, as quoted by the ancient Greek historian Thucydides (400 B.C.), "they will be more inclined to give way, since their land will still be untouched."[1] Moscow's daily *Red Star*, on November 6, 1963, expressed the message of deterrence in modern "nucleanese": "If you knew that before you stands a lieutenant or a colonel of Soviet strategic rockets—then, word of honor, you would doff your cap in his presence."

In a world in which territorial states have no reliable external guarantee of

[1] Thucydides, *History of the Peloponnesian War* (Baltimore: Penguin Books, Inc., 1954), p. 30.

301

their survival as independent units, "each state fends for its rights and seeks to maintain its existence" as well as the international situation permits, as Kenneth N. Waltz suggests (see Selection 38). The paradox of the process of mutual deterrence is that it is supposed to guarantee peace by making war credible. This paradox assumes apocalyptic proportions in today's age of thermonuclear missiles. Present-day deterrence consists, in Raymond Aron's words,

> . . . of threatening the enemy with thermonuclear retaliation should he act provocatively. With that being the present policy it is neither honest nor advisable to insist that "there is no alternative to peace." In strict logic, such a formula implies capitulation. If war is "impossible," how can one threaten a possible aggression with war?[2]

The thesis of nuclear deterrence (which is challenged by Etzioni and Green in Selections 36 and 37) rests on two pillars of credibility:

1. Credibility of the *technical capacity* to inflict nuclear damage of devastating proportions, especially the technical capacity of the victim of a first or sneak attack to strike back and destroy the assailant by means of independently targeted multihead missiles (MIRVs) that have been either well concealed (for instance, under the polar cap in submerged submarines, in hardened underground silos, or on the ocean floor in the nation's territorial waters) or so well protected (for instance, by an effective ABM system) as to escape the aggressor's first nuclear attack; and

2. Credibility of the *determination* to use the second-strike capacity, however devastating the aggressor's first attack may have been, however *sense-less* the retaliation may seem after nothing except the retaliatory missiles is left of the victim of the first attack.

The thesis of possible peace through mutual nuclear terror, as expounded succinctly by Robert McNamara, the United States Secretary of Defense in the Kennedy administration (Selection 34), is followed by two essays that attack the theory (closely related to the analysis by Herman Kahn in Selection 33) as translated into practice by the United States, the Soviet Union, China, and, to a lesser extent, France and England. These two essays are by Amitai Etzioni (Selection 36) and Philip Green (Selection 37).

The concept of nuclear deterrence is based on the so-called strategic thinking that has often been compared either to insurance calculations or the theory of games played by *rational* contestants. The concept is supposed to teach people to look at both sides of a contest and to take some account of probable options and capabilities of other nations who are doing the same calculations. Strategic

---

[2] Raymond Aron, "Introduction," in Herman Kahn, *Thinking about the Unthinkable* (New York: Horizon Press, Inc., 1962), p. 12.

thinking overcomes the dangers of following intuition, which is notoriously fallible, or wishful guessing, which may lead to disaster.

Analogies of strategic thinking to insurance or games are, according to Anatol Rapoport,[3] misleading. Insurance data are based on known frequencies of the events insured against. But no cases of nuclear exchanges are known, and an attempt to find out, mathematically or otherwise, could lead to a world catastrophy. Furthermore, insurance policies are usually written against natural disasters that cannot be really influenced; an insurance against flooding does neither decrease nor increase the likelihood of torrential rains. On the other hand, an "insurance-oriented" government-sponsored building of air-raid shelters may signal to the nuclear adversary that the probability of war has suddenly become part of the national calculations. This event may actually increase international tension, leaving the people less secure than before. Furthermore, the theory of rational games assumes (1) the almost unlimited ability of each player to think with no time factors intervening, (2) the perfect, flawless execution of a move—something that rarely happens in political and military contingencies, and (3) the deterrence theory assumes permanency of the current ambitions and goals of the participants. However, these goals are not so fixed and given as to be immune against changes in the near future.[4]

The word "conscience" is set by Rapoport to oppose the term "nuclear strategy" in his text *Strategy and Conscience*. These two terms should recall our earlier discussion of ideology and ethics in politics (Chapters 9 and 10), from which questions immediately arise concerning Rapoport's use of "conscience." We must ascertain whose and what type of conscience Rapoport has in mind when he proposes an intuitive, insight-seeking, and "conscience-driven" mode of thinking as an antidote for the inhuman, icily cold calculations of deterrence theorists. There is not much evidence that intuition and conscience necessarily lead to wiser and more human results, especially since conscience is very largely culture-bound. As Deutsch further points out, "the ideological fanatic who would tolerate no compromise with evil, the general who would accept 'no substitute for victory'—all these may be well following what they honestly perceive to be the voice of their conscience."[5]

The need for a change of perspectives is obvious. The costly arms race, almost everybody agrees, should be brought under control. The question is again *how*, since mutual suspicion and fears that have caused the arms race are also the main impediments to any real control or reduction of national armaments.

---

[3] Reference is made here to Anatol Rapoport's book *Strategy and Consicence* (New York: Harper & Row, Publishers, Inc., 1964) in which the author challenges the apparently rational and objective "sicence of nuclear strategy" as developed by Herman Kahn, Thomas Schelling, Henry M. Kissinger, and others.

[4] Karl W. Deutsch, "Introduction" to Rapoport, *Strategy and Conscience*, p. vii–xv.

[5] *Ibid.*, p. xiii.

34 / The U.S. Nuclear Strategy: Assumptions and Dangers

Robert S. McNamara

The following excerpt from an official United States statement on peace through nuclear terror was made in 1965; the official position of the United States has not been basically altered since. McNamara's words echo many of the concepts analyzed by Herman Kahn in Selection 33. This statement also focuses on the importance of civil defense on two accounts: first, because all the deterrents put together might fail to deter; and, second, because civil defense also serves as a deterrence message. The more poorly a population is protected, the more likely it is that that nation may yield to blackmail; therefore, its alleged retaliatory power becomes less credible.

The strategic objectives of our general nuclear war forces are:

1. To deter a deliberate nuclear attack upon the United States and its allies by maintaining a clear and convincing capability to inflict unacceptable damage on an attacker, ever were that attacker to strike first;

2. In the event such a war should nevertheless occur, to limit damage to our population and industrial capacities.

The first of these capabilities (required to deter potential aggressors) we call "assured destruction," i.e., the capability to destroy the aggressor as a viable society, even after a well-planned and executed surprise attack on our forces. The second capability we call "damage limitation," i.e., the capability to reduce the weight of the enemy attack by both offensive and defensive measures and to provide a degree of protection for the population against the effects of nuclear detonations.

The effectiveness of our strategic offensive forces in the damage-limiting role would be critically dependent on the timing of an enemy attack on the U.S. urban targets. Our missiles forces would be most effective against the enemy bombers if the attack on our urban centers were withheld for an hour or more after an attack on U.S. military targets—an unlikely contingency. Our manned bomber forces would be effective in the damage-limiting role

The United States Secretary of Defense statement made before the House Armed Services Committee, February 19, 1965, as quoted by *The New York Times* (February 20, 1965).

only if the enemy attack on our urban centers were withheld for several hours.

Based on the projected threat for the early nineteen-seventies and the most likely planning factors for that period, our calculations show that even after absorbing a first strike, our already authorized strategic missile force, if it were directed against the aggressor's urban areas, could cause more than 100 million fatalities and destroy about 80 per cent of his in-dustrial capacity. If our manned bombers were then to mount a follow-on attack against urban areas, fatalities would be increased by 10 to 15 million and industrial destruction by another per cent or two.

Although a deliberate nuclear attack upon the United States may seem a highly unlikely contingency in view of our unmistakable assured destruc-tion capability, it must receive our urgent attention because of the enormous consequences it would have. . . .

In order to assess the potentials of various damage-limiting programs we have examined a number of "balanced" defense postures at different budget levels. These postures are designed to defend against the assumed threat in the nineteen-seventies.

To illustrate the critical nature of the timing of the attack, we used two limiting cases. First, we assumed that the enemy would initiate nuclear war with a simultaneous attack against our cities and military targets. Second, we assumed that the attack against our cities would be delayed long enough for us to retaliate against the aggressor's military targets with our own missiles. In both cases, we assumed that all new systems will perform essentially as estimated since our main purpose here was to gain an insight into the overall problem of limiting damage. The results of his analysis are summarized below.

Estimated effect on U.S. fatalities of additions to the approved damage-limiting program:

MILLIONS OF U.S. FATALITIES

(Based on 1970 population of 210 million)

Additional Investment	Early Urban Attack	Delayed Urban Attack
$0 billion	149	122
5 billion	120	90
15 billion	96	59
25 billion	78	41

The $5 billion of additional investment (of which about $2 billion would come from non-Federal sources) would provide a full fall-out shelter program for the entire population. The $15 billion level would add about $8.5 billion for a limited deployment of a low cost configuration of a missile defense system, plus about $1.5 billion for new manned bomber defenses. The $25 billion level would provide an additional $8.5 billion for antimissile defenses (for a total of about $17 billion) and another $1.5 billion for improved manned bomber defenses (for a total of $3 billion).

35 / Are They Geese or Missiles?

Arkady S. Sobolev

This Soviet statement and warning was issued seven years before McNamara's explanation of the United States nuclear strategic assumptions. The Soviet representative at the United Nations Security Council demonstrated what Kahn had called "self-fulfilling prophecy" in the context of nuclear deterrence.

American generals refer to the fact that up to the present time the American planes have taken off on their flights and returned to their bases as soon as it became clear that it was a case of false alarm. But what would happen if American military personnel observing their radar screens are not able in time to determine that a flying meteor is not a guided missile and that a flight of geese is not a flight of bombers? Then the American planes will continue their flight and will approach the borders of the Soviet Union.

But in such a case the need to insure the security of the Soviet people would require the USSR to make immediate retaliatory measures to eliminate the oncoming threat. The Soviet Government would like to hope that matters will not go so far.

In order to get a clearer idea of the extremely dangerous character of acts of the United States [that are] dangerous to peace, it is enough to ask the question what would happen if the military Air Force of the Soviet Union began to act in the same way as the American Air Force is now acting? After all, Soviet radar screens also show from time to time blips which are

The Soviet official statement made at the United Nations Security Council on April 21, 1958, as quoted by *The New York Times* (April 22, 1958).

caused by the flight of meteors or electronic interference. If in such cases Soviet aircraft also flew out carrying atom and hydrogen bombs in the direction of the United States and its bases in other states, what situation would arise?

The air fleets of both sides, having discerned each other somewhere over the Arctic wastes or in some other place, apparently would draw the conclusion natural under those circumstances, that a real enemy attack was taking place. Then the world would inevitably be plunged into the hurricane of atomic war.

36 / Never Has a Non-War Cost So Much

Amitai Etzioni

In a direct polemic with Herman Kahn, Etzioni criticizes both the cost and the tremendous risks of the ever-accelerating arms race that the theory of deterrence seems to require on all levels, nuclear and conventional. Further elaborating the theme of nuclear risks, as presented by Kahn, and stressing that even according to Kahn the Americans and the Russians will have to agree on arms control measures ultimately, Etzioni concludes that the time for arms control and disarmament is now. The reader should be reminded of Kahn's interesting questions on the probability of war (1) if arms race is renewed at some future date, (2) if one side breaks the disarmament agreement, or (3) if one side fears that the opposite side is about to change its mind. It should be also recalled that no disarmament agreement now or in the future can eliminate our *knowledge* to produce doomsday weapons. (Introductory texts on nuclear physics describe the basic mechanism.)

The publication of Herman Kahn's study in nuclear strategy, *"On Thermonuclear War,"* has stirred up so many discussions and repercussions, motions and emotions, that it could in itself be a subject of sociological and psychological research. It is not just a book, but an event. Kahn does for nuclear arms what free-love advocates did for sex: he speaks candidly of

From pp. 4–12 *(passim)* of Amitai Etzioni, "Our First Manual of Thermonuclear War." Reprinted from the *Columbia Forum,* Fall 1961, Volume IV, Number 4. Copyright 1961 by the Trustees of Columbia University in the City of New York.

acts about which others whisper behind closed doors. By doing so, he may make the unavoidable more immediate, but he also makes us better prepared for it and reduces the chances of accident. . . .

The two most readily identified groups in the public argument over nuclear war are those who think it will be prevented by both sides perfecting nuclear bombs ("the balance of terror") and those who think it will be prevented by one side—ours—dropping its arms altogether. Kahn doubts that it can be prevented, only limited. The two groups agree on one assumption, that nuclear war would mean the end of civilization. Kahn denies this.

The choice, he insists, is not between possible mutual suicide and unilateral disarmament, for there is a whole range of other alternatives. He uses two main arguments to back up this assertion; one is technical, the other strategic. Technically speaking, bombs which can wipe the earth clean simply do not exist. . . . In addition, he points out, a carefully-planned civil defense system would greatly decrease potential death and destruction.

From a strategic viewpoint, Kahn says, only a completely irrational enemy would employ annihilation bombs. He who uses such bombs is quite likely to be blessed in kind, thereby doing away with himself as well as with the object of his attack. The most effective strategy for the enemy, according to Kahn, is to "blackmail" us, by bombing a military installation, a small region, or a city—or best of all, by merely threatening to bomb such targets. The USSR can simply say that either the US meets its demands or a nuclear bombardment will be launched. Any reasonable President can reach only one decision: he makes the concession. The blackmailer gets what he asks for—especially if he is clever, demanding "insignificant" concessions one at a time, and making each ultimatum seem like the last one. Obviously, no sensible American President will unleash a suicidal holocaust unless the concession demanded is huge. By keeping the stakes relatively low—a part of Southeast Asia, the American bases in Spain, two islands off China—the Communists will devour the West by inches.

As long as we rely almost exclusively on bigger and better versions of a few bombs, he argues, we will be blackmailed constantly and successfully, and we will have no alternative but to make one concession after another.

The only way out of this dilemma, Kahn says, is to develop more flexible means of deterrence, a "multi-deterrence" (my word), so that we can forestall not only an all-out attack on the American mainland, but also nuclear blackmail, limited provocations by conventional troops, and the challenge of local Communist rebel forces. The essence of multi-deterrence, therefore, is the possession of a force to counter every sort of threat the enemy might possibly make. If we have this, the enemy's threats will be neutralized and his blackmail will not pay off.

The list of the necessary components is a long one, but Kahn persuasively insists that every one of the items is vital. The effectiveness of each is contingent on the presence of the others. If one is eliminated, it leaves a gap in the Western defenses which the enemy can readily exploit.

1. Nuclear Bombs have to be built and improved in order to prevent an enemy who has such bombs from using them or threatening with them. Only the knowledge that homicide means suicide can stop an enemy from using these bombs to gain his objectives.

2. Limited War Capabilities, that is, conventional arms, must be greatly expanded so that "minor" provocations can be countered without resort to nuclear bombardment, on the one hand, or continuous "accommodation" on the other.

3. Insurance For Reliability is another necessity. The United States may have enough bombs to retaliate with ten tons of TNT for every man, woman and child in the Communist bloc, but we have no deterring power at all unless we can "deliver" them. What counts in the last analysis, Kahn says, is not the gross size of your stockpile but the net number of bombs you can actually drop on the target. This number is determined by the number of bombers and missiles the United States has at the outset of the conflict; minus those which would be destroyed in an enemy attack preceding the United States' strike; minus the bombers which will be shot down before they reach target and the missiles that will unexpectedly malfunction; minus, also, any unforeseeable effects of the post-nuclear attack environment on our "means of delivery" (e.g., communications jams may render much of the United States retaliatory force useless). A wide variety of weapons systems must be constructed since the power of any single weapon can be neutralized by the enemy on Judgement Day. We must have weapons of many types in order to be even relatively sure of having a retaliatory force when the crucial moment arrives. Weapons must be made invulnerable so that they will not be damaged or destroyed under attack. We must: develop an adequate warning system so that our planes can take to the air when an air attack is imminent; keep part of our bomber fleet constantly airborne; disperse the rest of the bombers among many bases; shelter our missiles in concrete silos ("harden" the missiles, in military jargon); station some missiles on moving platforms (trucks or railroad cars); hide some of our bombs and missiles underwater in nuclear submarines; and protect command positions from being hit by the enemy. . . .

. . . We must also develop an extensive system of civil defense, including, among other items, mass-produced and -distributed radiation meters for use by the survivors; surveys of and some construction of fallout shelters; and part-time 200,000-member cadres to train for civil defense and post-war restoration work. This much is for immediate implementation. Its total cost: about ten times the present Civil Defense budget. In the fairly near future, Kahn says, a much more far-reaching program will have to be undertaken.

Civil defense is necessary for two reasons, Kahn says. First, because all the deterrents put together might fail to deter. Nuclear war may break out in spite of them (and, as we shall see, in part because of them); when it does, a well-developed civil defense will reduce our losses. The recommendation of a large outlay for civil defense follows from Kahn's basic prognosis: nuclear war need not spell the end of a society, especially if the society is well-prepared. While an unprepared United States might suffer 80 million casualties, a prepared one might suffer "only" 40 millions.

But civil defense also serves as a central element of deterrence itself. The more poorly a population is protected, the more likely a nation is to succumb to blackmail, and the less credible is its alleged retaliatory power. Thus, in Kahn's view, an inadequate civil defense may itself invite an enemy provocation or attack.

In sum, Kahn advocates a strategy of deterrence, based not only on nuclear bombs, but on a large variety of other weapons, to counter the various kinds of threats the Communist bloc might pose; thus we may avoid not only annihilation but also becoming—some would say, continuing to be—the victims of blackmail.

It is easy to express one's feelings about a strategy which suggests not removing nuclear weapons, but adding to them all kinds of bombs and arms, the use of any of which might lead to a war in which nuclear bombs will be dropped. And certainly war is amoral, and those who advocate it are indeed prescribing amorality. But such declarations get us nowhere. International affairs are guided by political leaders and military strategists; moralists do not yet govern, or give counsel to those who do. Conventional and nuclear threats are made every day.

Thus we must examine Kahn's exposition as foreign and military strategy, that is, *on its own terms*. I am willing to grant Kahn's two main assumptions: that nuclear war is possible (hence we must plan for it and for what happens after it is over), and that nuclear blackmail is more likely to occur than, or before, nuclear Doomsday. But the central question is: will Kahn's strategy work? Can multi-deterrence really achieve the goals its advocates claim for it?

I believe the answer is no. Following Kahn's own logic, I shall explain why the monstrous military machine of multi-deterrence will yield no increase in security but a vast increase in risk; for the possibility of a small improvement in United States "posture," we may all be shoved "over the brink." It turns out that—even according to Kahn—to be able to continue such an accelerated arms race we must reach agreements with the Communists quite similar to the disarmament agreements which Kahn and Co. consider utterly Utopian.

On the face of it, multi-deterrence requires the construction of a vast, intricate military machinery. It demands high-speed computers to calculate its moves, teams of experts and electronic brains to think through its tactics, hundreds of millions of dollars per year to keep it going. It is a highly rational machine. That is, parts are all interdependent, each one is "justified" by the others. If you have bombers, for example, they are useless unless you supply them with runways; if you have runways, you have to protect them from bombs, hence you must have anti-missile missiles; both the bombers and missiles need someone to command them, hence you need to protect the headquarters and maintain "jam-free" communications networks at all times. Each item "makes sense" because of its contribution to the others, and the whole deterrence machine breaks down unless every part is present and functioning.

If this enormous ultra-complex system, this gigantic investment of resources, human energy and ingenuity, could yield a relatively assured peace—or at least a substitute for nuclear warfare—many of us might seriously consider buying it. In the bargain, we might have to give up a large part of our income, reducing our investment in schools, medical research, and economic development, not to mention private consumption. We might even have to turn our society into something resembling an immense fortress, live in concrete-walled bunkers, put our sons into trenches, subordinate many of our basic freedoms to security regulations, and sleep with our shoes on. If this garrison state would keep us from mass murder, and from being mass-murdered, it might be worth the price.

But it will not. First, as in any super-complex mechanism, something in this apparatus of automats and explosives, human commanders and computers, electronic beams and buck privates—something basic—is quite likely to go wrong. And the very fact that the parts are interdependent means that when one goes, the whole system collapses. It is simply impossible to have any assurance that so intricate a system will function realiably. It is madly rational. . . .

. . . In earlier wars, in which the means of destruction were primitive by comparison, such failures were rarely decisive. But now, a gap, a bungle, may cost some 20 million deaths beyond the 40 millions or so provided for in RAND's neat calculations.

In nuclear war, one Achilles heel is all anyone needs. . . . There is no more safety in a stockpile of bombs, missiles, and guns than there is in one powder keg. And the larger and more complex the stockpile, the more likely is Pandora's Box to spring open of its own accord—and the more awful its contents.

Many observers agree that a nuclear war is likely to take place in the next ten to fifteen years—*by accident*. Multi-deterrence itself can touch off that unintended nuclear war in any number of ways. Kahn himself cites the . . . dangers [of inadvertent war]. . . .

War may be started undeliberately in still another way: through *brinkmanship*—in my opinion the most likely immediate cause of an unintended World War III. Brinksmanship is a foolhardy game wherein one party declares that unless the other party grants a particular concession, the first party will carry out some threat which promises to do damage to both. The odds for being "called" are high; the damage, if "called," is tremendous; the concessions, if gained, are small. . . .

To reduce the damage from a war initiated by mistake, Kahn suggests various devices and procedures, collectively referred to as arms control. Among them is a direct communications line between the White House and the Kremlin.[6] This allows one side to ring up the other, if necessary, and say something like: "I'm sorry, old boy, one of ours just got loose and is coming your way. I'd appreciate it if you could forget the whole thing. But if you insist on wiping out one of my cities (or even an extra for revenge), I'll understand and explain to the folks." The offer to permit "moderate" retaliation is necessary; otherwise, the accident-victim—fearing the retaliation to his retaliation—may take the accident "seriously" and retaliate to begin with, with an all-out blow.

Such "logic" makes perfect sense if the two sides are playing chess: white takes one black pawn even if in the process he has to let black take one or even two of his pawns, but white will not agree to let black take his rook, much less his queen. Thus, revenge-allowance is an effective safeguard if we view life through the rationalistic, cool, blue glasses of a games-theorist —not, however, when we view it through a flickering radar screen propped up against a wall of suspicion.

Kahn presupposes that the United States and Russia can reach an agreement about the rules of the game and that each side trusts the other to play fair. It is implied that when the telephone rings in the White House and Khruschev says, "Sorry old man . . ." the President can be certain that only one missile is coming and that it is not carrying a bomb large enough to cripple the entire USA. It is likewise assumed that when Khrushchev answers the telephone, hears that Leningrad is accidentally doomed, and kindly agrees to accept Los Angeles in return, he will not give vent to his irritation by bombing San Francisco and Denver and Seattle as well. One might well ask: If the US and the USSR can confidently trust each other in such deadly matters, why can't they trust each other in calmer situations and negotiate disarmament? . . .

Many experts, including Kahn himself, agree that the emergence of new nuclear powers is likely to have disastrous consequences—none of which the multi-deterrence strategy is equipped to forestall: (1) While large countries are likely to survive and recuperate from nuclear war, smaller countries may be totally destroyed, or at any rate cease to be viable so-

---

[6] A direct communication link between Moscow and Washington, the so-called hot line, was established in 1963.——Ed.

cieties. (2) The more nuclear countries there are, the more decision-makers there will be who can touch off nuclear war, and the more likely it is that war will precipitated by mistake, accident, miscalculation, or brinksmanship. (3) The widespread dispersion of H-bombs means that some of them will fall into the hands of leaders who are far more irrational and aggressive than the leaders of the current nuclear powers. (4) Nuclear weapons ownership will give many countries as finger-hold on the nuclear triggers of the two super-powers. If a nuclear war breaks out between two lesser nations, the conflict can easily involve the United States and Russia whether or not they wish to become involved. . . . (5) It is even possible that a third power, hoping to benefit from the devastation of the two super-powers, may drop a bomb on one of them. Missiles can be very anonymous, especially when launched from an unidentifiable submarine in the wide blue ocean. (6) Finally, unless definite steps are taken to control the production and distribution of nuclear weapons, criminal organizations like the Mafia and rebel terrorists . . . will be able to afford their own nuclear arsenals before 1975!

. . . The spread of nuclear arms is the surest road—via many small disasters, several middling ones, or one big one—to Doomsday.

Multi-deterrence is not only incapable of averting these dangers, it even serves to increase them. The production of more and varied bombs at an ever-accelerating pace—a process which muti-deterrence necessitates—simply makes it easier for the Nth country to obtain the bombs. And once one small country obtains nuclear arms, many other countries will find inescapably that it is "in the interest of national security" for them to do likewise. Soon the whole earth will be piled with nuclear bombs and triggers. . . .

If nuclear war does occur, Kahn argues, no one will use the big bombs even if he has them. The danger of self-annihilation is too great; nuclear blackmail is a less risky, more promising course for a nuclear power. There are good reasons for denying this. One is the fact that Premiers and Presidents need not always be as rational as multi-deterrence requires them to be. Today both super-powers are governed by fairly level-headed leaders; some-day, a Hitler or Stalin may lead again. . . .

But nations that possess the Big Bombs are likely to use them even if level-headed rulers prevail. The reason is escalation. Escalation is the process by which, step after step, a country's leaders may be brought to "raise" the level of war by resorting to more and more powerful weapons until they reach the Last Escalation and unleash the most devastating bombs in their possession. . . .

Escalation can carry us not only from cold war to hot, from limited war to world war, and from conventional conflicts to nuclear attack—it may lead us that one step further to nuclear cataclysm.

Moreover, under certain circumstances, one may even deliberately choose to make the Last Escalation. It does, after all, grant the loser a last chance for survival if not for victory. His country is a ruin, his forces are demoralized; the enemy is breaking through his last lines. Pulling the biggest trigger gives him one slim, final opportunity to save the day, pull his scattered army together, and perhaps even be the war's sole survivor. A not-irrational leader might give it a try. He has nothing to lose, but if he succeeds he has a great deal to gain. Or with no chance whatever to win or to survive, a defeat-crazed leader—Hitler in his burning bunker, a dictator about to lose the last remnant of his semi-global empire—might still unleash the Doomsday Bomb. Men in such extremities may vow, "I shall drag them all into the grave with me." Deterrence is a strategy which assumes that people always make rational responses. But men with their backs to the wall are not in a "normal" psychological state; if there are buttons to push, they may very well push them.

There is really nothing in Kahn's multi-deterrence theory to deter Last Escalation, whether the motives behind it are rational or irrational. True, our theorist provides for some insurance. First, deter intermediate escalations (if the enemy is kept off the middle of the staircase, we need not fear that he will arrive at the top). We do this by convincing him that whenever he raises the level of warfare (by using more or deadlier weapons), we are more than ready to meet his challenge; he sees that the higher the level at which he is blocked, the larger his losses.

Last Escalation can also be forestalled if you deliberately and publicly limit your objectives in any given conflict. By so doing, you refrain from pushing the enemy to the wall. He realizes that as long as he does not escalate, he will suffer at worst only a limited setback, not total defeat.

But the hazards of such "insurance" are many. For one thing, it requires that the enemy have high faith in our promise to stop where we say we will, even if we are winning; it requires that we rely on the enemy's pledge not to escalate in situations where we are facing "limited defeat." To assume that all these requirements can be fulfilled is perfectly Utopian.

Second, insurance against escalation presupposes that our side is stronger than the other at each possible level of conflict, so that at no time will it pay the enemy to escalate to a higher level. Such a military "posture" is rarely, is ever, attained, and to bank our hopes on it is visionary.

Moreover, this insurance assumes that the seventh and eighth "limited setbacks" have the same psychological effect on the loser as the first and second. But it is clear that if one country—say the United States—loses a large number of rounds, it will feel more and more threatened. No matter how limited each individual setback, a long series will make the loser begin reacting like a man with his back to the wall. . . .

It may be a good sign for critics of armed deterrence that even Kahn—the high priest of multi-deterrence—is the first to admit that the whole vast machine, even if constructed just as designed and right on schedule, gives us at best only a short-run protection against disaster. We must also work for arms control. Kahn writes: "if we are to reach the year 2,000 or even 1975, without a cataclysm of some sort (in particular, if we are to obtain the time to work out the rivalry peacefully), we will almost undoubtedly require extensive arms control measures in addition to unilateral security measures." That is, we must reach some agreement with the Russians which, without giving either side an advantage, effectively controls the arms race, particularly the manufacture and distribution of nuclear weapons.

This raises two central questions which Kahn and other theorists of armed deterrence do not answer: If, in order to survive, we have to reach an agreement with the Communists despite all the armament and counter-armament, why not reach it without undergoing this wasteful, futile, perilous build-up? Does not the arms race itself create conditions preventing the kind of agreement which even proponents of the arms race see as absolutely essential?

Kahn's strategy—and the current military policy of the United States—yield us little besides an ever-accelerating arms race, an ever-increasing investment in an ever-growing pile of weapons which at best will never be used. Never has a non-war cost more: in money and resources as well as in energy, nerves, and intellect. All this sacrifice earns the illusion of an extra ounce of security in the shortest run, and in the process makes the world a vast field of powder kegs. It becomes more and more likely that at least some of the powder kegs will blow up, or be blown up.

At present, we have a last chance to avoid a nuclear disaster because the bombs and their means of delivery have not yet been perfected, because the worst—many more bombs, in many more countries—is still to come. The multi-deterrence strategy promises us nothing more than a chance to improve our "posture." At the same time, it greatly lowers the chances, at least for those of us who live in cities, to get to and survive the 1970's. Even if the first nuclear war is what Kahn calls a small one—say 20 million deaths on each side and ten years for recovery—the old enemies, or two new contenders, will soon be arming themselves for the next round. There is no safety in nuclear bombs, and never have arms established a lasting peace.

It is often stated that arms are merely symptoms of deeper ideological, political, and economic conflicts; that as long as no solution is found for these problems, there will be armies; that disarmament is a treatment of symptoms instead of the illness. It may be so. But we would be ill-advised to postpone treating the arms fever, symptom though it may be, lest, raging uncontrolled, it kill the patient before a cure for the disease can be effected. Moreover, reducing the fever seems necessary not just to keep the patient alive, but to gain access to deeper problems. The final round of arms reduction will require major changes in the international community, but we might never get started at all unless we bring the arms race under control. Halting *and* reversing the arms race, more than anything else, will alter our prospects from barren radioactive wastes to deserts watered by atoms-for-peace.

37 / Nuclear Deterrence and Moral Considerations

Philip Green

The following excerpt from Philip Green's critique of the theory of nuclear deterrence (see Herman Kahn, Selection 33) focuses on the conflict between ethical considerations and the deterrence logic. Five major themes may be identified: the deterrence theory (1) presumes that no conduct is absolutely prohibited, (2) treats all violence and destruction as quantitatively different but qualitatively indistinguishable, (3) justifies the indiscriminate killing of innocent persons under certain circumstances, (4) assumes that a commitment to wreaking destructive violence on foreign populations is morally neutral, and finally, (5) embodies some of the American cold war biases, notably the assumption of an irreconcilable and inevitable conflict between the communist and Western systems and the commitment to resist communist expansion and the ensuing diminishment of human freedom. In particular, Green attacks the assumptions of the "deterrence scientists" that claim that strategic analysis has been or can be separated from political goals, ideological preferences, and moral values.

. . . The basic impulse of deterrence theory is to defend American society—or "the West"—by threatening or committing any violence necessary to accomplish that task. There are only two grounds on which deterrence theorists appear to be capable of condemning a given proposal: (1)

The passages reprinted herein from Philip Green's *Deadly Logic: The Theory of Nuclear Deterrence* were published originally by the Mershon Center for Education in National Security, and are Copyright © 1966 by the Ohio State University Press. All rights reserved. Also published as a paperback by Schocken Books, New York, 1968; the material quoted is from this paperback edition, pp. 224–232, 238–239 *(passim)*. Author's footnotes have been omitted; footnotes added by the editor are so marked.

it would not "work" as well as some other proposal; (2) the end could be achieved with less loss of life. But any level of violence necessary to protect a given interest is approved, up to and including total annihilation of the enemy; as long as calculation is competitively self-interested, this is bound to be so.

Thus deterrence theory is the obverse, so to speak, of pacifism. To the pacifist's absolute prohibition against killing, deterrence theory responds with an absolute dispensation for killing. Nowhere is this seen more clearly than in this comment by Sidney Hook, one of America's most distinguished ethical philosophers and a "lay" supporter of deterrence policy:

> . . . If you were prepared to support the Second World War, then you were responsible for a decision which destroyed the lives of people who had no choice in making that decision and who did not want you to fight for them. . . .

In context Hook's reference is to the area bombing (and A-bombing) which the Allies used against Germany and Japan. Later in his remarks he refers to the "logical inconsistency" of those who supported World War II but opposed such actions, thus indicating his belief that the question of violence is a matter of kind, not degree: if one approves of an act of war, then one must *ipso facto* approve of an act of *total* war. . . . [O]ne is unhappily reminded of Ivan Karamazov's observation, that a moral relativist will inevitably be forced into the position that "anything goes."[7] . . .

. . . In many parts of the world it is legal for a private citizen to own a pistol or rifle, but nowhere may he own a machine gun. The reason for this universal prohibition is that the only thing one can do with a machine gun is commit a massacre; the means are disproportionate to any end private citizens may safely be allowed to contemplate achieving. But in the world of deterrence theory, pistols, machine guns, 100-megaton bombs and poisonous viruses are all alike. It is true that total war is not an invention of the Manhattan Project; and that, as some have argued, many weapons originally intended for self-defense or the use of professional armies have been used as weapons of extermination throughout history. But the obvious distinctive feature of *nuclear* weapons is that they are almost necessarily weapons of mass destruction—that is what they are for.

To be blunt, deterrence theory justifies the indiscriminate killing of innocent persons under certain circumstances. The English philosophers G. B. Anscombe and Walter Stein call this mass murder. The American theologian Paul Ramsey, agreeing with them, writes:

> Acts of war which directly intend and directly effect the death of noncombatants are to be classed morally with murder, and are never excusable.

[7] See a quote from Dostoevsky in Selection 30.——Ed.

One does not have to insist on that word; but to use a vocabulary that contains no word to indicate the true nature of what is called for, in relation to traditional ethical standards is to seduce one's readers into mistakenly thinking[8] that one's theory is ethically neutral. When Klaus Knorr writes that *"On Thermonuclear War* is not a book about the moral aspects of military problems," he has got the truth of the matter exactly reversed, for all deterrence theory is fundamentally concerned with moral issues.

To this insistence that there is a hidden ethical stance in deterrence theory, and to this description of the nature of that stance, several answers have been offered at various times by the supporters of a nuclear deterrence policy. They are all unsatisfactory or evasive. . . .

First, it is sometimes claimed that the United States proposes only to use nuclear weapons in self-defense, and self-defense does not raise the same moral issues as does wilful homicide. With regard to that assumption about the motives of the United States, one might make the cynical statement that war usually consists of a fight between two opponents each engaged in an act of self-defense. However, I shall let that point pass, and treat the claim on its merits. Thus Sidney Hook reasons as follows:

> As I read the history of Western culture it seems to me that survival at all costs is not among the values of the West. . . . I would . . . like to point out that in terms of the Western tradition, the view that it is not life but the good life which is the highest ideal . . . was not restricted merely to cases of individual heroism. Total war was also waged in the past. Let us stretch our imaginations a little. Imagine that we are living in Carthage and the Romans are at the gates. Carthage fought a total war. So did Judea. Many illustrations can be cited of cities and entire settlements which went down to destruction fighting for what they thought was the good life. . . . If we surrender our values, we open the floodgates for totalitarianism to sweep through the world. . . . (W)e bombed the Japanese islands, but what was the alternative? [9] The alternative was defeat, and acceptance of a system of infamy. . . . As a theoretical possibility, no matter what kind of moral economy one adopts, one can conceive of a situation in which the conditions of life for a people, like the conditions of life for an individual, would be unendurable. This, as I have said, was the decision made historically by Jewish people in fighting Rome.[10] It was made by many communities in fighting against Hitler.

[8] While Green condemns the deterrence theorists for their unquestioned assumption of enmity, they, in turn, could question Green's assumption that there is such a thing as "traditional ethical standards" known to and accepted by most men. See also Chapter 10 that contains controversies concerning the number of often contradictory codes of ethics as well as the ambiguity of their commandments.———Ed.

[9] I have made no attempt to analyze Hook's history, not being knowledgeable enough in that field. One can only hope his other references to historical events have more substance than his remarks about the war with Japan.

[10] See also the statement of the commander of the Jewish fortress Masada in A.D. 73 in the postscript to Chapter 10 (Selection 30).———Ed.

Such an argument answers itself. To present "total war" as the decision of a suffering community to martyr itself *in toto* is such a distortion of the actual situation that it is difficult to imagine how a distinguished philosopher can possibly have come to make such a statement. Deterrence theorists may incidentally propose that Americans fight to the last man (though I cannot think of any who actually do so), but that is obviously not the issue raised by deterrence theory. The prospect that nuclear weapons place before us is that our fighting *in extremis* to the last Russian, to the last Chinese, perhaps to the last European, perhaps to the last of some other peoples as well. The prospect, that is, is one of destroying objectively innocent persons in response to an attack upon ourselves. We propose to engage not in an act of self-defense, but in an act of punishment, and the punished may be legion.

The terrible fact is, as deterrence theorists themselves constantly point out, that the advent of strategic nuclear weapons has made complete defense of any kind almost impossible. There are only three ways in which one could defend one's self against someone who proposed to attack with strategic nuclear weapons. (1) One could defend against the weapons themselves. (2) One could attack those responsible for making the decision to attack before they had carried out their plan. (3) One could threaten to destroy those persons *after* they had implemented their attack.

The first alternative is generally agreed to be at best only a partial solution to the problem posed by strategic nuclear weapons. There is no antimissile weapon in sight that promises to do anything but make an attack more expensive—and after all, if there were a perfect defense, we would not need the deterrent. The other two alternatives require a discrimination in choosing victims that nuclear weapons do not possess. Thus deterrence theory proposes that we "defend" ourselves not by any of these means, but by the threat or reality of nuclear retaliation against the enemy, destroying indiscriminately those engaged in attacking us, and those who are not so engaged in any meaningful sense of the word. To equate such an event to the traditional morality of "heroic" self-defense is to commit a solecism. No one has described this situation of nuclear deterrence better than John Bennett, who remarks:

> When men in the West say "give me liberty or give me death" they rightly evoke a dual response. War is not likely to save liberty. And when men say this in the United States and in a few western nations, they hardly realize that they may be dooming hundreds of millions of people who never made any such choice. . . . [I]t would be well to ask a larger representation of mankind to have part in this decision since it may mean death for them before they have ever known the reality of liberty . . . I think that it was A. J. Muste who coined the phrase no "annihilation without representation" to indicate what is here involved.

The next three arguments I shall discuss are all attempts to salvage the claim that nuclear deterrence is clearly a form of legitimate self-defense and thus does not raise the grave ethical issues that are suggested above.

First, it is often assumed that since we will be "in the right" in a nuclear war, questions of ethical propriety will not arise. Such reasoning misses the point, however. The question whether one's cause is just is analytically separate from the question of what one may do to assert that cause. There is a difference too obvious to be ignored between shooting a man who is about to shoot you (unjustly, we assume), and throwing a bomb at him that can be expected to blow up six or seven million other people. In the latter case major questions of morality are present.

Second, it has at times been claimed that in modern warfare no one is "innocent." Now undoubtedly it is hard to draw a line, under conditions of modern warfare and particularly of nuclear warfare, between combatants and non-combatants. But this difficulty has lost most of its relevance for theory in the nuclear age, for in talking about the strategic use of nuclear weapons we are talking not merely about the slaughter of non-combatants in a warring nation but also sometimes of peoples who have never at any level of decisions opted to go to war.

In any event, even if somehow one manages to ignore this fact, the claim that the distinction cannot be made is still obviously false. Indeed it is so clearly false that it seems to be nothing but a transparent excuse for fighting those total wars that the authors of such statements wish to be morally free to fight. . . . [I]n the words of the English Catholic philosopher Walter Stein:

> It is common, indeed usual, to be uncertain of a boundary but quite certain of what lies well to the east or west of it. . . . Now the line between combatants and non-combatants is one of those which it is difficult to fix exactly . . . yet, nevertheless, there are large areas which unquestionably lie on either side of the line . . . a high proportion of any population consists of children, full-time mothers, pensioners and sick people. Of course, if someone is so inclined, he can reply that mothers rear children . . . that children will one day be workers or even soldiers . . . and that sick people frequently get well again. Moralizing can have its moments.

That is to say, we need only know that there *is* a fundamental moral difference between limited war and total war, to justify our insistence that the distinction be made—however difficult that may be. Indeed, the difficulty of "drawing the line" in modern war is precisely an argument, not in favor of fighting total wars, but in favor of *not* fighting them. . . .

. . . An alternative ground of argument suggested by some commentators is to deny that *nuclear* war need be *total* war. This is done either by postulating a kind of war called "counterforce war," or by asserting that a deterrence policy can be based purely on the *possession* of nuclear weapons, and not on their *use*. . . . [But] no *deterrence* theorist has advocated bluff . . . . nor, indeed, could any deterrence theorist who is committed to the idea that the assumption of rationality is useful propose the adoption of such a posture. For if rational, hostile, competitive men are making threats at each other, then the idea that we may ever use our countervalue forces is not credible *"unless we really intend to do it*. If we are only *pretending* that we would do it, the credibility and therefore the deterrent value of our force is almost certain to be lessened by the automatic and inevitable leaks." Furthermore, we can reverse that dictum and make the obvious point that given the traditional human manner of responding to aggressive violence, the only way an intent not to use nuclear weapons under any circumstances could be given psychological meaning would be for national leaders of all factions and parties inextricably to commit themselves to such a policy. That would be not deterrence, but unilateral disarmament. As to what is the present commitment of the American government to which so many deterrence theorists are advisers, we have the late President's [Kennedy] word for it:

> In the event of a major aggression that could not be repulsed by conventional forces we must be prepared to take whatever action with whatever weapons are appropriate.

Once one admits that the ultimate deterrent is not absolute bluff, therefore, the ethical issue is reinstated unchanged. . . .

13

Balance and Imbalance of Power

For a long time controversy has surrounded both the meaning and the usefulness of the concept and the practice of the balance-of-power politics. Originally, the term was used to describe the general pattern of European politics that had characterized peaceful coexistence as well as violent competition for mastery among five or more great powers (roughly from the Treaty of Westphalia in 1648—the accepted birthdate of modern territorial states—to World War II). Since the European balancing process did produce long periods of peace, usually by means of shifting alliances for the purpose of establishing a new equilibrium, it evoked praise on the part of some analysts; since, however, the same balancing process had also produced many wars for the purpose of readjusting the balance of power, it was also condemned as the primary cause of international conflicts.

Another controversy concerns the exact meaning of balance of power in a system of states whose inherent feature is a gross inequality of its component units. Today, for instance, over 120 medium, small, and microscopic powers have to coexist in the same world with two nuclear and industrial giants (the United States and Russia), three lesser nuclear powers (China, France, and England), and three nonnuclear great powers (Germany, Japan, and India). Still another complication should be noted: The "balance of power" is sometimes interpreted as meaning a *state* of a rough equilibrium of national capabilities or simply the opposite of a gross imbalance; at other times the term is used to describe a dynamic *process* of preventing imbalance.

Whatever the meaning may be, static or dynamic, the state of balance or the process of balancing must be analyzed simultaneously on many levels: not only between the nuclear superpowers and their blocs but also within these blocs among medium and small powers as well as among the nonaligned nations. In the final analysis, the balancing efforts between the mighty leaders of the two major alliance systems are the most important, since their success or failure will have a stabilizing or disruptive impact on the whole system of states.

One of the most frequent objections against balance-of-power politics is that the concept of quantifiable equilibrium, so definable in the world of physics and mathematics, cannot be transferred to the world of political behavior. The basic unit balanced in international politics is national power, which cannot be quantified and comparatively measured; it includes elusive ingredients such as national morale, national character, a nation's reputation, and the passions, intelligence, and skill of national leaders. Thus the concept of balance, which evokes an image of stability, security, and peace, produces, in fact, instability, insecurity, and wars. The possibility of miscalculation, the tendency to achieve a margin of superiority rather than an equilibrium to compensate for possible calculating errors, and the constant need to readjust national goals and capabilities to a changing international environment combine to make the concept and the ideal of a world power equilibrium a very shaky foundation of peace.

According to some of the writers represented in the following selections, national survival will supply the basic motivation to all states to engage in the balancing processes so long, as Kenneth N. Waltz concludes in Selection 38, "as states desire to maintain their political identities and so long as they must rely on their own devices in striving to do so." Beyond the survival motive, of course, the aim of nations may range from an ambition to conquer the world to a desire to be left alone.

A *minimum* response of states, which is necessary to the dynamics of balance, derives from the condition of coexistence of national states for whose survival there is no external guarantee. As Kenneth N. Waltz points out, perception of the peril that lies in unbalanced power encourages the behavior conducive to maintaining a balance-of-power system, or, as other authors express it, the international checks and balances. The process is therefore seen as an inevitable result of the existing system of sovereign states, an unorganized aggregate of coordinated rather than subordinated units. In the absence of any reliable supranational guarantee of their survival as independent units in the system (Selection 41 will show that "collective security" is not such a guarantee), nations are said to have no other choice than opposing power with power and determination with determination. Confrontation of more or less equal powers is never reassuring, but confrontation between an aggressive power and a weak one that has no defense is terrifying; such a situation invites blackmail and domination.

Nations engage in matching power by power by employing two basic methods:

1. *Individual* effort, usually in the form of mobilization of one's own resources, particularly armaments; and

2. *Cooperative* efforts by which nations combine their own power and efforts with the power and efforts of:

a) Foreign governments, usually in the form of *alliances* and other collective defense arrangements, or with the power and efforts of

b) Antigovernmental elements within the framework of an adversary state. Such a method of cooperation between a national government and foreign antigovernmental forces is usually referred to as *intervention* or interference in the domestic affairs of foreign nations. It is an integral part of the balancing process since its basic aim is to increase one's own strength by sapping the strength of the opposite side. In any balancing process an approximate equilibrium may be attained either by increasing the weight on one's scale or by taking off some weight from the opposite scale. The most usual methods by which a national government cooperates with antigovernmental individuals and groups within the framework of an adversary state are:

• *Psychological warfare,* especially radio propaganda, whose purpose is to undermine the allegiance of a foreign people to its own national government and so decrease that government's capacity to act effectively.

• *Infiltration and subversion* are terms that cover a great variety of usually clandestine operations, ranging from verbal instigation or support of insurgency to providing rebels or a guerilla movement with weapons, transportation, air cover, and detailed direction. The United States used this latter technique of interference with regard to Cuba (see Selection 18). Cuba openly maintains an organization for the purpose of revolutionary subversion in Latin American countries and elsewhere. Some forms of the balancing technique of interference easily blend into different types of subnuclear warfare, such as indirect aggression, war by proxy, or internationalized civil war.

• *Espionage* is a special form of interference, practiced by all nations for ages. The purpose is to deprive the adversary of the advantage that his secret plans or weapons provide in terms of their effectiveness and readiness. Evidently, a nation that has pierced all the secrets of the enemy while preserving all its own secrets would gain—all other things being equal—a significant advantage in both the balancing process and in an actual military conflict.

Nations rarely condemn the general practice of intervention in absolute terms; they either praise or condemn intervention after having evaluated its purpose. The end seems to justify the means of interference. Those who in 1968 condemned the Soviet intervention in Czechoslovakia may have simultaneously approved of the United States' intervention in Vietnam or, possibly, even recommended an American intervention against Soviet intervention in Prague. And vice versa.

Intervention in the domestic affairs of other nations for the purpose of international balance of power has always been practiced by governments. The ancient historian Thucydides introduced his account of the history of the Peloponnesian War with the attempt of the Greek city Corcyra to reinstall the exiled leaders in another city and thus to tilt the balance of power in Corcyra's favor. As means of illustrating the current hypocrisy about intervention—deplored by all but practiced by all—note the following official statements and their sources and consider them as a whole:

> I believe that it must be the policy of the United States to support free peoples who are resisting attempted subjugation by armed minorities or by outside pressures. ———(The Truman Doctrine, 1947)

> The Soviet Communists feel bound in sacred duty . . . to take active part . . . in support of the underground communist parties that are actively and courageously doing their work. ———(Pravda, Moscow, 1967)

> We are lending and will continue to lend aid to all those who fight against imperialism in whatever part of the world. . . . Imperialism never needs excuses to commit its crimes. Nor does the Cuban revolution need to ask for permission or for forgiveness to fulfill its duty of solidarity with all the revolutionaries of the world. ———(Radio Havana, May 18, 1967)

> No State has the right to interfere, directly, or indirectly, for any reason whatsoever in the internal and external affairs of any other state. ———(The United Nations General Assembly Resolution, unanimously adopted in 1966, including the votes of the United States, the Soviet Union, and Cuba)

Several analysts of international politics conclude that the generalized practice of intervention is a necessary consequence of the world's growing interdependence; in a global village everyone can be expected to be actively concerned with everyone else's private affairs. Other analysts point to the probable effects of mutual nuclear paralysis among the superpowers on the frequency of interventions. Terrorized by their respective thermonuclear defensive and offensive systems, superpowers tend to confront each other directly with extreme caution; they are more willing to confront each other indirectly, through and at the expense of smaller nations, and usually by means of wars by proxy or support of their respective puppets.

While the nuclear dimension of international politics may have increased the use of the balancing technique called intervention, it may have had a contrary effect on the traditional balancing techniques, notably alliances and counter-alliances; "internal effort has replaced shifting of alliances as the main means of maintaining an approximate balance of power," notes Kenneth N. Waltz (Selection 38). In a missile age the need for allies, their military resources, and bases on their territories seems to have declined. For the superpowers, acquisition and maintenance of alliances may become an unnecessary burden. And for the smaller powers, alignment with one of the superpowers in conflict with another superpower may mean only political and economic liabilities but no real protection, since nuclear weapons tend to paralyze the superpowers' usable force. "When a nation acquires independent nuclear capability," notes George Liska, "the responsibility for defense passes into its own hands symbolically and, as the last resort, in fact."[1]

Modern alliances may have, of course, functions other than deterrence and collective defense. Many alliances today provide for cooperation for the purpose of intraregional pacification, collective economic well-being, or ideological unity. They are, therefore, publicized as perhaps the first stepping stones toward the ultimate goal of an international government or supranational federal union, based on either regional or an ideological-economic community of interests. Initially this might have been the hope of the founding fathers of the two modern multilateral alliances, the Atlantic and the Warsaw pacts.

In conclusion, mention should be made of *collective security*, a concept and an ideal that marked the end of World War I—"the war to end all wars"—and was acclaimed as the end of the balance of power system and its by-products, armament race and shifting alliances. Unlike the balancing process in the usual sense (that is, prevention of imbalance and domination by adequate counter-power and counterwill), the concept of collective security aimed as creating a global "grand alliance" of all peace-loving nations against a potential or actual peace-breaker. The purpose was not a balance of power but, on the contrary, a terrifying *imbalance of power* that should frighten a potential aggressor into peaceful behavior or pulverize him if, despite the warning, he would insanely dare to break the peace. This concept was embodied in legal terms in the Covenant of the League of Nations (Article 16) and then again in the United Nations Charter (Chapter VII).

The concept of collective security has been based on two basic assumptions:

---

[1] George Liska, *Nations in Alliance: The Limits of Interdependence* (Baltimore: The Johns Hopkins Press, 1962), p. 277. A paperback of this book was published in 1968.

1. An extreme imbalance of power between a collectivity of peaceful nations that should include all the giants, on the one hand, and a few aggressive dwarfs, on the other. This assumption is very far from actual reality. In a nuclear age, in particular, the very idea of extreme imbalance is debatable, as the preceding selections on nuclear deterrence have indicated. A collectivity of nuclear giants can terrorize, at best, a nonnuclear dwarf but certainly it cannot frighten a single nuclear superpower or a small power that has either acquired its own deterrent or can count on a big nuclear brother. One hundred nations, acting rationally, can hardly outweigh one nation, insane or acting in despair, and equipped with a panoply of MIRVs. If the goals and nuclear arsenals of great powers are pitted one against the other, it is impossible to create the desired maximum disparity of power to deter and/or punish. Furthermore, the concept of collective security implies peacefulness on the part of great powers; in fact, however, peace has been more frequently and more seriously threatened by great powers and their direct or indirect conflicts than by small powers.

2. The second underlying assumption of collective security is the idea of an *indivisible peace*. Experience indicates that nations are quite willing to see the world half in war and half in peace if they can be left out. Unlike a national police establishment, nations are neither willing nor ready to engage in punitive military actions whenever or wherever peace is threatened. Their physical readiness depends on many variables such as an internal economic crisis, internal rebellion, or state of disarmament (a disarmed nation can hardly terrorize a potential aggressor into peaceful behavior); such factors may not permit implementation of an international commitment even if the leaders are otherwise willing. Their willingness depends on other variables, one of which may be simply the distance from the area of immediate concern. Many leaders do not feel impelled to send their influence half way around the world. More importantly, nations are rarely able to reach identical estimates in a concrete situation as to who is the aggressor and who is his victim. In 1950, the United States invoked the concept of collective security against Communist North Korea, but the Soviet Union labeled South Korea as the aggressor. In Chapters 6 through 10 we have sufficiently analyzed the problem of national interest, as conditioned by correct or false perceptions and ideological commitments, to realize how rarely can we expect the United States, Russia, China, France, and England (and Africa, India, and the Arabs) to reach an identical conclusion as to a given breach of peace, and establish the required imbalance of deterrent or punitive power.

Kenneth W. Thompson will deal with the assumptions and history of collective security more in detail in Selection 41.

38 / The Modern Balance of Power: Duopoly at the Top

Kenneth N. Waltz

The concept of balance of power as Europe had known it for the three hundred years preceding World War II cannot be applied without modification to a world in which only two nations so significantly exceed all others in the force at their disposal. The difference between the balancing processes in the past and now appears to some observers so fundamental that, as they conclude, international affairs can no longer be conducted or understood according to the balance-of-power concept. Four differences between then and now should be noted:

1. The balancing process, old style, was Europe-centered; the rest of the world was involved only indirectly, more often than not by means of competition over the limits of European colonial expansion. Today the competition is truly global.

2. The old balancing process centered around four to six great powers. Today, as a result of World War II, the international scene is dominated by only two superpowers. China, Japan, or Germany may later alter the present bipolarity but they have not done so yet.

3. In the past, one of the essential adjustments in the balancing process was the use or threat of force which did not, as today, imply the possibility of mutual annihilation of both the loser and the victor.

4. In the European balancing process the most frequent method of restoring a disturbed balance was the shift of alliances that could compensate for changes in the strength of competing nations. Today, excessive concentrations of power seems to negate the possibility of playing the game of shifting alignments.

Waltz's article recognizes the validity of the preceding four points but concludes that the balance-of-power analysis remains highly useful. Waltz sees a shift in perspective, however, from the previous concentration upon shifting alliances as a mode of adjustment to first, an examination of national power as a means of control and, second, to internal (national) effort as a way of compensating for incipient imbalance of power. Waltz's essay also critically

From Kenneth N. Waltz, "International Structure, National Force and the Balance of World Power." Copyright by the Board of Editors of the *Journal of International Affairs,* reprinted from Volume 21, No. 2, pp. 218–231 *(passim),* 1967. Permission to reprint is gratefully acknowledged to the Editors of the *Journal.* Some author's footnotes have been omitted; footnotes added by the editor are so marked.

examines the frequent assertion that the present inability of the two super-powers to use their awesome force effectively has resulted in substantial equality of great and small powers. While it is indeed true that strategic nuclear weapons deter the opposite strategic nuclear weapons and therefore cause a mutual paralysis, the superpowers' use of other-than-nuclear force has not been really as inhibited as it seems. Waltz also points to the difference between the power of a nation and its use of force. A nation is often impressively powerful when it does not need to use force and may become less powerful by using it.

. . . If two groupings of states have hardened or if the relation of major antagonism in the world is simply between two nations, the balance-of-power model no longer applies, according to the conventional definition. This conclusion is reached by placing heavy emphasis on the process of balancing (by realignments of states) rather than on altering power (which may depend on the efforts of each state). In a two-power world, emphasis must shift from the international process of balancing to the prospect of altering power by the internal efforts of each participant.

. . . With this shift in perspective, balance-of-power politics does not disappear; but the meaning of politics changes in a manner that can only be briefly suggested here.

In a world of three or more powers the possibility of making and breaking alliances exists. The substance of balance-of-power politics is found in the diplomacy by which alliances are made, maintained, or disrupted. Flexibility of alignment then makes for rigidity in national strategies: a state's strategy must satisfy its partner lest that partner defect from the alliance. . . . The alliance diplomacy of Europe in the years before World War I is rich in examples of this. Because the defection or defeat of a major state would have shaken the balance of power, each state was constrained to adjust its strategy and the deployment of its forces to the aims and fears of its partners. This is in sharp contrast to the current situation in NATO. . . . Though concessions to allies will sometimes be made, neither the Soviet Union nor the United States alters its strategy or changes its military dispositions simply to accommodate associated states. Both superpowers can make long-range plans and carry out their policies as best they see fit, for they need not accede to the demands of third parties. . . .

Disregarding the views of an ally makes sense only if military cooperation is relatively unimportant. This is the case in NATO, which in fact if not in form consists of unilateral guarantees by the United States to its European allies. The United States, with a preponderance of nuclear weapons and as many men in uniform as all of the Western European states combined, may be able to protect her allies; they cannot possibly protect her. Because of the vast differences in the capacities of member states, the approximately equal sharing of burdens found in earlier alliance systems is no longer conceivable. The gross inequality between the two superpowers and the members of their respective alliances makes any realignment of the latter fairly insignificant. The leader's strategy can therefore be flexible. In balance-of-power politics, old style, flexibility of alignment made for rigidity of strategy or the limitation of freedom of decision. In balance-of-power politics, new style, the obverse is true: rigidity of alignment in a two-power world makes for flexibility of strategy or the enlargment of freedom of decision.

Those who discern the demise of balance-of-power politics mistakenly identify the existence of balances of power with a particular mode of adjustment and the political means of effecting it. Balances of power tend to form so long as states desire to maintain their political identities and so long as they must rely on their own devices in striving to do so. With shrinking numbers, political practices and methods will differ; but the number of states required for the existence and perpetuation of balance-of-power politics is simply two or more, not, as is usually averred, some number larger than two.

The reduction in the number of major states calls for a shift in conceptual perspective. Internal effort has replaced external realignment as a means of maintaining an approximate balance of power. But the operation of a balance of power, as previously noted, has [also] entailed the occasional use of national force as a means of international control and adjustment. Great-power status was traditionally conferred on states that could use force most handily. Is the use of force in a nuclear world so severely inhibited that balance-of-power analysis has lost most if not all of its meaning?

[Three] reasons are usually given in support of an affirmative answer. First, because the nuclear might of one superpower balances that of the other, their effective power is reduced to zero. Their best and most distinctive forces, the nuclear ones, are least usable. In the widely echoed words of John Herz, absolute power equals absolute impotence. Second, the fear of escalation strongly inhibits even the use of conventional forces, especially by the United States or the Soviet Union. Nuclear powers must fear escalation more than other states do, for in any war that rose to the nuclear level they would be primary targets. They may, of course, still choose to commit their armies to battle, but the risks of doing so, as they themselves must realize, are higher than in the past. Third, in the nuclear age enormous military power no longer ensures effective control. . . .

Such arguments are often made and have to be taken seriously. In an obvious sense, part of the contention is valid. When great powers are in a stalemate, lesser states acquire an increased freedom of movement. That this phenomenon is now noticeable tells us nothing new about the strength of the weak or the weakness of the strong. Weak states have often found opportunities for maneuver in the interstices of a balance of power. This is, however, only part of the story. To maintain both the balance and its by-product requires the continuing efforts of America and Russia. Their instincts for self-preservation call forth such efforts: the objective of both states must be to perpetuate an international stalemate as a minimum basis for the security of each of them—even if this should mean that the two big states do the work while the small ones have the fun. . . .

. . . The cost of the American nuclear establishment, maintained in peaceful readiness, is functionally comparable to the costs incurred by a government in order to maintain domestic order and provide internal security. Such expenditure is not productive in the sense that spending to build roads is, but it is not unproductive either. Its utility is obvious, and should anyone successfully argue otherwise, the consequences of accepting his argument would quickly demonstrate its falsity. Force is least visible where power is most fully and most adequately present. The better ordered a society and the more competent and respected its government, the less force its policemen are required to employ. . . . Similarly in international relations, states supreme in their power have to use force less often. . . . Powerful states need to use force less often than their weaker neighbors because the strong can more often protect their interests or work their wills in other ways—by persuasion and cajolery, by economic bargaining and bribery, by the extension of aid, or finally by posing deterrent threats. Since states with large nuclear armories do not actually "use" them, force is said to be discounted. Such reasoning is fallacious. Possession of power should not be identified with the use of force, and the usefulness of force should not be confused with its usability. To introduce such confusions into the analysis of power is comparable to saying that the police force that seldom if ever employs violence is weak or that a police force is strong only when policemen are swinging their clubs. To vary the image, it is comparable to saying that a man with large assets is not rich if he spends little money or that a man is rich only if he spends a lot of it.

. . . Depending on a country's situation, it may make much better sense to say that military force is most useful when it deters an attack, that is, when it need not be used in battle at all. When the strongest state militarily is also a status-quo power, non-use of force is a sign of its strength. Force is most useful, or best serves the interests of such a state, when it need not be used in the actual conduct of warfare. . . .

Where power is seen to be balanced, whether or not the balance is nuclear, it may seem that the resultant of opposing forces is zero. But this is misleading. The vectors of national force do not meet at a point, if only because the power of a state does not resolve into a single vector. Military force is divisible, especially for the state that can afford a lot of it. In a nuclear world, contrary to some assertions, the dialectic of inequality does not produce the effective equality of strong and weak states. Lesser states that decide to establish a nuclear arsenal by slighting their conventional forces render themselves unable to meet any threat to themselves other than the ultimate one (and that doubtfully). By way of contrast, the military doctrine of the United States, to which the organization of her forces corresponds, is one of flexible response. Great powers are strong not simply because they have nuclear weapons but also because their immense resources enable them to generate and maintain power of all types, military and other, at different technological levels.

Just as the state that refrains from applying force is said to betray its weakness, so the state that has trouble in exercising control is said to display the defectiveness of its power. In such a conclusion, the elementary error of identifying power with control is evident. Absence of control or failure to press hard to achieve it may indicate either that the would-be controller noticed that, try as he might, he would have insufficient force or inappropriate types of force at his command; or it may indicate that he chose to make less than a maximum effort because imposition of control was not regarded as very important. One student of international relations has remarked that "though the weapons of mass destruction grow more and more ferociously efficient, the revolutionary guerrilla armed with nothing more advanced than an old rifle and a nineteenth-century political doctrine has proved the most effective means yet devised for altering the world power-balance." But the revolutionary guerrilla wins civil wars, not international ones, and no civil war can change the balance of power in the world unless it takes place in the United States or the Soviet Union. Enough of them have occurred since the Second World War to make the truth of this statement clear without need for further analysis. Even in China, the most populous of states, a civil war that led to a change of allegiance in the cold war did not seriously tilt the world balance.

Two states that enjoy wide margins of power over other states need worry little about changes that occur among the latter. Failure to act may then not betray the frustrations of impotence; instead it may demonstrate the serenity of power. The United States, having chosen to intervene in Vietnam, has limited the use of its military force. Because no realignment of national power in Vietnam could in itself affect the balance of power between the United States and the Soviet Union—or even noticeably alter the imbalance of power between the United States and China—the United States need not have intervened at all. Whether or not it could have safely "passed" in Southeast Asia, the American government chose not to do so; nor have its costly, long-sustained efforts brought success. If military power can be equated with control, then the United States has indeed demonstrated its weakness. The case is instructive. The People's Republic of China has not moved militarily against any country of Southeast Asia. The United States could successfully counter such a move, one would expect, by opposing military force with military force. What has worried some people and led others to sharpen their statements about the weakness of the power-ful is that the United States, hard though it has tried, has been unable to put down insurrection and halt the possible spread of Communist ideology.

Here again old truths need to be brought into focus. As David Hume long ago noted, "force is always on the side of the governed." The gover-nors, being few in number, depend for the exercise of their rule upon the more or less willing assent of their subjects. If sullen disregard is the re-sponse to every command, no government can rule. And if a country, be-cause of internal disorder and lack of coherence, is unable to rule itself, no body of foreigners, whatever the military force at its command, can rea-sonably hope to do so. If Communism is the threat to Southeast Asia, then military forces are not the right means for countering it. If insurrection is the problem, then it can hardly be hoped that an alien army will be able to pacify a country that is unable to govern itself. Foreign troops, though not irrelevant to such problems, can only be of indirect help. Military force, used internationally, is a means of establishing control over a territory, not of exercising control within it. The threat of a nation to use military force, whether nuclear or conventional, is pre-eminently a means of affecting an-other state's external behavior, of dissuading a state from launching a career of aggression and of meeting the aggression if dissuasion should fail.

Dissuasion or deterrence is easier to accomplish than "compellence," to use an apt term invented by Thomas C. Schelling.[2] Compellence is more difficult to achieve than deterrence, and its contrivance is a more intricate affair. In Vietnam, the United States faces not merely the task of compel-ling a particular action but of promoting an effective political order. . . . Military forces, whether domestic or foreign, are insufficient for the task of pacification, the more so if a country is rent by faction and if its people are politically engaged and active. To say that militarily strong states are feeble because they cannot easily bring order to minor states is like saying that a pneumatic hammer is weak because it is not suitable for drilling de-cayed teeth. It is to confuse the purpose of instruments and to confound the means of external power with the agencies of internal governance. Inability to exercise *political* control over others does not indicate *military* weakness. Strong states cannot do everything with their military forces, as Napoleon acutely realized; but they are able to do things that militarily weak states cannot do. The People's Republic of China can no more solve the problems of governance in some Latin American country than the United States can in Southeast Asia. But the United States can intervene with great military force in far quarters of the world while wielding an effective deterrent against escalation. Such action exceeds the capabilities of all but the strong-est of states.

[2] Thomas C. Schelling, *Arms and Influence* (New Haven: Yale University Press, 1966), pp. 70–71.

Differences in strength do matter, though not for every conceivable purpose. To deduce the weakness of the powerful from this qualifying clause is a misleading use of words. One sees in such a case as Vietnam not the *weakness* of great military power in a nuclear world but instead a clear illustration of the *limits* of military force in the world of the present as always. . . .

No political structure, whether domestic or international, can guarantee stability. The question that one must ask is not whether a given distribution of power is stable but how stable different distributions of power are likely to be. For a number of reasons, the bipolar world of the past two decades has been highly stable. The two leading states have a common interest in stability: they would at least like to maintain their positions. In one respect, bipolarity is expressed as the reciprocal control of the two strongest states by each other out of their mutual antagonism. What is unpredictable in such a two-party competition is whether one party will try to eliminate the other. Nuclear forces of second-strike capacity induce an added caution. Here again force is useful, and its usefulness is reinforced in proportion as its use is forestalled. Fear of major war induces caution all around; the Soviet Union and the United States wield the means of inducing that caution.

The constraints of duopolistic competition press in one direction: duopolists eye each other warily, and each is very sensitive to the gains of the other. Working in the opposite direction, however, is the existence of the immense difference in power between the two superpowers and the states of middle or lesser rank. This condition of inequality makes it unlikely that any shifts in the alignment of states would very much help or hurt either of the two leading powers. If few changes can damage the vital interests of either of them, then both can be moderate in their responses. Not being dependent upon allies, the United States and the Soviet Union are free to design strategies in accord with their interests. Since the power actually and potentially at the disposal of each of them far exceeds that of their closest competitors, they are able to control in some measure the possibly destabilizing acts of third parties or to absorb their effects. . . . The extent of the difference in national capabilities makes the bipolar structure resilient. Defection of allies and national shifts of allegiance do not decisively alter the structure. Because they do not, recalcitrant allies may be treated with indifference; they may even be effectively disciplined. Pressure can be applied to moderate the behavior of third states or to check and contain their activities. The Suez venture of Britain and France was stopped by American financial pressure. Chiang Kai-shek has been kept on a leash by denying him the means of invasion. The prospective loss of foreign aid helped to halt warfare between Pakistan and India, as did the Soviet Union's persuasion. In such ways, the wielding of great power can be useful.

The above examples illustrate hierarchical control operating in a way that often goes unnoticed because the means by which control is exercised are not institutionalized. What management there now is in international relations must be provided, singly and occasionally together, by the duopolists at the top. In certain ways, some of them suggested above, the inequality of states in a bipolar world enables the two most powerful states to develop a rich variety of controls and to follow flexible strategies in using them.

. . . For more than two decades, power has been narrowly concentrated; and force has been used, not orgiastically as in the world wars of this century, but in a controlled way and for conscious political purposes. Power may be present when force is not used, but force is also used openly. A catalogue of examples would be both complex and lengthy. It would contain such items, on the American side of the ledger, as the garrisoning of Berlin, its supply by airlift during the blockade, the stationing of troops in Europe, the establishment of bases in Japan and elsewhere, the waging of war in Korea and Vietnam, and the "quarantine" of Cuba. Seldom if ever has force been more variously, more persistently, and more widely applied; and seldom has it been more consciously used as an instrument of national policy. Since the war we have seen, not the cancellation of force by nuclear stalemate, but instead the political organization and pervasion of power; not the end of balance of power owing to a reduction in the number of major states, but instead the formation and perpetuation of a balance *à deux.*

39 / Nuclear Stalemate: Cause of Stability or Instability?

John H. Herz

The stabilization of mutual deterrence among superpowers has had, according to Herz, some unexpected and paradoxical effects on politics among nations. While it has pushed a major nuclear conflict up to the level of ever-present but perhaps never realized threat, it has also made nuclear weapons

Abridged from pp. 18–30 of John H. Herz, "The Territorial State Revisited," *Polity,* 1:1 (September 1968). Reprinted by permission of the author and the publisher. Some of the author's footnotes have been omitted; footnotes added by the editor are so marked.

unavailable for the protection (or blackmail) of nonnuclear nations. In addition, in the age of intercontinental missiles the importance of allies and foreign bases has become doubtful. The result is not only a vigorous reassertion of territorial nationalism and the emergence of microstates but also an increased attractiveness for the policy of nonalignment. (Another portion of Herz's study that focuses on new territorial nationalism was reproduced in Selection 3.)

Although the nuclear stalemate has reduced the probability of a major nuclear conflict, it tends to encourage the use of subnuclear violence, especially in the form of interventions in the domestic affairs of other nations.[3] Nevertheless, Herz also points to several countertendencies that may discourage the practice of subversion and intervention among nations.

"The dangerousness of war has reduced the danger of war." [4] The overkill machinery of nuclear armament, with all its potential pervasiveness in regard to the territory and boundaries of traditional international units, has had the unexpected, paradoxical, and encouraging effect of stabilizing a world most had believed destabilized in the extreme through the advent of the new weapon. At the dawn of the atomic age, when the new machinery for destruction had first become available to powers utterly at odds in regard to ways of life, types of regimes, and objectives of foreign policy, there had been general expectation that the holocaust was inevitable unless the enormity of the threat would make the superpowers agree on radical measures of disarmament and control. They did not, and yet, in twenty years of nuclear confrontation, the world has escaped nuclear war and even conventional war among major nations.

Chief cause of this development, of course, has been nuclear stalemate through nuclear deterrence. The boundaries of the blocs turned out to be the limits of spheres of tacitly agreed upon nonintervention. The United States and the Soviet Union emerged as the two great "conservatives," both intent on consolidating the status quo as it had been established after World War II, including its often abstruse and seemingly unmanageable arrangements, settlements, and boundaries (for example, the two Germanies, Berlin, and access routes to West Berlin; or the 38th parallel in Korea). A nuclear war, or any war that might escalate into one, was not to be risked over issues located in the sphere conceded to the other side (such as the

---

[3] Compare with a conclusion of another analysis: "Due to the unacceptable destruction that international war would in all likelihood bring today, the major contestants have turned to the manipulation of domestic revolutions as a means of maneuvering for power . . . revolution is replacing war. . . . The balance of power has come to depend to a great extent on the outcome of domestic revolutions." Cyril E. Black and Thomas P. Thornton, *Communism and Revolution: The Strategic Uses of Political Violence* (Princeton, N.J.: Princeton University Press, 1964), p. 446.

[4] Inis L. Claude, *The Changing United Nations* (New York: Random House, Inc., 1967), p. 9.

crises concerning Hungary, Berlin, or Cuba). In this way, at least in intention, the bloc frontiers have taken the place of the "trip-wire" lines of protection which national boundaries used to constitute in the age of territorial impermeability.

But this also meant protection of the respective actors and regimes and, by way of indirection, of the units controlled by these regimes. If Castro is protected in Cuba, or Chiang on Taiwan, or Ulbricht in East Germany, or whoever is in power at Seoul, this entails also the preservation of Cuba, the Republic of China, the German Democratic Republic, and the Republic of Korea *qua* territorial units. Force in the relationship between the United States and the Soviet Union, or their respective blocs, has been "unavailable" in the sense that the effects of nuclear action are considered unacceptable to either side. Although the weapon must remain available as a retaliatory threat, one not merely hopes that it will never be used but is more or less agreed that it will not function—except as retaliation—in one's policy calculations.

But the effect of the "unavailability of force" on the territorial stability of countries is not exclusively positive. It is somewhat ambiguous. For instance, we can see that, by way of curious reaction, force unavailable to the large may encourage the small to defy them and use force with impunity. What hampers the powerful—anxiety concerning nuclear confrontations, anticolonialist opinion, etc.—favors the small. They leave the nuclear worrying to the nuclear powers and bank on being backed up by world opinion and the world organization. To this may be added a frequent lack of responsibility or the parochialism of new nations and their leaders, who may be tempted to pursue grievances to the point of violence in disregard of the dangers this involves for world peace. They may even set out to create threats to the peace so as to draw attention to their particular problems.

Another ambiguity lies in the combined effect of nuclear "unavailability" and second-strike capacity. The latter protects the superpowers but seems to deprive the others, in and outside the blocs, of reliance on nuclear protection. This has been one of the reasons for the assertion of independence of bloc members and, in some instances, for the development of their own nuclear forces. . . .

. . . If the nuclear umbrella furnished their own allies by the United States and the Soviet Union has become dubious, can there be one for nonaligned countries? Verbal assurances of this sort tend to become "incredible," and even though they may be given in good faith, a counterpower not believing in them may be lured into risking confrontations that may end in nuclear war. In this way, far from creating protection and stability, a system of such guarantees may actually increase the danger of war. More likely than not, and whether there are nonproliferation agreements or not, if a nuclear power threatens a nonnuclear one, the latter will quickly be transformed into a nuclear power by a nuclear "friend" . . . ; in such an event, a treaty is unlikely to make much difference.

Thus we are warranted in anticipating a world of nuclear proliferation, with increasing numbers of both greater and lesser nuclear powers. This will certainly involve great instability and growing risks of actual nuclear war. On the other hand, it is at least imaginable that what happened in the post-war decades may repeat itself; that is, that at least for a period of time, *systems* of mutual deterrence may stabilize the situation. There may be regional systems, with regional nuclear balances, there may be agreed upon and inspected denuclearized areas, and so forth. Details depend on factors that are difficult to predict, such as the identity and distribution of the nuclear powers, the stage and level of their nuclear equipment, and the internal cohesion of the units in question. In any event, we may, by way of hypothesis, assume the emergence of a multipolar world of nuclear proliferation in which the territorial nature of the component units is preserved and is not entirely in jeopardy. . . .

Intervention and Nonalignment

In addition to nuclear permeability, certain new technological penetrabilities (for example, through observation and collection of information from space satellites and through telephotography) and the manifold opportunities created through economic, technical and military assistance, indirect penetration adds the power-political opportunities that emerge from an "international civil war" situation among competing systems and ideologies. This quasi-war situation renders possible political-military penetration of a country through promoting or lending assistance to indigenous insurrectionist forces, an assistance which, in turn, may range from diplomatic aid (for example, recognition) rendered to a rebel regime to making portions ("volunteer" or otherwise) or one's own armed forces available. It may further mean penetration of the top level of a country's regime through bribery or similar "purchase" of top personnel, or the doctrinal penetration of such levels on the part of revolutionary regimes. In the pursuance of such policies one may exploit all the weaknesses and dissensions which exist in the penetrated unit, whether they originate in ethnic, religious, or other groups discriminated against, in depressed socio-economic classes, or among ideologically opposed or alienated groups or individuals. . . .

Such penetration assisting the "revolutionary" side, or its threat, may in turn provoke similar penetration by powers interested in shoring up the existing unit and its regime. Defense agreements, military aid, training of troops, establishment of bases, economic-financial ties through investments, aid, exclusive or predominant trade relations, currency arrangements, all of these are common means to establish or maintain influence which, especially in the case of the newly independent, small, and weak units, frequently amounts to dependency coming close to what the "revolutionary" side (although engaging in similar policies in regard to "its" clients) denounces as "neo-colonialism." Not only American penetration of countries allegedly or actually threatened with "subversion," but also continued French influence in formerly French African units are cases in point. On the "Eastern" side, in addition to (and even in competition with) Soviet (and their clients') efforts, Chinese and Castroite forces may be at work.

Civil war assisted from abroad in this way may result in the dissolution of statehood (through secession) or of the prevailing regimes (through revolution). . . .

While not playing down the importance of these phenomena, one can point out countertendencies and advance the hypothesis that they may prevail in the long run.

One of these is the lessening of revolutionary penetration and interference that has resulted from the "deradicalization" of Communist regimes. Of late, there has been much discussion of a worldwide trend toward "deideologization," the "end" or, at least, the "erosion" or "decline" of ideologies and of the corresponding movements, whether leftist or rightist, West or East. There is little doubt of the presence of this phenomenon as far as the once world-revolutionary doctrines and policies of the core-Communist power are concerned.[5] It has been apparent not only in doctrines of peaceful coexistence, peaceful liberation from colonialism, and peaceful transition from capitalism to socialism but, more importantly, in Soviet moderation of her actual attitudes in the face of tempting situations abroad, most strikingly, perhaps, in Vietnam. Inasmuch as there has been aid to revolutionary forces, this has been due chiefly to the Chinese factor, the felt necessity not to lose face in the eyes of leftist movements and parties throughout the world. Even with the Chinese themselves, for whom Soviet deradicalization has been a golden opportunity to claim world-revolutionary leadership, action has not matched proclamation.[6] In a situation as close as the Viet-

---

[5] As Robert C. Tucker has pointed out, the process should be referred to as "deradicalization" rather than "deideologization," because less radicalism in action may be accompanied by doctrinal emphasis on symbols of "nonchange." "Intensified *verbal* allegiance to ultimate ideological goals belongs to the pattern of deradicalization" ("The Deradicalization of Marxist Movements," *American Political Science Review,* LXI [1967], 2, pp. 343 ff., 358). But even in this connection there is a decreasing line in regard to amount of and emphasis on doctrine running from Stalin through Khrushchev to the present Soviet rulers, and a corresponding decrease in expected reference and obeisance to ideology on the part of writers and scholars. Cf. Jean-Yves Calvez, "La place de l'idéologie," *Revue française de science politique,* XVII (1967), 1050 ff.

[6] Ed. note: In his study of new realism in the relations between the two nuclear superpowers, Hans J. Morgenthau includes the ideological decontamination of *both* the Soviet and the United States foreign policies with respect to each other (although

namese, assistance has consisted mainly of verbal advice rather than more forceful and substantial intervention. Only when danger struck really close to home, as in Korea after the U.N. forces crossed the 38th parallel, did they intervene more massively.

There seems to be growing realization among *all* Communist regimes that interference is promising only where conditions in the respective country or area are "ripe" for a revolution (or "war of liberation"), and that ripeness presupposes the readiness and ability of the indigenous forces to carry the brunt of the struggle. This has been stated repeatedly by both Soviet and Chinese spokesmen,[7] and it does not seem to be mere subterfuge. A long history of disappointment with Moscow-initiated and foreign-guided coups, uprisings, and riots from the Twenties (Hungary, Bavaria, Hamburg, China) to more recent times seems to have taught the Communist regimes a lesson. The situation that promises success cannot be created artificially; it must be based upon the "territorial imperative" motivating an indigenous population together with its leadership's revolutionary objectives.

But where indigenous forces are primarily responsible for a revolutionary victory, they are not likely to accept control or influence on the part of an assisting power—*vide* Yugoslavia and China herself. This, in turn, may lessen the temptation to intervene. And, by the same token, lessening of Communist interventionism may in due course diminish the West's concern with "world Communism" and its alleged "conspiracy" to control the world, and thus affect its policies of counter-interventionism. For twenty years

---

not with respect to other nations). In his article "Changes and Chances in American-Soviet Relations," *Foreign Affairs,* 49:3 (April 1971), 430, Morgenthau writes:

The emancipation of American and Soviet foreign policies from these dogmatic ideological stereotypes—again I must emphasize, limited to their mutual relations —has been the result of the impact the facts of life have made upon the thoughts and actions of the governments concerned. Foremost among these facts has been their failure to win the ideological allegiance of the nations of the third world in Africa, Asia and Latin America. The third world was supposed to be the decisive battleground in the struggle for men's minds, a struggle which would decide the fate of the world. Khrushchev, for instance, used to assure us that the third world would follow the lead of the Soviet Union and thereby seal the doom of the West. Nothing of the kind happened. The new nations of the third world have apparently preferred to be miserable in their own way to being made happy by the United States or the U.S.S.R.

This failure of ideological competition has led both superpowers to the conclusion that it is not worth the expense and the risk of a direct military confrontation, and they have given it up.

It is part and parcel of this victory of the facts of life over ideological blinders that the United States has for all practical purposes recognized the Soviet predominance in Eastern Europe.

[7] Interestingly, Trotsky, than whom no one was more "world-revolutionary," had declared in the Twenties that "only that revolution is viable which wins out of its own strength"—quoted in Ossip K. Flechtheim, *Bolschewismus 1917–1967: Von der Weltrevolution zum Sowjetimperium* (Vienna, 1967), p. 47.

there has not been a single Communist attempt to revolutionize a developed nation or society, or a corresponding attempt on the part of the West to "liberate" a Communist unit. . . .

We seem to be in a stage of transition from doctrinal-political splits, confrontations, and interventions toward a world of lessened antagonisms. In such a world, nation-states would be left in peace to develop their own systems and remain neutral themselves in regard to the great powers. Nonalignment is in line with nationalism as a legitimizing force; it also lessens the concern of the big that, by leaving small states alone, they might simply hand the opponent a chance to extend his influence. Under bipolar conditions, nonalignment could appear risky to the small because of absence of protection and guarantees. But even then alignment was not without dangers of its own—of becoming, for example, a target for the other side because of bases on one's soil. With the disintegration of the blocs noninvolvement will appear preferable to more and more of the weaker states. . . . If this tendency should spread, increased stability of nations and of the nation-state system would ensue.

40 / Limits to Intervention

Graham T. Allison, Ernest May, and Adam Yarmolinsky

"No more Vietnams," is a general and understandable reaction to the long and unsuccessful American intervention in Indochina. Perhaps isolationist retreat into our own fortress, America, may be the one possible guarantee that never more will the United States get involved in a wrong war at a wrong place at a wrong time. But is isolationism a realistic or a wise alternative? The following essay examines three types of possible future American involvement in the affairs of other nations or continents: (1) overt aggression against an

From pp. 245–260 (*passim*) of Graham T. Allison, Ernest May, and Adam Yarmolinsky, "Limits to Intervention." Abridged by special permission from *Foreign Affairs,* January 1970, Vol. 48, No. 2. Copyright by the Council on Foreign Relations, Inc., New York.

ally; (2) aggression against a nonally; and (3) internal violence, perhaps aided from outside and jeopardizing a friendly or neutral nation.

The credentials of the three authors are impressive: Allison and Yarmolinsky served in 1965 as deputy assistant secretaries of defense. May, Dean of Harvard College and professor of history, is the author of *The World War and American Isolationism, American Imperialism,* and other works. All three are professors at Harvard.

Not since World War II have Americans been so uncertain about the proper role of the United States in the world. The broad bipartisan consensus that characterized American foreign policy for two decades after the war has been overcome by widespread, bipartisan confusion about the nature of the world, the character of the challenges that policy-makers confront, and the proper employment of non-nuclear forces. Viet Nam is not the only cause of this confusion. Changes in American perceptions were evident earlier: as the fear of monolithic communism waned, hope grew that the United States and the Soviet Union could coexist peacefully; and the public showed diminishing interest in providing aid to less developed countries. But the expenditure of blood and treasure in Viet Nam has deepened fundamental doubts throughout our society—from the highest levels of government to college campuses and midwestern farms—as to whether the United States should in any circumstances become involved again in a limited war. A *Time*—Louis Harris Poll in May [1969] indicated that only a minority of Americans are willing to see United States troops used to resist overt communist aggression against our allies: in Berlin, 26 percent; in Thailand, 25 percent; and in Japan, 27 percent.

This pervasive uncertainty, confusion and discontent create an opportunity to reformulate the guidelines of American foreign policy and to educate the larger public about the responsibilities of the United States—their extent and their limits. . . .

Four general observations can be made about the character of the problem. First is the ubiquity of the visceral reaction: "No more Viet Nams!" This simplistic formula seems to guide the prescriptions even of some past participants in government. The impulse to avoid a future Viet Nam is as powerful today as was the impulse in the 1930s to avoid another World War I or the impulse after 1945 to avoid another Munich. The temptation to leap from the flagging horse we have been riding to any horse headed in the opposite direction seems compelling.

Second is the difficulty of the problem itself: Much of the traditional rationale for the size and shape of non-nuclear forces proves on examination to be highly questionable. It is not clear that such forces contribute to deterring major non-nuclear conflicts or that such conflicts are sufficiently likely to justify their standing by in readiness. Only military planners, professionally committed to belief in the worst contingencies, today assign significant probability to a sudden Soviet march across the north German plain, a surprise attack by the Red Army on the Mediterranean flank of NATO, or even an unheralded descent by Communist China on Burma or Thailand. Equally, it is unclear what role American non-nuclear forces can play in the kinds of minor wars that do seem probable. Viet Nam hardly encourages the conviction that they are suitable instruments for coping with insurgency in a foreign state. But the obvious alternatives to the traditional rationale do not pass muster either. One cannot say that there are no politico-military reasons for an American military presence of some sort in Europe or the Mediterranean. The ready availability of some U.S. force serves as a deterrent and therefore necessarily as a significant element in defense against possible overt attack on, say, Venezuela or South Korea. It is essential to recognize not only that no simple doctrines are readily to be discovered but that the questions themselves are not easy to understand.

Third is the impossibility of specifying any geographical area where developments are certain to be of such limited interest as never to raise the possibility that the United States should use non-nuclear force. If one could simply write off the less developed countries or Southeast Asia or Africa, the problem might be more manageable. But a reasonably thorough and unblinkered survey of the globe discloses conceivable situations in every area in which any responsible administration might have to consider introducing American forces.

Finally, there is no evidence that any set of principles can be identified which unambiguously distinguishes cases in which U.S. non-nuclear forces should and should not be used.

In attempting to design desirable, feasible guidelines for future uses of non-nuclear forces one must acknowledge that this issue is highly sensitive to the outcome of Viet Nam and the interpretation given that outcome in the United States. The argument here proceeds on the assumption that the likely settlement will be sufficiently adverse to American interests to assure disagreement both among decision-makers and among informed citizens about the degree to which we have achieved our initial objectives.

Even though there are no unambiguous guidelines, there is a fairly clear checklist of factors that would determine how any President or presidential adviser or even any responsible observer would judge a case of possible intervention. These factors include:

The American sense of commitment. Commitment can be based on formal treaties, letters exchanged between chiefs of state or high government officials, historical ties, past blood shed in defense of common goals, and the like.

The American sense of interest. Since this interest is no longer a function primarily of trading opportunities, territorial ambitions or imperialist pretensions, it is to be measured largely in terms of the sense of danger to the delicate equilibrium between the major world powers. Some situations will inevitably seem more dangerous than others, either because of possible immediate results or because of possible effects on expectations of leaders in either hostile or friendly states. National interest is also a function of substantive domestic concerns, as with the fate of Israel, or the possibility of a black-white confrontation in southern Africa.

The estimated probability of success, at various levels of cost and risk. The most attractive situation to decision-makers—and to the American public—will be one that seems to offer a high probability of success at relatively low risk.

Each of these factors involves judgment on the basis of uncertain estimates. Differences among reasonable men, especially over future dangers in acting or failing to act, are inevitable. Because of these uncertainties, there are large numbers of cases in which it is difficult to predict whether the United States would decide for or against intervention.

The uncertainties surrounding calculations about intervention are overshadowed by a second cluster of factors: the context in which the specific decision is made. This context includes:

The immediate background. A sudden event like the North Korean attack on South Korea or the collapse of the Dominican government in 1965 poses one kind of problem. A more slowly developing event like the Berlin Blockade or the North Vietnamese intervention in South Viet Nam poses another. A gradually festering situation such as that on the Israeli-Syrian frontier or in present-day Guatemala poses still another.

Comparative perspectives. Situations will vary also in similarity to past situations. The Dominican Republic in 1965 looked like Cuba in 1959. Reactions to, say, a coup in Guatemala could vary, depending on whether the situation was read as another Cuba or another Dominican Republic. A crucial question over the next few years will certainly be whether a situation does or does not look like another Viet Nam.

The historical trend. President Kennedy's decision to increase American advisers in Viet Nam seems inseparable from the sequence of events leading from the Bay of Pigs through Vienna, Laos and Berlin. There was a strong feeling that the line had to be drawn somewhere, even if that meant "the wrong war. . . ."

Congressional and public moods. Congress and the public might take one attitude toward North Korea and another toward, say, Bulgaria—not recently guilty of provocative behavior. Similarly, attitudes toward a situation in Africa could be affected by attitudes of and toward Blacks at home.

II

Conceding all the surrounding uncertainties, one can still distinguish three categories of cases: (1) overt aggression by a major communist power against a U.S. ally; (2) overt aggression by any state against a nation not a U.S. ally (*e.g.* Russia against Finland, China against India, a combination of Arab states against Israel or Jordan); (3) internal violence jeopardizing a friendly state, perhaps aided from outside but not involving significant overt action by foreign ground, air or naval units. (In the first two categories, overt aggression should be understood as comprehending any cases in which organized units of the armed forces of one nation move in significant numbers across the established frontiers of another nation; the term thus includes large-scale infiltration into insurgent-held territory and other situations sometimes described as "proxy war.")

Each category comprehends many kinds of cases. Even with regard to nations covered by the same alliance treaty, the United States does not have identical commitments. Within NATO, for example, we feel a greater sense of national commitment to Britain than to, say, Greece or even to Norway, despite our equal obligation to all. Some non-allies may have stronger moral claims than some allies. Israel, for example, certainly stands higher with the American public than Portugal or Paraguay. Persistent internal violence in South Korea would pose policy problems quite different from those presented by similar violence in Pakistan, and violence in Pakistan would wear a different appearance depending on whether outsiders numbered thousands or tens of thousands and whether they were Chinese or Russians. Even so, these categories are not only distinguishable but sufficiently different to admit differing policy guidelines.

The First Category: Overt Aggression against an Ally

Today the Rio Treaty, the North Atlantic Treaty, the Southeast Asia Treaty, the ANZUS Pact and mutual defense pacts with Japan, Korea, Taiwan and the Philippines commit the United States to the defense of 42 nations. Auxiliary arrangements, such as U.S. patronage of CENTO, have created a number of additional commitments. None of these commitments is in perpetuity. The obligations of the United States under these arrangements are of differing degrees and kinds. Thus the Rio and NATO treaties assert that "an armed attack against any [contracting] State shall be considered an attack against all and, consequently, each of the said contracting Parties undertakes to assist in meeting the attack," while the Southeast Asia Treaty provides that "aggression by means of armed attack against any of the Parties would endanger [each Party's] own peace and safety" and each Party agrees "to meet the common danger in accordance with [its] constitutional processes." In addition, some have been amplified by unilateral Executive or Congressional declarations. The Southeast Asia Treaty obligation to Thailand was markedly strengthened, for example, by a joint communiqué issued in 1962 by Secretary Rusk and Thai Foreign Minister Thanat Khoman which stated that the United States regarded Thailand's independence and integrity as "vital to the national interest of the United States;" it held that the American commitment to Thailand under the Southeast Asia Treaty was binding, regardless of whether other signers concurred or not. Statements by Secretary Dulles and a Congressional resolution of January 29, 1955, suggested that our obligation to the Republic of China included the defense of Quemoy and Matsu.

All such commitments deserve thoughtful reëxamination. Given the history of executive-legislative controversy over Viet Nam, some should be reviewed and either reaffirmed or revised in consultation with the Senate. With respect to all treaty commitments which the Government chooses to reaffirm, however, it seems appropriate that the President establish and announce a *presumption that the United States will intervene on behalf of an ally which is a victim of overt aggression.* Only by clearly reaffirming those commitments which are judged genuinely vital can the United States make clear that the aftermath of Viet Nam is not to be a withdrawal into a fortress America.

The Second Category: Aggression against a Non-Ally

The issue becomes more complex in cases of overt aggression against a nation not linked to the United States by a treaty of alliance. There is clearly a very considerable range of such cases in which the United States would not be prepared to intervene. If other governments judge the likelihood of American action by the three criteria of commitment, interest and risk of escalation, none will launch an overt attack on a nation friendly with the United States unless it judges the American commitment weak or the risk to the United States high. The critical question is likely to be one of U.S. interest, and that is likely to turn on whether other major powers are involved, on either side. In cases where no other major power is involved, there should be a *presumption against U.S. intervention.* Where the American response could be undertaken jointly with another major power, the risk of escalation might be reduced. This presumption, as stated, would not prejudice our responding to a United Nations Security Council decision to impose sanctions against an aggressor, up to and including military force.

The Third Category: Internal Disorder

Here more than elsewhere, there may be some ambiguity about what constitutes American military intervention. Various forms of intervention—*e.g.* diplomatic, economic, covert and military—are obviously related. Indeed, in the most visible cases—Laos and Viet Nam—military involvement has occurred in stages—from military aid missions, to arms, to advisers, to helicopters and finally to combat operations. But it is essential to draw a sharp line between official combat operations and the rest. For the admitted expenditure of American blood changes the character of subsequent choices about further investments of men and money. The term "military intervention" is therefore restricted here to cases involving either (1) the presence of American military personnel in sufficient numbers to cast doubt upon their claim to be traditional advisers, or (2) combat operations involving U.S. air or naval forces.

Before a decision on such intervention confronts the President, other government officials will have made many decisions and taken many actions that will critically affect his decision to intervene or not. Here, therefore, we must consider not only what presumptions should govern the expectations and behavior of officials, but also what procedures should be followed to place choices before the President.

Though Viet Nam provides no satisfactory and simple rules, it does suggest a number of relevant lessons. First, the effects of intervention are uncertain. Viet Nam suggests how hard it is to judge what makes for stability and instability in the developing world. Second, American power is more limited than many people have assumed. The massive application of our military power has not been able to achieve a military victory. Our best efforts have not been able to establish a stable popular government in Saigon. Third, any non-nuclear intervention in a nuclear world is likely to be a limited commitment; but once blood has been shed, it is extraordinarily difficult, especially as a matter of domestic policy, to cut losses.

These "lessons" seem all the more persuasive because the United States has no commitment to preserve any national régime. In few cases can one find a vital American interest that would be affected by a change of internal régimes. Our forces have a difficult time defeating national guerrillas that a government cannot overcome by itself. The belief that our troops and technology can be relied upon to cope with insurgency problems that national governments are unable to deal with encourages flabbiness in some existing régimes. It is highly uncertain what effect external military intervention will have on subversion, and what effect external efforts to control subversion will have on modernization. Indeed, nothing seems surer than that in some societies internal violence will be necessary for modernization.

These factors complement the overwhelming preference of the American public. Therefore, the Administration should make a serious effort to establish *a strong presumption against intervention in cases of internal disorder and/or subversion, even when there is outside encouragement and aid.*

Such a presumption need not be inconsistent with a willingness to supply economic aid, military equipment and even, in some cases, advisers.

III

Difficulties present themselves in connection with all three of the proposed presumptions. It is arguable, for example, that renewed evidence of U.S. fidelity to treaty obligations could dissuade NATO allies from contributing a "fair share" to their own defense. It could also be argued that the second presumption would encourage the Arabs to attack Israel. The most persuasive counter-arguments, however, are those against a presumption of nonintervention in cases of internal disorder. It can be contended that to establish such a presumption will encourage disgruntled groups in less developed countries to attempt insurgency, and will announce to nations bent on aggression that low-level aggression pays. These objections have bite. But they ignore two further considerations.

First, expectations about American willingness to intervene will be but one factor in the decision of disaffected citizens to rebel, of revolutionaries to fight on, and of régimes like those in Peking or Hanoi to support aggression beyond their frontiers. The factors that determine a choice to pursue revolution and insurgency are overwhelmingly local, and the factors that bear on a government's decision to support insurgency beyond its borders turn on a large number of considerations other than likely U.S. reactions. Indeed, it seems very uncertain what the effect will be on potential aggressors of statements by the United States about its intentions regarding intervention. Second, reduced expectation of U.S. intervention would create incentives for national governments to set their own houses in order, to be more responsive to citizens' interests, and to shore up their own counterinsurgency capabilities. Too often American support of rightist status quo régimes has resulted in restraints upon discontented religious and ethnic minorities, thus making the country more, rather than less, vulnerable to subversion. Although much uncertainty surrounds this entire set of calculations, it seems likely that a presumption against U.S. intervention will encourage insurgency by some small amount. On the other hand, this price is small in comparison with the cost of any alternative. . . .

Even if the suggested presumptions were in effect, the United States would still have obligations requiring substantial non-nuclear forces. Their adequacy could well determine the extent to which the margins of the presumptions might be tested. But the size of non-nuclear standing forces— and thus of the budget for what is identified as "general-purpose forces"— is primarily related to commitments to resist major overt aggression, and choices about the number of such contingencies. Forces that can be used to meet major contingencies can also be used in smaller contingencies. It has become as fashionable as it is obvious to assert that American non-nuclear forces can be reduced only as American commitments shrink. But this prescription neglects two further factors: contingency planning and force mixture. The Nixon Administration is reported to have examined the problem of contingency planning and to have reduced the preparedness requirement from a capability for simultaneously fighting two major wars and one minor war, to a capability for one major and one minor war at the same time. The question of the quantity and mix of forces required to deal with particular kinds of crises should be subjected to similar scrutiny.

The time is ripe for such reëvaluation for a number of reasons. First is the cost squeeze within the military budget, primarily the result of increasing unit costs and domestic needs and pressures. Second is the increasing mobility of general-purpose forces, which makes the same units available for a wide range of secondary contingencies; hence the requirements for these contingencies are not additive. Third is the fact that the chief determinant of force requirements is a psychological rather than a military variable, *i.e.* the conception in Russian minds of a credible American commitment to non-nuclear defense of Europe, and the conception in West European minds of a credible American deterrent, not only against attacks by the Soviet Union but against independent action by either of the two Germanys. This dual credibility at the non-nuclear level is important, both because of the political danger of unravelling NATO and the military danger of encouraging nuclear proliferation through European loss of confidence in non-nuclear defense. Recalculation of the forces necessary to meet the U.S. commitment in Europe may or may not produce a different result, but it should make the commitment more credible to the extent that the rationale is more realistic. The same sort of reevaluation could produce similarly useful results with respect to U.S. forces in Japan and Korea.

41 / The Concept of Collective Security

Kenneth W. Thompson

After both world wars, nations made a brave attempt to replace armaments, alliances, and interventions as major means of the international balancing process by a concept of indivisible peace. All nations would be equally

From pp. 753–766 *(passim)* of Kenneth W. Thompson, "Collective Security Reexamined," *American Political Science Review,* 27:3 (September 1953). Reprinted by permission of The American Political Science Association. Author's footnotes have been omitted.

interested and would equally participate in the maintenance and preservation of indivisible peace. Thus, all nations would place their national capabilities in the service of the global community. This concept of indivisible peace maintained by the collective effort of all peace-loving nations was named collective security. Basically, it envisioned the creation of "world police" *ad hoc* when, in the absence of a world state or government, general consensus manifests itself—also *ad hoc*. The League of Nations was the first international organization to incorporate the principle of collective security into its covenant. The United Nations modified the original concept, which was based on unanimous decision of all except the aggressor, and based collective security on the unanimity of the five great powers (U.N. Charter, Chapter VII). This hope for the enlightened dominance of the five peace-loving superpowers has so far proved unrealistic. Selection 12 contained J. G. Stoessinger's analysis of the implications of the veto provision.

From one standpoint it is a truism to say that collective security is something new under the sun. In past eras and especially in the eighteenth and nineteenth centuries, war was conceived of as a duel in which contestants should be isolated and restrained by the rest of international society. When nations engaged in armed conflict their neighbors sought to localize the struggle and alleviate its poisonous effects. However shortsighted their actions in not meeting the conflict directly and turning back aggression at its source, the nations pursuing these policies were sometimes successful for varying periods of time in preserving islands of peace in a warring world.

On August 8, 1932, however, Secretary of State Henry L. Stimson proclaimed the revolutionary fact that the modern state system was entering a new era in which warring powers were no longer entitled to the same equally impartial and neutral treatment by the rest of society. He announced to the New York Council of Foreign Relations that in future conflicts one or more of the combatants must be designated as wrong-doer and added: "We no longer draw a circle about them and treat them with the punctilios of the duelist's code. Instead we denounce them as lawbreakers."

This is the cornerstone of the universally recognized theory of collective security to which most Western statesmen profess loyalty today. . . .

In his first speech to the Senate, Harry S. Truman of Missouri declared: "The breaking of the peace anywhere is the concern of peace-loving nations everywhere." Senator Arthur H. Vandenberg announced following the San Francisco Conference in a dramatic speech to the Senate that he would support the ratification of the Charter with all the resources at his command. For, he explained: "peace must not be cheated of its collective chance. . . . We must have collective security to stop the next war, if possible, before it starts; and we must have collective action to crush it swiftly if it starts in spite of our organized precautions." . . .

It is important that we ask at the outset, then: What is collective security in theory? What are its precepts and main tenets? What, in simplest terms, is the philosophy of collective security? The rock bottom principle upon which collective security is founded provides that an attack on any one state will be regarded as an attack on all states. It finds its measure in the simple doctrine of one for all and all for one. War anywhere, in the context of Article 11 of the League of Nations, is the concern of every state.

Self-help and neutrality, it should be obvious, are the exact antithesis of such a theory. States under an order of neutrality are impartial when conflict breaks out, give their blessings to combatants to fight it out, and defer judgment regarding the justice or injustice of the cause involved. Self-help in the past was often "help yourself" so far as the great powers were concerned; they enforced their own rights and more besides. In the eighteenth and nineteenth centuries this system was fashionable and wars, although not eliminated, were localized whenever possible. In a more integrated world environment, a conflict anywhere has some effect on conditions of peace everywhere. A disturbance at one point upsets the equilibrium at all other points, and the adjustment of a single conflict restores the foundations of harmony at other points throughout the world.

This idea of collective security is simple, challenging and novel. It would do for the international society what police action does for the domestic community. If the individual is threatened or endangered in municipal society, he turns to the legitimate agents of law enforcement, the police. The comparatively successful operation of this system has meant relative peace and tolerable harmony for most local communities. Through the action of police or "fire brigades" on a world scale, collective security has as its goal two comparable objectives. It would *prevent* war by providing a deterrent to aggression. It would *defend* the interests of peace-loving states in war if it came, by concentrating a preponderance of power against the aggressor. These two ends have been the goals of both the League and the United Nations. . . .

Article 16 of the Covenant provided that any member resorting to war contrary to the Covenant had committed *ipso facto* an act of aggression against all other members. It was intended that first economic measures and then overt force should be applied against any offender. But although the international obligations of members were less ambiguous than in the Charter, there was no clear provision for their implementation or organization by a central enforcement agency. Each nation had full freedom to provide what troops it saw fit. The Council could then advise on additional measures. In contrast, Article 39 of the Charter of the United Nations commissions the Security Council to determine the existence of a threat to the peace or act of aggression and Articles 43-47 obligate the members, upon the completion of agreements, to supply troops to the Military Staff Committee. . . .

From the beginning, however, the real issue concerning collective security has had little to do with charters or compacts. The real issue has been the question of why the implementation of a system logically so flawless, and enjoying such impressive official devotion and popular support, should have been accompanied by a period of virtually unprecedented collective insecurity. It is a sobering fact that the nineteenth century was perhaps the most peaceful of modern centuries; the twentieth, by contrast, has been an epoch of unparalleled bloodshed. From 1815 to 1914 a system of old-fashioned balance of power contributed to the achievement of nearly a full century of uninterrupted peace. The past forty years have witnessed in rapid succession two great wars which the historian Arnold J. Toynbee compares to the double wars of the Romans and the Carthaginians and the two struggles of the Peloponnesian War which wrecked Hellenic Civilization. He has observed that quite possibly we have dealt ourselves the same "knockout blows" that these wars represented for the older civilizations. There were only eighteen months in the nineteenth century when France, Russia, Austria, Prussia, England and Spain found themselves at war with one another (excluding the Crimean War as a colonial struggle). By contrast, our experience thus far with the novel machinery of collective security has hardly warranted the unqualified postwar optimism of men like Mr. Hull that, with the new international organization, power politics and war were being left far behind in our progress toward utopia.

Instead the recent decades have been years of unceasing war or threats of war. What are the causes of this state of affairs? What are the reasons for the enormous gap between the theory and practice, the promise and performance of collective security? The most popular and reassuring answer has been that the radical doctrines of National Socialism and Communism have undermined the ideal system, and that modern technology has shattered the earlier limitations on conflict. Yet an equally dynamic creed challenged peace and order in the nineteenth century and provided a fighting faith for imperialist France.

The serious observer must look more deeply at the substance of political reality. In so doing he will find that collective security yesterday and today has been viewed unrealistically, and that its executors have been asked to perform tasks which could be performed with complete success only if certain objective conditions were realized. The most vital questions regarding collective security have seldom been asked; the real problems have often been evaded. The fundamental issues and problems which should have been boldly and realistically confronted have been concealed and obscured in constitutional verbiage and formal legalistic arguments. The . . . basic problems responsible for the tragic predicament of collective security include the problem of its basic preconditions [and] the political problem. . . . The first is from one standpoint most basic, for the preconditions of collective security, being frequently misunderstood, have presented the most stubborn obstacle to the maintenance of international peace.

Preconditions of Collective Security

Manifestly, collective enforcement is unattainable in the absence of appropriate international machinery and binding obligations clearly set forth in recognized legal instruments. Yet every informed citizen knows from experience that a legal arrangement imposed upon political and social conditions incompatible with its fulfillment makes successful political action difficult. Therefore it is essential in considering the reality of collective security that we understand fully its assumptions and requirements.

First, collective enforcement assumes a status quo, or situation of peace, on which the nations with predominant strength agree. In practical terms, the peace which a collective system must defend is the territorial status quo existing at the time the system is brought into being. There is nothing in past experience to indicate that all nations, or even a combination sufficiently powerful to defy the rest, will agree on the meaning of a particular status quo. Following every war, the defeated powers who feel they have suffered most by the terms of peace come to oppose the established status quo. In the aftermath of World War II, however, the question of satisfaction or dissatisfaction with the status quo has largely been superseded by an earlier and prior question. Up to the present time, no practical arrangement has been worked out acceptable to the major powers, who in this case are primarily the Soviet Union and the United States, on which the postwar status quo could be founded. The unresolved conflict between East and West has prevented the establishment of peace. Consequently, the latest experiment in collective security presents us with the anomalous picture of a system created to defend a status quo which has not yet been brought into being.

Moreover, the absence of accepted conditions of peace has been interpreted by some as a positive virtue. The wartime Secretary of State Cordell Hull argued that the League had been destroyed on the floor of the American Senate because of its intimate relationship with the Peace Treaty of Versailles. Better to establish a general international organization, he urged, and then, with passions less inflamed, work out a just and reasonable peace. James F. Byrnes, one of Mr. Hull's successors as Secretary of State in the postwar period, said that he was convinced, based upon his studies as a congressman of the proceedings of the Paris Peace Conference, that a "new approach" was essential. The negotiators at Paris had tried to settle too many difficult problems when the spirit of conflict and revenge still dominated their counsels. Mr. Byrnes prescribed a schedule of discussions in which the less controversial treaties, such as the Italian and Balkan settlements, would be negotiated first. Then the negotiators might turn from their initial successes to the more difficult questions of a German and a Japanese settlement. All agreements arrived at in this order would be introduced in the United Nations, where great and minor powers might participate in considering and amending them. In order to prevent the historic division of the nations into opponents and supporters of the postwar status quo, Mr. Byrnes reached the ingenious conclusion that: "We had to devise a system that would facilitate agreement among the major powers and at the same time provide the smaller states with ample opportunities to express their views." The newly created collective organization would intervene directly in the establishment of the postwar status quo.

In retrospect the problem inherent in the "new approach" has become plain for all to see. Its author, Mr. Byrnes, has observed: "It was a good theory. But it was faulty in one assumption." It assumed that the claims of the Soviet Union could be more readily accommodated to the vital interests of the West than has been the case. . . .

Second, collective security demands that nations subscribing to the status quo be willing and able at all times to muster overwhelming strength for collective defense at successive points of conflict. In theory, the supporters of the status quo might be capable in particular emergencies of mobilizing effective and decisive power against the single aggressor who sought to defy them. Or, by pooling the resources of all the nations in a permanently organized international force, collective enforcement could be made automatic, instantaneous, and preponderant. The former condition, however, is practically impossible of fulfillment, inasmuch as the threat to the status quo comes historically from more than one dissatisfied power or aggressor. The second condition would call for the unprecedented practice of international contingents operating under an international agency empowered to decide conclusively when and how they should be used.

The United Nations Charter seems to take a long step toward this objective by providing that all members are "to make available to the Security Council, on its call and in accordance with a special agreement or agreements, armed forces, assistance and facilities. . . . " (Article 43, Paragraph 1.) Through this provision, the incurable weakness of decentralized enforcement by which past international systems have been rendered impotent is ostensibly rectified. For the Achilles' heel of the earlier experiments was the decentralized character of the enforcement process; separate nations retained the right to determine whether or not miiltary forces would be made available to meet particular crises. In 1942, Cordell Hull had urged that "some international agency must be created which can—by force, if necessary—keep the peace. . . ." Yet Mr. Hull's proposition and Articles 43ff of the Charter, by which this historic difficulty apparently had been surmounted, in practice have remained a dead letter. No special agreements have been concluded by Members with the Security Council; talks in the Military Staff Committee soon reached an impasse. The Soviet Union has opposed proportionate contributions to an international air and naval force, which would leave it particularly vulnerable to forces overwhelmingly more powerful than its own. The United States has been concerned to make the United Nations Armed Force as strong as possible against the military preponderance of the Soviet Army in Europe and Asia, while the Russians have sought to keep it as weak as possible. It should be noted that the Russians have no monopoly on opposition to a powerful world police force. Senator Vandenberg declares in his Memoirs: "I am opposed to what is generally understood by the term 'international police force.' So, I believe, are the President, Secretary Hull and most realistic students of this problem. To be adequate, an international police force would have to be larger than the regular army and navy of any other power on earth. I think it is fantastic to believe that the people would long consent to the maintenance of any such enormous concentration of power in the postwar peace; and I also think that the temptation to reach for its ultimate control could become the greatest possible threat to peace in years to come." [Vandenberg, *Private Papers,* pp. 120-21.] The stalemate in the Military Staff Committee is fundamentally a symptom of the struggle between the two great powers and between supporters and opponents of the undefined status quo. In practice, the realization of the second condition of overwhelming strength for collective enforcement has constantly run afoul of special national demands for military security and supremacy.

There is a *third* and final prerequisite of collective security, however, to which we now turn, that was widely assumed to be in existence at the time preparations for the United Nations were first being made. It is essential to collective security in a world of unequal powers that at least the major powers enjoy a minimum of political solidarity and moral community. On October 13, 1944, Premier Stalin asked himself, in an article appearing in the Soviet *Information Bulletin,* if the world organization could be effective. He predicted that it would "be effective if the Great Powers, which have borne the brunt of the war against Hitler-Germany continue to act in a spirit of unanimity and accord."

The effectiveness of the United Nations and of the Security Council in particular was predicated upon the unanimity of the five great powers. It was an article of political faith in the Roosevelt Administration that trustworthiness and good will on the part of Americans would inspire the same qualities among the Russians. In a particularly revealing memorandum for President Harry S. Truman dated September 11, 1945, Mr. Stimson explained: "The chief lesson I have learned in a long life is that the only way you can make a man trustworthy is to trust him; and the surest way to make him untrustworthy is to distrust him and show your distrust." Unanimity among the great powers which alien ideologies and conflicting interests might otherwise undermine would be secured through the application of a code of social ethics that had in general been effective within the United States.

By October of 1947, Mr. Stimson, writing in *Foreign Affairs,* had cause to reformulate his proposition and to say: "I have often said that the surest way to make a man trustworthy is to trust him. But I must add that this does not always apply to a man who is determined to make you his dupe. Before we can make friends with the Russians, their leaders will have to be convinced that they have nothing to gain, and everything to lose, by acting on the assumption that our society is dying and that our principles are outworn." Thus the preconditions of collective security under the United Nations have either been wanting from the beginning, or have been corroded and destroyed by the all-consuming forces of the "cold war."

The Political Problem

The chief practical obstacle to collective security is the political problem deriving from the conflict of independent foreign policies. The loyalties and interests of nations participating in international organizations and collective security systems are of a different order from those of individuals taking part in the more intimate communities of the family and nation. Some years ago [Belgium's Foreign Minister] Paul Henri Spaak in an address before the Foreign Press Union declared: "There must be a hierarchy in international obligations. The nations of the continent cannot be asked to consider with the same realism and sincerity of judgment affairs which directly concern them and events which are taking place thousands of kilometres away in regions where they have neither interests nor influence. Indivisible peace, mutual assistance, and even collective security are general ideas whose practical effect must be clearly explained and clearly limited." Both individuals and nations pursue their own interests, but in some areas and on certain occasions the individual may forsake his egotistic motives for loyalty to some higher institution or nobler cause. There are institutions in integrated societies which provide common standards under which the individual can realize his aspirations. There need be no inherent conflict between an individual's private interests and his national loyalties, for the latter can often promote the realization of the former. On the other hand, conflicts are often inevitable between national and supranational loyalties, and when the projected policy of an international organization conflicts with that of a particular nation, at all times and in all places the national interest prevails. . . .

However, the pursuit of separate national interests by the various independent states presents the most troublesome issue we face in appraising collective security. The problem which impaired collective security under the League, and which was perhaps more decisive than the defection of the

United States in causing its downfall, was the unresolved conflict in the foreign policies of the principal powers. The conceptions of the national interests of France and England clashed with one another and with the principles of the League. France had one overarching objective: the absolute security of its territory. In French eyes, the one conspicuous threat it faced was Germany, which bordered France and perpetually endangered its northeastern frontier. In 1935–36, the second attack on the integrity of the League was launched with Mussolini's cruel "Rape of Ethiopia," which Il Duce preferred to describe euphemistically as a "civilizing mission." The dilemma with which France was confronted provides us with the classic instance of the political problem.

For France the sole threat against which sanctions had been prepared was Germany. Italy's aggressive action represented the wrong threat, at the wrong time, at the wrong border. Italy was the natural ally of France for, aligned with the much publicized Italian army, France hoped to balance the preponderance of the land forces of Germany, especially after Germany had moved into the Rhineland. The character of French foreign policy made it highly improbable that France could support sanctions up to the point where French loyalty to the Covenant would cost France its recent *entente* with Italy against Germany. British opinion appeared to accept this fact and Mr. Churchill observed that "the Foreign Secretary [Mr. Eden] was *justified in going as far with the League of Nations against Italy as he could carry France;* but I added that he ought not to put any pressure upon France because of her military convention with Italy and her German peroccupations; and that in the circumstances I did not expect France would go very far." In simplest terms, the choice for France was between the long range precedent which effective action might provide against the likelihood of German expansion and the immediately tangible results of not losing an ally against Germany. France compromised and sanctions were applied only half-heartedly.

The political problem also presents itself in regard to actual enforcement. Who is to apply sanctions? Who is to carry the burden of overt military action? In 1935–36, Britain alone was in a position to cut Mussolini's lines of communication and isolate his army. If genuine sanctions and force had been applied, the British navy would have shouldered the main burden. Yet there were murmurings by admirals and statesmen that the navy was ill-prepared, that there was ammunition for only about thirty minutes of fighting. British foreign policy, in contrast to that of France, directed that a stand should be taken. But the military component for action was lacking. In any enforcement action, since states are unequal, someone must bear more than his share. For this the British were unready in 1935–36.

. . . Unless nations have a margin of power beyond that essential to their survival, they can hardly be expected to share in the defense of a principle.

14

Conflict
and
Compromise

If conflicts of interest and opinion among men seem inevitable, then all effort should be made to seek solutions to such conflicts by peaceful means and mutual accommodation. Among nations such a civilized behavior means the use of diplomatic negotiations.

The possibility of settling an international issue by diplomatic negotiation depends on three factors:

1. Each of the conflicting sides must be aware that there is, first, conflict, and, second, that there is some common interest. As Fred Charles Iklé (Selection 42) notes: "Without common interest there is nothing to negotiate for, without conflict nothing to negotiate about." In other words, the issue must appear to both sides as susceptible to settlement through compromise. If one side wants what the other cannot concede even in part, "no amount of talk will make either party yield," as Hans J. Morgenthau noted, illustrating the problem of nonnegotiable issue by the following analogy.

The two women who came before King Solomon, each claiming the baby as her own, raised an issue which in its very nature could not be settled through negotiations. The issue itself called for all or nothing, and the wise King, by giving the appearance of treating it as though it could be settled by a compromise, demonstrated that it could not.[1]

It may be argued that conflicts among nations in the atomic age, however insoluble they may appear, should never be viewed as excluding settlement through compromise; any clash of interests and goals, at least among nuclear powers, is necessarily combined with one basic common interest: to avoid mutual annihilation. In our era international conflicts should be viewed, in essence, as bargaining situations, as Thomas C. Schelling argues in Selection 45. If this is so, then the second factor assumes an additional importance.

2. Policy-makers and negotiators must have not only the will but also sufficient energy, industry, and diplomatic skill. An inept ambassador may let a potential compromise slip through his fingers. As the Athenian orator and statesman Demosthenes (382-322 B.C.) noted:

> Ambassadors have no battleship at their disposal, or heavy infantry, or fortresses; their weapons are words and opportunities. . . . An ambassador who acts in a dilatory manner and causes us to miss our opportunities, is not missing opportunities only, but robbing us of the control of events.[2]

In the 1960s a former Ambassador of India to the United Nations (1954–1959) and professor of international relations similarly put an emphasis on the diligence and skill of diplomatic negotiators:

> An impatient and only moderately intelligent negotiator, or a negotiator whose timing is poor and who will be sitting at home or playing golf when the sequence of developments requires that he should be visiting his opposite numbers or refining his draft proposals, or doing both, will not help the cause of the negotiation. Of course, all negotiators must take time off and all of them have their human limitations. Yet again and again I have witnessed the effectiveness of constantly applied and alert diligence. Certainly Hammarskjöld[3] would not have been able to achieve what he did had it not been for the fact that he could work fifteen to eighteen hours a day without respite over long periods of time—and not only work long hours but be as alert at the end of his day as at the beginning.[4]

[1] Hans J. Morgenthau, "What the Big Two Can, and Can't, Negotiate," *The New York Times Magazine* (September 20, 1959), 9.

[2] Quoted by Harold Nicolson, *The Evolution of Diplomatic Method* (London: Constable and Co., Ltd., 1954), p. 13.

[3] Dag Hammarskjöld from Sweden was the second Secretary General of the United Nations (1953–1961); he was succeeded by U Thant from Burma. The first U.N. Secretary General was Trygve Lie from Norway (1946–1953).

[4] Arthur Lall, *Modern International Negotiation* (New York: Columbia University Press, 1966), p. 330.

3. There must be some direct or indirect communication between the two sides. Thomas C. Schelling (Selection 45) maintains that implicit communication may also produce results when explicit communication is impossible. In war or in a period of extreme tension, nations often are not or cannot be on speaking terms with each other. Yet, by logical deduction, guessing, or analogy, nations may become aware of their common interests, find an imaginary key to the closed door that has so far prevented any communication between them, and thus reach a *tacit* agreement or understanding and abide by it.

For the purpose of direct, constant, and intimate communications and negotiations, nations maintain in each other's capitals diplomatic missions. The establishment of embassies, legations, and consulates on a reciprocal basis is the usual consequence of mutual diplomatic recognition. Three basic assumptions underline the act of granting diplomatic recognition to a foreign government:

1. It is assumed that conflicts of interests among nations, though perhaps unavoidable, are susceptible to diplomatic solution. Logically, when diplomacy fails to provide a peaceful solution to a conflict and war ensues, diplomatic relations are severed.

2. The recognized foreign government is assumed to be capable of negotiating international agreements and abiding by them.

3. It is further assumed that the recognized government has authority over its people, institutions, and territory and is therefore deemed effective in the exercise of its power.

In theory, the diplomatic art of persuasion and compromise ends where the use or threat of violence (war or deterrence) begins. In practice, the dividing line is fluid. Diplomacy and violence often go hand in hand. The diplomatic negotiations between the United States and Communist North Vietnam, begun in 1969, continued while the changing intensity of constant fighting in Vietnam and Cambodia both shaped, and was shaped by, the Paris Conference. Wars that cannot be concluded at a battlefield as well as wars that have been won or lost are ultimately settled at a negotiating table.

One of the reasons for the simultaneity of diplomacy and violence is that harmony or conflict of interests among nations is rarely total. Good friends must sometimes engage in negotiations in order to eliminate or limit a conflict of their interests in a peripheral field so as to preserve their amity in other, more important fields. Enemies, on the other hand, sometimes negotiate and agree on marginal matters while the central area of implacable conflict remains untouched. In short, amity does not make negotiations unnecessary, and enmity does not preclude them. Statesmen and scholars derive conflicting conclusions from the possible simultaneity of partial harmony and partial conflict. Some of them point to the fact that one thousand agreements on secondary issues, dividing two enemies, cannot balance out the central conflict of vital security interests that both sides may consider worth an arms race or a war. In contrast, other observers recommend that enemy nations begin their cooperation at the periphery of their conflict and then, step by step, work toward the political center. This seemed to be the way in which the Soviet Union and United States have proceeded in the 1960s. While unwilling or incapable to solve their major conflicts in the sensitive areas of the world, from the Middle East and Vietnam to Berlin and Cuba, both superpowers have proved able to agree on many peripheral points of common interest: the suspension of atomic tests, ban on military uses of outer space and the ocean floor, cultural and trade exchanges, and a treaty on nonproliferation of nuclear weapons.[5]

Being an instrument of national policy, diplomacy is determined by rather than it determines the international political climate. For this reason diplomatic negotiations should not be credited with a greater potential than they possess: diplomacy is merely one of the remedies for international crises. Here one must warn against bewitchment by historical analogy—especially by nostalgic references to the so-called Golden Age of Diplomacy—roughly a period of one hundred years, from the final defeat of Napoleon at Waterloo (1815) to the beginning of World War I (1914). The question has been raised whether between 1815 and 1914 the art of aristocratic European diplomacy had created the "golden age" or whether it was the other way around. Charles Burton Marshall suggests that the successful performance of European diplomacy reflected but did not create the general European consensus, emerging after the final defeat of the heir of the French Revolution, Napoleon Bonaparte.[6] In the present era of emerging new nations and deep ideological cleavages, no miracles should be expected from diplomacy. The skill, industry, and dedication of professional diplomats cannot supply the will to compromise. If nations are not willing, diplomats have no other choice than to engage in empty ceremonies or, worse, in nondiplomatic name calling. In Marshall's words:

> What, most of all, distinguishes the present is a combination of unprecedented universality with unprecedented cleavages within the diplomatic framework— and therein lies a central part of the problem of order confronting diplomacy. . . . The proliferation of states without determined political character but with

[5] The treaty to halt the spread of atomic weapons and forbidding the existing nuclear powers to help other nations to enter the five-member "nuclear club" went into effect on March 5, 1970, when forty-seven nations deposited their instruments of ratification. Two nuclear powers refused to sign the treaty, China and France. Some states with nuclear potential hesitated to sign the treaty: India, Israel, Pakistan, Brazil, Argentina, and South Africa. On the other hand, some states with nuclear potential did commit themselves to the principle of nonproliferation: West Germany, Japan, Canada, Czechoslovakia, Sweden, and the United Arab Republic.

[6] Charles Burton Marshall, "The Golden Age in Perspective," Journal of International Affairs, 17:1 (1963), 13.

ambition to play a role in history occurs in a world already deeply riven over the meaning of history and, therefore, the character of a legitimate order. I refer to the confrontation called the Cold War. The interplay between that division and the sudden vast extension of diplomacy—a unification without unity—is truly unprecedented. "Never before have states belonging to the same diplomatic system differed as they differ today," according to Aron. "Never before have people involved in a common enterprise been so disunited on fundamental issues."[7]

Among nations it is sometimes difficult to ascertain at what point exactly a seemingly irreconcilable conflict has been transformed by the contending parties into a reluctant partnership, or, on the contrary, at what point friendship has collapsed under the impact of a new clash of interests and suspicion. Was, for instance, the Soviet-Nazi summit meeting in Moscow on the eve of World War II or the Soviet-American summit meeting at Yalta on the eve of the end of World War II the beginning of possible friendship (spoiled by subsequent events) or a cynically temporary cooperation between implacable enemies for the purpose of attainment of transient common goals? Or did President Nixon's initiative with regard to Mao's China in 1971 signal a truly new era in the relationship between the United States and the communist world or only a relatively short intermission in the continuing drama of an irreconcilable conflict?

Nations seem to move from conflict to cooperation and back with a lesser embarrassment than do individuals in family feuds or interpersonal relations. A pessimist is bound to deplore the ease with which international amity may change into violent conflict. An optimist rejoices that the reverse is also sometimes true and that new events, a new look at the situation, and diplomacy may transform enemies into partners and even friends.

42 / What Is Negotiation?

Fred Charles Iklé

Negotiation, like war, is only a tool of policy. It can be used on the side of angels as well as by the forces of darkness. It may settle conflicts short

[7] *Ibid.,* p. 15.

of war, divert governments from the use of force, or terminate fighting before destruction becomes complete. Yet, it may also prepare the way for aggression or be part of a blackmail. Iklé examines different aspects of diplomatic negotiations in his study *How Nations Negotiate*. The following excerpts are reproduced from that study.

Certain subjects seem quite clear as long as we leave them alone. The answers look obvious until we ask questions, the concepts appear to be well understood until we wish to define them, causes and effects are easily recognized until we seek to explain them, and all the rules pass for valid until we try to prove them. The social scientist, alas, shares the honor with the philosopher of often moving in his inquiries from the obvious to the obscure. Of course, he hopes to go beyond and to emerge with a clearer view of the whole and a better knowledge of the details than he first had on the basis of folklore and common sense. But to begin with, he must challenge the old answers with new questions.

Negotiation is a subject on which much has been said and written that seems self-evident until examined more closely. To resolve conflict and avoid the use of force, it is said, one must negotiate (Is this always the best way to settle conflict?). Negotiation requires a willingness to compromise (Why?), and both sides must make concessions (According to which law?). Neither side can expect to win all it wants (Not even if its objectives are modest?). If both sides negotiate in good faith (Who judges "good faith"?), they can always find a fair solution (And what is "fair"?). If there is a conflict about many issues, the less controversial ones should be solved first because agreement will lead to further agreement (Or will the postponed issues become harder to solve?). A negotiator should never make a threat he is not prepared to carry out (What is wrong with successful bluffing?). Each side has its minimum beyond which it cannot be moved (But how about moving the opponent's minimum?).

This book is concerned with the process and effects of negotiation between governments; in particular, it seeks to relate the *process* of negotiation to the *outcome*. To begin with, two elements must normally be present for negotiation to take place: there must be both common interests and issues of conflict. Without common interest there is nothing to negotiate for, without conflict nothing to negotiate about.

There are many ways in which governments—always subject to change, idosyncrasy, and pressure from within—relate their common interests to their conflicting interests. They may be isolationist and try to stay apart to avoid all conflict, while sacrificing the pursuit of possible common interests. Or they may simply follow habits and rules that regulate their interests and conflicts automatically without bargaining. The observance of some diplomatic practices is of this character. (So is routine buying and selling at fixed prices.) But usually a government takes account of the fact that its interests and its ability to pursue national objectives are influenced by decisions of other nations. Likewise it realizes that these other nations will be affected by its own decisions. It may try to coordinate this interaction without explicitly saying so—a process of "tacit bargaining." Or it may communicate with other governments for the explicit purpose of working out a particular combination of conflicting and common interests; that is, to reach an agreement.

One should perhaps distinguish between two kinds of common interests: a *substantive common interest* in a single arrangement or object, and a *complementary interest* in an exchange of different objects. In the substantive common interest, the parties want to share the *same* object or benefit from the same arrangement, which, however, they can bring about only by joining together. Hence they have to agree on the object's characteristics (concerning which they may have different preferences) and on the division of the costs and gains (where their interests are likely to conflict). Examples of agreements on such substantive common interests are the U.S.-Canadian treaty on the St. Lawrence Seaway, international fishery agreements to protect the supply of fish, and, in a sense, cease-fire agreements.

When parties are interested in an exchange, they want *different* things. These they cannot obtain by themselves but can only grant to each other. The clearest examples are barters and sales. Similarly, commercial aviation agreements, where each country wants to have its planes fly to the other country, have the purpose of settling an exchange. So do agreements for mutual tariff concessions.

In reality, however, most negotiations embrace a combination of substantive common interests and complementary interests. When the six European countries set up the European Economic Community, they had complementary interests in the exchange of tariff concessions and common interests in a large, unified European market. The nuclear test-ban treaty between the United States and the Soviet Union can satisfy the complementary interest in slowing down the opponent's development of new weapons and the common interest in preventing an increase in radioactive fallout or in discouraging the proliferation of nuclear weapons. Whether the substantive common interests or the complementary interests dominate depends on how the purposes of the agreement are defined.

The process by which two or more parties relate conflicting to common interests is the warp and woof not only of international relations but of human society; individuals, groups, and governments engage in it all the time. We become aware of it only when we call it something special—like Molière's Monsieur Jourdain when he discovered that for forty years he had been speaking "prose." There seems to be no established term for all the ways in which parties with conflicting and common interests interact—whether explicitly or tacitly—though "bargaining" is sometimes used that broadly.

"Negotiation" in a narrower sense denotes a process that is different from tacit bargaining or other behavior that regulates conflict. As used here, *negotiation is a process in which explicit proposals are put forward ostensibly for the purpose of reaching agreement on an exchange or on the realization of a common interest where conflicting interests are present.* Frequently, these proposals deal not only with the terms of agreement but also with the topics to be discussed (the agenda), with the ground rules that ought to apply, and with underlying technical and legal issues. It is the confrontation of explicit proposals that distinguishes negotiation (as here defined) from tacit bargaining and other types of conflict behavior. Beyond this confrontation appear other moves that the negotiating parties make to strengthen their own position, to weaken that of the opponent, or to influence the outcome in other ways. The subject matter of this book includes all these moves and the ways in which they relate to the outcome. That is, bargaining moves are included in the broader sense, to the extent that they serve pending or ongoing negotiations where explicit proposals are being put forward.

Only part of the frequent changes in relations between countries are the result of negotiation. Governments often revise their expectations and attitudes toward other countries as a result of unilateral actions or tacit bargains. Military and technological developments, growth or decline in economic strength, and internal political changes continually cause the rearrangement of conflicting and common interests between nations, and this happens whether or not diplomats negotiate.

There is no simple rule as to when negotiation is needed, and when tacit bargaining or even less conscious confrontations are more effective to restructure international relations. For certain arrangements negotiation clearly cannot be dispensed with; for others it is optional; and there are some issues which are better settled without it.

Negotiation is necessary for any arrangement that establishes complicated forms of collaboration, such as a joint war effort or Britain's attempted entry into the Common Market. (In contrast, the entry of, say, the Ivory Coast into the United Nations did not require significant negotiations.) Negotiation is needed for most exchanges, such as exchanges of prisoners or the granting of mutual consular facilities, and for all transactions involving monetary compensation, as in the payment of oil royalties or the leasing of air bases. Negotiation is, of course, necessary for the setting up of formal international institutions and for any arrangement where an *explicit* agreement is essential, such as a peace treaty or an alliance system.

On the other hand, certain undertakings are arrived at in such a delicate way that explicit proposals might interfere with the process. The mutually observed restrictions in the Korean War (for instance, no attacks on the supply lines leading into North and South Korea) is an example of arrangements that would not have been facilitated or might even have been upset by negotiation. The very uncertainties of a tacit understanding may have made these restrictions more stable, because both sides were unwilling to probe and push toward the limits of the "bargain," lest it all be upset. The negotiation of an explicit *quid pro quo* might have given rise to new demands and invited more haggling and tugging than the arrangement which the parties never discussed and never explicitly settled. Furthermore, while soldiers were being killed fighting the enemy, negotiations to establish rules and restraints for the battle or on the interdiction of supplies would have clashed with domestic opinion and perhaps adversely affected the morale of the troops.[8]

Likewise, if there is a deep-seated hostility between the populations of two countries, governments may be unable to negotiate because of public opposition but may work out some arrangements of mutual interest through tacit bargaining. The relationship between Jordan and Israel is an example.

In the field of arms control and disarmament, where we have become so accustomed to large and formal conferences, important understandings can at times be arrived at without negotiation. Formal talks might, in fact, make it more difficult to harmonize some arms policies insofar as they inevitably introduce political issues or questions of prestige and legal precedents.

Negotiation plays an important role in formalizing turning points in international relations, in catalyzing or at least clarifying changes that were caused by tacit bargaining or other processes, and in working out those finer shades in new arrangements between nations that the brute interplay of latent strength cannot define.

Although negotiation is necessary for any new relationship that is based on explicit agreement, an explicit agreement is usually only part of the outcome of negotiation. Negotiation may change the positions of the parties and their mutual relations in many other ways. The outcome may include, for example, tacit understandings between the parties, a clarification of the points of disagreement, a reorientation of national objectives, new commitments to third parties (allies, domestic groups, or world opinion), and propaganda effects. Many of these results may outweigh in importance whatever explicit agreement is arrived at. And even agreements themselves vary widely in their degree of specificity and the amount of disagreement that they leave unsettled.

[8] A pioneering analysis of the role of tacit bargaining in limited war is given by Thomas C. Schelling, *The Strategy of Conflict* [See Selection 45.——Ed.].

43 / Open Covenants Secretly Arrived At

Harold Nicolson

In the following selection a British historian, politician, and professional diplomat of world fame addresses himself to the problem of appropriate diplomatic method. In this age small nations and microstates as well as great powers tend to conduct "diplomacy" by loudspeaker, insult, and vote despite the fact that the voting strength of small nations is so blatantly disproportionate to their collective capacity to act. Sir Harold Nicolson recommends a return to some aspects of the old European diplomacy, which was based on the generally accepted rule that sound negotiations should be confidential, continuous, and courteous. In this context he attacks the first of Woodrow Wilson's Fourteen Points of January 8, 1918 (the fourteen principles of peace to be based on the allied victory), according to which nations emerging from World War I should commit themselves not only to "open covenants" but to "covenants *openly* arrived at after which there shall be no private understanding of any kind but diplomacy shall proceed always frankly and in public view" (*Italics added*).

. . . [T]he distinctive characteristics of the old diplomacy [were:] the conception of Europe as a centre of international gravity; the idea that the Great Powers, constituting the Concert of Europe, were more important and more responsible than the Small Powers; the existence in every country of a trained diplomatic service possessing common standards of professional conduct; and the assumption that negotiation must always be a process rather than an episode, and that at every stage it must remain confidential. . . .

. . . Every negotiation consists of stages and a result; if the stages become matters of public controversy before the result has been achieved, the negotiation will almost certainly founder. A negotiation is the subject of concession and counter-concession: if the concession offered is divulged before the public are aware of the corresponding concession to be received, extreme agitation may follow and the negotiation may have to be abandoned. The necessity of negotiation remaining confidential has never been more forcibly expressed than by M. Jules Cambon, perhaps the best professional

From pp. 72–91 *(passim)* of Harold Nicolson, *The Evolution of Diplomatic Method* (London: Constable and Co., Ltd., 1954). Reprinted with permission of the Literary Executor to Sir Harold Nicolson and the publisher.

diplomatist of this century. "The day secrecy is abolished," writes M. Cambon, "negotiation of any kind will become impossible." . . .

The speeding up of communications has certainly done much to alter the old methods of negotiation. In former days it took many months before a dispatch could be received and answered and ambassadors abroad were expected to use their own initiative and judgment in carrying out the policy outlined in the instructions they had received on leaving home. Some ambassadors profited by this latitude to pursue a personal policy. "I never," wrote Lord Malmesbury, "received an instruction that was worth reading." . . . Yet . . . most ambassadors during the period of slow communications were so terrified of exceeding their instructions or of assuming an initiative that might embarrass their home government, that they adopted a purely passive attitude, missed opportunity after opportunity, and spent their time writing brilliant reports on situations that had entirely altered by the time their dispatches arrived.

Today a Foreign Secretary from his desk in Downing Street can telephone to six ambassadors in the course of one morning or can even descend upon them quite suddenly from the sky. Does this mean that a diplomatist today is no more than a clerk at the end of a line? . . .

No, it was not the telephone that, from 1919 onwards, brought about the transition from the old diplomacy to the new. It was the belief that it was possible to apply to the conduct of *external* affairs, the ideas and practices which, in the conduct of *internal* affairs, had for generations been regarded as the essentials of liberal democracy.

It was inevitable, after the first World War, that some such experiment should be made. On the one hand, the ordinary citizen, being convinced that the masses in every country shared his own detestation of war, attributed the breach of the peace to the vice or folly of a small minority, which must in future be placed under democratic control. On the other hand, when the Americans arrived as the dominant partners in the coalition, they brought with them their dislike of European instituions, their distrust of diplomacy, and their missionary faith in the equality of man.

President Wilson was an idealist and, what was perhaps more dangerous, a consummate master of English prose. He shared with Robespierre the hallucination that there existed some mystic bond between himself and "The People,"—by which he meant not only the American people but the British, French, Italian, Rumanian, Jugo-Slav, Armenian, and even German peoples. If only he could penetrate the fog-barrier of governments, politicians and officials and convey the sweetness and light of his revelation to the ordinary peasant in the Banat, to the shepherds of Albania, or the dock-hands of Fiume, then reason, concord and amity would spread in ever widening circles across the earth. He possessed, moreover, the gift of giving to commonplace ideas the resonance and authority of biblical sentences, and, like all phraseologists, he became mesmerised by the strength and neatness of the phrases that he devised. During the long months of the Paris Peace Conference, I observed him with interest, admiration and anxiety, and became convinced that he regarded himself, not as a world statesman, but as a prophet designated to bring light to a dark world. It may have been for this reason that he forgot all about the American Constitution and Senator Lodge.

I have no desire at all to denigrate President Wilson, who was in many ways inspiring and inspired. He assumed a weight of responsibility greater than any single human being is constituted to support, and he was tragically crushed. Yet if we read again the tremendous sermons that he delivered during 1918 we shall find in them the seeds of the jungle of chaos that today impedes and almost obliterates the processes of rational negotiation. Let me, therefore, remind you, for a moment, of some of the Fourteen Points, the Four Principles, the Four Ends, and the Five Particulars.

The first of the Fourteen Points of January 8, 1918, provided that in future there should be nothing but "open covenants of peace openly arrived at," and that "diplomacy should proceed always frankly and in the public view." On reaching Paris, President Wilson quickly decided that by "diplomacy" he had not meant "negotiation," but only the results of that negotiation, namely treaties. He also decided that the phrases "openly arrived at" and "in the public view" were relative only and contained nothing that need deter him from conducting prolonged secret negotiations with Lloyd George and Clemenceau, while one American marine stood with fixed bayonet at the study door, and another patrolled the short strip of garden outside. I can well recall how startled I was, on first being admitted to the secret chamber, to discover how original was the President's interpretation of his own first rule. Today, being much older, I realize that the method he adopted was the only possible method which, in the circumstances, could have led to any result.

The general public, however, were not similarly constrained to test the validity of the President's pronouncements against the hard facts of international intercourse. They continued to assume that by "diplomacy" was meant both policy and negotiation, and to conclude that, since secret treaties were demonstrably evil things, negotiation also must never be secret but conducted always "in the public view." This is perhaps the most confusing of all the fallacies that we owe to President Wilson.

44 / The Pentagon Papers

Justice Potter Stewart
Justice Byron R. White
Justice John M. Harlan
Justice Hugo L. Black
Justice Harry A. Blackmun

The formula "open covenants secretly arrived at" is supposed to separate commitment to policy from negotiations. The government's commitment to international obligation or action must be made public in a free society to keep leaders accountable to the people, but diplomacy should be quiet and confidential to ensure success. The formula, however, does not offer a clear answer to the question of the time at which the public should be informed about an impending international commitment or action. Evidently it should be informed *before* it is too late for remedy but, on the other hand, not prematurely since publicity may reveal vital secrets to the enemy or jeopardize delicate negotiations. Foreign policy does not consist of unrelated and isolated actions but more often than not represents a continuum in which action, policy, and diplomacy are intricately intertwined. In practical terms, who can reliably determine what is "too late" and what is "premature" and by what means? The tendency of governments is to be on the safe side and classify as secret what the public could and should know.

The issue of "an open war secretly arrived at" was placed at the very center of American politics in 1971 in connection with the long and unsuccessful war in Vietnam.

In 1967 Robert S. McNamara, who was then the Secretary of Defense, commissioned what has since become known as the *Pentagon Papers*, a massive, top-secret history of the United States involvement in Indochina. The work, which took a year and a half to compile, consists of approximately 3,000 pages of narrative history and more than 4,000 pages of appended documents. The 47 volumes cover the involvement of four successive Administrations (Truman, Eisenhower, Kennedy, and Johnson) in the former French Indochina territory from World War II to May 1968, the month the peace talks began in Paris.

The New York Times obtained most of the documents and began publishing a series of articles based on them on June 13, 1971. After the first three daily installments appeared, the U.S. Department of Justice obtained a temporary restraining order against further publication from a federal district court in New York. The government's contention was that public dissemination of the secret Pentagon study would cause "immediate and irreparable harm" to the defense interests and security of the United States. A federal judge in the District of Columbia defined "harm" to mean "the death of soldiers, and destruction of alliances, the greatly increased difficulty of negotiation with our enemies, [and] the inability of our diplomats to negotiate."

The issue was fought through the courts for fifteen days. On June 30, 1971, the Supreme Court of the United States allowed *The Times* and other newspapers involved to continue publication of the Pentagon documents by a vote of 6 to 3.

Has the ruling of the Court, in fact, endorsed President Wilson's formula according to which diplomacy should "proceed always frankly and in public view"? Hardly. As the following excerpt indicates, the majority of the Court that had ruled in favor of the mass media did so for six different reasons and, with the exception of Justices Douglas and Black, the ruling certainly cannot be construed as a guarantee of an unqualified, absolute freedom of the press, regardless of circumstances. If in the future an immediate threat of an irreparable harm to the nation's security can be proved, the conflict between the freedom of the press and the government's duty to protect the nation's survival by secrecy remains as unresolved as before.

The ambiguity of the Court was subsequently matched by a similar ambivalence toward governmental secrets on the part of the mass media. The same media that had vehemently condemned the excessive governmental secrecy in the case of Vietnam expressed a general approval of, if not admiration for, the deceitful way in which the trip by Henry A. Kissinger to Peking had been arranged and his secret negotiation with Chou En-lai conducted. Paradoxically, the new secret attempt at a rapprochement between China and the United States was made at the same time that the national controversy on the subject of governmental secrecy had reached its peak. Ironically, it was the vice-president and columnist of *The New York Times,* James Reston, who, in his conversation with Premier Chou in Peking on August 6, 1971, said: "If we leave [the solution of world problems] to journalists, the world will be in a mess. It has to get down to quiet diplomacy."

The following excerpt reproduces a conflict of views among the members of the Supreme Court when called upon to determine whether the classified documents, illegally appropriated by a research specialist at M.I.T., Dr. Daniel Ellsberg, could be published by the press, or whether the government had the right then—or ever—to prevent the publication of governmental secrets. The full text of the judicial opinions, reproduced below, as well as the whole series of *The New York Times* articles and selected Pentagon documents, may be found in a paperback edition, published by Bantam Books, under the title *The Pentagon Papers as Published by The New York Times.*

Justice Potter Stewart

In the governmental structure created by our Constitution, the executive is endowed with enormous power in the two related areas of national defense and international relations. This power, largely unchecked by the legislative and judicial branches, has been pressed to the very hilt since the advent of the nuclear missile age. For better or for worse, the simple fact is that a President of the United States possesses vastly greater constitutional independence in these two vital areas of power than does, say, a prime minister of a country with a parliamentary form of government.

In the absence of the governmental checks and balances present in other areas of our national life, the only effective restraint upon executive policy and power in the areas of national defense and international affairs may lie in an enlightened citizenry—in an informed and critical public opinion which alone can here protect the values of democratic government. For this reason, it is perhaps here that a press that is alert, aware, and free most vitally serves the basic purpose of the First Amendment. For without an informed and free press there cannot be an enlightened people.

Yet it is elementary that the successful conduct of international diplomacy and the maintenance of an effective national defense require both confidentiality and secrecy. Other nations can hardly deal with this nation in an atmosphere of mutual trust unless they can be assured that their confidences will be kept. And within our own executive departments, the development of considered and intelligent international policies would be impossible if those charged with their formulation could not communicate with each other freely, frankly, and in confidence. In the area of basic national defense the frequent need for absolute secrecy is, of course, self-evident.

I think there can be but one answer to this dilemma, if dilemma it be. The responsibility must be where the power is. If the Constitution gives the executive a large degree of unshared power in the conduct of foreign affairs and the maintenance of our national defense, then under the Constitution the executive must have the largely unshared duty to determine and preserve the degree of internal security necessary to exercise that power successfully. It is an awesome responsibility, requiring judgment and wisdom of a high order. I should suppose that moral, political, and practical considerations would dictate that a very first principle of that wisdom would be an insistence upon avoiding secrecy for its own sake.

For when everything is classified, then nothing is classified, and the system becomes one to be disregarded by the cynical or the careless, and to be manipulated by those intent on self-protection or self-promotion. I should suppose, in short, that the hallmark of a truly effective international security system would be the maximum possible disclosure, recognizing that secrecy can best be preserved only when credibility is truly maintained. But be that as it may, it is clear to me that it is the constitutional duty of the executive—as a matter of sovereign prerogative and not as a matter of law as the courts know law—through the promulgation and enforcement of executive regulations, to protect the confidentiality necessary to carry out its responsibilities in the fields of international relations and national defense.

This is not to say that Congress and the courts have no role to play. Undoubtedly Congress has the power to enact specific and appropriate criminal laws to protect Government property and preserve Government secrets. Congress has passed such laws, and several of them are of very colorable relevance to the apparent circumstances of these cases, and if a criminal prosecution is instituted, it will be the responsibility of the courts to decide the applicability of the criminal law under which the charge is brought. Moreover, if Congress should pass a specific law authorizing civil proceedings in this field, the courts would likewise have the duty to decide the constitutionality of such a law as well as its applicability to the facts proved.

But in the cases before us we are asked, instead, to perform a function that the Constitution gave to the executive, not the judiciary. We are asked, quite simply, to prevent the publication by two newspapers of material that the executive branch insists should not, in the national interest, be published. I am convinced that the executive is correct with respect to some of the documents involved. But I cannot say that disclosure of any of them will surely result in direct, immediate, and irreparable damage to our nation or its people. That being so, there can under the First Amendment be but one judicial resolution of the issues before us.

I join the judgments of the court.

Justice Byron R. White

I concur in today's judgments, but only because of the concededly extraordinary protection against prior restraints enjoyed by the press under our constitutional system. I do not say that in no circumstances would the First Amendment permit an injunction against publishing information about Government plans or operations. Nor, after examining the materials the Government characterizes as the most sensitive and destructive, can I deny that revelation of these documents will do substantial damage to public interests. Indeed, I am confident that their disclosure will have that result. But I nevertheless agree that the United States has not satisfied the very heavy burden which it must meet to warrant an injunction against publication in these cases, at least in the absence of express and appropriately limited Congressional authorization for prior restraints in circumstances such as these.

Justice John M. Harlan

Forced as I am to reach the merits of these cases, I dissent from the opinion and judgments of the Court. Within the severe limitations imposed by the time constraints under which I have been required to operate, I can only state my reasons in telescoped form, even though in different circumstances I would have felt constrained to deal with the cases in the fuller sweep indicated above. . . .

. . . It is plain to me that the scope of the judicial function in passing upon the activities of the executive branch of the Government in the field of foreign affairs is very narrowly restricted. This view is, I think, dictated by the concept of separation of powers upon which our constitutional system rests.

In a speech on the floor of the House of Representatives, Chief Justice John Marshall, then a member of that body, stated:

> The President is the sole organ of the nation in its external relations, and its sole representative with foreign nations. *(Annals,* 6th Cong., Col. 613 (1800).)

From that time, shortly after the founding of the nation, to this, there has been no substantial challenge to this description of the scope of executive power. See *United States* v. *Curtiss-Wright Export Corp.,* 299 U.S. 304, 319–321 (1936), collecting authorities.

From this constitutional primacy in the field of foreign affairs, it seems to me that certain conclusions necessarily follow. Some of these were stated concisely by President Washington, declining the request of the House of Representatives for the papers leading up to the negotiation of the Jay Treaty:

> The nature of foreign negotiations requires caution, and their success must often depend on secrecy; and even when brought to a conclusion a full disclosure of all the measures, demands, or eventual concessions which may have been proposed or contemplated would be extremely impolitic; for this might have a pernicious influence on future negotiations, or produce immediate inconveniences, perhaps danger and mischief, in relation to other powers. (J. Richardson, "Messages and Papers of the Presidents" 194–195 (1899).)

But in my judgment the judiciary may not properly go beyond these two inquiries and redetermine for itself the probable impact of disclosure on the national security.

> The very nature of executive decisions as to foreign policy is political, not judicial. Such decisions are wholly confided by our Constitution to the political departments of the Government, executive and legislative. They are delicate, complex, and involve large elements of prophecy. They are and should be undertaken only by those directly responsible to the people whose welfare they advance or imperil. They are decisions of a kind for which the judiciary has neither aptitude, facilities, nor responsibility and which has long been held to belong in the domain of political power not subject to judicial intrusion or in-

quiry. (*Chicago & Southern Air Lines* v. *Waterman Steamship Corp.,* 333 U.S. 103, 111 (1948) (Jackson, J.).)

Even if there is some room for the judiciary to override the executive determination, it is plain that the scope of review must be exceedingly narrow. . . .

Justice Hugo L. Black

I adhere to the view that the Government's case against *The Washington Post* should have been dismissed and that the injunction against *The New York Times* should have been vacated without oral argument when the cases were first presented to this Court. I believe that every moment's continuance of the injunctions against these newspapers amounts to a flagrant, indefensible and continuing violation of the First Amendment. Furthermore, after oral arguments, I agree completely that we must affirm the judgment of the Court of Appeals for the District of Columbia and reverse the judgment of the Court of Appeals for the Second Circuit for the reasons stated by my brothers Douglas and Brennan. In my view it is unfortunate that some of my brethren are apparently willing to hold that the publication of news may sometimes be enjoined. Such a holding would make a shambles of the First Amendment.

Our Government was launched in 1789 with the adoption of the Constitution. The Bill of Rights, including the First Amendment, followed in 1791. Now, for the first time in the 182 years since the founding of the Republic, the Federal courts are asked to hold that the First Amendment does not mean what it says, but rather means that the Government can halt the publication of current news of vital importance to the people of this country. . . .

. . . Both the history and language of the First Amendment support the view that the press must be left free to publish news, whatever the source, without censorship, injunctions or prior restraints.

In the First Amendment the Founding Fathers gave the free press the protection it must have to fulfill its essential role in our democracy. The press was to serve the governed, not the governors. The Government's power to censor the press was abolished so that the press would remain forever free to censure the Government. The press was protected so that it could bare the secrets of government and inform the people. Only a free and unrestrained press can effectively expose deception in government. And paramount among the responsibilities of a free press is the duty to prevent any part of the Government from deceiving the people and sending them off to distant lands to die of foreign fevers and foreign shot and shell. In my view, far from deserving condemnation for their courageous reporting, *The New York Times, The Washington Post,* and other news-papers should be commended for serving the purpose that the Founding Fathers saw so clearly. In revealing the workings of government that led to the Vietnam war, the newspapers nobly did precisely that which the founders hoped and trusted they would do.

Justice Harry A. Blackmun

Two Federal District Courts, two United States Courts of Appeals, and this Court—within a period of less than three weeks from inception until today—have been pressed into hurried decision of profound con-stitutional issues on inadequately developed and largely assumed facts without the careful deliberation that, hopefully, should characterize the American judicial process. There has been much writing about the law and little knowledge and less digestion of the facts. In the New York case the judges, both trial and appellate, had not yet examined the basic ma-terial when the case was brought here. In the District of Columbia case, little more was done, and what was accomplished in this respect was only on required remand, with *The Washington Post,* on the excuse that it was trying to protect its source of information, initially refusing to reveal what material it actually possessed, and with the District Court forced to make assumptions as to that possession.

With such respect as may be due to the contrary view, this, in my opinion, is not the way to try a lawsuit of this magnitude and asserted importance. It is not the way for Federal Courts to adjudicate, and to be required to adjudicate, issues that allegedly concern the nation's vital welfare. The country would be none the worse off were the cases tried quickly, to be sure, but in the customary and properly deliberative manner. The most recent of the material, it is said, dates no later than 1968, already about three years ago, and *The Times* itself took three months to formulate its plan of procedure and, thus, deprived its public for that period.

The First Amendment, after all, is only one part of an entire Constitu-tion. Article II of the great document vests in the executive branch primary power over the conduct of foreign affairs and places in that branch the responsibility for the nation's safety.

Each provision of the Constitution is important, and I cannot subscribe to a doctrine of unlimited absolutism for the First Amendment at the cost of downgrading other provisions.

First Amendment absolutism has never commanded a majority of this court. . . . What is needed here is a weighing, upon properly developed standards, of the broad right of the press to print and of the very narrow right of the Government to prevent. Such standards are not yet developed. The parties here are in disagreement as to what those standards should be. But even the newspapers concede that there are situations where restraint is in order and is constitutional. Mr. Justice Holmes gave us a suggestion when he said in Schenck:

> It is a question of proximity and degree. When a nation is at war many things that might be said in time of peace are such a hindrance to its effort that their utterance will not be endured so long as men fight and that no court could regard them as protected by any constitutional right. (249 U.S., at 52.)

It may well be that if these cases were allowed to develop as they should be developed, and to be tried as lawyers should try them and as courts should hear them, free of pressure and panic and sensationalism, other light would be shed on the situation and contrary considerations, for me, might prevail. But that is not the present posture of the litigation.

The Court, however, decides the cases today the other way. I therefore add one final comment.

I strongly urge, and sincerely hope, that these two newspapers will be fully aware of their ultimate responsibilities to the United States of America. Judge Wilkey, dissenting in the District of Columbia case, after a review of only the affidavits before this Court (the basic papers had not then been made available by either party), concluded that there were a number of examples of documents that, if in the possession of *The Post,* and if published, "could clearly result in great harm to the nation," and he defined "harm" to mean "the death of soldiers, and destruction of alliances, the greatly increased difficulty of negotiation with our enemies, the inability of our diplomats to negotiate. . . ." I, for one, have now been able to give at least some cursory study not only to the affidavits, but to the material itself. I regret to say that from this examination I fear that Judge Wilkey's statements have possible foundation. I therefore share his concern. I hope that damage already has not been done.

If, however, damage has been done, and if, with the Court's action today, these newspapers proceed to publish the critical documents and there results therefrom "the death of soldiers, the destruction of alliances, the greatly increased difficulty of negotiation with our enemies, the inability of our diplomats to negotiate," to which list I might add the factors of prolongation of the war and of further delay in the freeing of United States prisoners, then the nation's people will know where the responsibility for these sad consequences rests.

45 / Tacit Coordination of Expectations and Behavior

Thomas C. Schelling

Foreign policy decisions usually reflect the outcome of a prior process of political calculations in which national leaders weigh the advantages and the disadvantages that are likely to result from their adoption of one of available alternative courses of action. International conflicts in which the participants act *rationally* to optimize their choices in the face of their opponents, who are also expected to behave rationally and optimize their choices, are susceptible to game-theory analysis. Game theory is a mathematical technique for the analysis of the logic and strategy of conflict (games of strategy). The term game is not employed here in its ordinary sense, even if some relationship to poker or chess may be recognized. As Morton Kaplan noted, "many objections to the theory of games stem from a misplaced objection to its ordinary connotations of 'playful,' 'frivolous,' and so forth." [9] Knowledge of game theory does not make a national leader a better strategist. Game theory is not primarily concerned with advising the optimum strategy for any particular conflict, but merely with its logic. Its technique of logical and mathematical analysis may give "men an opportunity to bring conflicts of interest up from the level of fights, where the intellect is beclouded by passions, to the level of games, where the intellect has a chance to operate." [10]

The focal point is, of course, rationality, a controversial concept in itself (see also Selection 37 by Philip Green). Rationality requires that each participant has a set of mutually consistent and relatively well-defined policy objectives and should not try to run in two different or even opposite directions at the same time. Rationality also requires that national leaders choose strategies consistent with the expectations they can rationally entertain about other leaders' behavior. This assumption of rational expectation and rational behavior, if taken quite literally, is certainly unrealistic, as John C. Harsanyi pointed out, with the following warning and observation:

From pp. 19–36 *(passim)* of Thomas C. Schelling, "Bargaining, Communication, and Limited War," *The Journal of Conflict Resolution*, 1:1 (March 1957). Reprinted by permission of the Journal and the author whose help in abridging his essay for this volume is gratefully acknowledged. The article forms the basis of Chapter 5 in Schelling's book *The Strategy of Conflict* (New York: Oxford University Press, 1960). Some author's footnotes have been omitted.

[9] Morton A. Kaplan, "A Note on Game Theory and Bargaining" in Morton A. Kaplan (Ed.), *New Approaches to International Relations* (New York: St. Martin's, Inc., 1968), p. 486.

[10] Anatol Rappoport, "The Use and Misuse of Game Theory," *Scientific American*, 207:6 (1962), 108.

Policy makers are human and therefore occasionally make mistakes. Moreover their policy objectives are seldom quite consistent. For one thing, when people have to choose between two or more very unpleasant alternatives, they often find it very hard to make up their minds and follow any of these policies in a consistent manner. For another thing, every policy maker is subject to conflicting pressures from his own constituents, and these may make it very difficult for him to adopt any unambiguous policy line. For instance, both in international and in internal politics, one often has to choose between trying to reach a mutually acceptable *agreement* with one's opponents, and trying to keep them in check by mere superior *strength*. But usually the worst possible policy is to antagonize and provoke one's enemies even further without the will and the ability to face a showdown with him. Yet this is precisely the irrational policy that many countries have often been following against countries unfriendly to them.[11]

In the following analysis, Thomas C. Schelling applies the technique of logic to conflict situations in which there is minimal or imperfect communication between adversaries—a frequent case in international politics in peace and war. Yet, even in such situations logic and guessing may discover a key that will permit the adversaries to coordinate their respective rational expectations about each other's behavior, behave accordingly, and so limit war or bring a dangerous situation under reasonable control. The possibility of such tacit or implicit agreement between noncommunicating rivals can be demonstrated in the case of the Sino-American limited war in Korea. Schelling's analysis further assumes that most international conflicts are nonzero-sum games [12] in which the gain of one does not imply the loss for the other, and vice versa.

The problem of opening direct communications with an adversary with whom a nation had only "tacitly bargained" for a quarter of a century was well described by Henry A. Kissinger, President Nixon's adviser on national security. After his return from Peking, where he had gone to prepare a summit meeting between President Nixon and Chairman Mao, Kissinger said (*The New York Times,* July 17, 1971): "When you have not been in touch with a country for 25 years, it is amazing how technically difficult it is simply to find out where you should talk, and with whom. That is something they don't teach in textbooks on diplomacy."

Limited war requires limits; so do strategic maneuvers if they are to be stabilized short of war. But limits require agreement or at least some kind of mutual recognition and acquiescence. And agreement on limits is

---

[11] John C. Harsanyi, "Game Theory and the Analysis of International Conflict," *The Australian Journal of Politics and History,* 11 (December 1965), 292.

[12] In game theory, "nonzero-sum game" is one in which the sums of the payoffs to the respective players are not equal in all outcomes. "Zero-sum game" is one in which the sum of the payoffs to the respective players is equal or zero regardless of the outcome.

difficult to reach, not only because of the uncertainties and the acute divergence of interests but because negotiation is severely inhibited both during war and before it begins and because communication becomes difficult between adversaries in time of war. Furthermore, it may seem to the advantage of one side to avoid agreement on limits, in order to enhance the other's fear of war; or one side or both may fear that even a show of willingness to negotiate will be interpreted as excessive eagerness.

The study of tacit bargaining—bargaining in which communication is incomplete or impossible—assumes importance, therefore, in connection with limited war, or, for that matter, with limited competition, jurisdictional maneuvers, jockeying in a traffic jam, or getting along with a neighbor that one does not speak to. The problem is to develop a modus vivendi when one or both parties either cannot or will not negotiate explicitly or when neither would trust the other with respect to any agreement explicitly reached. The present chapter will examine some of the concepta and principles that seem to underlie tacit bargaining and will attempt to draw a few illustrative conclusions about the problem of limited war or analogous situations. It will also suggest that these same principles may often provide a powerful clue to understanding even the logically dissimilar case of explicit bargaining with full communication and enforcement.

The most interesting situations and the most important are those in which there is a conflict of interest between the parties involved. But it is instructive to begin with the special simplified case in which two or more parties have identical interests and face the problem not of reconciling interests but only of coordinating their actions for their mutual benefit, when communication is impossible. This special case brings out clearly the principle that will then serve to solve the problem of tacit "bargaining" over conflicting preferences.

Tacit Coordination (Common Interest)

When a man loses his wife in a department store without any prior understanding on where to meet if they get separated, the chances are good that they will find each other. It is likely that each will think of some obvious place to meet, so obvious that each will be sure that the other is sure that it is "obvious" to both of them. One does not simply predict where the other will go, since the other will go where he predicts the first to go, which is wherever the first predicts the second to predict the first to go, and so ad infinitum. Not "What would I do if I were she?" but "What would I do if I were she wondering what she would do if she were I wondering what I would do if I were she . . . ?" What is necessary is to coordinate predictions, to read the same message in the common situation, to identify the

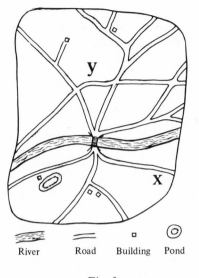

River   Road   Building   Pond

Fig. 1

one course of action that their expectations of each other can converge on. They must "mutually recognize" some unique signal that coordinates their expectations of each other. We cannot be sure they will meet, nor would all couples read the same signal; but the chances are certainly a great deal better than if they pursued a random course of search.

The reader may try the problem himself with the adjoining map (Fig. 1). Two people parachute unexpectedly into the area shown, each with a map and knowing the other has one, but neither knowing where the other has dropped nor able to communicate directly. They must get together quickly to be rescued. Can they study their maps and "coordinate" their behavior? Does the map suggest some particular meeting place so unambiguously that each will be confident that the other reads the same suggestion with confidence?

The writer has tried this and other analogous problems on an unscientific sample of respondents; and the conclusion is that people often can coordinate. The following abstract puzzles are typical of those that can be "solved" by a substantial proportion of those who try. The solutions are, of course, arbitrary to this extent: any solution is "correct" if enough people think so. The reader may wish to confirm his ability to concert in the following problems with those whose scores are given in a footnote.[13]

[13] In the writer's sample, 36 persons concerted on "heads" in problem 1, and only 6 chose "tails." . . . The upper left corner in problem 2 received 24 votes out of a total of

1. Name "heads" or "tails." If you and your partner name the same, you both win a prize. . . .

2. Put a check mark in one of the sixteen squares. You win if you all succeed in checking the same square.

3. You are to meet somebody in New York City. You have not been instructed where to meet; you have no prior understanding with the person on where to meet; and you cannot communicate with each other. You are simply told that you will have to guess where to meet and that he is being told the same thing and that you will just have to try to make your guesses coincide.

4. You were told the date . . . but not the hour of the meeting in No. 3; the two of you must guess the exact minute of the day for meeting. At what time will you appear at the meeting place that you elected in No. 3? . . .

These problems are artificial, but they illustrate the point. People *can* often concert their intentions or expectations with others if each knows that the other is trying to do the same. Most situations—perhaps every situation for people who are practiced at this kind of game—provide some clue for coordinating behavior, some focal point for each person's expectation of what the other expects him to expect to be expected to do. Finding the key, or rather finding *a* key—any key that is mutually recognized as the key becomes *the* key—may depend on imagination more than on logic; it may depend on analogy, precedent, accidental arrangement, symmetry, aesthetic or geometric configuration, casuistic reasoning, and who the parties are and what they know about each other. Whimsy may send the man and his wife to the "lost and found"; or logic may lead each to reflect and to expect the other to reflect on where they would have agreed to meet if they had had a prior agreement to cover the contingency. It is not being asserted that they will always find an obvious answer to the question; but the chances of their doing so are ever so much greater than the bare logic of abstract random probabilities would ever suggest.

41, and all but 3 of the remainder were distributed in the same diagonal line. Problem 3, which may reflect the location of the sample in New Haven, Connecticut, showed an absolute majority managing to get together at Grand Central Station (information booth), and virtually all of them succeeded in meeting at 12 noon. In the map most nearly like the one reproduced here (Fig. 1), 7 out of 8 respondents managed to meet at the bridge.

A prime characteristic of most of these "solutions" to the problems, that is, of the clues or coordinators or focal points, is some kind of prominence or conspicuousness. But it is a prominence that depends on time and place and who the people are. Ordinary folk lost on a plane circular area may naturally go to the center to meet each other; but only one versed in mathematics would "naturally" expect to meet his partner at the center of gravity of an irregularly shaped area. Equally essential is some kind of uniqueness; the man and his wife cannot meet at the "lost and found" if the store has several. The writer's experiments with alternative maps indicated clearly that a map with many houses and a single crossroads sends people to the crossroads, while one with many crossroads and a single house sends most of them to the house. Partly this may reflect only that uniqueness conveys prominence; but it may be more important that uniqueness avoids ambiguousness. Houses may be intrinsically more prominent than anything else on the map; but if there are three of them, none more prominent than the others, there is but one chance in three of meeting at a house, and the recognition of this fact may lead to the rejection of houses as the "clue."

But in the final analysis we are dealing with imagination as much as with logic; and the logic itself is of a fairly casuistic kind. Poets may do better than logicians at this game, which is perhaps more like "puns and anagrams" than like chess. Logic helps . . . but usually not until imagination has selected some clue to work on from among the concrete details of the situation.

Tacit Bargaining (Divergent Interests)

A conflict of interest enters our problem if the parachutists dislike walking. With communication, which is not allowed in our problem, they would have argued or bargained over where to meet, each favoring a spot close to himself or a resting place particularly to his liking. In the absence of communication, their overriding interest is to concert ideas; and if a particular spot commands attention as the "obvious" place to meet, the winner of the bargain is simply the one who happens to be closer to it. Even if the one who is farthest from the focal point knows that he is, he cannot withhold his acquiescence and argue for a fairer division of the walking; the "proposal" for the bargain that is provided by the map itself—if, in fact, it provides one—is the only extant offer; and without communication, there is no counter-proposal that can be made. The conflict gets reconciled—or perhaps we should say ignored—as a by-product of the dominant need for coordination.

"Win" and "lose" may not be quite accurate, since both may lose by comparison with what they could have agreed on through communication. If the two are actually close together and far from the lone house on the map, they might have eliminated the long walk to the house if they could have identified their locations and concerted explicitly on a place to meet between them. Or it may be that one "wins" while the other loses more than the first wins: if both are on the same side of the house and walk to it, they walk together a greater distance than they needed to, but the closer one may still have come off better than if he had to argue it out with the other.

This last case illustrates that it may be to the advantage of one to be unable to communicate. There is room here for a motive to destroy communication or to refuse to collaborate in advance on a method of meeting if one is aware of his advantage and confident of the "solution" he foresees. In one variant of the writer's test, A knew where B was, but B had no idea where A was (and each knew how much the other knew). Most of the recipients of the B-type questionnaire smugly sat tight, enjoying their ignorance, while virtually all the A-questionnaire respondents grimly acknowledged the inevitable and walked all the way to B. Better still may be to have the power to send but not to receive messages: if one can announce his position and state that his transmitter works but not his receiver, saying that he will wait where he is until the other arrives, the latter has no choice. He can make no effective counteroffer, since no counteroffer could be heard. . . .

The writer has tried a sample of conflicting-interest games on a number of people, including games that are biased in favor of one party or the other; and on the whole, the outcome suggests the same conclusion that was reached in the purely cooperative games. All these games require coordination; they also, however, provide several alternative choices over which the two parties' interests differ. Yet, among all the available options, some particular one usually seems to be the focal point for coordinated choice, and the party to whom it is a relatively unfavorable choice quite often takes it simply because he knows that the other will expect him to. The choices that cannot coordinate expectations are not really "available" without communication. The odd characteristic of all these games is that neither rival can gain by outsmarting the other. Each loses unless he does exactly what the other expects him to do. Each party is the prisoner or the beneficiary of their mutual expectations; no one can disavow his own expectation of what the other will expect him to expect to be expected to do. The need for agreement overrules the potential disagreement, and each must concert with the other or lose altogether. Some of these games are arrived at by slightly changing the problems given earlier, as we did for the map problem by supposing that walking is onerous.

1. A and B are to choose "heads" or "tails" without communicating. If both choose "heads," A gets $3 and B gets $2; if both choose "tails," A

gets $2 and B gets $3. If they choose differently, neither gets anything. You are A (or B); which do you choose? (Note that if both choose at random, there is only a 50-50 chance of successful coincidence and an expected value of $1.25 apiece—less than either $3 or $2.) . . .

2. You and your partner (rival) are to be given $100 if you can agree on how to divide it without communicating. Each of you is to write the amount of his claim on a sheet of paper; and if the two claims add to no more than $100, each gets exactly what he claimed. If the two claims exceed $100, neither of you gets anything. How much do you claim? $————. . . .

3. Two opposing forces are at the points marked X and Y in a map similar to the one in Fig. 1. The commander of each force wishes to occupy as much of the area as he can and knows the other does too. But each commander wishes to avoid an armed clash and knows the other does too. Each must send forth his troops with orders to take up a designated line and to fight if opposed. Once the troops are dispatched, the outcome depends only on the lines that the two commanders have ordered their troops to occupy. If the lines overlap, the troops will be assumed to meet and fight, to the disadvantage of both sides. If the troops take up positions that leave any appreciable space unoccupied between them, the situation will be assumed "unstable" and a clash inevitable. Only if the troops are ordered to occupy identical lines or lines that leave virtually no unoccupied space between them will a clash be avoided. In that case, each side obtains successfully the area it occupies, the advantage going to the side that has the most valuable area in terms of land and facilities. You command the forces located at the point marked X (Y). Draw on the map the line that you send your troops to occupy.

4. A and B have incomes of $100 and $150 per year, respectively. They are notified of each other's income and told that they must begin paying taxes totaling $25 per year. If they can reach agreement on shares of this total, they may share the annual tax bill in whatever manner they agree on. But they must reach agreement without communication; each is to write down the share he proposes to pay, and if the shares total $25 or more, each will pay exactly what he proposed. If the proposed shares fail to add up to $25, however, each will individually be required to pay the full $25, and the tax collectors will keep the surplus. You are A (B); how much do you propose to pay? $————.

The outcomes in the writer's informal sample are given in the footnote.[14] In those problems where there is some asymmetry between "you" and

[14] In the first problem, 16 out of 22 A's and 15 out of 22 B's chose heads. Given what the A's did, heads was the best answer for B; given what the B's did, heads was the best answer for A. Together they did substantially better than at random; and, of course, if each had tried to win $3, they would all have scored a perfect zero. . . . In

"him," that is, between A and B, the A formulations were matched with the B formulations in deriving the "outcome." The general conclusion, as given in more detail in the footnote, is that the participants can "solve" their problem in a substantial proportion of the cases; they certainly do conspicuously better than any chance methods would have permitted, and even the disadvantaged party in the biased games permits himself to be disciplined by the message that the game provides for their coordination.

The "clues" in these games are diverse. Heads apparently beat tails through some kind of conventional priority. . . . Roads might seem, in principle, as plausible as rivers, especially since their variety permits a less arbitrary choice. But, precisely because of their variety, the map cannot say *which road;* so roads must be discarded in favor of the unique and unambiguous river. (Perhaps in a symmetrical map of uniform terrain, the outcome would be more akin to the 50-50 split in the $100 example—a diagonal division in half, perhaps—but the irregularity of the map rather precludes a geometrical solution.)

The tax problem illustrates a strong power of suggestion in the income figures. The abstract logic of this problem is identical with that of the $100 division; in fact, it could be reworded as follows: each party pays $25 in taxes, and a refund of $25 is available to be divided among the two parties if they can agree on how to divide it. This formulation is logically equivalent to the one in problem 4, and, as such, it differs from problem 2 only in the amount of $25 instead of $100. Yet the inclusion of income figures, just by *suggesting* their relevance and making them prominent in the problem, shifts the focal point substantially to a 10-15 split rather than 12.5-12.5. And why, if incomes are relevant, is a perfectly *proportional* tax so obvious, when perhaps there are grounds for graduated rates? The answer must be that no *particular* graduation of rates is so obvious as to go without saying; and if speech is impossible, by default the uniquely simple and recognizable principle of proportionality has to be adopted. First the income figures take the initial plausibility away from a 50-50 split; then the simplicity of proportionality makes 10-15 the only one that could possibly be considered capable of tacit recognition. The same principle is displayed by an experiment in which question 4 was deliberately cluttered up with *additional* data —on family size, spending habits, and so on. Here the unique attraction of the income-proportionate split apparently became so diluted that the preponderant reply from both the high-income and the low-income respondents

---

problem 2, 36 out of 40 chose $50. (Two of the remainder were $49 and $49.99.) In problem 3, 14 of 22 X's and 14 of 23 Y's drew their boundaries exactly along the river. The "correctness" of this solution is emphatically shown by the fact that the other 15, who eschewed the river, produced 14 different lines. Of 8×7 possible pairs among them, there were 55 failures and 1 success. Problem 4 showed 5 out of 6 of those with incomes of $150 and 7 out of 10 of those with incomes of $100 concerting on a 15-10 division of the tax. . . .

was a simple 50-50 division of the tax. The refined signal for the income proportionate split was drowned out by "noise," and the cruder signal for equality was all that came through. . . .

In each of these situations the outcome is determined by something that is fairly arbitrary. It is not a particularly "fair" outcome, from either an observer's point of view or the points of view of the participants. Even the 50-50 split is arbitrary in its reliance on a kind of recognizable mathematical purity; and if it is "fair," it is so only because we have no concrete data by which to judge its unfairness, such as the source of the funds, the relative need of the rival claimants, or any potential basis for moral or legal claims. Splitting the difference in an argument over kidnap ransom is not particularly "fair," but it has the mathematical qualities of problem 2.

If we ask what determines the outcome in these cases, the answer again is in the coordination problem. Each of these problems requires coordination for a common gain, even though there is rivalry among alternative lines of common action. But, among the various choices, there is usually one or only a few that can serve as coordinator. . . .

Explicit Bargaining

The concept of "coordination" that has been developed here for tacit bargaining does not seem directly applicable to explicit bargaining. There is no apparent need for intuitive rapport when speech can be used; and the adventitious clues that coordinated thoughts and influenced the outcome in the tacit case revert to the status of incidental details.

Yet there is abundant evidence that some such influence is powerfully present even in explicit bargaining. In bargains that involve numerical magnitudes, for example, there seems to be a strong magnetism in mathematical simplicity. A trivial illustration is the tendency for the outcomes to be expressed in "round numbers"; the salesman who works out the arithmetic for his "rock-bottom" price on the automobile at $2,507.63 is fairly pleading to be relieved of $7.63. The frequency with which final agreement is precipitated by an offer to "split the difference" illustrates the same point, and the difference that is split is by no means always trivial. More impressive, perhaps, is the remarkable frequency with which long negotiations over complicated quantitative formulas or *ad hoc* shares in some costs or benefits converge ultimately on something as crudely simple as equal shares, shares proportionate to some common magnitude (gross national product, population, foreign-exchange deficit, and so forth), or the shares agreed on in some previous but logically irrelevant negotiation.

Precedent seems to exercise an influence that greatly exceeds its logical importance or legal force. A strike settlement or an international debt settlement often sets a "pattern" that is followed almost by default in subsequent negotiations. Sometimes, to be sure, there is a reason for a measure of uniformity, and sometimes there is enough similarity in the circumstances to explain similar outcomes; but more often it seems that there is simply no heart left in the bargaining when it takes place under the shadow of some dramatic and conspicuous precedent.[15] In similar fashion, mediators often display a power to precipitate agreement and a power to determine the terms of agreement; their proposals often seem to be accepted less by reason of their inherent fairness or reasonableness than by a kind of resignation of both participants. . . .

There is, in a similar vein, a strong attraction to the *status quo ante* as well as to natural boundaries. Even parallels of latitude have recently exhibited their longevity as focal points for agreement. Certainly there are reasons of convenience in using rivers as the agreed stopping place for troops or using old boundaries, whatever their current relevance; but often these features of the landscape seem less important for their practical convenience than for their power to crystallize agreement.

These observations would be trivial if they meant only that bargaining results were *expressed* in simple and qualitative terms or that minor accommodations were made to round off the last few cents or miles or people. But it often looks as though the ultimate focus for agreement did not just reflect the balance of bargaining powers but provided bargaining power to one side or the other. It often seems that a cynic could have predicted the outcome on the basis of some "obvious" focus for agreement, some strong suggestion contained in the situation itself, without much regard to the merits of the case, the arguments to be made, or the pressures to be applied during the bargaining. The "obvious" place to compromise frequently seems to win by some kind of default, as though there is simply no rationale for settling anywhere else. Or, if the "natural" outcome is taken to reflect the relative skills of the parties to the bargain, it may be important to identify that skill as the ability to set the stage in such a way as to give prominence to some particular outcome that would be favorable. The outcome may not be so much conspicuously fair or conspicuously in balance with estimated bargaining powers as just plain "conspicuous."

This conclusion may seem to reduce the scope for bargaining skill, if the outcome is already determined by the configuration of the problem itself and where the focal point lies. But perhaps what it does is shift the locus where skill is effective. The "obvious" outcome depends greatly on how the problem is formulated, on what analogies or precedents the definition of the bargaining issue calls to mind, on the kinds of data that may be available to bear on the question in dispute. . . .

[15] This and the preceding paragraph are illustrated by the speed with which a number of Middle Eastern oil-royalty arrangements converged on the 50-50 formula a few years after World War II.

Most bargaining situations ultimately involve some range of possible outcomes within which each party would rather make a concession than fail to reach agreement at all. In such a situation any potential outcome is one from which at least one of the parties, and probably both, would have been willing to retreat for the sake of agreement, and very often the other party knows it. Any potential outcome is therefore one that either party could have improved by insisting; yet he may have no basis for insisting, since the other knows or suspects that he would rather concede than do without agreement. Each party's strategy is guided mainly by what he expects the other to accept or insist on; yet each knows that the other is guided by reciprocal thoughts. The final outcome must be a point from which neither expects the other to retreat; yet the main ingredient of this expectation is what one thinks the other expects the first to expect, and so on. Somehow, out of this fluid and indeterminate situation that seemingly provides no logical reason for anybody to expect anything except what he expects to be expected to expect, a decision is reached. These infinitely reflexive expectations must somehow converge on a single point, at which each expects the other not to expect to be expected to retreat.

If we then ask what it is that can bring their expectations into convergence and bring the negotiation to a close, we might propose that it is the intrinsic magnetism of particular outcomes, especially those that enjoy prominence, uniqueness, simplicity, precedent, or some rationale that makes them qualitatively differentiable from the continuum of possible alternatives. We could argue that expectations tend not to converge on outcomes that differ only by degree from alternative outcomes but that people have to dig in their heels at a groove in order to make any show of determination. One has to have a reason for standing firmly on a position; and along the continuum of qualitatively undifferentiable positions one finds no rationale. The rationale may not be strong at the arbitrary "focal point," but at least it can defend itself with the argument "If not here, where?"

There is perhaps a little more to this need for a mutually identifiable resting place. If one is about to make a concession, he needs to control his adversary's expectations; he needs a recognizable limit to his own retreat. If one is to make a finite concession that is not to be interpreted as capitulation, he needs an obvious place to stop. . . .

If some troops have retreated to the river in our map, they will expect to be expected to make a stand. This is the one spot to which they can retreat without necessarily being expected to retreat further, while, if they yield any further, there is no place left where they can be expected to make a determined stand. Similarly, the advancing party can expect to force the other to retreat to the river without having his advance interpreted as an insatiable demand for unlimited retreat. There is stability at the river—and perhaps nowhere else.

This proposition may seem intuitively plausible; it does to the writer, and in any event some kind of explanation is needed for the tendency to settle at focal points. But the proposition would remain vague and somewhat mystical if it were not for the somewhat more tangible logic of tacit bargaining. The latter provides not only an analogy but the demonstration that the necessary psychic phenomenon—tacit coordination of expectations—is a real possibility and in some contexts a remarkably reliable one. The "coordination" of expectations is analogous to the "coordination" of behavior when communication is cut off; and, in fact, they both involve nothing more nor less than intuitively perceived mutual expectations. Thus the empirically verifiable results of some of the tacit-bargaining games, as well as the more logical role of coordinated expectations in that case, prove that expectations can be coordinated and that some of the objective details of the situation can exercise a controlling influence when the coordination of expectations is essential. *Something* is perceived by both parties when communication is absent; it must still be perceptible, though undoubtedly of lesser force, when communication is possible. The possibility of communication does not make 50-50 less symmetrical or the river less unique or A B C a less natural order for those letters.

If all we had to reason from were the logic of tacit bargaining, it would be only a guess and perhaps a wild one that the same kind of psychic attraction worked in explicit bargaining; and if all we had to generalize from were the observation of peculiarly "plausible" outcomes in actual bargains, we might be unwilling to admit the force of adventitious details. But the two lines of evidence so strongly reinforce each other that the analogy between tacit and explicit bargaining seems a potent one.

To illustrate with the problem of agreeing explicitly on how to divide $100: 50-50 seems a plausible division, but it may seem so for too many reasons. It may seem "fair"; it may seem to balance bargaining powers; or it may, as suggested in this paper, simply have the power to communicate its own inevitability to the two parties in such fashion that each appreciates that they both appreciate it. What our analysis of tacit bargaining provides is evidence for the latter view. The evidence is simply that *if* they had to divide the $100 without communicating, they could concert on 50-50. Instead of relying on intuition, then, we can point to the fact that in a slightly different context—the tacit-bargaining context—our argument has an objectively demonstrable interpretation.

To illustrate again: the ability of the two commanders in one of our problems to recognize the stabilizing power of the river—or, rather, their inability not to recognize it—is substantiated by the evidence that if their survival depended on some agreement about where to stabilize their lines *and communication were not allowed,* they probably could perceive and appreciate the qualities of the river as a focus for their tacit agreement. So the tacit analogy at least demonstrates that the idea of "coordinating expectations" is meaningful rather than mystical. . . .

. . . [I]f this general line of reasoning is valid, any analysis of explicit bargaining must pay attention to what we might call the "communication" that is inherent in the bargaining situations, the signals that the participants read in the inanimate details of the case. And it means that tacit and explicit bargaining are not thoroughly separate concepts but that the various gradations from tacit bargaining up through types of incompleteness or faulty or limited communication to full communication all show some dependence on the need to coordinate expectations. Hence all show some degree of dependence of the participants themselves on their common inability to keep their eyes off certain outcomes.

This is not necessarily an argument for expecting explicit outcomes as a rule to lean toward exactly those that would have emerged if communication had been impossible; the focal points may certainly be different when speech is allowed, except in some of the artificial cases we have used in our illustrations. But what may be the *main* principle in tacit bargaining apparently may be at least *one* of the important principles in the analysis of explicit bargaining. And, since even much so-called "explicit" bargaining includes maneuver, indirect communication, jockeying for position, or speaking to be overheard, or is confused by a multitude of participants and divergent interests, the need for convergent expectations and the role of signals that have the power to coordinate expectations may be powerful.

Perhaps many kinds of social stability and the formation of interest groups reflect the same dependence on such coordinators as the terrain and the circumstances can provide: the band wagon at political conventions that often converts the slightest sign of plurality into an overwhelming majority; the power of constitutional legitimacy to command popular support in times of anarchy or political vacuum; the legendary power of an old gang leader to bring order into the underworld, simply because obedience depends on the expectation that others will be obedient in punishing disobedience. The often expressed idea of a "rallying point" in social action seems to reflect the same concept. In economics the phenomena of price leadership, various kinds of nonprice competition, and perhaps even price stability itself appear amenable to an analysis that stresses the importance of tacit communication and its dependence on qualitatively identifiable and fairly unambiguous signals that can be read in the situation itself. . . .

Tacit Negotiation and Limited War

What useful insight does this line of analysis provide into the practical problems of tacit bargaining that usually confront us, particularly the problems of strategic maneuver and limited war? It certainly suggests that it is *possible* to find limits to war . . . without overt negotiation. But it gives us no new strong sense of *probability*. War was limited in Korea, and gas was not used in World War II; on the possibility of limited war these two facts are more persuasive than all the suggestions contained in the foregoing discussion. If the analysis provides anything, then, it is not a judgment of the probability of successfully reaching tacit agreement but a better under-standing of where to look for the terms of agreement.

If there are important conclusions to be drawn, they are probably these: (1) tacit agreements or agreements arrived at through partial or haphazard negotiation require terms that are qualitatively distinguishable from the alternatives and cannot simply be a matter of degree; (2) when agreement must be reached with incomplete communication, the participants must be ready to allow the situation itself to exercise substantial constraint over the outcome; specifically, a solution that discriminates against one party or the other or even involves "unnecessary" nuisance to both of them may be the only one on which their expectations can be coordinated.

Gas was not used in World War II. The agreement, though not without antecedents, was largely a tacit one. It is interesting to speculate on whether any alternative agreement concerning poison gas could have been arrived at without formal communication (or even, for that matter, with communica-tion). "Some gas" raises complicated questions of how much, where, under what circumstances: "no gas" is simple and unambiguous. Gas only on military personnel; gas used only by defending forces; gas only when carried by vehicle or projectile; no gas without warning—a variety of limits is con-ceivable; some may make sense, and many might have been more impartial to the outcome of the war. But there is a simplicity to "no gas" that makes it almost uniquely a focus for agreement when each side can only conjecture at what rules the other side would propose and when failure at coordination on the first try may spoil the chances for acquiescence in any limits at all.

The physical configuration of Korea must have helped in defining the limits to war and in making geographical limits possible. The area was sur-rounded by water, and the principal northern political boundary was marked dramatically and unmistakably by a river. The thirty-eighth parallel seems to have been a powerful focus for a stalemate; and the main alternative, the "waist," was a strong candidate not just because it provided a shorter de-fense line but because it would have been clear to both sides that an advance to the waist did not necessarily signal a determination to advance farther and that a retreat to the waist did not telegraph any intention to retreat farther.

The Taiwan Straits made it possible to stabilize a line between the Com-munist and National government forces of China, not solely because water favored the defender and inhibited attack, but because an island is an integral unit and water is a conspicuous boundary. The sacrifice of any part of the island would have made the resulting line unstable; the retention of any part of the mainland would have been similarly unstable. Except at the water's edge, all movement is a matter of degree; an attack across water is a declaration that the "agreement" has been terminated.

In Korea, weapons were limited by the qualitative distinction between atomic and all other; it would surely have been much more difficult to stabilize a tacit acceptance of any limit on size of atomic weapons or selection of targets. No definition of size or target is so obvious and natural that it goes without saying, except for "no size, on any target." American assistance to the French forces in Indochina was persuasively limited to material, not people; and it was appreciated that an enlargement to include, say, air participation could be recognized as limited to air, while it would not be possible to establish a limited *amount* of air or ground participation. One's intentions to abstain from ground intervention can be conveyed by the complete withholding of ground forces; one cannot nearly so easily commit *some* forces and communicate a persuasive limit to the *amount* that one intends to commit. . . .

In sum, the problem of limiting warfare involves not a continuous range of possibilities from most favorable to least favorable for either side; it is a lumpy, discrete world that is better able to recognize qualitative than quantitative differences, that is embarrassed by the multiplicity of choices, and that forces both sides to accept some dictation from the elements themselves. The writer suggests that the same is true of restrained competition in every field in which it occurs.

Prior Arrangements

While the main burden of this paper has been that tacit bargaining is possible and is susceptible for systematic analysis, there is no assurance that it will succeed in any particular case or that, when it succeeds, it will yield to either party a particularly favorable outcome compared with alternatives that might have been available if full communication had been allowed. There is no assurance that the next war, if it comes, will find mutually observed limits in time and of a sort to afford protection, unless explicit negotiation can take place. There is reason, therefore, to consider what steps can be taken before the time for tacit bargaining occurs, to enhance the likelihood of a successful outcome.

Keeping communication channels open seems to be one obvious point. (At a minimum, this might mean assuring that a surrender offer could be heard and responded to by either side.) The technical side of this principle would be identification of who would send and receive messages, upon what authority, over what facilities, using what intermediaries if intermediaries were used, and who stood in line to do the job in what fashion if the indicated parties and facilities were destroyed. In the event of an effort to fight a restrained nuclear war, there may be only a brief and busy instant in which each side must decide whether limited war is in full swing or full war has just begun; and twelve hours' confusion over how to make contact might spoil some of the chances for stabilizing the action within limits.

Thought should be given to the possible usefulness of mediators or referees. To settle on influential mediators usually requires some prior understanding, or at least a precedent or a tradition or a sign of welcome. Even if we rule out overt arrangements for the contingency, evidences by each side of an appreciation of the role of referees and mediators, even a little practice in their use, might help to prepare an instrument of the most extreme value in an awful contingency.

But all such efforts may suffer from the unwillingness of an adversary to engage in any preparatory steps. Not only may an adversary balk at giving signs of eagerness to come to agreement; it is even possible that one side in a potential war may have a tactical interest in keeping that war unrestrained and aggravating the likelihood of mutual destruction in case it comes. Why? Because of the strategy of threats, bluffs, and deterrents. The willingness to start a war or take steps that may lead to war, whether aggression or retaliation to aggression, may depend on the confidence with which a nation's leaders think a war could be kept within limits. To be specific, the willingness of America to retaliate against local aggression with atomic attack depends—and the Russians know that it depends—on how likely we consider it that such retaliation could itself remain limited. That is, it depends on how likely it is in our judgment that we and the Russians, when we both desperately need to recognize limits within which either of us is willing to lose the war without enlarging those limits, will find such limits and come to mutually recognized acquiescence in them. If, then, Russian refusal to engage in any activity that might lead to the possibility of limited war deters our own resolution to act, they might risk forgoing such limits for the sake of reducing the threat of American action. One parachutist in our example may know that the other will be careless with the plane if he is sure they can meet and save themselves; so if the first abstains from discussing the contingency, the other will have to ride quietly for fear of precipitating a fatal separation in the terrain below.

Whether this consideration or just the usual inhibitions on serious negotiation make prior discussion impossible, there is still a useful idea that emerges from one of our earlier games. It is that negotiation or communication for the purpose of coordinating expectations need not be reciprocal: unilateral negotiation may provide the coordination that will save both parties. Furthermore, even an unwilling member cannot necessarily make himself unavailable for the receipt of messages.... If one of our parachutists, just before the plane failed and while neither of them dreamed of having to jump, idly said, "If I ever had to meet somebody down there, I'd just head for the highest hill in sight," the other would probably recall and know that the first would be sure he recalled and would go there, even though it had been on the tip of his tongue to say, "How stupid," or "Not me, climbing hurts my legs," when the plane failed. When some signal is desperately needed by *both* parties and both parties know it, even a poor signal and a discriminatory one may command recognition, in default of any other. Once the contingency is upon them, their interests, which originally diverged in the play of threats and deterrents, substantially coincide in the desperate need for a focus of agreement.

46 / The Impenetrable Blank of the Future: A Postscript

Charles Burton Marshall

A sense of editorial neatness usually requires a clear-cut conclusion. A study of international politics should, for instance, conclude with either a documented forecast of an inevitable doom or a reasoned anticipation of a glorious future for men and nations.

Neither conclusion seems possible. The preceding chapters recorded the observable facts of aggressive competitiveness of groups and individuals as well as enlightened arguments and hopes for tolerance and cooperative coexistence within and among nations. We should not hide from ourselves, as the French sociologist Raymond Aron put it,

> ... the virtual contradiction between the realism of the short term and the hope in the long term of passing beyond international politics as they have been for a millennia. It is perhaps our historic situation to be placed at the center of this contradiction.[16]

The ages-old struggle between the irrational and foolish, on the one hand, and the rational and wise, on the other, keeps on being waged among men and

From pp. 12–17, 26–27 *(passim),* of *The Limits of Foreign Policy* by Charles Burton Marshall. Copyright 1954 by Holt, Rinehart and Winston, Inc. Reprinted by permission of Holt, Rinehart and Winston, Inc., and the author.

[16] Raymond Aron, "Political Action in the Shadow of Atomic Apocalypse," in Harold Lasswell and Harlan Cleveland (Eds.), *The Ethic of Power* (New York: Harper & Row, Publishers, Inc., 1962), p. 458.

nations with no certainty as to its outcome. Nations and men, as Abba Eban of Israel once quipped, behave rationally and wisely only after they have exhausted all other resources. "What makes our age unique," suggested Carlos Romulo, the foreign minister of the Philippines,

> . . . is that the immediate questions and the ultimate question are locked together. . . . Our clients are the next generation. . . . but there may be no next generation unless we do today what has to be done for the two billion clients who are now alive.[17]

What about the future then? Will it be much worse or better than the present? We cannot really answer this basic question. The reason is simple enough: We do not know and we cannot know; as Charles Burton Marshall suggests, we are only men, not supermen. And in all human situations, optimism and hope alternate with pessimism and despair. In his 1969 *Annual Report* to the United Nations on the state of the world, Secretary General U Thant concluded:

> I can report very little progress of the world at large towards the goals of the United Nations Charter—to maintain international peace and security, develop friendly relations among nations, and achieve international cooperation. Futhermore, I have a strong feeling that time is running out.

Nothing comes more easily or does less good than the engaging pastime of thinking up bold and imaginative schemes for improvement in disregard of the means for realizing them. This is true in all human endeavor. Here I wish to apply the thought to the subject of foreign policy. . . .

In the life of the state as in the life of the individual, problems foreseen may often be beyond the scope of one's power of ordaining. The situation in the conduct of foreign policy often reminds me of the story of the boastful pilot. While steering a ship into port, he remarked to the skipper, "I know every rock in this harbor." A rending contact between ship and reef interrupted him. Then he added, "That's one of them now." . . . I stress the obvious but often overlooked externalness of foreign policy. The fundamental circumstance giving rise to foreign policy is that most of the world is outside the United States. The areas in which our foreign policy has its effects are those lying beyond the range of our law. They include about fifteen-sixteenths of the world's surface and contain about sixteen-seventeenths of its peoples. We cannot ordain the conditions there. The forces do not respond to our fiat. At best we can only affect them. . . .

The terms *state* and *government* convey ideas of hugeness, majesty, and impersonality. These overtones should not mislead us. The state—and this is true also of its agent, government—remains, in Plato's phrase, man written large.

[17] Carlos Romulo, a speech commemorating the tenth anniversary of the world organization at the United Nations General Assembly in 1955.

It is only man. It is not superman. It is man written large, not limitless. The individual is multiplied in the frame of the state. The individual's limitations are not transcended. The institutions of political life do not add to the dimensions of the human mind. They have no insights denied to individuals. They produce no wisdom beyond the compass of man's mind. The intelligence operating in the lines of decision and execution is but human intelligence. It has the inherent attributes of contingency, fallibility, and subjectivity. Service to the state does not bring to the minds of the servants any additional endowments for perceiving the future. For all its majesty, the situation of the state is still the human situation. . . .

Anyone who has dealt responsibly with foreign policy must have felt the meaning of Whitman's lines:

> How can I pierce the impenetrable blank of the future?
> I feel thy ominous greatness, evil as well as good;
> I watch thee, advancing, absorbing the present, transcending the past;
> I see thy light lighting and thy shadows shadowing, as if the entire globe;
> But I do not undertake to define thee—hardly to comprehend thee . . .

To perceive the great extent to which a foreign policy, attempting to cope with the future, must be speculative and chancy is not a source of weakness. To the contrary, in Edmund Burke's phrase, "We can never walk surely but by being sensible of our blindness." The gravest errors are consequent from deceiving oneself that it is possible by some prodigy of planning to overcome this inherent circumstance.

Something of this fallacy is basic to every proposition for a perfect, all-embracing solution of our problems in foreign relations. The young Gladstone's mentor advised him that politics was an unsatisfactory business and that he would have to learn to put up with imperfect results. That advice has wisdom akin to the lessons of *Faust* and *Paradise Lost:* that grace derives from a sense of one's limitations and that tragedy is the wage of losing that sense.